BRIGHT YOUNG PEOPLE

BRIGHT YOUNG PEOPLE

THE LOST GENERATION OF
LONDON'S JAZZ AGE

D. J. TAYLOR

FARRAR, STRAUS AND GIROUX • NEW YORK

FARRAR, STRAUS AND GIROUX
18 West 18th Street, New York 10011

Printed in the United States of America
Originally published in 2007 by Chatto & Windus, a division of the
Random House Group Limited, Great Britain
Published in 2009 in the United States by Farrar, Straus and Giroux
First American paperback edition, 2010

Grateful acknowledgment is made for permission to reprint text from the following: "From Patrick, aetat: LXX" and an unpublished letter by John Betjeman, reprinted by permission of Candida Lycett Green. "Where Engels Fears to Tread" by Cyril Connolly, reprinted by permission of Deidre Levi. *Afternoon Men* by Anthony Powell, reprinted by permission of the Powell family archive. "Bright Young People" by Noël Coward, reprinted by permission of The Overlook Press.

The Library of Congress has cataloged the hardcover edition as follows:
Taylor, D. J. (David John), 1960–
    Bright young people : the lost generation of London's jazz age / D. J. Taylor.—1st U.S. ed.
        p.   cm.
    "Originally published in 2007 by Chatto & Windus, a division of the Random House Group Limited, Great Britain"—T.p. verso.
    Includes bibliographical references and index.
    ISBN: 978-0-374-53211-6
    1. Great Britain—Social life and customs—1918–1945.   2. Children of the rich— Great Britain—Social life and customs—20th century.   3. Bohemianism—Great Britain—History—20th century.   4. Anxiety in youth—Great Britain—History—20th century.   5. Great Britain—Social conditions—20th century.   I. Title.

DA566.4.T39 2009
305.242094109042—dc22

                                                                            2008031366

Paperback ISBN: 978-0-374-53211-6

Designed by Gretchen Achilles

www.fsgbooks.com

PRAISE FOR BRIGHT YOUNG PEOPLE

"[An] incisive social history . . . [A] richly detailed work."
—CARYN JAMES, *The New York Times Book Review*

"A poignant study of the elusive relationship between art and the social world from whence it springs . . . D. J. Taylor, author of a first-rate life of George Orwell, shows the sharp instincts of an expert biographer in his approach to 1920s English youth culture."
—DAMIAN DA COSTA, *The New York Observer*

"Absorbing . . . The book really takes hold when Taylor seizes on the actual trajectory of the lives of individual members, most . . . poignantly that of Elizabeth Ponsonby . . . The pages devoted to her, enriched by Taylor's access to the Ponsonby family papers, are all the biography her lack of accomplishments and frittered-away youth warrant; yet they greatly deepen this study of a social phenomenon."
—KATHERINE A. POWERS, *The Boston Globe*

"Deft . . . [A] captivating new history of the age . . . Mr. Taylor's book is at once elegy and critique. And this is just as it should be."
—EMILY WILKINSON, *The Washington Times*

"A note of genuine pathos is struck in [Taylor's] description of how the increasingly straitened economic and political circumstances of the '30s began rendering this gaudy subculture obsolete. Immensely readable, and of real value as a sharply pointed cautionary tale."
—*Kirkus Reviews*

"There are . . . plenty of juicy anecdotes to go around . . . The text is enlivened by several *Punch* cartoons from the period, vividly depicting the hold these rich young partygoers once held on the public's imagination."
—*Publishers Weekly*

"[Conveys] precisely the aspect of the Bright Young People that is most difficult to give expression to on paper: not books or parties, but 'an atmosphere . . . An outlook, a gesture, an essence.'"

—MARK BOSTRIDGE, *The Independent on Sunday*

"Sharp, insightful . . . Atmospheric and thoroughly vivid . . . [Taylor] succeeds entirely in transporting his readers to the frenzied 1920s world of Bath and Bottle parties, scavenger hunts, scandalous night-clubs, and ruinous amounts of alcohol."

—HONORIA ST. CYR, *Open Letters Monthly*

"Compelling and ultimately touching . . . A witty and sensitive account of the pathos and the glamour of the generation fated to 'sorrow in sunlight.'"

—ROSEMARY HILL, *The Guardian*

"Excellent . . . The brightest of the Bright Young People [make] their fictional counterparts in Waugh's *Vile Bodies* pale into insignificance . . . Taylor lays bare their cavortings with an archeological eye."

—PHILIP HOARE, *The Independent*

"Taylor, for years a journalist, is fascinated by—and authoritative on—the lucrative relationship forged between the shrewdest of the Bright Young People and the glamour-hunting press . . . Shrewd and absorbing in his analysis of the way Waugh and Nancy Mitford . . . promoted the world they would soon skewer in fiction."

—MIRANDA SEYMOUR, *The Sunday Times* (London)

"Fascinating . . . A complex study of family, fear and breakdown . . . Taylor's achievement is to remind us that there are few periods of recent history more culturally interesting than the years between the wars."

—FRANCES WILSON, *New Statesman*

"A goldmine . . . If I had to choose one book as a summing up of the BYP, it would be Taylor's." —BEVIS HILLIER, *The Spectator*

Katie Vandyck

D. J. TAYLOR

BRIGHT YOUNG PEOPLE

D. J. Taylor is a literary critic and the author of two acclaimed biographies: *Thackeray: The Life of a Literary Man* and *Orwell: The Life*, which won the Whitbread Prize for Biography in 2003. He has written seven novels, including *Kept: A Victorian Mystery*. He lives in Norwich, England.

ALSO BY D. J. TAYLOR

FICTION

Great Eastern Land

Real Life

English Settlement

After Bathing at Baxter's: Stories

Trespass

The Comedy Man

Kept: A Victorian Mystery

Ask Alice

NONFICTION

A Vain Conceit: British Fiction in the 1980s

Other People: Portraits from the Nineties (with Marcus Berkmann)

After the War: The Novel and England Since 1945

Thackeray: The Life of a Literary Man

Orwell: The Life

On the Corinthian Spirit: The Decline of Amateurism in Sport

FOR LAURA PONSONBY
AND KATE RUSSELL

The Bright Young People have never been appraised at their true valuation.

—PATRICK BALFOUR, *Society Racket* (1933)

An entire book could be written about that period in London between 1924 and 1930, the last days of post-war youth which I shall vulgarly call "the bright young people's era."

—BRENDA DEAN PAUL, *My First Life* (1935)

The social life of London in "the twenties" must, to the censorious young of the present day, appear like a prolonged and rather vulgar orgie. Over-indulgence in sex and gin was its main surface characteristic . . . The Universities produced an astonishing number of effeminates of the type known as "fairies," and a mannerless crowd of young hooligans, with money to burn, was turned out by the larger public schools. Brought up in a dishonored world, without the salutary criticism of their fathers and elder brothers, these irresponsibles and their female counterparts, started a "wild party" which lasted as long as their money did. Finding the gossip writers ready to para-graph their antics they called themselves "Bright Young People," popularised gate-crashing, took drugs, indulged or pretended to indulge in unnatural vices, and drove their cars about at high speed, when under the influence of drink, in the hope, if there was a smash, that the case would be reported in the Sunday newspapers . . . Time has dealt harshly with many of them.

—DOUGLAS GOLDRING, *Odd Man Out* (1935)

Evelyn Waugh's *Decline and Fall* and *Vile Bodies* have been taken as satiri-cal fantasies, but they describe a real manner of life with total accuracy.

—ALAN PRYCE-JONES, *The Bonus of Laughter* (1987)

CONTENTS

ACKNOWLEDGMENTS

My most substantial debt in the writing of this book is to Laura Ponsonby and Kate Russell, granddaughters of Arthur and Dorothea Ponsonby and nieces of Elizabeth Ponsonby, who not only allowed me unlimited access to their family papers and photographs and lavish hospitality but answered countless questions with unfeigned enthusiasm. I am profoundly grateful to them.

Among other providers of hitherto unpublished material, I should like to thank Jonny Gathorne-Hardy and the family of the late Lady Anne Hill for allowing me to make use of material relating to Eddie Gathorne-Hardy; John Powell and his family for supplying me with letters written by Anthony Powell to Henry Yorke (Henry Green) in the late 1920s; and Sebastian Yorke for allowing me to quote from his father's side of the correspondence. Deirdre Levi very kindly allowed me to quote from an unpublished letter written by her husband, Cyril Connolly, to Tom Driberg, and Candida Lycett Green performed the same service with a letter written by her father, Sir John Betjeman, to Lady Anne Hill.

Parts of chapters five and twelve began life as a lecture entitled "Henry Green and the Bright Young People," given at Warwick University at a conference staged in October 2005 to mark the centenary of Green's birth. I am very grateful to Jeremy Treglown, Green's biographer, whose idea this was. Similarly, part of chapter seven reproduces the introduction to a reprint of Marie-Jaqueline Lancaster's *Brian Howard: Portrait of a Failure*, published by the Timewell Press in 2005. I should like to thank Andreas Campomar both for commissioning this piece and allowing me to reproduce it.

Several people professionally engaged on the social and literary life of the 1920s and 1930s offered valuable help, suggestions and introductions. I should particularly like to thank Mark Amory, Bryan Connon, Max Egremont, Philip Hoare, Selina Hastings, James Knox and Hugo Vickers. Of the many other people who responded to letters or requests for information, I should like to thank Mark Everett, the Honorable Desmond Guinness, Anthony Hobson, Ian Irvine, Marie-Jaqueline Lancaster, Michael Meredith, the late Anthony Powell, Lady Rumbold and Paul Willetts.

Among institutions where I undertook research, Lucie Gosling and her colleagues Marcelle Adamson and Katie Simpson at the *Illustrated London News* archive, owners of copyright in, among other publications, the *Tatler*, the *Bystander* and the *Sketch*, were a mine of information. I should also like to thank Janet McMullin, assistant librarian of Christ Church, Oxford, holders of the Tom Driberg papers. The staff of the London Library were as indefatigable as ever.

At Chatto & Windus, I should like to thank my publisher, Alison Samuel, and editor, Jenny Uglow, for their customary support and tact. I should also like to thank my agent, Gill Coleridge, and her former assistant Lucy Luck.

Numerous literary editors supplied me with relevant books to review. They include Mark Amory, Clare Asquith, Boyd Tonkin, Christina Patterson, Suzi Feay, Nicola Smyth, Will Skidelsky, Alan Jenkins, Holly Eley, Caroline Gascoigne, Andrew Holgate, Nancy Sladek, Claire Armitstead, Justine Jordan and Josh Lacey.

The account of a Bright Young People's party taken from the *Daily Express* "some time in 1929" is wholly imaginary.

Love and thanks to Rachel, Felix, Benjy and Leo as always.

D. J. TAYLOR

February 2007

A NOTE ON NAMES

What with marriage, remarriage and accession to hereditary titles, the Bright Young People were more than usually prey to changes of name. Several had two, some as many as three or four. The Honorable Daphne Vivian, for example, became, successively, Lady Weymouth, the Marchioness of Bath and Mrs. Xan Fielding. In general, I have tried to refer to people by the names they went under at the time to which I am referring to them. Thus, Diana Mosley at the time of her engagement to Bryan Guinness is "Diana Mitford." From her wedding to the breakup of her first marriage she is "Diana Guinness." Looking back on the twenties in old age, she is "Diana Mosley." Nancy Mitford, on the other hand, remains "Nancy Mitford" rather than "Mrs. Rodd," as this is the name by which she is generally known. I have also inclined towards concision. The correct name for the Earl of Rosslyn's son Hamish is "The Honorable Hamish St. Clair Erskine." Here he is plain "Hamish Erskine."

THE CAST

"The Dragoman" writes . . .

Mrs. ANTROBUS's entertainments have always been acknowledged as the height of Mayfair *ton*, and last Thursday's fancy dress ball in honour of her daughter MYRTLE's twenty-first birthday was no exception. Indeed the guests were unanimous that it was the best small party of its kind to be held in London in recent months. In deference to the hostess's association with the smart younger set, the Bright Young People were out in force. Miss ELIZABETH PONSONBY was charm itself in an acrobat's costume, very prettily adorned with a scarlet sash, and seemed determined to confound her father's reputation for Socialist austerity. Miss BRENDA DEAN PAUL, as befits a baronet's daughter, was in court dress, while Mr. BRIAN HOWARD impersonated Lillie Langtry with the thespian vigour for which he is so rightly renowned. The misses TERESA and ZITA JUNG-MAN, the highly accomplished daughters of Mrs. Richard Guinness, came—most amusingly—as each other, while the Hon. STEPHEN TEN-NANT made a "good" late entrance as Taglioni in the role of La Sylphide, a vision in white taffeta which so ravished Mr. CECIL BEATON that he instantly rushed forward to photograph him.

It was by now unconscionably hot and, the french windows being thrown open, a number of guests debouched on to Mrs. Antrobus's lawn, almost overturning the stout impediment of Mr. ROBERT BYRON, who, attended by the Hon. GAVIN HENDERSON in the guise of Miss Ponsonby's grandfather Sir Henry, had contrived a startling representation of Her late Majesty Queen Victoria. Lingering at the buffet, I found myself in earnest conversation with the elegant figure of Mrs. PLUNKET GREENE, whose stepfather Mr. Bendir the racing fraternity knows so well, attired as Cleopatra. The Hon. EDWARD GATHORNE-HARDY, who happened to be passing, remarked in his inimitable way that she lacked only her asp.

Mr. BEVERLEY NICHOLS, whose last novel caused such a sensation, and is recently returned from America, was poetical as Shelley, while Mr. BRYAN GUINNESS and his wife the Hon. Mrs. GUINNESS wandered through the rooms in a haze of satisfaction which only the newly married may appreciate. I looked for Mrs. Guinness's sister, the Hon. NANCY MITFORD, but, alas, found her absent. She is, I believe, away in Banffshire with her friend the Countess of Seafield.

As for the other guests, where Beauty led, Art had followed. Mr. HENRY YORKE, whose industrial adventures are apparently at an end, was saturnine and the Hon. PATRICK BALFOUR meekly attentive. Mr. EVELYN WAUGH, with whom I enjoyed a lively talk, announced, to great consternation, that he was engaged on that very shocking but oh so fascinating endeavour, the writing of a novel about Mayfair life. Despite Miss Ponsonby's assertion that the result would be both "blush-making" and "bogus," I received the distinct impression that Mrs. Antrobus's guests awaited the book with the keenest anticipation . . . [*continues*]

DAILY EXPRESS, "some time in 1929"

BRIGHT YOUNG PEOPLE

DIONYSIUS IN MAYFAIR

It was an age of "parties." There were "white" parties in which we shot down to the country in fleets of cars, dressed in white from head to foot, and danced on a white floor laid in the orchard, with the moonlight turning all the apples to silver, and then—in a pale pink dawn—playing races with champagne corks on the surface of the stream. There were Mozart parties in which, powdered and peruked, we danced by candlelight and then—suddenly bored—rushed out into the street to join a gang excavating the gas mains at Hyde Park Corner. There were swimming parties where, at midnight, we descended on some municipal baths, hired for the occasion, and disported ourselves with an abandon that was all the fiercer because we knew that the press was watching—and watching with a very disapproving eye.

—BEVERLEY NICHOLS, *All I Could Never Be* (1949)

Toward the end of June 1928, a curious invitation began to descend upon certain doormats in the southwestern postal districts of London. It was the height of the metropolitan season and the mantelpieces of Chelsea and Belgravia were crammed with requests to attend debutante balls and evening parties—the Countess of Ellesmere's ball at Bridgwater House was shaping up to be the summer's most talked-about social event—and yet this particular rectangle of stiff white cardboard seemed unusually distinctive. Printed, rather than engraved—an economy that any Mayfair hostess would have instantly remarked—issuing from 44 Grosvenor Square, SW1, but without the customary instruction to RSVP, it advertised what, in the context of postwar London society, was a unique entertainment. Here, in short, irregularly set out lines of script, "Mrs. Plunket Greene, Miss Ponsonby, Mr. Edward Gathorne-

Hardy and Mr. Brian Howard" requested the pleasure of the invitee's company

at St George's Swimming Baths, Buckingham
Palace Road, at 11 o'clock, p.m. on Friday,
13th July, 1928.
Please wear a Bathing Suit and bring a Bath towel and a Bottle.
Each guest is required to show his invitation on arrival.

Who were the hosts? None of the prospective guests—idle young men living in Mayfair mewses, blooming specimens of aristocratic girlhood from Pont Street and Lowndes Square, tatterdemalion "artists" hunkered down in Chelsea basements, gossip columnists on the London society magazines—had the least trouble in identifying them. Young—at twenty-seven, Elizabeth Ponsonby was the oldest by a year—louche, irregularly employed, they were all indefinably glamorous, well-connected, and, as such, had been a fixture of newspaper society columns for the past three years. Elizabeth Ponsonby was the daughter of a former government minister destined to become Labour leader of the House of Lords; "Babe" Plunket Greene, stepdaughter of Arthur Bendir, the chairman of Ladbroke, was married to Elizabeth Ponsonby's cousin David, grandson of the composer Sir Hubert Parry; the Honorable Eddie Gathorne-Hardy was a younger son of the Earl of Cranbrook; Brian Howard the scion of a successful art dealer and impresario who conducted his business from Bryanston Square and spent his leisure in a sixteen-bedroom country house (which his son thought inconveniently small) in Sussex. Together they were the embodiment of a group of twenty-something men and women—fast, rackety and pleasure-seeking—sometimes known to the newspapers who wrote up their goings-on as "the younger set" but more often filed under the name by which history now remembers them: the Bright Young People.

Convened beneath the darkness of a sultry summer night, the "Bath and Bottle Party," as it came to be known, was the Bright Young People's apotheosis. No subsequent gathering approached it either in terms of novelty or notoriety. Gossip columnists who had failed to secure invitations hastily defended their absence. Nobody believed "Johanna" of *The Lady*, who, inveigled to the dirt-track racing at the White City, pronounced that she "did not regret a bit missing the amusing 'bathing party.'" Among several press reports, the most authentic was provided by Tom Driberg, a young Oxford graduate who assisted Colonel Percy Sewell on the *Daily Express*'s "Talk of London" column. Driberg's eye-witness account, which appeared in the next morning's edition, mixed resolute attention to detail with what, to most of his middle-class readers, would have been the whiff of scandal. "Bathing costumes of the most dazzling kinds and colors were worn by the guests," he gravely reported, while dancing took place to the strains of a Negro orchestra and the hardy leaped into the bath, "of which the water had been slightly warmed." Roving across the assembled throng, Driberg's copy-hungry eye noted:

> Great rubber horses and flowers floated about in the water, which was illuminated by colored spotlights. Many of those present brought two or three bathing costumes, which they changed in the course of the night's festivities. Cocktails were served in the gallery, where the cocktail-mixers evidently found the heat intolerable, for they also donned bathing costumes at the earliest opportunity. A special cocktail, christened the Bath-water Cocktail, was invented for the occasion.

As for the guests, Driberg found he could recognize the Honorable Stephen Tennant, son of the late Lord Glenconner, in "a pink vest and long blue trousers." A less obvious reveler was Clive Bell, the Bloomsbury art critic, while among the ladies "Miss Elizabeth Ponsonby looked most attractive in a silk bathing costume of which the lower part was red and the bodice rainbow-like with its stripes of blue and red." Amid much preening and carousing, a certain amount of bona fide swimming took place. Brenda Dean Paul remembered Mary Ashley Cooper giving "some really wonderful exhibitions of diving," while a group of Mayfair debutantes "remained in the pool the whole time ducking those who came their way." Meanwhile, an older category of guests looked more or less benignly on. The only available seats were in the changing cubicles, Brenda recorded, "but by this time the older generation of dowagers had acclimatized themselves to almost anything. Nothing seemed to surprise them any more." Looking back on the scene, the baronet's daughter could still picture this group of elderly ladies, "quite contented like plump hens in cubby holes, sitting in dim solitude . . . with lorgnettes fixed at the dripping parade."

No photographs of the Bath and Bottle Party survive. Written accounts, on the other hand, confirm that most of the activities associated in the popular imagination with the Bright Young People were triumphantly on display, a compound of cocktails, jazz, licence, abandon and flagrantly improper behavior. The party continued beyond dawn: policemen had to be brought in to encourage the final guests to leave; passersby on their way to work were startled by the sight of scantily clad young men and women in search of buses and taxis. Much more disquieting, from the angle of newspaper moralists, was the musical accompaniment. "Great astonishment and not a little indignation is being expressed in London over the reports that in the early hours of yesterday morning a large number of Society women danced in bathing dresses to the music of a Negro band at a 'swim and dance' gathering organized by some of Mayfair's Bright Young People," the *Sunday Chronicle* observed. A "well-known society hostess" remarked that her principal objection to the party was "the colored element."

Disapproval of this kind was routine for the England of 1928. But what also floats across the surface of the Bath and Bottle Party, along with the rubber horses and the deliquescing flowers, is the scent of elegy. Brenda Dean Paul remembered it as one of the last of the "big" parties before the late-twenties diaspora and the gradual debasement of an ideal. Looking back from the wasteland of the mid-1930s, she had "the recollection of turgid water and thousands of bobbing champagne corks, discarded bathing caps and petal-strewn tiles as the sun came out and filtered through the giant skylights of St. George's Baths, and we wended our way home." This is a characteristic image from the Bright Young People's world: the thought of sorrowing in sunlight, good times gone, the myriad champagne corks bobbing away on a stream turned unexpectedly chill.

Who were the Bright Young People? Answering that question is one of the principal objects of this book, for all the obstacles thrown across the pursuer's path—either out of a sense of self-preservation or from sheer mischief—by the Bright Young People themselves. To give only the most obvious example, Evelyn Waugh's *Vile Bodies* (1930) is always taken as the definitive exposé of this restless, rackety Mayfair world, its endless flights to nowhere in particular, its fractured alliances and emo-

BEAUCHAMP. *)

The Woman. "ARE YOU ONE OF THE BRIGHT YOUNG PEOPLE? *I AM.*"

tional dead ends. Yet the typescript of the novel contains a prefatory warning: "Bright Young People and others kindly note that all characters are entirely imaginary (and you get far too much publicity already whoever you are)." This is the reddest of red herrings. Waugh knew exactly who "they" were. A letter of July 1929 to his friend and fellow novelist Henry Yorke, when *Vile Bodies* was a quarter done, notes, "It is rather like P. G. Wodehouse and about bright young people." Waugh, then staying in the country, goes on to discuss a party invitation from their mutual friends Bryan and Diana Guinness: "I might go up for it if I thought there wouldn't be anyone who wouldn't be too much like the characters in my new book." The novel contains half a dozen skits on, or versions of, identifiable Bright Young People, as well as up-to-the-moment facsimiles of the vocal stylings of the Guinness set. Publicly, though, Waugh was anxious to distance himself from his material, to feign ignorance of his sources, put clear water between the satirist and the things he was supposed to be satirizing. This was a common affectation among 1920s partygoers. The laughter, if it could be heard at all, was always coming from the next room.

If individual Bright Young People were chary of acknowledging their status, so the group as a whole defies instant analysis. It was at once too heterogeneous, too far-flung and at the same time too precisely located, too blatant and too interior, too promiscuous and yet too inbred. Its members ranged from the rich and aristocratic—Bryan Guinness on his marriage to Diana Mitford in 1929 was supposed to have acquired an income of £20,000 a year—to the downright disreputable. Some Bright Young People became successful writers, journalists or artists, while others plumbed the depths of drink, drugs and disappointment. They were much written about and much misrepresented. At an early stage their behavior acquired a generational focus, to the point where they were assumed to reflect the attitudes of thousands of people who barely knew that they existed. In the end, as the social historian Alan Jenkins noted, the words "Bright Young People" became a label for *all* the young in Britain who did anything unusual at all. Given that many of the Bright Young People were artists, albeit sometimes in very minor and inconsequential ways, their spoor can be tracked across vast acreages of British cultural life. Their style—brisk, affected, outwardly impersonal, inwardly often deeply vulnerable—influenced a host of descendants who knew nothing of their ancestry, and their echoes can be found in the pages of books written long after the movement's original members were gone.

The mythological baggage that accumulated around individual Bright Young People could last half a lifetime. Frequently it persisted until death.

Toward the end of February 2006, the four British broadsheet newspapers carried full-page obituaries of an elderly woman the exact nature of whose celebrity their readers would probably have struggled to locate. "Mrs. Zita James," dead at the ripe age of 102, turned out to be the former Miss Zita Jungman, and together with her younger sister, Teresa (aka "Baby"), a figure of supreme importance to the Bright Young People's legend. Beneath the obituarists' admiring gaze, a bygone world came creaking into life, composed of the tables at her mother's house, as recalled by Cecil Beaton, "groaning with caviar, oysters, pâté, turkey, kidney and bacon, hot lobsters and delicious meringues," of guest lists aflame with lustre and *éclat*, of Ivor Novello, Gladys Cooper and Tallulah Bankhead bidden to dinner, of Stephen Tennant emerging into the hall at Wilsford Manor in a white Russian suit with silver train and a bandeau round his head. Pursued—fruitlessly—across the twenties by Sacheverell Sitwell, married—briefly—to a grandson of the Duke of Wellington, Zita had apparently preserved her original outlook on life into her eleventh decade. Rising at midday in the annex she shared with Baby on the Guinness estate a dozen miles from Dublin, she was accustomed to devote at least some part of the day to watching her favorite film, *The Sound of Music*, before retiring to bed in the small hours.

What, one wondered, had Zita done with her 102 years on the planet? Here and there came stray references to the three-quarters of a century she had spent beyond the orbit of the Bright Young People, in particular her wartime service with a Canadian-Polish ambulance unit trapped in a remote corner of Brittany in May 1940 as the German tanks sped west. All this, though, seemed of much less account than the Rolls-Royces jostling each other in Piccadilly or the evening on which, for a bet, she and Lord Birkenhead's daughter Lady Eleanor Smith tried to spend the night in the Chamber of Horrors in Madame Tussaud's. And then, of course, there were the photographs, culled from Beaton's archive: Zita with pageboy haircut as Romeo, about to attend a fancy dress ball; the two sisters lying horizontally, head to head and with eyes closed, on plastic sheeting.

The most memorable of all is a group portrait taken at Wilsford in the summer of 1927. Here, got up in the style of a Watteau fête champêtre, sit seven of the most dandified exquisites ever placed before a camera. Zita, on the extreme left, stares out at an angle to the lens, one hand on her outstretched knee. The composer William Walton, looking like Punchinello, wears a floral jerkin and carries a feathery straw hat. Cecil Beaton, at the rear of the group, has the waxed, rigid face of a doll. Stephen Tennant and Georgia Sitwell, Sacheverell's wife, sit side by side. Baby, next in line, looks directly at the photographer, while Rex Whistler, on the extreme right, eyes closed beneath heavily accentuated eyebrows, pouts coyly with one hand balanced tremulously on his hip. It is an extraordinary portrait—stylized, sophisticated, ultramodern, and yet, in its dandy posturing, hugely frivolous and self-centered, an image that, in the end, conveys nothing except its own artificiality. By chance, Lytton Strachey arrived at Wilsford while the pictures were being taken. "Strange creatures," he is supposed to have remarked, "with just a few feathers where brains should be."

Zita lived for another eighty years, through the Second World War, Suez, the sixties, the three-day week, Thatcherism and beyond, yet this is the picture that encapsulates her existence. From the angle of the observing world, nothing of any significance happened to her beyond this point: she exists forever on the edge of the Wilsford charivari. Curiously enough, one of Zita's obituarists, the biographer Philip Hoare, noted that having filed a piece about the Bright Young People to mark the opening of Stephen Fry's 2003 film *Bright Young Things*, he received a letter from one of her relatives suggesting that she had achieved rather more than a succession of cameo appearances at the parties of the 1920s. On the contrary, all the evidence suggests that the reverse is the case and that Zita's life stopped here on a bridge in Wiltshire, on a bright summer's morning in 1927, with Cecil and Stephen capering in the foreground, and Lytton Strachey marching silently toward them over the dusty Wilsford drive.

"Even to want to write about so-called artists who spend on sodomy what they have gained by sponging betrays a kind of spiritual inadequacy," George Orwell declared, in a review of Cyril Connolly's solitary novel, *The Rock Pool* (1936). Orwell's point becomes all the more marked when you realize that Connolly's collection of remittance men and seedy self-gratifiers idly languishing on the French Riviera can be taken as the down-at-heel, bohemian end of the Bright Young People *en vacance*. Stark warnings over the perils of dealing with frivolity, and frivolity's myriad guises, litter the late-twentieth-century literary landscape. "This book is richly stocked with people whom any person of decent instincts will find loathsome," John Carey once wrote—sounding rather like Orwell himself—in a review of *Children of the Sun* (1976), Martin Green's chronicle of interwar English "decadence."

The appearance, some years before, of Marie-Jaqueline Lancaster's massive compendium of the life of Brian Howard provoked Julian Symons, another critic in the Orwell mold, to fury. To Symons, Mrs. Lancaster's six hundred pages of debt, dereliction and despair was an epic distillation of false values, caste and clique triumphing over genuine merit: "Today the gentlemen are on the defensive, but there are still reasons to be miffed about (to take a small instance) the seriousness with which a book about the talentless Brian Howard, talentless perhaps, but amusing and *one of us*, was recently treated." The thought that seriousness is automatically the preserve of people with cheery proletarian values and prosaic lifestyles—that a barfly with a private income and a web of well-connected friends has already damned himself beyond redemption—is one of the great consolations of English literary life. I am not immune to it myself. "The humblest coal miner who ever tried to write a sonnet is of more intrinsic literary—and social—interest than Steenie Tennant," *Private Eye*'s anonymous critic pronounced in an appraisal of Philip Hoare's *Serious Pleasures: The Life of Stephen Tennant* (1990), "but alas, the toff hagiography strain of English letters endures."

In fact, I was that anonymous critic. Seventeen years later, I'm not sure that I agree with my younger self. Neither is it possible to write off Brian Howard and his associates as a gang of gilded triflers. The influence of the Bright Young People can be felt throughout twentieth-century artistic life. To take only the most flagrant examples, the London society world of the mid- to late 1920s was a crucible in which were forged the careers of several of England's greatest novelists, one of its best-loved contemporary poets and half a dozen leading figures in ballet, photography and surrealist painting. Beneath the surface hubbub lay, too, a deep strain of unease, often extending to outright melancholy. Raised in the shadow of the Great War, denied most of the social and economic certainties of their parents' generation, the Bright Young People knew, if they had any sense of perspective, that their pleasures came at a price, that somewhere in the middle distance a reckoning awaited. "It is a queer world which the old men have left them," Evelyn Waugh wrote in a valedictory editorial for his school magazine, considering the plight of what he called "the youngest generation," "and they will have few ideals and illusions to console them when they 'get to feeling old.' They will not be a happy generation."

It was a prophetic remark. Born into an atmosphere of marked cards and unpaid debts—moral, spiritual and economic—their relationships were prone to fracture, their marriages to collapse. In the diaspora of the 1930s, when the Mayfair alliances had broken up, they searched desperately for political and religious certainties—became socialists, communists, fascists and Catholics, wrote poems against the dictators, fought in Spain and resisted the men bent on appeasing Hitler. If the social baggage they brought with them from the 1920s occasionally compromised their efforts to "connect" ("25th August—end of everything for us; 31st August—back from party 3:30 a.m.," runs Brian Howard's record of a stay in the south of France immediately before the outbreak of the Second World War), this isn't to extinguish the seriousness of the attempt. Even their failures—the chronic inability of a Howard or a Stephen Tennant to leave anything behind them for posterity except their legend—have a desperate human interest. As for salvaging anything from Howard's microscopic oeuvre, there is hardly anything to salvage. Yet the dandy posturing is undercut by an occasionally lacerating self-awareness. "At least I'm a has-been," he is once supposed to have snapped to a fellow member during a late-period entanglement at the Gargoyle Club, "and that's something you can never be." It was the same with Elizabeth Ponsonby, whose career in the 1930s is a kind of object lesson in the futility of thinking that you can go on living the life of your gilded youth in a world of marching armies and three million unemployed. Elizabeth, it is fair to say, is one of the twenties' enduring symbols: a bright, capering spirit with a weekly berth in every gossip column in Fleet Street who died before she was forty.

Perhaps this is just the inevitable fate of youth movements, that degeneration of early sparkle into a "revolt into style," to borrow George Melly's phrase, which leaves the founders washed up on a shore from which the tides of fashion have long since receded. In the end, the Bright Young People's legacy is not a shelf of books or even an album full of photographs but an atmosphere, a way of communicating, an outlook, a gesture, an essence. Looking back on his lost youth in the early 1960s, Evelyn Waugh suggested that "there was between the wars a society, cosmopolitan, sympathetic to the arts, well-mannered, above all ornamental even in rather bizarre ways, which for want of a better description the newspapers called 'High Bohemia.'" This book is an attempt to trace the contours of that society, to examine its origins, the particular elements of style, culture and language that existed at its core and the wreckage that accumulated in its wake after the dance was over.

CHAPTER ONE

FIGURES IN A LANDSCAPE

Human nature being what it is, trivial and surface manifestations of revolutionary exuberance will always have a fascination for the average reader.
—DOUGLAS GOLDRING, *The Nineteen-Twenties* (1945)

The 1920s were the great age of the press sensation. The defrocked vicar, the nightclub raid, the genteel murder, the man swallowed whole by the whale and regurgitated onto the sand bleached white by its gastric juices—all these were served up by mass-market news-papers as indiscriminately as a packet of hundreds and thousands. Middle-class readers who opened their copies of the *Daily Mail* on July 26, 1924, found a yet more enticing phenomenon: the discovery, alive and kicking on the streets of central London, of nothing less than a brand-new youth cult. CHASING CLUES, the report proclaimed. NEW SOCIETY GAME.

MIDNIGHT CHASE IN LONDON
50 MOTOR CARS
THE BRIGHT YOUNG PEOPLE

This, the *Mail*'s reporter continued, using the language of the hunting field, was the "final meet" of the "Society of Bright Young People," a nebulous body that had inaugurated a series of treasure hunts through the capital. The society had apparently grown from "a few enthusiastic couples hunting for a prize of a few pounds" to a movement that had "captured all smart London." There followed a description of the "meet" and the celebrities present—these included the actresses Gladys

Cooper and Tallulah Bankhead—then a graphic account of the hunt itself, written up in a style halfway between the report of a race meeting and a fashion page.

> By this time slow cars had given place to high-powered ones, and slow wits to faster wits, so that the field, which had started some 50 cars strong, all closely packed, jostling for position, was straggled out, though still traveling well.
>
> Lovely coiffures and beautiful dresses deftly arranged were no longer in that form. Shingled heads scored heavily, for long hair was in many cases streaming in the breeze. Dressmakers should rejoice for the birth of the Bright Young People, for few of the frocks which went to Seven Dials yesterday morning will ever see the light of a ballroom again. A crawl on all fours in that none too clean neighborhood . . . in search of an elusive clue chalked on the pavement, has soiled the majority beyond repair.

After cruising around the seedier purlieus of Covent Garden, members of the convoy concluded their evening at Norfolk House, St. James's, where in addition to the final clue "a splendid breakfast had been prepared and a string band to cheer them after their strenuous adventures."

Thus set down, the account introduces most of the elements that would subsequently be associated with the Bright Young People: glamour, money, famous names and lashings of snob appeal. The baton was soon taken up by other papers: *Punch* published a cartoon the very next month in which a burglar claims to be a Bright Young Person. It was entirely appropriate that the initial unveiling should take place in the *Daily Mail*. One of the features of the cultural landscape of the immediately postwar period was the emergence of a new middle-class press, one step up from lowbrow tabloids such as the *Mirror*, several rungs down from the sonorities of *The Times* and the *Telegraph*, less keen on straightforward news and political debate than on what were known as "talking points," personages and personalities. "Get more names in the paper. The more aristocratic the better, if there's a news story around them," Lord Northcliffe, the *Mail*'s proprietor, had instructed his staff, sounding rather like Lord Copper of the *Daily Beast* in Evelyn Waugh's *Scoop*. "Everyone likes reading about people in better circumstances than his or her own ... Write and seek news with at least the £1,000 a year man in mind."

By the standards of the mid-1920s the "£1,000 a year man" was a fabulous plutocrat: the average provincial clerical wage, for example, was barely a tenth of this figure. Such discrepancies between the profile of the average reader and the moneyed exquisites whom journalists were supposed to have in mind brought an odd or, from the angle of modern journalism, thoroughly conventional focus in which readers were silently encouraged to aspire to a condition, an income and a way of life that hardly any of them could ever hope to achieve. At the same

Disturbed Intruder. "Sh! Not a word, Guv'nor. I belongs to the League o' Bright Young People, an' this is one of our 'unts fer missin' clues."

time, as part of its campaign to render journalism less staid and more attractive to the potential purchasers, the *Mail* was keen on "stunts"—sand castle competitions at holiday resorts, improvements to the British loaf, the "*Daily Mail* hat," halfway between a Homburg and a bowler, and, despite the fact that Winston Churchill was persuaded to be photographed in it, one of the paper's few failures. Nothing could have been more of a "stunt" than the handful of socialites who jammed their expensive cars into the narrow byways of Seven Dials. Not only did the "society" already exist, contain recognizable figureheads and pursue favorite recreations, its members seemed perfectly happy to assist in their own exploitation. If the Bright Young People had shunned publicity and kept themselves to obscure country houses or Mayfair cellars, their individual destinies might have been very different. As it was, they concluded an instantaneous compact with the press which, in the end, was to prove their undoing.

As the *Mail*'s reporter had deduced, the origins of the Bright Young People predated their lavishly framed public debut. Essentially they grew out of the activities of a small and initially faintly exclusive group that included Lady Eleanor Smith, Elizabeth Ponsonby, Zita and Baby Jungman and Elizabeth's cousin, with whom she was frequently confused, Loelia Ponsonby. Loelia dated the origin of the treasure hunt to the day sometime in 1922 or 1923 when

> Zita and Teresa and Eleanor and another friend, Enid Raphael, had nothing to do so they invented a new kind of paper-chase. Zita and Eleanor were the hares with five minutes start and they zig-zagged about London using buses and undergrounds and leaving clues behind them as they went. This turned out to be such an exciting game that they asked me and some other girls to join in and we used to amuse ourselves on blank afternoons by chasing each other round London.

All these young people fitted Lord Northcliffe's criteria for newsworthiness. Eleanor Smith was the daughter of Lord Birkenhead, formerly lord chancellor and soon to be appointed secretary of state for

India; Mrs. Jungman's second marriage had attached her daughters to the great brewing house of Guinness; Loelia's father was "Fritz" Ponsonby, later Lord Sysonby, and at this point in a long courtier's career comptroller to King George V. The girls, and their biddable male associates, specialized in small-scale practical joking. Eleanor, Brian Howard and their friend Alannah Harper, for example, once broke into the Surrey mansion of the Richard Guinnesses—Zita's and Baby's mother and stepfather—stole Mrs. Guinness's pearls and burned the flannel nightdress brought by her guest Mrs. Asquith in that lady's bedroom. The police were called and a scandal averted only by an apologetic telephone call from Mrs. Howard.

Generally, these early manifestations were greeted with a certain amount of indulgence. Low-key at first, the spoofs became more and more elaborate. Baby, for instance, pretended to be a reporter from a nonexistent newspaper and interviewed Beverley Nichols at Claridge's while her sister and Eleanor hid under the table. One treasure hunt led to the Hovis factory on the Embankment, where a clue had been baked into a loaf of brown bread, and on another to a special edition of the *Evening Standard*, printed with the amused connivance of its proprietor, Lord Beaverbrook. In the course of one small-hours foray on Buckingham Palace, the captain of the guard took fright at the convoy of cars and telephoned for reinforcements. As the field increased the pool assembled at the outset could rise to as much as £100, while spin-off activities became increasingly complex. There were "scavenger" parties, where guests were bidden to bring back a spider in a matchbox, a policeman's helmet or one of Stanley Baldwin's pipes, and devious hoaxes in which Eleanor masqueraded as a Russian princess or a young man introduced to his fellow guests at a country house party as "Prince Michael of Serbia" kept up the deception throughout the weekend, telling fantastic stories of his motoring exploits and being allowed to get away with some spectacular cheating at bridge.

The point about these early exploits, other than irritating the people who came within their orbit, is that they established the celebrity of individual members of the Bright Young People long before the movement had any deliberate focus. John Rothenstein remembered meeting

Elizabeth Ponsonby for the first time at a lunch party in 1923: "a stylishly slender girl of about twenty-two, with an oval pale face especially modeled, it seemed to me, to express an aristocratic disdain . . . Already she was something of a legend." Elizabeth's mother, the formidable Dorothea Ponsonby, was alarmed by the rise of a new, ostentatiously moneyed, younger "set" in which her much less well-off daughter had become all too willingly entangled. "E's standard of riches angers me," she confided to her diary late in the same year. "Taxis always—everywhere. It doesn't amuse her to dine anywhere but at the Berkeley. She lives like a person with £3,000 a year who spends £800 on her dress." Where her daughter, supposedly sustained by a tiny parental allowance, got her money from Dorothea didn't care to inquire, she decided. But whatever its source, "the standard set by her *nouveau riche* friends is impossible."

Dorothea's complaints would be restated on countless occasions during the next few years by parents bewildered by what they perceived as reckless extravagance and bad company. Meanwhile, there are two fundamental questions to be asked. Who were the Bright Young People and, perhaps more easily answerable, where did the phrase originate? Etymologically, "Bright Young Person" is only one among a number of sobriquets that came into being in the 1920s to describe a part of the social demographic usually on the right side of thirty but in some cases many years or even decades beyond it. The most resonant of these was the collective tag of "the lost generation," whose echoes were still faintly resounding as late as the eve of the Second World War. " 'You are all a lost generation!' remarked Gertrude Stein of us post-war age groups," runs the second line of "Where Engels Fears to Tread," Cyril Connolly's spoof on the noncareer of Brian Howard, "and now . . . we know who lost us." Stein had supposedly coined the phrase to describe the evocations of jeunesse dorée pioneered by F. Scott Fitzgerald and Ernest Hemingway in novels such as the former's *The Beautiful and Damned* (1922) and the latter's *The Sun Also Rises* (1926). Alec Waugh, alternatively, remembered a never-to-be-published book of this title by Douglas Jerrold coming his way in 1920. This suggested to him that the expression was in current usage only a year or so after the Great War.

Whatever its origin it had, essentially, two meanings. On the one hand, large numbers of young men had been literally "lost," that is, wiped out by the conflict of 1914–18. Looking through the Sherborne old boys' circular in 1942, Waugh calculated that exactly half the forty-two boys admitted to the school in his own year of entry, 1911, were dead, the majority of them on the Western Front. The survivors of this carnage were lost in a different way: set adrift in a postwar world that had changed beyond recognition and whose new protocols were ominously difficult to comprehend. "And of those who had so far survived," Waugh went on, surveying the thousands of young ex–army officers like himself who had seen their lives thrown into disarray, "how many had not had their chances of making an effective contribution to the world of their generation ruined by the interruption of their education, the dislocation of their plans?" But however "lost," dispersed and vagrant, and irrespective of whether they had fought in the war, young people of the kind who followed the early 1920s treasure hunts, or went scavenging in search of a celebrated actress's corsets, nearly always considered themselves homogenous, part of the same broadly defined social group, sustained if not by social or economic ties then by a communal view of the life they led.

Brian Howard once inscribed a book to "Harold Acton, the poet of my generation"—which is subtly proprietorial, perhaps, but also acknowledges the existence of a collective spirit. Evelyn Waugh, writing in 1929 to Henry Yorke about their mutual friend Diana Mitford, newly married to Bryan Guinness, wondered "Do you and Dig [Yorke's wife] share my admiration for Diana? She seems to me the one encouraging figure in this generation." One doesn't have to regard the young Guinnesses as the idlest of social butterflies to think that this is a rather extraordinary claim to be made of a girl not yet past her twentieth birthday, and to assume that there are secret codes at work, a kind of quietly canvassed spiritual consanguinity of which only Waugh and his immediate circle were aware. What made Diana Mitford exceptional? The outsider cannot tell, but Waugh's assumption of hidden depths is intriguing, and yet more so in that it exists in direct contrast to a surface world of partygoing, expensive cars and rentier lucre.

Much less exact is the description "Bright Young Thing." Again, this was in general use very soon after the end of the First World War, but the meaning is all-purpose, as imprecise in its way as "flapper." A Bright Young Person may have been a Bright Young Thing, but not all Bright Young Things were Bright Young People. The chattering twenty-somethings who infest literary parties attended by Gordon Comstock, the disaffected hero of Orwell's *Keep the Aspidistra Flying* (1936)— "troops of bright young things who dropped in for half an hour, formed circles of their own and talked sniggeringly about other bright young things whom they referred to by nicknames"—have nothing to do with Elizabeth Ponsonby and her friends: this is simply Orwell's shorthand for anything juvenile, bumptious and loud. Used in this way, "Bright Young Thing" had a wide currency throughout the 1920s and beyond, variously employed as a means of identification, an archetype (as in newspaper articles about "What the bright young thing is thinking") and as an advertising tool designed to reach anyone between the ages of eighteen and thirty-five.

"Bright," in any case, was one of the key adjectives of the decade, regularly applied—again, mostly by newspapers and society magazines—to any activity that seemed to represent a departure from the prewar groove or a challenge to prewar staidness. A "Brighter London Society" had been founded as early as 1922—patrons included the Bishop of Birmingham and Gordon Selfridge—with the aim of making London "economically the most worthy and beautiful city in the world." Among the usages identified by *Punch* in the 1920s, for example, were campaigns for "Brighter Clothes for Men," "Brighter Motoring," "Brighter Pantomimes" and even "Brighter Bridge." It was inevitable that some of this luster should rub off on youth. In the late-twenties press advert for Abdulla cigarettes a group of dandified exquisites, in what looks like elaborate fancy dress, are greeted by their hosts at the door of a smart-looking town house. The accompanying poem by F. R. Holmes brings together several contemporary assumptions about Bright Young People—"smartness," partygoing, the thought of a great deal of extravagance achieved on the cheap—while misnaming them. The cast of "The Bright Brigade," in fact, look remarkably like the real-life faces to be seen every week in the *Tatler*. In contrast to "Bright Young Thing," or more concrete social groupings that gossip columnists of the period occasionally infiltrated (Mrs. Dersingham in J. B. Priestley's *Angel Pavement* tries to impress her guests by claiming a remote attachment to "all that young smart set, Mrs. Dellingham, young Mostyn-Price, Lady Muriel Pagworth, and the famous Ditchways"), "Bright Young Person" had a much more distinctive framing. Bright Young People, all the late 1920s evidence suggests, were that much more exclusive, better connected, the initiators of trends and fads rather than the acolytes who followed in their wake. In the last resort a Bright Young Thing was a stereotype, a Bright Young Person an identifiable individual whose footprints could be tracked all over the landscape of the London society magazines.

None of this, though, tells us who the Bright Young People actually *were*. The first ever Bright Young Person, according to Osbert Sitwell,

was Beverley Nichols. But Nichols had no real connection with the Jungman sisters and their immediate circle: he was an up-and-coming literary man with one eye on the stage and a weakness for the society of elderly aristocratic ladies. And yet, with his serial appearances in gossip columns and his ability to seem "in the swim and of the moment," as one journalist put it, he seemed to personify the mid-twenties cult of youth. In middle age, former members invariably emphasized the smallness of the movement's scale, its exclusiveness and impenetrability: "a gang of boisterous juveniles," Nichols himself decided in 1949, acknowledging that the phrase "Bright Young People" had now become "painfully evocative." According to Douglas Goldring, a novelist and social chronicler of a rather older generation, "In the 'twenties a very small handful of Bright Young People secured a great deal of publicity by throwing wild parties and indulging in kindergarten orgies of gin, sex and drugs which caused their faces to be printed in the Sunday newspapers."

The ranks of this "boisterous little gang of publicity hunters"—note again the use of the adjective "boisterous"—might have reached two thousand in all, Goldring calculated, "with a fringe of socialites and intellectuals of the kind portrayed in novels by Arlen, Huxley and later Waugh." Even allowing for hangers-on, two thousand looks like an overestimate. Newspaper unmaskings of key personnel tended to produce mixed results. To examine press coverage of the Bright Young People over the period 1924–30 is to find periodic shifts of emphasis as different sets and subsets move in and out of the limelight. Many of the original treasure hunters gave up by the mid-1920s, put off by the clamor of press attention. Loelia Ponsonby claimed that she never attended a Bright Young People gathering after 1925, and that even scavenger parties were a vulgar dilution of their animating spirit: as she rather disdainfully put it of the list of objects, "the embarrassment of trying to borrow them in the middle of the night can only have been equalled by the boredom of taking them back next day."

The acknowledged star of 1926–27, long after Miss Ponsonby's retirement, was Stephen Tennant. ("His appearance alone is enough to make you catch your breath—golden hair spreading in flowing waves across a delicate forehead; an ethereally transparent face; clothes which mold themselves about his slim figure," gushed the *Daily Express*.) By the end of the decade, on the other hand, press interest had shifted to the unassuming figure of Bryan Guinness and his fiancée, Diana Mitford, whose house, after their marriage in 1929, became a center for Bright Young Person activity: *Vile Bodies* owes a great deal to the "Guinness set." Meanwhile, a core element remained. Elizabeth Ponsonby and the Jungman sisters were gossip columnists' staples throughout the period, Brian Howard, Eddie Gathorne-Hardy and "Babe" Plunket Greene only slightly less so. The *Sunday Dispatch*, reflecting on the phenomenon long after it had ceased to exist, decided that in the end there were "only four" true Bright Young People and that they were the hosts of the Bath and Bottle Party.

It was all very well for newspapers to "name" Bright Young People: frequently those identified wanted nothing to do with the exposure. To a certain kind of partygoer, usually one connected with the Guinness network, these affiliations were there only to be disdained. In his memoirs Bryan Guinness lamented that a society magazine "implied that we belonged to a set called the Bright Young People." Even in old age Guinness professed to be horrified by these imputations of juvenile license: "I remember at the time suggesting that this set was entirely alien to us and our friends, and even suggesting that the appellation was libelous." The real Bright Young People, he proposed, "were those we read about in the newspapers and who were rightly satirised by Evelyn Waugh. We saw an immense distance between our group of talented friends and the sensation-mongering crowd to whom the name was applied." Although Guinness concedes that "it is possible that the distinction was less apparent to others than it was to us," this kind of distancing was very common. At Zita Jungman's wedding to Arthur James in 1929, "Johanna" of *The Lady* was "assured by Guinness after Guinness . . . that there are not and never were any Bright Young People." Diana Guinness, too, in later life was concerned to debunk some of the myths that she assumed to have grown up about her bygone London life. Most Bright Young People, she declared, "played no part in London society." Among various names regularly proposed as paid-up members of the clan, Evelyn Waugh was "definitely *not* one," owing to his intense distaste for parties.

To counter these disconcerting refusals to be drawn, one can only point out that *Vile Bodies* borrows much of its language from the Guinnesses' own drawing room. All the same, a strict chronology of Bright Young personnel and involvement is difficult to come by. Contemporary press reports are notoriously fallible. Gossip columnists ordered to cover a particular social event had a habit of recording the names of people whom they only assumed to be present. Diana Mosley had no memory of having attended the Bath and Bottle Party: "We went to lovely balls, but *not* in St. George's Swimming Baths." Many of the links forged by ambitious young men to the movement were cheerfully opportunistic. Responding to a suggestion that he, Evelyn Waugh and Noël Coward were the Bright Young People's chief illuminati, Beverley Nichols was keen to point out that "we had far too much work to do, and we were in fact their most energetic critics." Nevertheless, as he admits, "there seemed no particular object, at that moment, in denying our depravity." One sees Nichols's point, while wondering if a certain amount of cake isn't being had and eaten, too, and if the man who elsewhere in his autobiography turns sentimentally nostalgic about the champagne corks bobbing on the surface of the moonlit stream wasn't himself occupying a ringside seat at the twenties circus.

Happily, there were some former Bright Young People who were prepared both to name names and to locate them in a recognizable period milieu. Daphne Fielding's biography of Rosa Lewis, legendary chatelaine of the equally legendary Cavendish Hotel in Jermyn Street, imagines a summer night in 1923 and somebody suggesting "Let's go round to Rosa's." As one, the young people

pile into taxis which draw up outside the Cavendish. The night porter, Moon, looking like a cross old turtle, reluctantly opens the door, and in they troup: Brian Howard, Hugh Lygon, David and Olivia Plunket Greene; Lord Ribblesdale's grandson Martin Wilson, Lettice Lygon, the lily-fair daughter of Earl Beauchamp, and Mark Ogilvie-Grant, giving his impersonation of Clara Butt singing "Land of Hope and Glory," followed by his cousin Nina Seafield, a red-haired edition of the young Queen Victoria; Henry Weymouth and Daphne Vivian twanging ukuleles, Michael Rosse and his sister Bridget Parsons, pioneers of the Charleston in Mayfair ballrooms; Nancy Mitford and Hamish Erskine, Elizabeth Ponsonby and Robert Byron, John Sutro and Babe McGusty.

All those mentioned here played at least some part in the Bright Young People world: all that jars is the date. To particularize, in 1923 Brian Howard, Robert Byron and Mark Ogilvie-Grant were still at Eton and Henry Weymouth still at Harrow, the teenaged Nancy Mitford still firmly under the thumb of her parents, Lord and Lady Redesdale, and Hamish St. Clair Erskine a boy of fourteen. In fact, each of Nancy's biographers suggests that her first meeting with Hamish did not take place until several years later.

At the same time, whether the kind of after-hours carouse described here dated from 1923 or, as seems much more likely, 1928, we have the beginnings of a world, an ambience and, more important, a cast. But where did it, and they, come from? Youth movements seldom emerge, fully fledged, out of the ether. They need originators, conduits, seed beds, links with other groupings that preceded them. Early anatomists of the Bright Young People were inclined to associate them with recent outbreaks of London bohemianism, such as the almost mythical parties given by Gwen Otter and her brother Frank in Edwardian days, or the "green carnation" partygoers of Wilde-era aestheticism. Certainly, there were interesting continuities: Elizabeth Ponsonby at one point lodged with the ageing Miss Otter, to the consternation of her parents; Evelyn Waugh's midtwenties diaries are full of references to lunching with "Gwen," of being shown her collection of Wilde pamphlets, of going with her to meet the actor Ernest Thesiger; Vyvyan Holland, a fixture of the twenties party circuit, was Oscar Wilde's son; Wilde's niece Dorothy was a friend of Stephen Tennant. Bright Young People themselves emphasized links with a glamorous yet recherché metropolitan social life of which they had been dimly aware in childhood. Defending his lifestyle to his mother, and simultaneously distancing himself from his much-loathed father, Brian Howard maintained that "years ago, such a group was led by Nancy [Cunard], and Iris [Tree] and Diana Cooper. Daddy—and it is simply no USE denying it—would have been proud to have been at their parties . . ." Several figures from this era, and some eras even further removed in time, survived to ornament the world of the Bright Young People. Osbert Lancaster remembered his youthful fascination with Harry Melville, the octogenarian theatrical impresario, "one of the last of the professional diners-out," whose social calendar in his salad days was said to have been fully booked from early May through to Goodwood. For Lancaster and his contemporaries, Melville's interest was practically archaeological: "an attested friend of Oscar Wilde, one who had encountered Proust when both were sitting to Blanche, he seemed to embody all the fabled sophistication of a period of which we were disposed to take the rosiest view."

The movement's early sponsors, on the other hand, tended to be men in their late twenties who had served in the Great War and moved on into Fleet Street or literature. Beverley Nichols, for example, born in 1898, was already established as a journalist by the mid-1920s, his homosexuality concealed behind a veneer of boyish charm. ("There is not much of the superficial bright young person about a young man who will take you round his garden and tell you how the lupins and larkspur are coming on," one female profile writer enthused.) A pet of society hostesses, the confidant of Dame Nelly Melba, whose memoirs he ghosted, Nichols supplied a bridge between the staider environment of the London ballroom and the more raffish social life that had grown up since the armistice. Alec Waugh, Nichols's exact contemporary, a novelist who had published his wartime best seller *The Loom of Youth* (1917) at a precocious nineteen, offered connections to the world of literary magazines and publishers' parties.

The gap in years between some of the older Bright Young People and their younger contemporaries was not unbridgeably wide: Alec Waugh was born in 1898, Brian Howard in 1905. Other factors, notably the experience of war service, could turn this discrepancy into a chasm.

The great 1920s joke peddled by newspapers about the Bright Young People was the presence in their ranks of moonlighting middle age. A *Punch* cartoon from 1927 shows an unfashionably dressed woman, well beyond her first youth, confronting a balding gentleman in a dinner jacket. "Are *you* one of the Bright Young People?" she demands. "*I* am." Sharp-eyed observers were occasionally conscious that the social scene of which they were a part was in danger of turning into an old person's racket. At a night club party on New Year's Eve 1929, Henry Yorke noted the presence of "old men with red faces and bald heads with their eyes knocking against their spectacles, yelling and shrieking." Evelyn Waugh was even more scathing: "In Society indefatigable maiden ladies of Chelsea and Mayfair, dyspeptic noble-men and bald old wits still caper in the public eye as 'the Bright Young People,' " he warned readers of the *Evening Standard*.

Like much of what Waugh wrote about the Bright Young People, this is an exaggeration. The specimen Bright Young Person—and this includes most of the people who appear on Daphne Fielding's list—was, in fact, almost absurdly youthful. Elizabeth Ponsonby, born in December 1900, was a distinctly older figure. The median date of birth was around 1905. Diana Mitford, on her engagement to Bryan Guinness, was a mere eighteen. If age brought consanguinity, then so did the alliances of school and university. Eleanor Smith and Zita Jungman had been at Miss Douglas's establishment at Queen's Gate with Alannah Harper. The founding members of the Eton Society of the Arts in 1920 included Howard, Yorke, Harold Acton and Anthony Powell. Evelyn Waugh and Tom Driberg first came across each other at Lancing College. Oxford, too, became a Bright Young Person's nursery. The legacy of the war, manifested in gruff ex-servicemen who referred to the dining hall as "mess" and the legend of the misbehaving former officer apprehended by a proctor's bulldog who turned out to be his batman, had dissipated by about 1922, after which the most fashionable colleges, Magdalen and Christ Church, were dominated by a new breed of undergraduates, predominantly Old Etonians notable for the flamboyance of their dress and manner. The undergraduate magazine *Isis* produced this account of the Hypocrites' Club:

The Hypocrites are perhaps the most entertaining people in the University. They express their souls in terms of shirts and gray flannel trousers and find outlet for their artistic ability on the walls of their clubrooms. To talk to they are rather alarming. They have succeeded in picking up a whole series of intellectual catch-phrases with which they proceed to dazzle their friends and frighten their acquaintance: and they are the only people I have ever met who have reduced rudeness to a fine art.

Anthony Powell, who went up to Balliol from Eton in the autumn of 1923, preserved a photograph of a fancy dress party held at the club in March 1924 under the auspices of Robert Byron and John "The Widow" Lloyd, so nicknamed after one of his friends saw an advertisement for a shaving preparation called "The Widow Lloyd's Euxesis." Byron masquerades as his namesake; Harold Acton is in uniform, topped with a white mask; Powell himself wears antique military garb and carries a sword. The whole thing—costumes, attitudes, expressions—strongly anticipates some of the press portraits of Bright Young gatherings held later in the decade in London.

Vast acreages of Bright Young People life—its extravagance, its whimsicality, its calculated excess—seem to have come under the plow somewhere between Christ Church's Peckwater Quadrangle and Oxford High Street, with occasional excursions into the surrounding countryside. John Fothergill, landlord of the Spread Eagle at Thame, remembered a "wake" held to mark the (temporary) closure of the Hypocrites by the university authorities at which fifty guests drank sixty bottles of champagne. Again, exotic costumes were a feature of the proceedings. Lord Emley, Earl Beauchamp's eldest son, wore a purple dress suit, while Byron came "shrouded with lace trimmings." Evelyn Waugh, inscribing a copy of *Decline and Fall* to Fothergill, noted that he might recognize some of the characters. Most prophetic of all, though, was the foundation of the Oxford University Railway Club, which specialized in cross-country excursions to the Midlands and lavish banquets in dining cars, the whole supported by a Gallic mythology of *chefs de gare* and *conducteurs*.

In November 1923, when fourteen people left Oxford early one evening on the Penzance–Aberdeen express, a three-course meal was rapidly consumed, including hors d'oeuvres at Bletchingdon (7:20), roast chicken and sausage at King's Sutton (7:51) and dessert and coffee at Lutterworth (8:43). Arriving at Leicester, the club debouched across the platform to catch the train returning in the opposite direction. During a brief annual general meeting, Richard Pares, later to become a Fellow of All Souls, was elected *chef de gare*, the Honorable Gavin Henderson appointed "guard" and Harold Acton installed as *conducteur*, while toasts were drunk to King Edward VII, the railway companies and the steward of the train. Back in Oxford, "holding aloft the signals which had decorated the table, a procession of fourteen in dinner jackets ascended the hill from Oxford station with thankfulness in their hearts for their journey of 150 miles." Composed of well-born, if not positively aristocratic, former public school boys, the membership list of the Railway Club reads like a gazetteer of future Bright Young People. A photograph from a 1925 excursion includes Henry Yorke, Lord Weymouth, David Plunket Greene, Brian Howard, John Sutro, Hugh Lygon, Bryan Guinness, Patrick Balfour and Mark Ogilvie-Grant. These are exactly the kind of Oxford circles in which Basil Seal, the scapegrace hero of Evelyn Waugh's *Black Mischief* (1932), is remembered to have moved:

> He played poker for high stakes. His luncheon parties lasted until dusk, his dinner parties dispersed in riot. Lovely young women visited him from London in high-powered cars. He went away for weekends without leave and climbed into college over the tiles at night. He had travelled all over Europe, spoke six languages, called dons by their Christian names and discussed their books with them.

Such guests, needless to say, were always welcome in Mayfair drawing rooms. A feature of the Bright Young People's hold on London society at the movement's zenith was the way in which leading hostesses—Lady Carisbrooke, the Duchess of Sutherland, Mrs. Keigwin—could be persuaded to stage entertainment of a Bright Young Person's character. To straightforward society figures could be added a more ramshackle layer of pleasure seekers: dress designers like Norman Hartnell and Willie Clarkson, mysterious foreign nobility such as Count Anthony Bosdari ("Tony Bosdari"), supposedly related to the king of Italy, the hard-drinking baronet Sir Francis Laking, and well-connected but hard-up young women like Brenda Dean Paul. Brenda (born 1907) is a pattern example of the kind of social connections that might lead their bearer into the world of the Bright Young People. The daughter of a baronet, and on her mother's side the granddaughter of a celebrated Polish violinist, she was inducted by her mother into London society in her early teens, met Noël Coward and fraternized with Mrs. Benjamin Guinness's daughters Meraud and Tanis. In 1923, aged sixteen, she attended her first adult party, hosted by the theatrical impresario Ned Lathom, in honor of Tallulah Bankhead, and watched the principal guest arrive after midnight, "breathless and glamorous, like a tornado in bright blue chiffon," to conclude her performance on the dance floor with several cartwheels. Instantly seduced, the wide-eyed teenager would spend the next ten years adrift on a sea of parties, rarely going to bed before four or five in the morning, seldom eating and sustaining her existence on a diet of cocktails, double brandies and salted nuts.

Exclusive, blue-blooded and moneyed at the top, the movement also extended to a much less presentable basement, consisting of harder-core bohemians such as Ed Burra, Billy Chappell and Barbara Ker-Seymer, who had first met as students at the Chelsea School of Art. There were Bloomsbury connections, notably with Clive Bell and Lytton Strachey—Nancy Mitford remembered having a "jolly dance" with Strachey when he came, dressed as an admiral, to the famous "Sailor Party" of summer 1927—but also links to other literary groupings of the period diametrically opposed to Bloomsbury and its influence. Edith Sitwell, for example, was an early sponsor of Brian Howard's poetry, promoted Anthony Powell's first novel and found Tom Driberg his first job. Beneath this modernist topsoil lay the relics of an older bohemia, made up of such phenomena as the Chelsea Arts Ball and Augustus John's parties. Inevitably, the publicity that attended most of the major Bright Young

People stunts encouraged the presence of intrigued outsiders: minor literary figures from a previous generation in search of kindred spirits, journalists in search of copy, visiting Americans lured east from New York or north from Paris by the rumor of a new kind of café society.

The variety of contending constituencies could sometimes make a specimen Bright Young entertainment seem uncomfortably heterodox. At other times it was possible to blend the individual elements into a predominantly seamless whole. To celebrate the publication of a book of short stories by the novelist Mary Butts, a quintessential twenties figure who later became addicted to opium, Alec Waugh had the idea of throwing a large party at the author's flat in Belsize Park. The guests, according to Butts's friend Douglas Goldring, were equally divided between the "respectable" and "bohemian" ends of Waugh's acquaintance. The hired butler and the famous names left early; the remainder of the guests kept it up until breakfast time and finally lit a bonfire in the garden. Goldring remembered a last glimpse of Evelyn Waugh, still at this time an Oxford undergraduate, playing football with the butler's hat in the hall. The famous "Bruno Hat" hoax, from a much later date in the Bright Young People trajectory, in which guests were invited to an exhibition of faked modernist paintings, mixed several outwardly disparate elements: Bryan and Diana Guinness provided the venue; Brian Howard manufactured the art; the surrealist painter John Banting contrived the frames (out of rope); Evelyn Waugh, signing himself "A. R. de T," wrote the spoof catalogue; Lytton Strachey was among the guests.

Similarly, the social round recorded in Eddie Gathorne-Hardy's engagement diary for 1927 draws on nearly every layer of Bright Young Person society: appointments with "Babe," "Brian," "Beverley" and Sandy Baird, dinners with Harry Melville, rendezvous at fashionable clubs, a party of David Tennant's. The list of telephone numbers include "Olivia" (Plunket Greene), "Elizabeth" (Ponsonby) and "Tallulah" (Bankhead).

Multi-tiered, descending effortlessly through an almost infinite number of interconnected layers, the social unit of which the Bright Young People were a part had several distinguishing marks. The most obvious was its link to the uppermost layers of the interwar British establishment. Individual Bright Young Persons were the heirs to marquisates and earldoms; they owned broad acres in Ireland; had fabulous sums set aside by admiring parents for their upkeep. Bryan Guinness's mother is supposed to have fretted over the difficulty her son had in spending his £6,000 a year Oxford allowance. Inevitably, there were political connections. Elizabeth Ponsonby's father finished his parliamentary career as Labour leader of the House of Lords. Beverley Nichols, a high-profile president of the Oxford Union in the year after the Great War—where his achievements included persuading Winston Churchill to speak against a motion calling for the immediate dissolution of the coalition government—had his name canvassed as an Asquithian Liberal candidate. Many Conservative MPs, including Nichols's friend Victor Cazalet, and the young newcomer Bob Boothby (who in old age noted that "The Twenties were well worth a visit to this planet"), had Bright Young connections: the distance between a Tory Party gathering and a Bright Young Person's entertainment was often no more than the length of a couple of Mayfair thoroughfares, as on the night in 1929 when several guests at a party for defeated Conservative candidates in the recent general election ended up at Norman Hartnell's celebrated "Circus Party" in Bruton Street.

Senior politicians, too, had their part to play in the movement's mythology. Evelyn Waugh, Robert Byron and Gavin Henderson all knew Stanley Baldwin's daughter, Betty. The scene in *Vile Bodies* in which "Miss Brown," the prime minister's daughter, invites some Bright Young People back to her home for a late-night supper party ("It was a lovely evening for Miss Brown . . . To think that all these brilliant people, whom she had heard so much about . . . should be here in papa's dining-room, calling her 'my dear' and 'darling'") is supposedly based on a night in the mid-1920s when the Ladies Mary and Sibell Lygon, daughters of Earl Beauchamp, returning to Halkin House in the small hours from a dance without a front-door key, discovered that the footman instructed to wait up and admit them had fallen asleep. Stranded on their Belgravia doorstep in white ball gowns, they decided that the sole solution was to walk round to the only other local family they knew, the Baldwins at Downing Street, and demand a bed for the night.

However exalted some of these personal connections, they were altogether dwarfed by a far more glamorous lure: the cult of the Prince of Wales. The future King Edward VIII was one of the chief media preoccupations of the 1920s. His clothes minutely itemized, his social engagements forensically set out, his dance partners avidly discussed, the "Little Man," as the newspapers christened him, dominated front pages like no previous royal personage. Photographed during his 1924 American tour in Oxford bags, dancing, at the wheel of a motorboat or playing polo, his lifestyle—for press purposes—was that of the Bright Young Person *in excelsis*: extravagant, pleasure-seeking, fast-moving. The activities in which he involved himself, too, had all the characteristics of the twenties stunt: students from the University of Southampton dancing round him to shouts of "Here We Go Round the Prince of Wales"; the owner of the Café de Paris assuring him that only his presence on the dance floor could arrest the establishment's decline. Frequently at large in classic Bright Young Person's milieux—the nightclub, the West End party—the prince was, in a certain sense, the movement's unofficial patron. There was an ominous symbolism, again, in his detachment from the world of his parents. Compared to his playboy son, George V, with his stamp collection and his fondness for musical comedy, seemed a figure from the remote past. Such glimpses of the royal presence as he offered to late-twenties partygoers were warmly appreciated. Escorting Nina Seafield to a party at Lady Cunard's in February 1928, Cyril Connolly experienced a "snobbish thrill" at the sight of the prince walking up the wide staircase and shaking hands with Maurice Baring and Diana Cooper as he reached the summit.

It would be a mistake to exaggerate this air of exclusiveness. If the upper rungs of the Bright Young People were populated by the wealthy and the well-connected, their lower reaches could be determinedly out at elbow. However conscious they may have been of these distinctions—see Diana Mosley on the Bath and Bottle Party—most Bright Young People were keen to display a sense of solidarity. Attacks on the movement produced an instant closing of ranks. Evelyn Waugh's literary journalism from the period is marked by his eagerness to take sides against the Bright Young People's disparagers. When the writer Charles Graves abused some gate-crashing partygoers (people arriving unasked to private parties was a long-running scandal), Waugh wondered frostily whether it was conceivable "that Mr. Graves is suggesting in print that there are houses where it is natural for him to be received but not these ladies." The novelist Ethel Mannin, who had supposedly "made free" with the names of several of his friends in her autobiography, was given similarly rough treatment.

If they were anxious to defend themselves against assaults of this kind, Bright Young People were also eager to analyze exactly what being a Bright Young Person meant. Significantly, most of them stressed the movement's artistic achievements (Bryan Guinness and his "talented friends") and its pronounced bohemian slant. Writing to his mother in 1931, in response to a complaint about the notorious "White Party" which effectively set the seal on the whole Bright Young People's era, Brian Howard—not as it happened present himself—suggested that it sounded like "an amusing, wildish party given by the only group of people outside the Continent who—motley in social status though they may be—know genuinely how to enjoy themselves, rid as they are of most of the restraints self-imposed by their more titled fellows—restraints of social aspirations and sexual taboos." Howard is writing in the early 1930s, at a point when the original Bright Young People groupings had all but disintegrated, but the characteristics that he locates applied to many a gathering held several years before in the movement's heyday.

In the end the classic Bright Young Person's environment was curiously democratic: a self-contained space in which, however briefly, and in however artificial the circumstances, a duchess and an avant-garde painter could meet on equal terms. No doubt such spaces have always existed in English life, but the particular conditions of the 1920s gave them an unexpected resonance. The party at Milly Andriadis's hired house to which Nick Jenkins accompanies Charles Stringham in the second part of Anthony Powell's *A Buyer's Market* (1952) deftly reproduces this atmosphere—much more so than the deb dance which precedes it. Here, under Milly's welcoming but no-nonsense gaze, all kinds of celebrities are gathered—foreign royalty, Oxford dons, city eminences—but also an abundance of queer fish: "quite an elegant crowd," as one onlooker puts it, while including, as someone else points out, "one or two extraordinary figures from the lofts of Chelsea." What united the Bright Young People and made them seem a discrete unit was not a shared political or social outlook or an economic standing but what Patrick Balfour called "a community of impulse." On paper the connection between, say, Brenda Dean Paul, Evelyn Waugh, Diana Mitford and Ed Burra barely exists. Yet the magnets that drew together the contemporary It girl, the aspiring novelist, the peer's daughter and the avant-garde painter were far stronger than the demarcations of class, wealth and temperament that might have pushed them apart. All were intimately connected to the distinctive twenties environment in which they operated and the wider social world beyond.

THE BURRA LINE

Ed Burra (1905–76) was an odd fish. A curious-looking "goblin child," as he put it, denied a formal education by chronic ill health, he began his professional career with an early-twenties stint at the Chelsea Polytechnic. The friends made there, and during a further two years at the Royal College of Art—these included the dancer William Chappell and the avant-garde photographer Barbara Ker-Seymer—sustained him for the rest of his life. Emotionally, Burra was an enigma. Anthony Powell recalled an interrogation by Hermione Baddeley. "Have you ever loved a man?" "No." "Have you ever loved a woman?" "No." "Not even your mother?" There was a pause, while Burra thought about it. "No."

Burra's pictures are no less puzzling: surreal, Firbankian fantasies, rife with rococo embellishment, in which outlandish figures parade across dense, otherworldly landscapes, the general effect consistently undercut by stealthy intimations of menace and disquiet; metaphorical grave goods lie everywhere about. In *The Two Sisters* (1929) two Identi-Kit women, dressed in the fashions of the day, drink tea as a pair of onlookers in pierrot hats pick fruit from a tree and a young man in a tunic bearing a tray stands apprehensively by. In *Show Girls*, from the same year, an extraordinarily sinister line of dancers with black hats and carrying black-bowed shepherd's crooks descends into view.

For all his continual appearances on the margins of smart bohemia, it would be wrong to claim Burra as a "Bright Young Artist." At the same time, many of his preoccupations are those of the Bright Young People: that delight in the sharp, bright colors of the society magazine (see *Girl in a Windy Landscape*, from 1923–24, which looks like a *Vogue* front cover); the absorption in mirrors, surfaces, narcissistic reflection—a whole set of pictures recording the interiors of snack bars and cafés, with faces glinting back at themselves out of the chromium surround.

Much of his early work, too, comes crammed with Bright Young symbols: pierrots, sailors, acrobats, figures from the commedia dell'arte. Like many another partygoer of his time, Burra was deeply impressed by contemporary black culture, and visited the Bal Nègre in Paris and Harlem, where he produced vigorous sketches of the local dance floors. Or there is his sketch from 1930 of a couple performing the Charleston: two grotesque figures, each storklike on one leg, symmetrically poised, on one level surreally detached from the milieu that prompted it, on another rich, sinuous and concentrated, and perfectly in keeping with the world of Brian Howard, Stephen Tennant and Brenda Dean Paul.

CHAPTER TWO

THE SOCIETY RACKET

Mother's advice, and father's fears
Alike are voted—such a bore.
There's negro music in our ears,
The world is one huge dancing floor.
We mean to tread the Primrose Path,
In spite of Mr. Joynson-Hicks.
We're people of the Aftermath
We're girls of 1926.

—JAMES LAVER, "The Women of 1926"

S ometime toward the end of 1932, Patrick Balfour, formerly the
Daily Sketch's "Mr. Gossip" and the model for Simon Balcairn,
"Mr. Chatterbox" of *Vile Bodies*, settled himself down at one of
the stout oak tables of the Easton Court Hotel, Chagford in Devon, and
began to write a study of London social life in the 1920s. Evelyn Waugh,
given the first draft to read, affected to be unimpressed. "Pauper Balfour
wrote a book saying all rich people lived in blocks of flats," he later complained to their mutual friend Lady Diana Cooper, "which doesn't seem
to me to be true." For all its grounding in newspaper gossip pages, *Society Racket: A Critical Study of Modern Social Life* (1933) is a substantial
piece of work. Its most significant moment comes when Balfour—
anticipating a shelf full of future social historians—attempts to define
the animating spirit of the twenties. Predictably enough, he diagnoses
"a period of change," but of a democratic sort, in which one kind of
upper-class existence was turning imperceptibly into another, whose
surface manifestations seemed uncannily symbolic: from quails in aspic

to eggs and bacon; from champagne to lager; from mansions to mansion flats; and from balls to cocktail parties. It was an age

> in the course of which peers became Socialists, and Socialists became peers, actors and actresses tried to be ladies and gentlemen and ladies and gentlemen behaved like actors and actresses, novelists were men-about-town and men-about-town wrote novels, persons of all ranks became shopkeepers and shopkeepers drew persons of rank to their houses.

The participants might have been drawn from a wider social catchment area than had previously been the case, but the dance—an enduring metaphor for the London social world of the 1920s—continued. Moreover, the end in view was the same as it had always been: the creation, whether consciously or otherwise, of a more or less exclusive caste for the benefit of an impressionable public who viewed it from a distance: the "racket" of Balfour's title.

If the London ballrooms of the 1920s were the venue for a "society racket," then the Bright Young People were both its chief beneficiaries and its enduring talisman. Other survivors who looked back from the vantage point of the 1930s, a time when some of the excesses of the previous decade loomed sharply into focus, tended to produce versions of the Balfour line. Writing her memoirs in 1935, at the tender age of twenty-eight, Brenda Dean Paul decided that after the war "a state of society prevailed quite unparalleled in the social history of the country." There were three reasons for this, Brenda deposed: punitive taxation, the greater independence of women and something that, sounding a great deal older than twenty-eight, she categorized as "general social laxity." The great estates were sold up and their owners forced to earn livings. Young people, "being faced with the problems of life far earlier than our parents, had no inclination to conform to stereotyped private dances and other formal social innovations and broke gradually away, forming little groups or 'coteries,' which came to be known by the papers as 'the bright young people.'" The combination of relatively impoverished young men and newly independent young women, who no longer expected to be "paid for" or minded being taken to the less conventional entertainments of the postwar era, created "a new camaraderie of youth . . . an independence, an equality, which gave birth to a new code of social manners."

No doubt many of these distinctions would have escaped the readers of daily newspapers. To Mr. Smeeth, the desiccated accountant in J. B. Priestley's *Angel Pavement* (1930), browsing impressionably through his newspaper on the bus from Stoke Newington to the City, a dinner jacket is a dinner jacket. On the other hand, the cult of "youth" was one to which practically every inhabitant of the British Isles in the 1920s would have unhesitatingly subscribed. One can see this everywhere in postwar life: in the determination of political parties to repopulate their ranks with youthful, media-friendly war veterans (Eden, Macmillan, Mosley), in the vogue for twenty-something playwrights and entertainers (Noël Coward, Ivor Novello). It seemed obvious even to schoolboys that middle-aged maturity was in sharp retreat. Evelyn Waugh's Lancing diary canvasses "the extraordinary boom of youth, which everyone must have noticed . . . Every boy is writing about his school, every child about the doll's house, every baby about its bottle. The very young have gained an almost complete monopoly of bookshops, press and picture gallery." Courtesy of Waugh's older brother Alec, this juvenile route march toward the citadels of power had, in the title of his novel *The Loom of Youth* (1917), a slogan, expressly calculated to alarm all the hard-faced and necessarily old men who had done well out of the war.

Seen in this light, the Bright Young People were a symptom of the continuing reaction against the stuffiness of prewar social arrangements, the rigidity of their dress codes and the formality of their relationships, the restrictions of their hours, what Balfour—again—calls "a sort of public demonstration against the dullness of social life." At the same time, and for reasons that had nothing to do with the boisterousness of this new younger element, that social life itself was subject to rapid reinvention. "Society," most informed commentators of the interwar era agreed, was in flux, to the point where fundamental questions had to be asked about its scope, scale and composition. Of what, when it came down to it, did this social abstract—an almost phantasmal institution in which newcomers could rise unhindered to the surface or sink unmourned to the depths, succeed triumphantly, fail ingloriously, or, worse perhaps, simply be ignored—actually consist?

On one level, "society" was as subject to the same economic and demographic pressures as any other part of the postwar national fabric. Its most significant catchment area—upper-class young men in their early twenties—had been sharply depopulated by the war. Their replacements were not always so young or so well connected. Then again, the old political axes on which a great deal of prewar social life had turned had been thrown into disarray by the changing landscapes of Westminster. Mr. Balfour had been one thing, and Mr. Asquith another, but what did one do with a Ramsay Macdonald or a Philip Snowden, upstart newcomers over whom no Conservative or Liberal hostess of a previous generation would have cared to fight? Far more important, in the long term, was the new mass-market commercialization, the world of the Hollywood actress, the tycoon, the successful sportsman (or woman), the popular entertainer.

There had always been a space in English society's upper echelons for people of this kind: prizefighting MPs and Brummagem industrialists hustled into the peerage. Suddenly there were more of them and the commercial arrangements that produced them were expressly calculated to solidify their hold. Worse, the social system that regulated these incursions, that gave precedence to landed wealth and ancient alliances, seemed to be breaking down. The result was that the society of the twenties was driven by an odd mixture of compromises and concessions to a new way of living. Ascot, Cowes, the debutante dance and the regimental ball survived more or less unaltered from their prewar shape. Joining them, on the other hand, came the fancy dress party, the nightclub and the treasure hunt, and the world of the Chelsea bohemians, which before the Great War had largely confined itself to Chelsea, could now be found conjoined with Mayfair to form a new kind of "smart bohemia" open both to an avant-garde artist and a baronet's daughter. In exceptional circumstances, it was possible to shut oneself away from these manifestations of a changing landscape—Queen Mary famously refused to have divorcées to tea and, confronted with the bathing-suited chorus of *No, No, Nanette*, ostentatiously averted her gaze—but for the majority of party-givers and dinner convenors on whom society depended for its existence, some kind of accommodation had to be reached.

At the heart of these seismic shifts lay a series of financial readjustments. Taxation may not quite have pauperized the aristocracy, as many aristocrats continued to complain, but its effect on the average upper-class income could hardly be shrugged off. Between 1914, the year that the Great War began, and 1925, the year before the General Strike, the number of people in the United Kingdom whose annual income, net of tax, exceeded £10,000 fell by two-thirds, from around 4,000 to 1,300. Price rises, income tax, super tax, death duties—each of these fiscal assaults combined to weaken the economic, and ultimately the social, position of many an upper-class family whose ranks, in many cases, had already been depleted by the war. Mrs. Kent-Cumberland in Evelyn Waugh's short story "Winner Takes All," her husband dead in Flanders, who closes down a wing of her house, reduces the number of her servants, "lets the flower gardens go," is stingy about new tennis balls and covers her front lawn with grazing sheep, was not alone in her purposeful economizing.

Compared to Mrs. Kent-Cumberland and her kind, the people now conducting society's operations seemed more cosmopolitan, less trammeled by convention, mercurially self-made. Several of them, if it came to that, were not even British. Of the half-dozen society hostesses who presided over the London entertainments of the 1920s, Mrs. Corrigan had been born Laura-Mae Whitrock in backyard Wisconsin, while Lady Cunard came originally from San Francisco and had swapped her baptismal name of "Maud" for the more exotic "Emerald."* Even homegrown equivalents lacked the social sheen of their aristocratic forebears. Mrs. Ronnie Greville, whose invitations were perhaps the most highly regarded of all, was the illegitimate daughter of a brewer.

---

* *The source of several legendary exchanges. What would Lady Cunard be wearing to the opera that evening, Mrs. Corrigan once inquired. "Just a tiara and my own hair," Lady Cunard replied (Barbara Cartland,* We Danced All Night *[1970], p. 201).*

Lady Colefax, left badly off by her late husband's debts, set up as an interior designer and combined high-powered lunch parties with house refurbishment. It was all a far cry from the chatelaines of the Edwardian era, and Mrs. Greville, whatever the grandeur of her country house at Polesden Lacey, was merely "a common, waspish woman," Harold Nicolson told James Lees-Milne, "who got where she did through persistence and money."

In all kinds of ways the old boundaries of the Edwardian age—"open," but not to a degree that threatened their controlling hierarchies—were annually dissolving. Young men who would previously have been labeled "outsiders" had to be admitted or there was a danger that society, as traditionally conceived, would cease to exist. Existing stock, meanwhile, seemed acutely susceptible to the kind of young women who would previously have had the greatest difficulty in establishing themselves in the grander kind of drawing room. In this frenetic game of musical chairs, not everyone was guaranteed a seat. An entry in Evelyn Waugh's diary from October 1925 considers David Plunket Greene's engagement to "Babe" McGustie, the stepdaughter of Arthur Bendir, the chairman of Ladbroke, the bookmaker's: "She is quiet and good-natured and pretty and well dressed with round eyes and rather a shiny nose ... I should have supposed her the last person to excite David, particularly as, apparently, none of the Bendir money will come to her. I gather too that her mother's position in the society to which David aspires is very uncertain." The problem, though never stated in so many words, was that these alien elements had a tendency to adulterate the purity of what lay within. As Balfour breezily summarized it, the standards of behavior of these incoming hordes were not the standards of the pre-1914 era. Neither, unhappily enough, were the standards of those who would have been on the list anyway. "Society to them was just a means of enjoying themselves in as easygoing a manner as possible."

This juxtaposition of a social elite, keen on the principle of formal entertaining, and a younger element keener still to rebel against social convention led to several symbolic standoffs, nearly all of them involving Bright Young People. By coincidence, reports of the Bath and Bottle Party in July 1928 began appearing at the fag end of a controversy known as the "Great Mayfair War." This had broken out at Lady Ellesmere's ball, held a week or so before at Bridgwater House, when the hostess pounced on four guests she did not recognize—Stephen Tennant, David Plunket Greene, Nancy Beaton and Elizabeth Lowndes—and asked them to leave. Tennant and Plunket Greene, it turned out, had invitations; the girls did not, but had simply been invited to make up a party. For such an apparently minor social squabble, the Ellesmere gate-crashing scandal occupied what might seem to be a wholly disproportionate amount of newspaper space. Attitudes were struck on both sides. Stephen Tennant took to the pages of the *Evening Standard* to admit that, like Plunket Greene, he had brought a partner whose name was not on the guest list, and that the trouble began when Lady Ellesmere heard Elizabeth Lowndes say, "Isn't this a joke? I have not been invited." Nancy Beaton declared, "I am innocent. It is not true." Lady Ellesmere, meanwhile, maintained that she was standing up for the principle of homes being open only to the people who were wanted in them. Yet it quickly became clear that the principle being defended was highly confused. Tennant and Plunket Greene argued that in the changed conditions of the 1920s, when invited to a ball it was quite usual to bring a few friends along as well. On the other hand the force of Lady Ellesmere's complaints was somewhat weakened by the fact that she did not know many of the invited guests even by sight and, it could be inferred, was quite self-consciously presiding over a free-for-all. Lord Castlerosse, who wrote the *Sunday Express*'s "Londoner's Log" column, weighed into the argument by observing that a week rarely passed without his receiving several invitations from people he didn't know. Clearly, as Balfour remarked, "social attitudes had become very confused."

Beneath the surface clamor about gate-crashers and social climbers lurked a rather more salient question: whom was all this for? Or rather, for whose benefit other than that of the partygoers summoned to it on a daily, or more accurately nightly, basis? To the majority of the newspaper-reading populace the upper classes—with whom society was presumed to be aligned—figured as the embodiment of all that was glamorous, successful and wealthy. The relationship between this group of people, at best no more than a few thousand strong, the media who packaged their activities for public consumption and the public itself was not at all straightforward. As social historians have pointed out, the upper classes were, broadly speaking, compliant in this presentation: they allowed themselves to be photographed for society columns; they gave interviews; society women regularly accepted commissions from advertising firms for endorsing beauty products or even foodstuffs ("I sat next to Lady Birkenhead, who told me she got £85 for saying she used Lyons Coffee Extract which she had never tasted," Beverley Nichols reported back from one lunch engagement). Rather than offering a front of unimpugnable rigidity, society allowed itself to be satirized, whether in print or on the stage, was prepared to tolerate occasional denunciations of its supposed "decadence" and enthusiastically played up to its stereotypes. It encouraged the idea that it was in some degree accessible, that a man (or woman) who was not born into it could arrive there by the exercise of some special talent or distinction.

Above all, and in a remarkably consistent way, it dominated the national consciousness. Then, as now, Sunday papers aimed at a working-class readership tended to restrict themselves to scandal and high jinks. Dailies such as the *Mail* or the *Express*, alternatively, were interested in minutiae: the interiors of upper-class homes; the vagaries of upper-class dress styles; the shades of upper-class opinion. As Ross McKibbin puts it, "No reader of the middle-class press, however cursorily he or she in fact read it, could escape society and it was not intended that they should." The world thereby conveyed to middle-class and lower-middle-class readers may have been stylized and self-mythologizing, but this, in a certain sense, was the point: the absence of stylization and myth would have robbed it of mystique. By comparison, the reality of upper-class life could seem deeply peculiar. In "Winner Takes All" Evelyn Waugh charts the relationship between Tom Kent-Cumberland and a lower-middle-class girl named Gladys Crutwell. Hitherto, Tom has kept rather silent on the subject of his family; Gladys's conception of it, consequently, is derived entirely from the media.

She understood, vaguely, that they lived in a big house, but it was a part of life that had never been real to her. She knew that there were duchesses and marchionesses in something called "Society'; they were encountered in the papers and the films. She knew there were directors with large salaries; but the fact that there were people like Gervase [Tom's elder brother] or Mrs. Kent-Cumberland, and that they would think of themselves as radically different from herself, had not entered her experience.

However startled she might be by the reality of snobbish Mrs. Kent-Cumberland, Gladys is still a victim of Balfour's "racket": the suborning of large parts of the population to an illusory upper-class myth of glamour and style.

Naturally enough, illusions of glamour and style work both ways. How far were the millions of people beyond society's gates fooled by this deception? While conceding that one mustn't assume too easily that such a strategy worked, McKibbin concludes that "it does seem that, at least in the inter-war period, Society, as the public, glamorous (and histrionic) manifestation of the social and political elite, promoted the interests of that elite." Perhaps, in the end, this doesn't mean very much: the same thing, with a few temporal adjustments, could have been said of the social arrangements of Thackeray's day. All the same, if society, as conceived of in the popular mind, helped to perpetuate the upper classes as a social institution, then—as it could hardly fail to do—it also helped to perpetuate the existence of the Bright Young People. Perhaps the most remarkable thing about the movement by the late 1920s was how comfortably certain elements of it had been assimilated into the mainstream of upper-class London life. By July 1930, six months after the publication of *Vile Bodies*, Evelyn Waugh had clambered high enough up the Belgravian north face to rate a dinner invitation to Lady Cunard's. Here he noted the latter's "restlessness" ("obviously dissatisfied with me as a lion") but found himself welcomed into a throng that included Sir Oswald Mosley, Princess Bibesco, George Moore and Lord Ivor Churchill. Waugh, as Lady Cunard correctly surmised, was no threat to the social citadels whose walls he had now breached. Like Thackeray, again, he took a positive relish in the company of people whom he was occasionally prone to mock. By the time of *Put Out More Flags* (1942), fourteen years on from his knockabout debut in *Decline and Fall* (1928), Alastair Digby-Vane-Trumpington has quietly metamorphosed into one of Waugh's heroes.

In other ways this small, incestuous metropolitan world was unusually constrained. Reinvented by posterity as a time of unbridled license, the 1920s were, in reality, one of the most tightly regulated eras in English history. Even by their close, most of the restrictions introduced during the war and contained in the Defence of the Realm Act, always known by its acronym DORA, were still going strong. Such was the general air of repressiveness that the 1921 Licensing Act, which allowed patrons of licensed premises to continue drinking after eleven provided they had something to eat, was seen as a relatively enlightened measure. The prospect of any further concessions to gaiety was extinguished by the appointment as home secretary in 1923 of the barnacled figure of Sir William Joynson-Hicks. DORA and Sir William, whose moment of political glory had come fifteen years earlier when he defeated Winston Churchill at Oldham, were clearly made for each other. The rash of nightclubs that had grown up in the aftermath of the Licensing Act was vigorously policed. Brenda Dean Paul remembered a raid on a club in Piccadilly in which Elizabeth Ponsonby was forced to eat the piece of antique sausage meat left on their table by the management to support the legal fiction that patrons were enjoying a late-night snack. If "Jix," whom even Conservative newspapers found irresistible ("the gay Lord Jix" as *Punch* christened him), had an overriding weakness, it was that he could not discriminate: to the Home Office the respectable supper restaurant and the brothel in all but name were both symptoms of the same disease. As a contemporary critic once put it, he expected nightclubs to be filled with prostitutes and instead found their dance floors seething with people he knew from the Mayfair social round. The Night Light, for example, had four peers and two princesses on its committee. One raid on the Kit-Kat took place only twenty-four hours after the Prince of Wales had danced there. For most of the 1920s central London was subject to a "cleanup" prosecuted by Jix and his enthusiastic side-kick Lord Byng, the commissioner of police, but its only real effect was to give some of the demimondaines involved a celebrity which the pre-war era would probably have denied them.

Consider, for example, the career of Mrs. Kate Meyrick, who founded the notorious Forty-three at 43 Gerrard Street in 1921. The club, whose early patrons included Augustus John, Jacob Epstein and Joseph Conrad, was first raided in 1923, when its proprietress was fined £300. A year later thirty-three men and eight women apprehended on the premises appeared at Bow Street Magistrates Court and were fined forty shillings each. Mrs. Meyrick, charged with serving intoxicating liquor without a license, was sentenced to six months in Holloway. Here her spirits were kept up by the sympathy of such distinguished clients as the Crown Prince of Sweden and Tallulah Bankhead, while one of her daughters managed the business in her absence ("Tony and I went off to 43 Gerrard Street where Miss Meyrick is carrying on in her mother's place exactly the same as ever," runs an entry in Evelyn Waugh's diary from around this period). For the rest of the decade, and some way beyond it, Mrs. Meyrick was a recognized part of the diversions offered up by middle-market newspapers to their readers: perpetually harassed, charmingly unflustered ("The police are always so kind to me," she commented after one bust), always discreetly expanding her empire and refining her clientele. In 1925, at the height of the London nightclub craze, she opened the Manhattan, whose patrons included Sophie Tucker and Rudolph Valentino. Then, two years later, came a yet grander venture: the Silver Slipper in Regent Street, on to whose immense glass floor more than a score of policemen emerged on Christmas night 1927 just as the Cossack dance was being performed.

Mrs. Meyrick bore these afflictions with fortitude. In June 1928 she was in court again for selling alcohol without a license, admitted all charges and was given six months. Let out of Holloway a month early, she was greeted at its gates by her daughter Mary, now the Countess of Kinnoull—two of her daughters ended up marrying into the aristocracy—and shortly afterward charged under the Prevention of Corruption Act when £12,000 was found in safe deposit under the name of a policeman called Goddard. Several other nightclub owners were implicated: none possessed Mrs. Meyrick's notoriety. At the Old Bailey wads of £10 notes with which it was alleged she had bribed Goddard were displayed to the jury. "I swear on my soul that I have never paid Goddard one penny piece," the defendant declared. She was sentenced to fifteen months hard labor. By this time her establishments had taken on a wholly iconic significance. Bright Young People novels are full of cryptic nods in her direction. "'I say,'" inquires Barlow's naval officer brother in Anthony Powell's *Afternoon Men* (1931), "'do any of you ever go to the Forty-Three?'" Stringham, drunkenly meditating a retreat from Milly Andriadis's party, decides that "'the Forty-Three would be too stuffy—in all senses—for my present mood.'" It is to a thinly disguised version of Gerrard Street ("Sink Street"), too, that Charles Ryder, Sebastian Flyte and "Boy" Mulcaster repair in *Brideshead Revisited*.

At least Mrs. Meyrick was a real live club owner. Two of the other leading figures in whom newspaper columnists of the period enthusiastically dealt were the most flagrant of archetypes. The "Modern Girl," occasionally referred to by more genteel commentators as the "Modern Young Woman," was a press fixation from the early 1920s on. Her origins lay not so much in the wave of female emancipation brought about by the Great War, when numbers of upper-class girls were encouraged to work as hospital nurses, but in a social category defined by Anthony Powell as "slightly (only very slightly) 'liberated' girls, mildly highbrow, of immediately pre-war vintage." As a child, Powell could actually remember some of them and "the great to-do made about their drinking and smoking." Mildred Blaides, who first appears in *At Lady Molly's* (1957) as a wartime voluntary nurse, scandalizing her sister Mrs. Conyers with her incessant "gaspers" and floods of army slang, is a fine early specimen of the breed. Variously stigmatized by popular newspapers as "brassy" or, worse, "gold-digging," the Modern Girl—in which category Bright Young People such as Elizabeth Ponsonby effortlessly reposed—looks in retrospect to have been a fairly innocuous creature. Tending to live at home with her parents—the "bachelor girl" who inhabited her own flat was still a rarity—she could frequently be found demonstrating her independence by means of some relatively undemanding job. According to Balfour, the debutantes of his generation often worked in dress shops or high-class beauty parlors. Elizabeth Ponsonby had a sporadic career as a fashion model. When Brenda Last in Evelyn Waugh's *A Handful of Dust* (1934) is denied a lucrative divorce settlement by her outraged husband, her first thought is to work as a saleswoman for her boyfriend's conniving mother: Mrs. Beaver converts Belgravia houses into genteel apartment blocks and sells her tenants embroidered cushions and other household appurtenances from a shop-cum-showroom.

Full-scale economic autonomy, on the other hand, lay some way off. "Gals like us, our allowances were tiny," Diana Mosley later recalled: her sister Nancy Mitford got by on £125 a year. But however constrained by disapproving parents, the Modern Girl was still capable of provoking outrage in the minds of the people she knocked up against. Jessica Mitford, Nancy's younger sister, remembered mid-1920s family life as a kind of ongoing guerrilla war, with skirmish after skirmish fought over the latest symbol of twenty-something rebellion: "the hushed pall that hung over the house, meals eaten day after day in tearful silence, when Nancy at the age of twenty had her hair shingled . . . Nancy using lipstick, Nancy playing the newly-fashionable ukelele, Nancy wearing trousers, Nancy smoking a cigarette . . ." Even Bright Young People occasionally balked at some of the excesses of female behavior. Balfour recalled Elizabeth Ponsonby coming to Oxford to display her recently shingled hair, cut short like a boy. "This was the first shingle I had seen and it induced in me a feeling of astonishment coupled with faint horror."

These were, on the face of it, modest rebellions—minor adjustments to conventional behavior, a revolt symbolized by short skirts, high heels and cigarette cases—yet their effect on large sections of upper-class society was profoundly unsettling. Press forums agonized over the annual retreat of women's hair: one newspaper advanced the case of a Lancashire mill girl who, newly shingled, was thrown over by her fiancé and committed suicide. Sexual irregularity was everywhere suspected ("What I always wonder, Kitty, is what they actually do at these parties of theirs? I mean, do they . . . ?" muses Lady Throbbing in *Vile Bodies*.

"My dear," Lady Blackwater assures her, "from all I hear, I think they do"). All this gave rise to an enduring stereotype of young, upper-class female behavior which, although it bore very little relation to general attitudes, lodged irrevocably in the public mind. James Laver's "The Women of 1926" is a mixture of field guide and moral critique:

> *In greedy haste, on pleasure bent,*
> *We have no time to think or feel.*
> *What need is there for sentiment,*
> *Now we've invented Sex-Appeal?*
> *We've silken legs and scarlet lips,*
> *We're young and hungry, wild and free,*
> *Our waists are round about the hips.*
> *Our skirts are well above the knee*
> *We've boyish busts and Eton crops,*
> *We quiver to the saxophone,*
> *Come, dance until the music stops,*
> *And who can bear to be alone?*

Significantly, Laver's satire ends with a nod in the direction of the Forty-three ("Come all you birds / And sing a roundelay / Now Mrs. Meyrick's / Out of Holloway").

If the Modern Girl was occasionally given the benefit of the doubt—admired, for example, for her enterprise, enthusiasm and charm—no such indulgence extended to that symptom of national decline, the Modern Young Man. The *Daily Express* produced a celebrated attack on "The Modern Girl's Brother," in the course of which this hapless nonentity was condemned as weary, anemic, feminine, bloodless, "dolled up like a girl," "an exquisite without masculinity" and "resembling a silken-coated lap-dog." Clearly the specter of homosexuality lurks behind these complaints, although the *Express* hastened to reassure its readers that "it is not suggested that he is sexually depraved." Snob appeal sometimes allowed certain members of the Bright Young People to deflect these criticisms, or even make them work to their advantage—Stephen Tennant, for example, was commissioned to write newspaper beauty tips for "Today's Lady"—but in general, just as the Bright Young Woman became the symbol of a much wider complaint about feminine style, so the Bright Young Man was regarded as thoroughly representative of the "decadence" with which postwar England was presumed to have become infected.

Naturally, most of the fissures that newspaper columnists claimed to have detected between "youth" on the one hand and a disappearing establishment on the other were wholly artificial. In some ways a Brian Howard or a Stephen Tennant—exotic figures whose exoticism alarmed even their friends—represented nothing but themselves. As ever—something that historians of youth movements nearly always choose to ignore—the usual patterns of young people's education and development proceeded more or less unhindered. The early career of Alec Douglas-Home, for instance, born in 1903 and an exact contemporary of several leading Bright Young People, offers an instructive contrast. Educated at Eton and Christ Church, where he occupied himself not in the activities of the Railway Club but on the cricket field, Lord Dunglass, as he was then styled, left Oxford in 1925. He subsequently joined an MCC cricketing eleven captained by Pelham Warner on a three-month tour of South Africa. Back in England he spent time on his family's Lanarkshire estates, supported the local Boys' Brigade and joined the Lanarkshire Yeomanry. Then, in 1928, he "let it be known" that he would like to be considered for any suitable Scottish vacancy at the forthcoming general election. Defeated at Coatbridge and Airdrie in 1929, he was elected for nearby Lanark in the National Government landslide of 1931, thereby inaugurating a political career that lasted for the next four decades. As a Conservative peer in the 1960s, Lord Home would have seen at least one former Bright Young Person regarding him from the government benches—Lord Faringdon, the former Gavin Henderson—but this was as far as the association went.

Small-scale, essentially confined to a tiny quarter of the metropolis, the Bright Young People, like the Modern Girl and the Modern Girl's Brother, wielded an influence on the popular conception of "youth" out of all proportion to their numbers. Coming only a few years after a devastating war that obliterated hundreds of thousands of young men, the antagonism between youth and seniority that characterized the 1920s was of far greater significance than previous intergenerational disturbance. For all the enthusiasm for "youth," the talk of "new blood" and the need to sweep away prewar stuffiness, the twenties, practically every commentator of the period agrees, was a difficult time to be a young man. Part of this difficulty lay in the simple fact of his existence. Orwell, a decade later, noted the tremendous feeling of guilt experienced by the young man born in the years after 1900 who, consequently, had managed to avoid military service. "The very fact of his being alive was against him," Balfour declared, "for he was thus prevented from standing level with 'the boys who had died.'" Whatever feats he accomplished, he would always be compared, and nearly always unfavorably, with the war generation lost in the Flanders mud.

But there was more to these anxieties than a sense of generational inferiority. To a failure to emulate the achievements of those killed in the war could be added the insecurities of the new postwar landscape, where jobs were scarce and whole areas of employment seemed set aside for the jealous middle-aged. On the one hand the peculiarly charged atmosphere of the 1920s, with its promise of good times and limitless horizons, had raised expectations among the young; on the other the reality of its economic pressures had simultaneously let them down. Cyril Connolly noted the reluctance of his contemporaries to accept the routine compromises that had done for their fathers: "They could not settle down to boring jobs and unprofitable careers with prewar patience and their cleverness seemed a liability rather than an asset." Balfour, alternatively, identified a gap between the kind of person that the public school system had launched on to the social world of the 1920s ("a gentleman and a gentleman of leisure") and the kind of person—tough-minded, competitive and hardworking—required by the postwar labor market. The Bright Young Man, Balfour thought, was "a hybrid, hovering between two worlds and two systems."

Evelyn Waugh, who quickly established himself as a spokesman for "youth" and youth's difficulties—"I think it would be so convenient if the editors could be persuaded that I embodied the Youth Movement so that they would refer to me whenever they were collecting 'opinions,'" he told his agent a month after *Decline and Fall* was published—agreed. It seemed to him that a young man in his early twenties must have "an almost insane buoyancy of temperament" if he didn't at times feel that he was not wanted, he told radio listeners in 1932. A very early piece of journalism from 1929 notes that "things have not been particularly easy for those of us who have grown up in the last ten years." Everywhere the young man looked, in fact, he found his path blocked by "the phalanx of the indestructible forties." All this had led to a kind of "arrested development" in which youth kicked its heels in frustration, denied the chance to shine, its dreams of glory perpetually deferred.

Certainly the careers of many of Waugh's Oxford contemporaries bore this out. Balfour became a gossip columnist. Gavin Henderson ended up working for a firm of interior decorators. Connolly, after a promising start as a *New Statesman* reviewer, married an heiress and settled for the comfortable life of the Continental exile. Brian Howard, when taxed with idleness, informed his mother that sooner than become a journalist he would kill himself. None of these destinies could have been inferred from Eton careers in which Connolly and Howard, albeit in rather different ways, had carried all before them. Even for those with substantial private incomes—a Bryan Guinness, a Stephen Tennant—the road ahead could look surprisingly cheerless. Newspaper columns were full of newfangled "careers for our sons"; novels of the period cheerfully canvassed employment prospects. Trapped by Mrs. Fosdick, at a rehearsal for the Passenger Court pageant in Anthony Powell's *From a View to a Death* (1933), the upwardly mobile painter Arthur Zouch has to listen to a considerable monologue on the subject of her undergraduate son Torquil: "And they say that they are getting a very nice type of young man in the BBC now . . ." Zouch advises interior decorating. Neither niche would have been thought appropriate for the son of a minor county gentleman thirty years before.

Pressures of this sort—minor deprivations, perhaps, in a world of mass unemployment and fiscal uncertainty, but calculated to sap the morale of an entire social class—built up a widespread resentment. This was most dramatically displayed in attitudes to the war and the generation who had fought in it. More so than any of the trivial distinctions of dress and behavior, the Great War offered the 1920s their great symbolical divide, parceling society up into groups of people who, it was implied, could never hope to understand each other. In a *Spectator* piece written in early 1929, Evelyn Waugh maintained that the war had divided the whole of Europe into three "perfectly distinct classes between whom none but the most superficial sympathy can ever exist." These were "a) the wistful generation who grew up and formed their opinions before the war and who were too old for military service; b) the stunted and mutilated generation who fought; and c) the younger generation." Waugh is choosing his words carefully. The adjectives "stunted" and "mutilated" carry a particular freight of meaning. To Waugh and his contemporaries the gap between veterans and noncombatants was all the more marked for its chronological slightness. Alec Waugh had commanded a machine-gun unit and spent time in a POW camp; his brother sat out the war years at school. Maurice Bowra, who survived the Western Front to become a fellow of Wadham and a gray eminence to generations of Oxford undergraduates, was, when Anthony Powell first met him, twenty-five to Powell's eighteen.

Confronted on all sides by evidence of the war's impact, most of it brought home to them by the war's survivors, Bright Young Men—and Women—tended to react with what was seen at the time as an unforgivable flippancy. The war veteran, seen at large in a Bright Young Person's novel, is not much more than a figure of fun—Jasper Fosdick, say, in *From a View to a Death*, who, vacant and unemployable, fritters away time on the golf links, or Captain Grimes, the pederastic schoolmaster in *Decline and Fall*. "I subscribed a guinea to the War Memorial fund, I felt I owed it to them," Grimes remarks to Paul Pennyfeather of his alma mater. "I was really sorry," the disgraced and nearly court-martialed Old Harrovian goes on, "that that cheque never got through." Later in the novel, Grimes reminisces: "You're too young to have been in the war, I suppose? Those were the days, old boy . . . I don't suppose I was really sober for more than a few hours." This sort of thing caused great offense in 1928, and yet the lightness of the tone allows it to harmonize with the novel's wider framework. Nancy Mitford's *Highland Fling* (1931), in which a group of Bright Young People descends on a Scottish house party, contains several peculiar scenes in which the customary bantering tone is brought sharply down to earth. At one point greenery-yallery Albert Gates tells a war veteran, "We haven't exactly forgotten it, but it was never anything to do with us. It was your war and I hope you enjoyed it." On another occasion, when choleric General Murgatroyd declines to shake hands with a "filthy hun," Albert loses his temper: "Even when you have brought another war on us, it won't be any good. None of my generation will go and fight." Another guest, middle-aged Mr. Buggins, takes it upon himself to remonstrate:

> I know you did not really mean to say much, but remember that sort of thing does no good and only creates more bitterness between our two generations, as though it did not exist already. I know that many of us seem to you narrow-minded, stupid and unproductive. But if you look a little bit below the surface you might realize that there is a reason for this. Some of us spent four of what should have been our best years in the trenches . . .

Here, you suspect, Mitford is being serious and the effect—amid a deluge of cocktails, pajama parties and practical jokes—is wholly incongruous.

Flippancy about the war would be used by the right-wing press as a stick with which to beat the light-minded young throughout the 1920s. A *Punch* cartoon from August 1928 shows two fashionably dressed young women in conversation. "'What? You engaged to Arthur? But, my dear, he's *quite* an old man. *He was in the war you know.*" "Arthur," who stands meekly by, is all of thirty-five.

All this was highly symbolic of the social landscapes brought into being by the war: constrained by the past, restoring much of the pomp and glamour of the prewar era, but increasingly infiltrated by new groups of colonists. Another standard *Punch* joke of the period features the social climber, the *h*-dropping arriviste, H. M. Bateman's social naïf throwing a snowball at St. Moritz or talking about "horse-riding" in the regimental mess. In its own increasingly stylized way, the world of the Bright Young People reflected these tensions. Its upper levels may have included a Bryan Guinness or a Stephen Tennant; precariously perched on its lower rungs, alternatively, came young men and women surviving on their wits, exalted connections and an ability to adapt to circumstance. Two of the milieu's characteristic figures, ominously enough, are the adventuress and the young man on the make. When someone remarks of Harriet Twining's relationship with the American publisher Scheigan in *Afternoon Men*, "She won't come near him. She's got his gold cigarette case. He's very upset," one knows exactly the sort of girl Harriet is: predatory, acquisitive, using love affairs as an opportunity to feather her nest.

There were real-life Harriets, purposefully at large in the world of the West End nightclub and the *Bystander* portrait. A representative specimen might be Doris Delavigne, supposedly the model for Iris Storm in Michael Arlen's *The Green Hat*, who, having run through a selection of guards officers, politicians and statesmen, eventually brought down the substantial figure of Viscount Castlerosse. When Lord Berners once offered to lend her money, she remarked that it was very sweet of him but anything he could afford would not keep her going for a week. Though less open to moral censure, the paths cut through the late-1920s Mayfair jungle by male adventurers such as Evelyn Waugh and Cecil Beaton were quite as emphatic. In the end, ironically enough, the key roles in public perception of the Bright Young People in their late-twenties heyday tended to be played by relative outsiders. Having observed, recorded and exploited the movement, it was they who survived to preserve its memory in the years after it ceased to exist.

CHAPTER THREE

YOUNG MEN ON THE MAKE: LONDON 1924–28

Bright young people
Making the most of our youth,
They speak in the Press
Of our social success,
But quite the reverse is the truth.

— NOËL COWARD

"Do you know what we're doing?"
"No."
"Shall I tell you?"
"Yes."
"We are wasting our youth."

— ANTHONY POWELL, *Afternoon Men*

To a newcomer to the mid-1920s London party circuit, one not yet *au fait* with its complex codes and protocols, Cecil Beaton and Evelyn Waugh would have seemed very similar young men. Too similar, perhaps. Each, having first traveled through the English public school system, was recently down from university—Waugh had been to Oxford, Beaton to Cambridge—bearing a poor degree but a certain amount of notoriety. Each, in contrast to their highborn friends, the proud heirs to landed estates or giant manufacturing concerns, could be counted as thoroughly middle class: Waugh was the son of a London publisher; Beaton's father worked in the timber business. Each, more to the point, was snobbishly disaffected by his upbringing, fearful of the taint of "trade," and in Waugh's case prepared to walk several hundred yards to post a letter so that its frank should come from the Hampstead sorting office in upmarket NW3 rather than the Golders Green establishment in downmarket NW11.

Here, though, the comparison ends. Tallish, wavy-haired and with a cultivated—possibly overcultivated—elegance of manner, Beaton was intensely ambitious, all his unshakeable energies concentrated on what he referred to in his diaries as the "uprise." Waugh, in contrast, seemed to have no ambition at all. His Oxford reputation—Anthony Powell remembered having Waugh pointed out to him as a freshman as one of the notabilities of the place—derived from a talent for drunken buffoonery. Down from Hertford in the summer of 1924 with a third-class degree in modern history, he merely loafed around his parents' house and sponged off the despairing Arthur Waugh before taking the first of the succession of badly paid schoolmastering jobs that would sustain him for the next two and a half years.

If nothing else, the contrast between this pair of twenty-one-year-olds—Evelyn and Cecil, Oxford drunk and Cambridge fop—newly hatched into an adult world of work and responsibility illustrates the point about human quiddity made in Powell's *A Dance to the Music of Time*: that what might, on one level, appear to be identical products of the same environment may, in the end, turn out to be fundamentally detached from each other in terms of aims, attitudes and outlook. Yet, by the end of the decade, there was far more to bring Waugh and Beaton together than to drive them apart. Each had made a resounding success of his early career, Waugh as a novelist, Beaton as a society photographer. Each, moreover, had used his professional triumphs as a social calling card, smoothing an entry into circles where the sons of middle-class professional men were not always to be found. And in each case, as both Beaton and Waugh happily acknowledged, the catalyst had been provided by the world of the Bright Young People, which each had infiltrated, used as the raw material for his art and finally come to dominate.

If there was one desideratum that this joint trajectory lacked, it was friendship. In fact, Waugh's relationship with Beaton was characterized by outright antipathy: a "fathomless mutual hatred," as Anthony Powell put it, dating back to prep-school days in prewar north London and periodically renewed until Waugh's death. As late as 1961, reviewing the first expurgated tranche of Beaton's self-serving diaries, Waugh claimed that they told the story of a man "unashamedly on the make." Here, Waugh thought, was a diarist who revealed himself quite openly as a "young man consumed by worldly ambition, not for power nor creation; he merely wanted to get himself known and accepted." In case there should be any doubt over the roots of this antagonism, Waugh tracked his distaste for Beaton back to the school playground. He was "an extremely pretty little boy," Waugh recalled, whose offense was that he was thought to enjoy his music lessons. "The bullying of little Beaton was ... repeated many times. Our chief sport was to stick pins into him." Many other pins—metaphorical, but no less painful to their victim—would be stuck into Beaton's abnormally sensitive hide over the next half century.

To do Beaton justice, he would cheerfully have admitted the charge of opportunism. He was a howling arriviste and he knew it: "She doesn't know I'm a scheming snob," he remarked of a hostess with whose charitable work he assisted in the mid-1920s. "She thinks I'm just charming." Whatever the moral emptiness that may lie behind it, this kind of candor can be unexpectedly bracing. Beaton's diaries, consequently, conjure up the odd spectacle of social advancement being pursued simply as an end in itself, extraordinary amounts of energy and enthusiasm invested in a task about whose ultimate goals even Beaton occasionally had the gravest doubts. Waugh's diaries, alternatively, are merely a chronicle of wasted time: opportunities not taken up and talent squandered. Taken together, they offer a route into the two main quadrants of the early Bright Young People world: Waugh's more random and bohemian, its professional connections mostly gratis of his brother Alec, its destiny always in doubt; Beaton's a calculatedly upmarket projection of his photographs into the society magazines of the day, and his person into the drawing rooms of some of the grandest country houses in England.

The social forays of Waugh, first employed at a school in North Wales (the Llanabba Castle of *Decline and Fall*), then at an establishment at

Aston Clinton in Buckinghamshire, were largely confined to the holidays. Back in London in the autumn of 1925, he contrived to attend his second party at the home of the novelist Mary Butts in Belsize Park. Here he discovered "some very odd painters quite drunk and rather naked" belonging to a social category which his hostess called "Paris Queer." The party was supposedly in honor of the black American actor Paul Robeson, "but he had a fit in his dressing room and could not come." Five days later Waugh found himself at the Savoy Hotel with a mixed party including his cousin Claud Cockburn, his friend Alastair Graham and an unknown American actor. He climbed onto the actor's bed while Cockburn "sat on the lavatory and worked the plug with his foot for hours." The host, meanwhile, "carried round packets of tooth-powder which he said was heroin & everyone took."

Set against these chronicles of dissipation, Beaton's journal is a model of poorly concealed purpose. There was to be no seedy schoolmastering for a man who, even by the time of his departure from Cambridge, had managed to get two pictures of his sister Nancy into the *Tatler* and another of his mother into the *Bystander*. Already there were several useful names in his address book: he had met Dorothy Todd, the editor of *Vogue*, and hatched a plan to become a professional photographer, learning trade secrets from the society portraitist Paul Tanqueray. Beaton senior, while not positively discouraging, had begun to make noises about the necessity of earning a living and the advantages of the family business. Cecil could barely bring himself to attend to these rumblings of bourgeois discontent. He was basking in the friendship of a young woman named Alannah Harper, important to him not merely for her own (considerable) wealth and social position—her father was a consultant on the Aswan Dam project—but for the conduit she offered to the world of her old school friends Lady Eleanor Smith and Zita Jungman.

Having admired Cecil's photographs of his mother and sister, Miss Harper suggested that he ought to broaden his range. She also invited him to tea. Cecil was ecstatic. "I was looking forward to that," he crowed, "as the Harpers were terrifically rich and I've lately found that Alannah Harper has an artistic appreciation and is thoroughly well read and amusing without being brilliant." Rich, artistically aware, amusing without being tiresomely highbrow—clearly Cecil had struck oil with his new friend. Yet, however enticing, the promise of these exalted connections could not be instantly transformed into an income. He was barely twenty-one and the doors of society, much less those of its magazine editors, were still closed to him. Mr. Beaton, too, was proving fractious. Come November he announced that he would like Cecil to "get a little idea of business" by going to his office and keeping accounts. Outraged by this display of philistinism, Cecil allowed himself to be borne reluctantly away to the city, installed in an office which smelled "like an underground lavatory" and introduced to a career in the timber trade that lasted all of eight working days.

The world of the Bright Young People's first colonizing army was already divided into several distinct compartments. Simultaneously, the smallness of the milieu encouraged a certain amount of cross-fertilization. Waugh, though he did not move in the same circles as Beaton, was connected to one of the chief Bright Young People groups through his friendship with Richard and David Plunket Greene, whom he had known at Oxford, and their younger sister Olivia, with whom he was fruitlessly in love. Gwen Plunket Greene, the children's mother, was the sister of Dorothea Ponsonby and through them he met their cousin, Elizabeth. The diary entry in which this encounter is recorded makes it plain that Waugh knew all about Elizabeth Ponsonby's reputation as a leader of the "bright young set." Up from Aston Clinton for the day in late October, he and Richard joined a party at the Café Royal. "Julia [Strachey] came & Elizabeth Ponsonby, whom I met for the first time. Two years ago, or less even, I suppose I should have been rather thrilled by her." Four years later Waugh would place Elizabeth center stage in one of his novels. For the moment he was content to observe her in action.

There were other people quietly monitoring the antics of the Plunket Greenes and their satellites. Not all of them were as admiring as Waugh. Dorothea Ponsonby, in particular, had a vigilant eye trained on the doings of her nephews and niece and the company they kept, and was not impressed by either. Over the years Dorothea would develop into a seasoned chronicler of the Bright Young People, noting with glacial distaste the behavior of the friends her daughter brought back to the family house at Shulbrede in Sussex. As early as March 1924, her gaze had been fixed on her nephew David, whose visit had coincided with a period of mounting industrial unrest: "[He] takes not the *least* interest in *anything* that goes on," Dorothea complained. "Doesn't ask about the strike which is raging & very serious . . . or ask to see the papers. But he brought with him about 7 picture-papers filled photographs of naked women & legs & a cinema paper—which I had never seen before & was really like a nightmare in its sordid garishness." Olivia, subjected to the same steely scrutiny during a visit with her mother later in the year, seemed if anything worse. "By the end of the day I could have smacked Olivia," Dorothea grimly recorded: "—a chit—a rude, egotistical frivolous vain painted child who takes no truck whatever with anyone over 40—unless they are smartly dressed." Attending a polo match at Cowdray with Olivia, David Plunket Greene and a family friend, Olivia Robinson (her niece "showed no joy or amusement—only thinking she wasn't smart enough—or somebody else was smarter & never glancing at the polo"), Dorothea eavesdropped on the young people's chatter: "The snatches of conversation I caught between her & Olivia & David were something so futile it's impossible to say."

Elizabeth Ponsonby was already gone from the parental home, but Dorothea feared the influence of these three egotistical young hedonists on her younger child, Matthew, then an undergraduate at Balliol College, Oxford. Matthew, she noted, during the expedition to Cowdray, was easily led, "gets inveigled & feels he'd like to be in . . ." These suspicions were confirmed on an evening in the following spring when Matthew was found incapably drunk in charge of a car in the Strand, fined twenty guineas and deprived of his driver's license. Arthur Ponsonby, as remorseless a diarist as his wife, was anxious to spread the blame. "It turned out that he had taken a disreputable friend of the Greenes with him and had had beer on an empty stomach," he recorded, shortly after the case came to court. "The actual incident arose out of his good nature and weakness in being led astray by a set of which Richard Greene is the leader who regard drunkenness as something amusing and fine." The "disreputable friend," investigation revealed, was Evelyn

Waugh. Piecing the incident together—it turned out to be one of many preliminaries to a party given by Waugh and Olivia at the Greenes' house in Hanover Terrace—and convinced that her son had been enticed into mischief, Dorothea made inquiries. A conversation with John Rothenstein cast Waugh's behavior in the blackest imaginable light:

> As he told me he had just been dining with the Waughs, I asked him what he thought of Evelyn. He said he liked him—he was very clever. I said something about how angry I'd been at his behavior & J. R. described to me how E. Waugh had appeared at the Savile Club to see him after luncheon of the celebrated day. He asked J. R. to go to a certain club or restaurant with him for a drink . . . J. R. went with him but could not drink the gin & sodas offered him. He asked J. R. to go to the Greenes party that night which he was arranging with Olivia & was getting tons of wine. J rather demurred said he did not feel up to being rowdy. Evelyn W. then persuaded J to go with him to Hanover Terrace & bought 3 bottles of champagne one of which he opened & proceeded to drink in the taxi on his way there. At Hanover Terrace he filled Gwen's white china ducks with champagne & persuaded everybody to drink out of them—he himself appears to have drunk the larger quantity & when J departed after tea spoke thickly & confidentially to J saying "I am sorry I made Olivia drunk." This was not true.

Dorothea was aghast to find that Rothenstein, previously assumed to be a respectable young man, "seemed to think the whole thing very amusing." To make matters worse, Richard Greene had written claiming that Waugh was not drunk when Matthew joined them. "I think it disgusting a sort of orgy in the afternoon," Dorothea declared. "It does make me angry." The battle lines were drawn up. Thereafter both Ponsonbys regarded their nephews, niece and associates as a collection of gilded layabouts, out to make trouble and liable to entice impressionable youth into mischief. Waugh, affecting to be annoyed by Arthur's success in springing Matthew from Bow Street while leaving his accomplice behind bars for the next five hours ("rather ill-naturedly I thought"), sat on the episode for the next twenty years before recasting it as the climax of Charles Ryder's, Sebastian Flyte's and "Boy" Mulcaster's late-night carouse in *Brideshead Revisited.*

There are distinctions to be drawn. What Dorothea Ponsonby complained about was essentially private behavior, the immaturity and deceit of a tiny group of young people whose failings were exaggerated by the distorting mirror of family ties. Simultaneously, the world of the Bright Young People had already begun to transform itself, to leave the background of the private party and the car chase for a series of activities that were, on the one hand, a great deal more public and, on the other, a great deal more self-conscious. The treasure hunt was still in vogue—the newspapers of October 1925 carried excited reports of a young man scaling Cleopatra's Needle and the Sloane Square traffic being brought to a halt—but it was about to be overtaken by what the gossip columns christened the "stunt" or "freak" party—a fancy dress ball on the grand scale, themed around a particular era, color or costume. It was at this point, old hands thought, that the Bright Young People's transformation from private amusement to public spectacle was complete. Loelia Ponsonby's complaint about press reporters sent to cover the gatherings of the mid-1920s was that they did not distinguish between the original treasure hunters and "the friends of my cousin Elizabeth," who organized parties that "we thought exhibitionist—they always seemed to be held where there were photographers and where they would create the maximum disturbance."

David Tennant's Edwardian Party, staged at the Gargoyle Club early in 1926, was thought to have inaugurated this kind of ceremony. Bidden to "come as you were twenty years ago," Brenda Dean Paul, her mother and brother arrived *en trio,* Lady Dean Paul in an original dress of 1906 topped with a white leghorn and trimmed with bows and a stuffed osprey, wheeling her daughter—clad in baby clothes—in a pram and accompanied by her sailor-suited son bowling a hoop. Within the scene resembled "a crazy children's party," with the band got up in Eton suits, stiff collars and school caps. This was classic old-style bohemian behavior, imported from nearby Chelsea and set to work in a Soho club, and yet the freak party template was quickly taken up by mainstream hostesses and reproduced in smarter society settings. In July of the same year, for example, Mrs. Corrigan staged an "All Star Theater" at a borrowed house in Grosvenor Street, with an entertainment provided by an amateur cast including Lady Louis Mountbatten, Lord Brecknock, Daphne Vivian and Lord Ashley, with Lady Plunket masquerading as "Beauty Nimble Legs . . . the favorite of Terpsichore." The Duchess of Sutherland's fancy dress ball, held a few days later and featuring a gang of fashionable debutantes dressed as the Eton rowing eight, followed the same pattern—Mayfair taking its cue from the much rowdier subworld that existed on its fringe.

Beaton, meanwhile, was moving ever nearer to the celebrity he craved. At New Year 1926 he designed his sisters Nancy's and Baba's dresses for the Peter Pan Party, an annual society event in which the newspapers took an obsequious interest. They won second and third prizes and their pictures appeared in the press. On the strength of this Beaton extended his contacts: Mrs. Whish of the *Daily Express* commissioned him to take photographs for her social column at half a guinea a time. Still, the bells of hearth and heritage clanged in his ear. Pining for his son to acquire some serious commercial expertise, Beaton senior next sent him to work for a Danish associate named Schmiegelow. The man proved unexpectedly sympathetic and allowed his protégé to mark time. He was happier at the first performance of Edith Sitwell's *Façade* at the Chenil Galleries, to which Alannah Harper escorted him in April, and where his attentive eye caught sight of Augustus John, Harold Acton, Miss Todd of *Vogue* and the Jungman sisters. The mark of Beaton's obsessions, his absolute fixation on "uprise" and leaving the down-at-heel world of the timber trade in his slipstream, was the way in which they colored not merely his imaginative life but the innermost reaches of his subconscious. He had odd dreams in which he saw his mother's photograph in the *Tatler* and longed for his sisters to make successful marriages. "I couldn't help picturing vividly the lurid scene when Nancy and Baba get married to some titled person and they appear looking marvelous in silver." The beau monde never had a sincerer aspirant. He went to Venice to cover the Baroness d'Erlanger's costume ball, felt overawed by the phalanx of professional photographers, but consoled himself by meeting Diaghilev.

Polite yet purposeful, an ornament to the grandest dinner party and, like his mentor Beverley Nichols, much admired by elderly ladies, Beaton combined his talents with a thoroughgoing ruthlessness if he thought the situation demanded it. Mrs. Beaton, who helped in the preparation of his luncheon parties, held at the family house in Bayswater, was understandably hurt by her son's refusal to let her meet his guests. "It's so silly," Cecil rationalized to his diary. "One doesn't want to waste time making the silly conversation that Mummy makes." All of a sudden all the hard work, the suave attendance on Mrs. Whish, the afternoons spent retouching his portraits or waiting nervously for Manley the butler to summon him to the phone, looked as if they might be about to pay off. Alannah introduced him to Brenda Dean Paul and Lady Eleanor Smith, and invited him to a tea party where the photographs he had taken of her were "raved over" and commissions arranged for portraits of Eleanor and the Jungman sisters. Zita came to lunch in November 1926. "She is a perfect young lady," Beaton wrote approvingly. "She has a completely different personality to anyone I know, thoroughly unflashy, quiet but very original." Eleanor Smith and Baby turned up four days later for a photo session in the Beaton nursery, where the girls ended up "almost naked—just bits of gold tinsel round their middles . . . one a dashing brunette, the other a dashing blonde." The afternoon brought what, to Beaton, was a spectacular incidental benefit in the shape of an invitation from Zita's and Baby's mother, Mrs. Richard Guinness.

Already, a year into his London career, Beaton found himself reposing in what, as the phenomenon of the Bright Young People continued to develop, became a very common category: the talented young man accepted by "smart" society on account of that talent who, while enjoying the amenities that smart society had to offer, made no bones about exploiting it for his own advancement. Significantly, the first thing Beaton did with his invitation to the Guinness party was to let Mrs. Whish in on the secret. Yet, for all this early success—he was barely twenty-two— Beaton knew that there was a particular Bright Young sanctum which he had yet to penetrate. Alannah's, Zita's and Baby's friends tended to be Oxford-educated Old Etonians—an exclusive group to which he had few connections and whose presence could take the shine off gatherings at which he might otherwise have performed to advantage. But Alannah continued to shuffle new friends his way: Edith Sitwell was brought round to be photographed; in the scattering of pre-Christmas parties he was introduced to Elizabeth Ponsonby and a young man named Frederick Ashton. There was a significant moment in December—significant in that it symbolized both his acceptance into this alluring new world and the nervous terror it inspired in him—when he delivered some portraits of the Jungman sisters to Baby as she sat having her portrait painted in Oliver Messel's studio. Social antennae delicately attuned, Beaton instantly felt himself out of place. "I was also afraid of meeting a lot of snobby young men, who all knew one another well and were coming to tea a bit later. They are the sort of people who think more of one if one is a bit distant and so far I'd never met them . . ." All Beaton's worst suspicions were confirmed by the arrival of Brian Howard. "The Queen of the Troupe," he decided, "with his floppy eyes and fish face. His voice so terribly cultured and affected. Oh God give me the open spaces and the plowed fields." Ringing up Alannah, at whose own tea table he was expected, he was joined at the receiver by a line of "smart people anxious to say a word of love." Conscious of his own talent for insincerity, Beaton was furious when he detected this failing in others. "It was disgraceful, insincere, disgustingly smart and was so dreadfully like the party in a Noël Coward play." Alannah having been communally saluted, someone announced that Stephen Tennant was in London. This produced "screams and more telephonic rot."

Here Beaton features as the middle-class observer, acutely aware of his less than exalted background, fearful of being snubbed, conscious, in the last resort, that his status is no more than that of the superior tradesman. But he continued to make a good impression. At a dance given by Tanis Guinness's mother, Mrs. Benjamin Guinness, just before Christmas 1926, both Howard and Tennant made friendly overtures: by the end of the evening he had been invited to accompany Tennant, Tanis and her sister Meraud to the amusement park on the following day. Nervous of the excursion, Beaton managed to enjoy himself, while noting that the gap in social class made him more self-conscious at the coconut shies than his companions. "They were so earnest about enjoying themselves and thinking about nothing else, but I, rather middle-class-ly, was noting that people stared and glared and even laughed at us." Like Evelyn Waugh (who, as he once put it, had always thought himself a gentleman until he met his future mother-in-law, Lady Burghclere), Beaton's awareness of his social origins was a source of perpetual irritation to him, but it is also what gives his observations their sharpness. He wanted to be like his grander friends, he admired their airs and luxuriated in their company while remaining faintly conscious of their absurdity.

Not that this awareness ever lessened the force of his ambition: like Thackeray in an earlier age, he preferred to mock a duke from the comfort of the duke's drawing room rather than from the street beyond it. At all times, too, he was careful not to let his professional career lag behind his social climbing. Or rather, he knew that the two were so intimately connected as to be indistinguishable. In the first few days of 1927 the different strands of his life came triumphantly together. Nancy and Baba made spectacular repeat performances at the Peter Pan Party, the latter sumptuously arrayed as Mary, Queen of Scots' lady-in-waiting, Lady Mary Beaton (to whom, it was later pointed out, the Bayswater Beatons bore no relation). On the next day Beaton learned that his pictures of his mother, Baba, Edith Sitwell, the du Mauriers and the Jungmans would shortly be published in the *Tatler*. Then came an invitation to the Tennants' country house, Wilsford Manor, in Wiltshire. There was no doubt about it. The timber merchant's son from Bayswater had arrived.

Naturally, there was a downside to this series of personal and professional triumphs. Beaton's absolute ubiquity in the society magazines of the late 1920s did not always commend itself to his contemporaries, especially those with more substantial claims to artistic talent. "Have you seen the December *Vogue*?" Ed Burra demanded of Barbara Ker-Seymer after a particularly lavish spread of Beaton photographs and Beaton sketches. "It's Cecil Beaton Baba Beaton Annie Beaton Mrs Beaton Father Beaton Lizzie Beaton Beaton Beaton and even one of those amusing drawings by Cecil Beaton of Cecil Beaton impersonating a fragrant old Staffordshire piece representing Apollo . . ." But for the next few years Beaton was a fixed and irremovable part of the Bright Young Person's landscape, photographed at its parties, satirized in its novels, dancing attendance on its aristocratic *jeunes premières*. It was he, perhaps more than any impresario of the day, who gave coherence to what had for the first two or three years of its existence been no more than a rather slapdash collection of personalities and parties. Caught in the wash of these individual trajectories, the movement had begun to enter a new phase: a period in which everything they did was zealously recorded by gossip columnists, in which groups of Bright Young People exerted themselves to emulate and surpass each other in the range and the oddity of their entertainments. A distinctive social environment began to take shape, in which the Bright Young Men and Women could operate on their own terms, untrammeled by society hostesses or disapproving elders.

There were a dozen venues in central London that could be regarded as definitive Bright Young People's territory. A few were private residences: the flat that Brian Howard shared with Eddie Gathorne-Hardy at 39 Maddox Street and Patrick Balfour's flat-cum-studio in Yeoman's Row, Knightsbridge, where John Betjeman remembered:

> *The spurt of soda as the whisky rose*
> *Bringing its heady scent to memory's nose*
> *Along with smells one otherwise forgets:*
> *Hairwash from Delhez, Turkish cigarettes,*
> *The reek of Ronuk on a parquet floor*
> *As parties came cascading through the door:*
> *Elizabeth Ponsonby in leopard-skins*
> *And Robert Byron and the Ruthven twins . . .*

One step up from the lodgements of individual Bright Young People came a series of faintly disreputable nightclubs like the Cave of Harmony, initially in Charlotte Street, later at other addresses, or the Blue Lantern in Ham Yard, a club with a slightly intellectual tinge where once, greatly daring, Anthony Powell asked Tallulah Bankhead to dance. Higher up the social scale reposed the "smart" nightclubs such as the Embassy Club, the Kit-Kat and Chez Victor. The two most characteristic settings, on the other hand, were a club that sometimes seems to have been founded merely to give the movement a *locus operandi*, and a private hotel which, by this point in its long history, had all but vanished into clouds of bygone Edwardian glory.

From its earliest days, the Gargoyle Club at 69 Dean Street was a quintessential twenties institution. Brought into being for entirely frivolous reasons—its founder, David Tennant, claimed that he simply wanted somewhere to dance with his girlfriend—it also maintained a quite genuine commitment to the arts: a chic nightclub for dancing, according to the original press release, but also a daytime refuge for the avant-garde, where "still struggling writers, painters, poets and musicians will be offered the best food and wine at prices they can afford." There was, additionally, evidence of that typical twenties hankering after artistic freedom. "Above all," Tennant declared, "it will be a place without the usual rules where people can express themselves freely." In practice, the Gargoyle combined its inherited bohemianism with a scent of glamour: Hermione Baddeley, Tennant's dancing partner, appeared in Noël Coward's *On with the Dance*, whose big number "Poor Little Rich Girl" was the hit song of 1925; the first subscription list included Somerset Maugham and members of the Guinness, Rothschild and Sitwell families; the club committee brought together Clive Bell, A. P. Herbert and Arnold Bennett: the doyen of Bloomsbury critics, a journalizing independent MP and one of the wealthiest novelists of the day.

If 69 Dean Street—where on mild nights guests made their way to the door through a gaggle of Soho prostitutes—seemed an incongruous setting for a social experiment of this kind, its interior sprang an even greater surprise. Through his artistically minded friends, Tennant knew Matisse. Asked to advise on décor, the veteran post-Impressionist proposed that the walls of the main room on the first floor should be covered with a mosaic of mirrored tiles, assembled out of the fragments of ancient French looking-glasses. Two of the artist's paintings—*The Red Studio* and *The Studio, Quai St. Michel*—were displayed on the premises, the first in the dining room, the second halfway down the main staircase. All this gave the place a pronounced air of chic. Sixty years after being taken to it by her father, the novelist Elizabeth Jane Howard could still remember the squares of mirror glass lining restaurant and dance floor, "which made it larger and much more glamorous."

The club's tone was correspondingly smart. A seven-guinea subscription, and an enlightened scheme whereby the "deserving artistic poor" were given honorary membership, brought in genuine bohemians. On the other hand the presence of ancient Soho landmarks such as Nina Hamnett and Augustus John was balanced by regular incursions from the Howard and Acton generation of Oxford aesthetes. Occasionally Bright Young People could overrun the place completely: one party of Alannah Harper's was thought to have lasted for forty-eight hours. Much more congenial to Tennant's original conception was the presence of up-and-coming artists in search of a refuge. Ed Burra, for example, appreciated an easygoing atmosphere not always found in other ports of call. "I find the Gargoyle comes a bit more expensive than our dear old Maison [Lyons]," he told Barbara Ker-Seymer, "but when you are surrounded by lovely new Matisses whose price runs into 4 figgers and get a squint at *Vogue* without paying it's not so expensive." Once its habitués were in place—Lady Dean Paul, Brenda's mother, say, installed at the bar, or David Tennant eating sausages and mushrooms in the dining room—there was something about the club's atmosphere that kept social exclusiveness at bay. As Daphne Fielding put it, "the Gargoyle seemed to transform ordinary conventional people into bohemians; on becoming members they even began to dress quite differently." Detractors took a more prosaic view, maintaining that the place was quickly colonized by suburban interlopers who had nothing to do with its inaugural spirit: "packed with the two hundred nastiest people in Chiswick," as Constant Lambert once observed of its heaving Saturday night dance floor.

Quite as central to the Bright Young People's mythology was the Cavendish Hotel in Jermyn Street, less for its amenities—now somewhat faded—than the reputation of its legendary proprietress, Rosa Lewis, immortalized by Evelyn Waugh as "Lottie Crump," owner of "Shepheard's Hotel" in Dover Street. Famously down-to-earth—Waugh claimed that the last words she spoke to him were "Take your arse out of my chair"—unimpressed by the grandest connections, should they fail to chime with her mood, Rosa was a startling example of the essential fluidity of the late-Victorian era, an enduring symbol of the distances which the talented but humbly born could sometimes expect to travel on the way to its summit. A watchmaker's daughter and former kitchen maid from the East End, she began her career proper as cook to Lady Randolph Churchill before carving out a niche as a kind of freelance caterer to the Prince of Wales during his weekend round of country house visiting. At twenty-five, in time-honored Victorian fashion, she married a butler, the extravagantly named Excelsior Lewis, and opened an exclusive lodging house in Eaton Place. There were problems with Lewis, who drank and mismanaged the accounts, but by 1902, buoyed up by her success as a supper provider to the balls of Coronation Year, she had amassed sufficient funds to buy the Cavendish. Thereafter she maintained a dual existence, combining an intensely lucrative high-class catering business with the management of an equally patrician but eccentrically run hotel.

The Great War was Rosa's apogee. Subsequently her profits declined and her premises turned gradually into a period piece, a sepia-tinted throwback to a vanished age, sustained by the memory of lost aristocratic laughter and the remnant of King Edward VII's personal wine cellar. Aldous Huxley, who stayed there in the early thirties, compared it to a run-down country house: "large, comfortable rooms, but everything shabby and a bit dirty." The Huxleys' visit was enlivened by a young man in evening dress who came swaying into their room in the small hours and had to be thrown out. The connection between Rosa and the Bright Young People was, if anything, dynastic: many of them were the children—increasingly, as time went on, the grandchildren—of her original patrons. Keen on the spectacle of well-bred young people enjoying themselves, notoriously indulgent of youthful foibles, she featured as a kind of eccentric aunt, turning up at smart wedding receptions in her trademark garb of white Busvine coat and skirt, and a dark green homburg hat trimmed with a selection of small stuffed birds.

The Cavendish itself remained a late-night haunt on which party-goers descended after midnight, when drinks were available in the large drawing room on the first floor and Rosa held court amid a motley collection of guests and loiterers. Half a century after his attendance at these rackety soirées, Anthony Powell tried to convey something of the extraordinarily eclectic nature of the people habitually gathered there: a couple of guards ensigns, say, an American tourist or two, a handful of Bright Young Men, but also a peculiar assortment of waifs and strays, vague people "whose presence seemed absolutely inexplicable." Powell also noted the "tense, menacing atmosphere" of the place—in part attributable to the faintly seedy late-night ambience, but also a result of the regular appearance of communal drinks bills, which the most affluent person in the room was expected to settle. Flanked by her long-term companion Edith Jeffery, Rosa combined an Alice in Wonderland–style amnesia over her guests' identities—Powell was once introduced to the company as "Bimbash Stewart," an Edwardian man-about-town who had died in 1907—with considerable shrewdness. "Young Doris may go far on those legs of hers," she once remarked of Doris Delavigne, later Viscountess Castlerosse, "but, mark my words, she doesn't know how to make a man comfortable."

Mid-1920s Bright Young People territory contained several other outposts: the Restaurant de la Tour Eiffel in Percy Street, for example, with its celebrated proprietor, Stulik; nightclubs like the Bat or the Night Light; out-of-the-way small-hours nooks such as the Windmill in Windmill Street, where at any time until dawn bacon and eggs could be procured from a grave butlerlike personage in a tailcoat, whom Anthony Powell imagined that a duke would have been proud to employ. Veering as it did between the smartest society function and the thoroughly disreputable carouse, a Bright Young Person's progress around London could accommodate a bewildering variety of different compartments. Determined to enjoy himself once on his first night back in town, Alfred Duggan, Lord Curzon's stepson, began the evening by dining formally with his mother, Lady Curzon, at her house in Carlton Terrace, proceeded to a West End play, followed this up with supper at the Café Royal, moved on to "a lurid attic in Ham Yard" (probably the Blue Lantern) and concluded the night's entertainment at the Forty-three with "Mrs. Meyrick, Miss Meyrick and the entire staff at his feet."

While the movement's focus was firmly metropolitan, there were acknowledged Bright Young Person's retreats beyond London: country houses or stately homes where the presence of weekending sons and daughters and their friends was guaranteed to shake up the rural torpor. These included the Ponsonbys' country house at Shulbrede on the Surrey-Sussex border; Faringdon, the Oxfordshire home of the eccentric Lord Berners; Maresfield in East Sussex, owned by the Vorticist painter Edward Wadsworth; and Swinbrook, the Mitford seat in Oxfordshire ("At weekends they would swoop down from Oxford or London in merry hordes," Jessica Mitford remembered, "to be greeted with solid disapproval by my mother and furious glares from my father"), where Nancy Mitford was welcomed as a highly desirable recruit. "A delicious creature," Brian Howard informed Harold Acton, "quite pyrotechnical, my dear, and sometimes even profound, and would you believe it, she's hidden among the cabbages of the Cotswolds." Oxford remained a popular weekend destination, long after the original Bright Young Oxonians had gone down: Osbert Lancaster, who went up to Lincoln College in 1926, remembered summer visits from "contemporary celebrities" such as Elizabeth Ponsonby, Brenda Dean Paul and even Tallulah Bankhead.

Other destinations were yet more remote. A popular summer retreat was Cullen Castle in Banffshire, home of Nina, the youthful Countess of Seafield. "We haven't once been to bed before 2," Nancy reported back from one such gathering, "pajama parties every night in Nina's sitting room which is like a gala night at the Florida." On one of these evenings, Nancy continued, she, Nina, Mark Ogilvie-Grant and Hamish Erskine embarked on a fancy dress dinner: "Hamish & I draped our middles in calf-skin chiffon & wore vine leaves. I had a wreath of red roses & I curled Hamish's hair with tongs, he looked more than lovely. Mark just came in a bathing dress & a wreath & Nina was a lady of the court of Herod."

Nancy's account of life at Cullen offers a characteristic picture from this light, bright and strangely garish twenties world: the thought of a collection of grown-up children—wanton and yet curiously innocent— loudly amusing themselves in a hermetically sealed bubble, while the real world, with all its pressures and obligations, grinds on in the distance. For all its surface delights, the image carries with it the seeds of its own destruction. One knows, somehow, that here in 1928, with the General Strike two years gone and economic meltdown lurking beyond the Highland heather, that epicene young men cannot go on curling their hair in Scottish castles for much longer, that all these willed high spirits, these shriekings over nothing, will be reckoned up in future unhappiness, that the dancers—to use the metaphor of the day—are stepping ever closer to the precipice's edge.

For the moment all this lay far beyond the horizon. Most contemporary chroniclers insist that 1927 was the high-water mark of the first phase of Bright Young People activity. "London in that early summer of 1927 was very gay," Alec Waugh wistfully recalled. In a hotly competitive atmosphere, hosts and hostesses strove desperately to surpass each other in the originality of their invitations, closely watched by society columnists. "London's Bright Young People have broken out again," the *Daily Express* informed its readers in mid July. "The treasure hunt being *passé* and the uninvited guest already *démodé*, there has been much hard thinking to find the next sensation. It was achieved last night at a dance given by Captain Neil McEachran at his Brook Street house." The "Impersonation Party," at which each of the guests was asked to represent some well-known personality, attracted widespread publicity. The *Tatler* was on hand to photograph the revelers, who included Tallulah Bankhead in flannels and shirt, and Elizabeth Ponsonby in a red wig as Iris Tree. In terms of Bright Young People mythology, its significant feature is its reflexiveness, a vigilant self-absorption that led several of the guests to come not as stars of stage or screen but as each other. Tom Driberg, for instance, disguised himself as Brian Howard, making up his face, giving one of his eyebrows an exaggerated twist and carrying a packet of cigarettes in his hand in order not to spoil the line of his suit. Olivia Plunket Greene, alternatively, had her hair peroxided and styled to resemble Brenda Dean Paul.

And if individual Bright Young People had already begun to feed off each other's reputations and identities, so their idiosyncrasies had begun to filter down into the wider public consciousness. Parents who came across specimen Bright Young Men generally did not like what they saw. "I never remember that he is quite as awful to look at and it gives me a shock," Dorothea Ponsonby complained, on being reintroduced to Brian Howard at about this time. "I can't look at him. He is like an obscure footman." Eddie Gathorne-Hardy, while a "gentleman" and displaying a sense of humor, was "feeble—foppish with eye glass and squeaky laugh—luxurious with no back bone & superior." Patrick Balfour, brought home by Matthew Ponsonby during an Oxford vacation, fared even worse. "Typical of a certain section of the young of these days," the Shulbrede sybil lamented. "Like a satire [sic] to look at—with Chinese eyes & hair only beginning to grow from the back of his head . . . Appears to be heartless and rootless—a freak with a touch of the *chien de poche* [Ponsonby slang for a supposed, but not necessarily practicing, homosexual]."

These laments were not confined to private diaries. The Bright Young People "joke" had already begun to make its way into the newspapers, and in particular to that barometer of middle-class conservative opinion, *Punch*. Ever attentive to the vagaries of youth, *Punch* had been keeping a hard and unyielding eye on what it regarded as adolescent foolery from the early 1920s onward. There were "Charleston" jokes—a gyrating young man splayed over a doormat of whom it is said approvingly that now at least he can wipe his feet; an American who claims proficiency on the grounds that he has Saint Vitus' dance—or the "Diary of a Mondaine," a 1926 spoof indicted from "Mayfair Mansions" in super-fashionable argot.

By the following year this generalized distaste for nightclubs, short skirts and staying up late assumes a more deliberate focus. Several *Punch* cartoons of 1927 take up the idea of generational divide. "Sorry I'm late," one fashionably dressed girl apologizes to another as they meet in some late-night vestibule, "I've been dining with my parents." "I expect they were terribly bucked," her companion responds. Others mock the supposed casualness of Bright Young People's relationships. But at heart, *Punch*'s attitude was more ambivalent than its running commentary suggests: even at their most censorious, complaints about juvenile license tended to be balanced by a kind of exasperated fascination.

More to the point, perhaps, the Bright Young Person, like the lion-hunting society hostess or the bohemian "hartist" of the mid-nineteenth century, was too good a joke to ignore. In the end, he—or she—became a *Punch* staple, brought out at regular intervals to emphasize the gap between a hidebound elder generation and its feckless youthful offshoots. "I should have thought that a nightclub was the very *last* place a daughter of mine would go to," a disapproving paterfamilias sternly rebukes a sylphlike young woman. "It usually is, darling," she carelessly replies. These ambiguities were noticeable in the wider coverage of Bright Young People's antics that emblazoned middle-market newspapers until at least the end of the decade. On the one hand journalists—often with the sanction of their proprietors—were keen on "youth" in all its manifestations, even if that youth could be seen to be conducting itself in foolish or irresponsible ways. On the other, the suspicion of "decadence," triviality or outright immorality could always bring this fixation crashing down to earth. In an atmosphere where a good deal of indulgence came mingled with the iciest gusts of puritanical disapproval, Stephen Tennant, who began his long, dandified progress through the society columns at about this time, was impossible to resist.

Uncle. "I SAY, MY DEAR, DO YOU KNOW IT'S NEARLY THREE O'CLOCK?"
Niece. "GRACIOUS! I'D NO IDEA WE'D BEEN HERE SO LONG; YOU MUST BE BORED. WELL, WHERE DO WE GO NEXT?"

"It would be impossible, I feel, to be as decadent as Lambert Orme looked," Harold Nicolson wrote in "Lambert Orme," a fictional composite largely based on the novelist Ronald Firbank. Much the same could be said—frequently was said—of Stephen Tennant. Tall, with elaborately coiffed blond hair set in marcelled waves, and pale, flapping hands, he walked, as Thomas Hardy once remarked to Siegfried Sassoon, like the young Swinburne: as he sauntered affectedly around a room it could sometimes seem as if his legs were tied together at the knee. No account of Tennant's upbringing, in the cosseted surroundings of the parental home at Wilsford, omits his infant narcissism. As a toddler, coming across a particularly luxuriant pansy in the garden, he is supposed to have observed, "Someone's looking." Later, asked by his father, Lord Glenconner, what he wanted to "be" in life, he answered, "A great beauty, sir." Spoiled and quite possibly sexually confused by his indulgent mother, who dressed him in girls' clothing way beyond infancy, he had been launched into the world as a precocious teenage artist. At twenty he was a wholly exotic figure: eccentric, self-absorbed, flamboyant in a way that most of the twenties partygoers could never hope to emulate, either—depending on how you looked at it—drenched in the scent of moral contamination or grievously misunderstood. "Nowadays so many boys are *girlish*, without being effeminate," his chum Edith Oliver loyally declared. "It's the sort of boy that has grown up since the war." Driberg included him in a *Daily Express* checklist of the Bright Young People's finest, suggesting that, "should he favour you with speech, with an epigram, perhaps, that reveals an intuition as searching as a woman's, you will feel that condescension, indeed, can go no further."

Inevitably, there were literary leanings. These realized an unpublished society novel titled *The Second Chance* ("It is high life with a capital H & full of crude impossibilities—however one has to begin like that. I hope one day to be a great novelist"). In general, though, Tennant's aesthetic hankerings were ornamental. There were long hours spent planning the décor of the Wilsford interiors, or the costumes of fancy dress balls. Beaton, invited down for the first time in early 1927 ("and now oh joy of heaven I was asked to stay at Wilsford"), was aware that in the presence of such exotic good taste his own role could only be that of respectful acolyte. Amid a spirited company that included the Jungman sisters and Oscar Wilde's niece Dorothy, he enjoyed himself extravagantly: "I undressed & wore a flimsy pair of speckled pyjamas which completely went with the room . . . I wanted to eat all the books & all the flowers & Stephen as well: I am sure I went to bed with a beam of happiness on my face." Clearly, Cecil went down well, for in February he was invited to stay with Tennant and his mother on the Riviera, in a ménage that included Zita, Dorothy and Rex Whistler, together with the Guinness sisters and Loelia Ponsonby.

Back in England in the spring, the relationship continued to prosper. At a charity pageant early in May, Stephen took the role of Prince Charming with Cecil as Lucien Bonaparte and appearances by Zita, Tallulah Bankhead and Oliver Messel. A month later Beaton was bidden to a literary party at Wilsford, where the guests included Sacheverell Sitwell and his wife, Georgia; Eddy Sackville-West; Rosamond Lehmann; and the American writer Elinor Wylie. He took a much-reproduced photo of the assembled company as they lay on the floor covered with imitation leopard skins. The shivaree of the London season found Tennant and Beaton—the latter in the role of foil-cum-factotum—in their element. At Mrs. Benjamin Guinness's fancy dress ball, Tennant attempted to impersonate a beggar but arrived "elegant as a fairy" with a billowing silk cloak to hide the rags.

At the Impersonation Party, Tennant masqueraded as Queen Marie of Romania, a virtuoso performance requiring hours in front of the mirror and minute attention to detail. Clad in white silk, with pearls, gloves and meticulous coiffure, he seemed, as his biographer notes, a professional in a roomful of amateurs. But a professional what? His talent—if that is what it was—was essentially evanescent: the gesture, the smart remark, the pajamas that "went with the room." Taken beyond the spangled palisades of the Mayfair drawing room or the country house revel, more exotic specimens of the Bright Young People could run into serious trouble. There was a symbolic standoff at the Earl of Pembroke's ball, held on August 5 at Wilton House, to celebrate his son's coming of age. Cecil, in an episode recounted so many times that it became one of the great dramatic events of his life, far outstripping the reality of a brief upending in a few inches of muddy water, was thrown into the river Nadder by a gang of hearties. Stephen, who had arrived "looking like a gilded butterfly," his half-inch eyelashes combed out to their fullest extent and with gold dust sprinkled liberally in his hair, seemed set to follow Beaton over the bank. In the end, though, the bullies stayed their hand: the experience, Tennant managed to convince them—no doubt with truth—would have killed him.

Evelyn Waugh, meanwhile, was living an altogether different life, far out upon the margins of the Bright Young People world. Such parties as he attended in the holidays from his schoolteaching jobs were firmly located at its bohemian end. In September 1926, for example, he was present at a gathering "given by the lesbian girls I met the other day," where Sir Francis Laking, dressed first as a girl and then stark naked, attempted a Charleston. Waugh's real involvement with the Bright Young People began in 1927 when, sacked from his position at Aston Clinton, he found himself once more in London in search of paid employment but also eager to enjoy himself in agreeable company. Thereafter his diaries are crammed with references to Bright Young haunts and personalities. The tone, though—in contrast to the blasé, *Tatler*-ish style of his later journal keeping—is notably unworldly. Clearly Waugh, discovering these things for the first time, is uncertain of the territory being mapped out and the impression made. An excursion in February 1927 to "a night club called Victors" was obviously his inaugural visit. Still following the chaotic trail blazed through London society by Olivia Plunket Greene, he accompanied her to the celebrated Negro revue *The Blackbirds*, which had taken London by storm the previous year. A week later, with his brother Alec and Harold Acton, he was invited to a party at Oliver Messel's:

Alec and Harold and I dined first at the Ritz ... It was a crowded party with all the Blackbirds and all the Oxford Brian Howard set and stray and squalid stragglers uninvited from Otter's and Francis. Cecil Roberts became insensible with drink and, curled in overcoat, vomited and pissed intermittently. Robert Byron made an ostentatious entry as Queen Victoria. The Earl of Rosse and I cut each other throughout the evening. Olivia and I both felt more than a little lonely.

The last sentence is significant. Waugh is still observing this world: he is not yet a part of it. But the course on which he was now embarked would take him steadily closer to its center. Early in March 1927 he began working on a trial basis at the *Daily Express* as a trainee reporter. The newspaper tryout was a popular standby for Oxford graduates of the 1920s—a chance to demonstrate enterprise and zeal in the atmosphere of a Fleet Street newsroom with the prospect of a full-time post three months afterward. Whereas Driberg, who arrived later in the year, used the job as the springboard to an immensely successful journalistic career, Waugh—capricious and not amenable to office discipline— calculated that not one of the stories he worked on ever appeared in print. On the other hand the *Express* trial gave him carte blanche to spend time loitering in the West End of London. His diary entries for the next few months are full of what would prove to be highly significant connections. In early April he met "such a nice girl called Evelyn Gardner." Starting his fifth week on the *Express* early in May, he noted that "a charming girl called Inez Holden works on the paper. I have been to a few parties and joined a club called the Gargoyle." Six weeks later he records visiting a cinema with Inez, "Then to the Gargoyle, then to the Night Light where she spent all my money on a shilling in the slot machine then back to the Gargoyle." Sacked by the *Express*—not at all to his surprise—in early July, he devoted the rest of the summer to his social life. Three weeks on he attended a party given by Richard Plunket Greene and his wife in Eddie Gathorne-Hardy's rooms, shortly afterward gate-crashing the Impersonation Party in Brook Street ("I don't know who the host was"), noting that "everyone was dressed up and for the most part looking rather ridiculous," and thinking that Olivia, in her Brenda Dean Paul costume, "seemed so unhappy."

Later in the month he escorted Olivia and Eddie to a cocktail party, went to the ballet with John Sutro and attended a gathering hosted by

David Tennant and Brian Howard, which was "quite amusing." There was still the problem of work, although the publishing firm of Duckworth, on the recommendation of Anthony Powell, had commissioned a biography of Rossetti. But the pattern of Waugh's life had changed, grown smaller, more metropolitan, more ambitious, even. There were still evenings such as that memorialized in the entry of August 30 ("Then to the Gargoyle where we found Bobbie and with him, he drunk, to the 43. Talked to a whore about Bulgaria where she had clearly never been. Then to another club called Manhattan which turned out to be a brothel"), but in general his diaries from the autumn of 1927 are more purposeful: seeing people about jobs; interviewing Pre-Raphaelite survivors for *Rossetti*; reviewing books for the *Bookman*; and, early in September, starting work on "a comic novel."

A comparison with Beaton is instructive. Indefatigable and omnipresent, obsequious when the grandeur of the occasion demanded it, imperious when his professional dignity was at stake, Cecil combined his aerie in the upmarket society magazines with a steely determination to move beyond them. The *Tatler* and the *Bystander* were all very well, but Beaton had his eye on *Vogue*, and in particular its lucrative American edition. Happily, Edna Woolman Chase, who had founded the magazine with Condé Nast, liked his work and recommended him to Alison Settle, the new London editor: Miss Todd, Beaton's former sponsor, had been sacked for making the paper too highbrow. As ever, social and professional triumphs marched side by side. In November 1927 he had his first exhibition at the Cooling Galleries in Bond Street, loyally patronized by the beau monde: *The Lady*'s correspondent saw Tennant there with Oliver Messel and Sir Oswald Mosley. Previously more or less separate from each other in terms of milieu and ambition, Beaton and Waugh were now increasingly launched on a parallel track. Anthony Powell, a reliable observer of Waugh throughout his life, noted the change that seemed to have come over his friend toward the close of 1927. Powell, now a year into his job at Duckworth, had begun a printing course at Holborn Polytechnic, which took him to the institution's premises in Southampton Row several nights a week. By chance, on an evening in October, he came upon Waugh hurrying along one of its corridors. ("His appearance had the familiarity, combined with complete improbability, which one associates with dreams," Powell remembered.) Asked what he was doing, Waugh volunteered the information that he had decided to take up carpentry as a profession. There was also mention of Tolstoy. To Powell this suggested that "writing need not be absolutely barred as a sideline."

Meeting him again a few weeks later, on a tube train, Powell discovered that his friend had a yet more radical end in view. Without preamble, Waugh announced that he was going to be married. Powell, by his own admission, thought he was joking. Waugh was a week or two short of his twenty-fourth birthday. "Marriage . . . was something unthought of among contemporaries at that date, an undertaking well outside the consideration of the possible; or so it seemed to me." But he knew of Evelyn Gardner, whose name had been mentioned to him by Alec Waugh, significantly enough in the context of a discussion of the Modern Girl. Alec, who had run into Powell in the neighborhood of Sloane Square, revealed that Miss Gardner—the Honorable Miss Gardner—inhabited a flat in the vicinity with her friend Pansy Pakenham. Contradicting newspaper articles about the Modern Girl putting on too much makeup, drinking too many cocktails, being brassy, bad-mannered and gold-digging, these two, Alec suggested, "couldn't be nicer, prettier, quieter, more intelligent." Looking back at Waugh's engagement, which had still to circumvent the substantial obstacle of his fiancée's mother, the formidable Lady Burghclere, Powell thought it symbolic of an altogether larger development. The scope of his life was widening, Powell thought. The old Waugh—feckless, improvident, bohemian—was fading into the past on the night they met on the tube when he announced "I'm going to be married." Already, Powell noticed, he had begun to slough off bohemian acquaintances who failed to correspond to the view he now took of himself. Naturally, his eagerness to marry the younger daughter of the first Lord Burghclere was a testimony to the feelings that this slender, gamine-looking girl aroused in him, but it also marked a sea change in the scope of his social aspirations.

Waugh's diary for 1927 ends with an entry for December 13: "Evelyn rang up to say she had made up her mind to accept." It was not resumed until the day of his marriage, June 27, 1928. This hiatus is a pity as Waugh's comments on the Bright Young People gatherings of the early summer would, you feel, have been worth having. Their undoubted stars, if only by weight of press cuttings, were Beaton and Tennant. Stephen had spent the winter of 1927–28 abroad in the Bavarian highlands, for the sake of the winter sunshine his mother thought necessary to his health. Back in London in the spring he attended his brother's wedding to Hermione Baddeley on April 16 and then, four days later, cohosted a party with Brenda Dean Paul and his cousin Olivia Wyndham at the latter's house in Sloane Square. Driberg, covering the event for the *Daily Express*, thought that it marked the return of the Bright Young People after a winter's hibernation: "Intelligence—determined and natural—and beauty turned up in crowds." The guest list was a cornucopia of Bright Young personalities: Cecil, Rex Whistler, Harold Acton, Brian Howard. The cynosure, however, was the cohost. Driberg reported that he wore earrings and a football jersey. Mr. Tennant, the report went on, "when in London drives about in an electric brougham of the Edwardian period. He says it is like riding in a bow-window."

Elusive and protean, Stephen flitted from one gossip column to the next: "a fantastic figure in silver and gray" at a party given by Elizabeth Ponsonby in the Royal Hospital Road, with Cecil alongside him as "an Edwardian dude, with golden wig and topper"; arriving at his brother's post-honeymoon pajama party at Adelphi Terrace in white satin, but, according to the *Evening Standard*, changing halfway through into green. Later on in May, Nancy Mitford wrote to her brother, Tom, about a visit made with Nina Seafield and Patrick Balfour to the Pageant of Hyde Park Through the Ages, staged at Daly's Theatre. "Alas old B [Howard] wasn't Disraeli: he ran out at the last moment . . . Mark [Ogilvie-Grant] looked lovely in a white wig & knee breeches & Oliver Messel was *too* wonderful as Byron . . . Stephen Tennant as Shelley was very beautiful." A fortnight later came the annual extravaganza of the Chelsea Arts Ball, when the Tennant party formed what one newspaper called "a large group in a fantastic range of chiffon and velvet, showing the Picasso scheme of coloring."

Evelyn Waugh's marriage took place less than three weeks later.

Most contemporary witnesses adjudged Lady Burghclere to be irreconcilable, although Nancy Mitford claimed to remember her "saying how pleased she was that her daughter should marry into a good literary family." The ceremony was conducted without her knowledge, before a minuscule congregation, at St. Paul's, Portman Square. Harold Acton was best man. Robert Byron gave away the bride. Alec Waugh and Pansy Pakenham, the bride's former roommate, were witnesses. Returning from a honeymoon in Beckley (Lady Burghclere, now apprised of the situation, was, according to her son-in-law, "quite inexpressibly pained"), Waugh sat down to correct the proofs of *Decline and Fall*, set for publication in the autumn. Fifty years later Anthony Powell attempted to re-create the atmosphere of the Waughs' Islington flat, at which he was a regular visitor ("Tony Powell came to see us after dinner full of scandal about the Sitwells," ran a diary entry of October 4), and the personalities of the two young people who inhabited it. Waugh, he thought, on settling down as a married man, made no secret of the fact that he wanted his life in some ways to change, expressing a wish to know "only the intelligent and smart." She-Evelyn, as Evelyn Gardner had now become known, though "brought up in an aristocratic world," wanted, Powell thought, "to diminish, rather than increase, those aspects of aristocratic life that become tedious if taken too seriously." Insofar as one can summarize these aspirations, Waugh aspired to "smartness"; his wife, on the other hand, was keen on amusement, a pursuit in which smartness might or might not play a part. Though not yet in the Tennant-Beaton class, the couple had become personalities. They dined with Osbert Sitwell and their photographs appeared in the *Sketch*.

Cecil, meanwhile, had his sights set on even grander quarry. On November 3, encouraged by Beverley Nichols, who had recently been appointed editor of the *American Sketch*, he set sail for New York. Though disappointed that no press reporters were on hand to witness his departure, he was gratified by his reception. Condé Nast invited him to lunch; American *Vogue* accepted his pictures; fashionable New York flocked to his studio. Beaton being Beaton, the impression he contrived to make on Manhattan society was carefully orchestrated. The room in which he welcomed clients was littered with strategically placed debris: piles of press cuttings, unfinished drawings, discarded envelopes with smart addresses scribbled carelessly on their flaps. Only his habit of making up his face attracted disapproval: Nichols advised him to stop. But the triumphs of his American expedition were there for all to see. Mrs. Harrison Williams had invited him to spend the weekend at her Long Island estate. Lady Mendl had underwritten his exhibition at the de Wolfe Gallery on Fifth Avenue. Shortly before Christmas 1928 he wrote an exuberant letter home to "Johanna" of *The Lady*. "The atmosphere is so electric that one cannot stop. I have done, in my three weeks here, just as much as any American tripper would have done in England at the same time, which is a lot . . . Every party seems more expensively done than the last." Above all, he was impressed by the profusion of flowers, knowing that a rose cost a dollar and an orchid eight or nine. "Life is very exciting," he signed off, "and it is glorious fun being treated as though one were a celebrity."

Just before he left England, he had received tangible proof that another, previously unregarded, member of his generation was also moving forward into the limelight. "Is it true," Tennant had wondered in October, "that you and I appear in a novel by Waugh?" It was. Stephen's and Cecil's cameos in *Decline and Fall* were symptomatic of a wider trend. The Bright Young People had ceased to be a cult, a private joke or an exclusive sect. Increasingly their activities would move out into the mainstream of national life, to be recorded, analyzed and satirized like any other phenomenon. In this lay the seeds of their undoing.

MR. PRYCE-JONES'S CONNECTIONS

One talks routinely about individual Bright Young People being "well connected." What did this mean in practice? Good connections, after all, are relative. Evelyn Waugh, who complained loudly of his middle-class poverty, was the son of a publisher and the younger brother of an established novelist-about-town, which, from his own professional vantage point, were the best connections of all. Lieutenant-Colonel Philip Powell was a friend of Thomas Balston, the junior partner at Gerald Duckworth & Co., for whom his son Anthony went to work: the same point applies. But in the wider scheme of things these were minor affiliations, passkeys to salaried employment of the kind that practically every upper-bourgeois family kept up its sleeve. How did they work higher up the scale? There were certain Bright Young People whose every movement was monitored by a chorus of well-placed helpers, whose address books were mini-*Debrett's* and *Almanachs de Gotha*, whose ramifications came screaming with well-nigh princely éclat. How did they get on?

Inspect, for example, the career of Alan Pryce-Jones, too young, perhaps—he was born in November 1908—to have moved among the Bright Young People in their heyday, but a keen observer of their early-thirties decline. Pryce-Jones senior was a guardsman who "went into the City," but his paternal grandfather was a bona fide Victorian magnate, founder of the "Royal Welsh Warehouse," knight of the realm and long-term Tory MP for Montgomery Boroughs. Elsewhere among his father's family, "Uncle Pryce" was a baronet, while his aunt Nell's husband acted as chairman of the Humber car company, from which the family bought their motor vehicles at a discount. But if the Pryce-Joneses smelled occasionally of "trade," in however sanitized and respectable a form, the other side of the family were impeccable Whig aristocrats. Mrs. Pryce-Jones was the great-granddaughter of Lord Grey, architect of the 1832 Reform Bill, and through him connected to a half-dozen of the great Victorian clans—Ponsonbys and Dawnays and Bulteels, Barings and Lytteltons and Beresfords—their collective luster fading a little here in the demotic twentieth century but never to be disregarded in the realm of quiet words and surreptitious influence. Not to be outdone, Mr. Pryce-Jones retired from the city to the post of gentleman at arms, occupied an apartment at Windsor and was offered occasional invitations to dine with the king and queen. Later in life, the young Pryce-Jones would wonder whether he didn't spend too much time with "elderly people who were my contemporaries."

But younger friends had their own particular distinction. Arriving at Eton early in 1922, he was immediately called upon by an older boy named Dunglass—Lord Dunglass, later fourteenth Earl of Home, and as Sir Alec Douglas-Home, Conservative prime minister in 1963–64—at the behest of some shared relative. The school's serious literary talent, Connolly and Orwell, had already moved on to Oxford and the Burma Police, but even so there were Peter Watson, later proprietor of *Horizon*, James Lees-Milne and the Earl of Rosslyn's son Hamish St. Clair Erskine to smooth his path. It was the same at Oxford, where his first visitor was John Betjeman. Sent down from the university, he was rescued by Watson and deposited on his parents' doorstep from the seat of a hired Rolls-Royce. A friend suggested devilling for J. C. Squire, editor of the *London Mercury*, who introduced him to G. K. Chesterton and Hilaire Belloc. Christmases were spent at Hever Castle, whose owner, John Astor, proprietor of *The Times*, had married a cousin of his mother; holidays at such far-flung retreats as the Winter Palace Hotel, on the banks of the Nile, where he accompanied Dame Nellie Melba on an upright piano while she sang "You Are My Heart's Delight" to another of the establishment's guests, Queen Marie of Romania.

The roster of influence, connection and tip-top fashionable society goes on: afternoon teas with Lady Randolph Churchill; research work for her son while the latter, then chancellor of the exchequer, wrote *Great Contemporaries*; a friendship with Somerset Maugham . . . And yet all the available evidence suggests, to be "well connected" was not, here in the early 1930s, quite enough. Dinner with Their Majesties was all very well, but the royal guest remained an unpaid editorial assistant on a relatively obscure literary weekly. Slowly, incrementally, and to the great annoyance of those left behind in its wake, England was turning more democratic. In the smaller world of the Bright Young People, it was the middle-class meritocrats—Beaton, Waugh and others like them—who would have the last laugh.

CHAPTER FOUR

PARENTS AND CHILDREN

We parents of today are having a poorish time. We have no control whatever.
— ARTHUR PONSONBY'S diary, April 22, 1925

I think she is made for better things, but I am helpless.
— ARTHUR PONSONBY on his daughter, February 11, 1923

I f a single characteristic defined the Bright Young People, made them conspicuous and saturated the reports that were filed about them, it was the deeply ambiguous relationships which they enjoyed with their parents. Patrick Balfour described the young men of the 1920s— by which he meant young upper-middle-class Oxbridge graduates—as a "rebel army," and the institution they were rebelling against was, for the most part, parental suzerainty. The father worrying about his son's future, the mother alarmed by her daughter's chronic unfittedness for the part that nature presumably intended her to play, are such a commonplace of the interwar novel that one forgets their significance and the intergenerational truce that preceded them. Naturally, these distinctions can be overstated. Throughout history certain kinds of children have always got on badly with their mothers and fathers, and certain kinds of mothers and fathers have returned the compliment. In the 1920s these attitudes—smoldering resentment on the one hand, puzzled incomprehension on the other—grew sharply opposed, moved out of their private spawning ground and became a source of widespread public comment, endlessly disputed in newspaper articles and books, and argued over at dinner tables from Belgrave Square to the remotest provincial suburb. Fictional chroniclers were always keen to emphasize the seriousness of the issues at stake. Christopher Isherwood, reappraising *All the Conspirators* (1928) nearly thirty years after it was first published, claimed that it was a souvenir of "the days when parents were still heavies." Like Balfour, Isherwood describes these disputes in military terms. The novel, he thought,

> marks a minor engagement in what Shelley calls "the great war between the old and the young." And what a war it was! Every battle of it was fought to a finish, with no quarter asked or shown. The vanquished became love-starved old maids, taciturn bitter old bachelors, chronic invalids, harmless lunatics; or they died, if they were lucky. You may call the motives of these characters trivial, but their struggle is mortal and passionate.

Isherwood is exaggerating his case, yet an echo of its martial clamor can be found in the careers of nearly every Bright Young Person of the period. This hostility took a variety of forms. Between some Bright Young sons and their fathers there was an absolute severance. "Estranged from parents (as we all were then)/Let into Oxford and out again," runs a couplet from John Betjeman's seventieth-birthday tribute to Balfour. Betjeman's father, Ernest, a manufacturer of dressing tables and household ornaments, was characterized by one of his son's closer friends as "a tyrant." Balfour's dealings with his own father, Lord Kinross, were chronically strained: Dorothea Ponsonby, when her son brought him back to Shulbrede, instantly identified "one of the class that hates parents & avoids going home."

At one remove from Balfour-style estrangement came a number of homosexual Bright Young Men who despised their fathers while remaining fixated on their mothers. Brian Howard and Beverley Nichols, who later wrote a book portraying John Nichols as a drunken sadist, spent much of their lives, and in Nichols's case many thousands of words, dramatizing these oppositions into mythological tableaux where the son—sissified, artistic but courageous—heroically replaces the father in his wife's affections. Beneath this second echelon came a procession of young men and women whose dealings with their parents followed a switchback ride of contending emotions. Nancy Mitford, the eldest of an extraordinary six-strong brood of sisters, domineered over by the exacting and eccentric Lord Redesdale and frequently ignored by his reticent wife, regarded her father and mother—"Farve" and "Muv" in the private language of the Mitfords—with a peculiar mixture of tolerance and exasperation. The battles fought in this decade-long war may have been the usual skirmishes about hairstyles, unsuitable friends and staying up late, but they were given an added dimension by the extravagance of Lord Redesdale's response: on one occasion, genuinely shocked by the news that Nancy had been escorted to a cinema in Oxford by Brian Howard, he informed her that, had she been a married woman, this could be considered grounds for divorce.

Nancy's letters from the 1920s are full of woeful despatches from the front line of generational conflict: a stand-up row with Lady Redesdale over an invitation to stay with Nina Seafield in the baronial splendor of Cullen ("I had a terrific fight with Muv about staying with Nina & she said at last go if you like but I'd rather you didn't which is always so unsatisfactory so I said I'd go . . . I think at 22 one is old enough to choose one's own friends don't you, especially as I'm to pay for it myself"); a string of innocuous-sounding escapades sternly rebuked; tentative relationships dismissed out of hand. In October 1926, staying with her friend Middy O'Neill at the latter's grandmother's house in Queen's Gate, she tried to liven up an afternoon party by hiring a Punch and Judy show from Harrods. Appalled by the suggestion of rowdiness, Lady O'Neill accused the girls of staging an orgy and sent Nancy home in disgrace.

All this was harmless enough. Yet it took place in and was to some extent conditioned by an atmosphere of intense propagandizing, in which parent-hating proselytizers were bent on mischief. Writing to her brother, Tom, in 1926, after a trip from Paris to Victoria Station in the company of Brian Howard, Nancy remembered the latter "imploring me to break with the family as soon as I could." For home-loving Nancy this would have been unthinkable. She respected her parents, tolerated their vagaries, was prepared to conciliate their wildest whims, yet the Redesdales continued to treat her as a wayward and unreliable child, issuing a regular series of behavioral fiats which she was expected uncomplainingly to obey. To her younger sister Jessica, these disputes offered a dreadful object lesson on the need for independence. Looking back to her childhood, Jessica believed that "how she [Nancy] loathed Swinbrook & longed to be free of Muv etc.—her fate, to be stuck in that life because she hadn't got any way of escape being without money even after she started writing, was a huge influence on me, then and forever." As late as 1930, when Nancy was a grown woman in her mid-twenties, there was trouble over her friendship with Evelyn Waugh. "The family have read *Vile Bodies*," she reported to Mark Ogilvie-Grant, "& I'm not allowed to know him, so right I think."

Waugh's relationship with his own avuncular but theatrical father, Arthur, was complicated by the favoritism lavished in childhood on his brother Alec. As a teenage boy, Alec's return from boarding school would be greeted by banners welcoming home "the heir of Underhill," the Waughs' modest house on the borders of Hampstead. By his early twenties Waugh found his father dull, fogeyish and aesthetically out-of-date. His house filled with his son's disreputable friends, his modest finances gravely impaired by his son's reckless extravagance, Arthur was deeply upset by this contempt. "The fact is that he [Evelyn] is thoroughly ashamed of his parents," he later complained to a friend, "and does his best to banish them from his conscience." In the roster of objections compiled by Lady Burghclere in her efforts to forestall her daughter's marriage to Waugh in the spring of 1928, "ill treatment of his father" is second on the list.

How did Lady Burghclere know? Perhaps it was simply that her antennae were finely tuned to this kind of failing, that the scars picked up in her own skirmishes in the late-1920s generational war encouraged her to suspect the worst. Her daughter specialized in lightning engagements to wildly unsuitable young men: her nine previous fiancés included the purser of a cruise ship on which she had been exiled to get over a previous attachment. At the heart of these exercises in mutual incomprehension lay an inbred reluctance, on the parental side, to abandon the prewar codes and conventions that sent daughters to debutante dances and sons, if not to manage their estates, then into respectable professions and time-sanctioned modes of life. In the febrile atmosphere of the postwar years, none of this was at all easy to accomplish. More-over, upper-class parents tended further to alienate their children by combining a lack of interest in what the child wanted from life with a savage predisposition to interfere. In old age Evelyn Gardner acknowl-edged that her serial engagements were a mark of her desperation to es-cape Lady Burghclere at all costs: she found her mother domineering and unresponsive. A Hampstead maisonette was preferable to the chill interiors of "home." Parents wanted security for their children; they de-sired them to be "happy"; at the same time they were suspicious of the younger generation's motives; whatever emotional preferences they cared to express were instantly marked down as proof of immaturity. Anthony Powell remembered the "extraordinary disfavor in which marriage was held by the parental generation of that day." He could re-call half a dozen couples from the world of deb dances and smart recep-tions who were prevented, or severely hindered, from getting married for no other reason than parental bloody-mindedness.

Equally suspect, perhaps, were the small number of parents—often, but not exclusively, mothers—who, rather than condemning youthful high spirits on principle, made a point of sympathizing with their off-spring. Some of the sharpest passages in Dorothea Ponsonby's diaries are those that touch on her sister Gwen Plunket Greene's dealings with her children, Richard, David and Olivia. An entry from July 1924 re-ports a conversation with Gwen in which the latter "talked of how much she preferred the young to the old & she makes one feel old in be-ing able to adapt herself to modern conditions & to feel that all the young do is attractive and right." For her own part, Dorothea confessed to liking youth only "in the abstract." At other times she suspected that her sister was merely disguising her own deeply felt convictions for the sake of family harmony. At the end of the memorable afternoon in which she had marked down her niece Olivia as "a rude, egotistical vain painted child," she decided that her sister "swam with the tide—is shocked at nothing—& only wants to please Olivia. 'Is she happy' or 'is she enjoying herself' she says to her with a fond expression during the day." Dorothea wondered whether this outward serenity came at a price. Detached from her children, Gwen became "quite different" and acknowledged that many aspects of their behavior disturbed her. "It seems to me that the grown ups ought to put some kind of brake on," Dorothea purposefully concluded. "But we haven't the moral courage. It is not life to lie in bed in the morning & to gossip & dress up & to tear about in a car—& to go to night clubs without any assertion. They never get their teeth into anything."

Applying this brake to juvenile behavior was easier said than done, as Dorothea, of all people, should have known. Even more so than Lady Burghclere, with her stream of prospective sons-in-law, "Dolly" and her husband, Arthur, were classic victims of the generational conflict of the 1920s. Seen through the prism of their voluminous diaries, and the letters exchanged between all three parties, their relationship with their daughter, Elizabeth, can be read as a constantly unfolding family tragedy that dragged on for nearly twenty years, full of pious hopes and false dawns, unpleasant truths and grim resignation, expressing itself in painful public scenes and heartfelt private misery, in which more straightforward considerations tended to be brushed aside by the murmur of heredity. The Ponsonbys belonged to a small yet significant redoubt of early-twentieth-century English life—the poor but high-minded up-

IDEAS FOR OUR "BRIGHT YOUNG PEOPLE."

[Since a section of the "Bright Young People" literally "set the Thames on fire," things have been a little quiet. The following suggestions from other well-known phrases may help to restore their brilliance.]

"COMING HOME WITH THE MILK."

per class: wellborn and well connected (Arthur's father had been Queen Victoria's private secretary, Dorothea's the composer Sir Hubert Parry), but by the standards of their contemporaries subsisting in a state of genteel poverty. Arthur's letters from the 1920s are full of the difficulties of making ends meet, and the elegant economies involved in keeping up Shulbrede, their antique priory on the Surrey-Sussex border, and a London town house on an income that rarely exceeded £1,200 a year.

Politically, too, Arthur belonged to an exclusive class: one of that small band of pacifist Liberals who, having lost their seats in the "coupon" election of 1918, migrated to the Labour benches. By 1922, Sir Henry Ponsonby's son had reinvented himself as Labour member for the defiantly working-class constituency of Sheffield Brightside, to the great distress of some of his county neighbors. Thoughtful, well-meaning, on easy terms with many of the great minds of the age, Arthur is an attractive figure and by no means the intellectual or emotional middleweight that his modest nature sometimes seems to suggest. Weighed down by stirrings of conscience, he came to believe that he and Dorothea had, through no particular fault of their own, failed in their

IDEAS FOR OUR "BRIGHT YOUNG PEOPLE."

"ASKING A POLICEMAN THE TIME."

duty to their children: he by his long absences on political business, his wife through the chronic ill health that confined her to bed or low-key pottering around the Shulbrede garden. These circumstances, he thought, had allowed Elizabeth, and to a lesser extent her brother, Matthew, to grow up more or less unsupervised, with disastrous consequences for her moral well-being.

Stage-struck since childhood—there were drawers crammed with theater programs, family albums thick with hoarded reviews—Elizabeth had originally wanted to be an actress. A tactful letter survives in which Sir Gerald du Maurier, asked for an estimate of her prospects, quietly pours water on the scheme. Father and daughter would have been equally disappointed. Arthur himself was a haunter of first nights and matinées and had tried his hand as an amateur playwright. A diary entry from 1922 mentions "two little plays I have written for E . . ." Although much of Elizabeth's early twenties were taken up in an attempt to establish herself on the stage, her engagements were limited to walk-ons and a stint in rep at Nottingham. All the same, what career she had was always attended by publicity, most of it connected to her father's burgeoning status in the Labour Party. A brief tryout as a mannequin—Arthur was by then a Foreign Office minister in Ramsay Macdonald's short-lived government of 1924—brought lavish headlines. There were other jobs in fashionable dress shops, none of them long-lived. Even by this stage the Ponsonbys—Arthur reticent and sorrowful, Dorothea sharp and plain-spoken—were beginning to regard their daughter as a hopeless case, a more or less insoluble problem dragging them down into misery, there only to strip them of resources and peace of mind. "E here for the weekend," Arthur recorded in May 1922. "It is difficult to know what she is to do and where she is to live etc. She certainly feels no pleasure in this place." To an early talent for extravagance—guaranteed to wreak havoc on the Ponsonbys' straitened finances—could be added a hankering for unsuitable company. In the autumn of the same year, Arthur found himself criticizing a group of her cronies brought down to Shulbrede: "I cannot understand the youth of today as represented by E and her friends. Nothing but incessant giggling and the reduction of everything under the sun to absurdity. You feel that if they leave off there will be nothing to fall back on."

From the angle of the uncomprehending twenties paterfamilias, aghast at the supper table twitter, this was a common enough complaint. But what was it about Elizabeth that made her so exasperating, intractable and apparently irredeemable? Arthur's diaries are full of rueful little character sketches of a daughter he loved beyond measure but whose lifestyle he found thoroughly unhealthy: "all the crudest faults of the modern girl," he lamented in 1923, combined with "virtues of her own which she seems bent on suppressing." Photographs of Elizabeth from the early 1920s show a slender, rather haughty-looking demoiselle with a long nose and an oddly wistful expression. Arthur, who admired her tenacity in pursuit of good causes and lame dogs, was simultaneously cast down by what he regarded as her fondness for bad company ("Her preference for disreputable people is, I am afraid, incorrigible") and a determination to please herself at all costs. She had no real ambition, he constantly complained, was interested only in her high-powered social life and took trivial jobs in Mayfair boutiques and fashion houses simply to keep close to the two or three square miles of central London that formed her daily beat.

One looks for a gap between the real person—a rather noisy, purposeless and unhappy girl—and the legend of the society gossip columns, only to find the one shading effortlessly into the other. Her romantic attachments came and went. The young man who basked in her favor one evening could find it unexpectedly withdrawn on the next. In January 1926, Evelyn Waugh attended a dinner party at his brother Alec's where, "rather to my surprise but considerably to my gratification Elizabeth Ponsonby made vigorous love to me which I am sorry now I did not accept. She has furry arms." On the following day, however, "We fetched Elizabeth Ponsonby who seems entirely to have overcome her attraction to me." Summing up his twenty-something contemporaries forty years later, Tom Driberg was aware that some of his gossip column paeans ("Eternal sophistication looks out a little uneasily, from under her heavy eyelids, and her mouth, smiling as enigmatically as that of the Giaconda, can utter all knowledge and all wisdom," ran one encomium in the *Daily Express*) exaggerated a rather prosaic reality. "She was a very emphatic and rather pathetic character at the same time," he remembered, "rather thin and scraggy but quite pretty—a bit older than the others," but above all possessed of a tremendous energizing spirit: "one of those vital sparks who got the parties going."

Back in Shulbrede, meanwhile, Arthur and Dorothea continued to fret: the one plaintively, the other with mounting irritation. Dorothea's diary contains the text of a no-nonsense letter sent in the autumn of 1923:

> But it hurts us to see you getting coarse in your speech & outlook in life & it spoils your chance . . . There were girls I knew like you & one knew by the way they were going that their lives were eventually going to be dust and ashes . . . Surely you ought to enlarge your sphere of enjoyment—not only find happiness in night clubs & London parties & a certain sort of person. If you only find amusement in these things in fact if you are only looking for amusement you will be bound to decline.

All this strikes an oddly prophetic note. Mingled with it is a hint of the fatalism that, even at this early stage, characterized the Ponsonbys' attitude to their daughter. No amount of lectures on the evils of late nights, frivolous conversation and low company would ever have any effect on Elizabeth: these were the hours she liked; the topics she wanted to talk about; the people she needed to have around her. As for guiding her daughter into seemlier modes of behavior, Dorothea knew that she possessed neither the resources nor the stamina. "The truth is to cope successfully with these young people—you need both money and health," the wife of Ramsay Macdonald's foreign minister acknowledged. "E would respect me more if I could afford to dress well & go about . . ." Gradually, Elizabeth's conduct, friends and future became an obsession with them. "The thought of certain people keeps me awake at night," Dorothea recorded in October 1924. "E.P. What is she going to do with her life?" In odd hours away from his political commitments—and sometimes during them—Arthur was reaching the same conclusions.

Like his wife, he was darkly conscious of his inability to act. "E in bed till 11 a.m. often not in bed until 4 a.m. leads a life which is beyond belief," he wrote a few months before Dorothea's small-hours heart-searching. Repeatedly he worried away at the question of what Elizabeth wanted from life. "She has been a mannequin and a super on the stage. It seems to satisfy her as owing to her being my daughter she has received an inordinate amount of publicity. I think she is made for better things but I am helpless."

The accounts of Elizabeth's activities that filtered back from London did not inspire confidence. An undated letter, sent from a relative's house in Chelsea, describes a fatal accident in breezy period slang: "The most appalling thing happened last night about 12:15 ... a man fell from the balcony at the back of the house + was killed, it was the most awful nightmare. He didn't die at once, that is I think he took about 15 minutes. We got masses of doctors + an ambulance + he was taken to hospital, but of course it was no good."

Arthur and Dorothea looked for positive signs, balancing Elizabeth's careless amusements with her genuine liking for their company, the closed circuits of her social round with her loyalty to the people to whom, however misguidedly, she clung. Casting her circumspect eye on other parents, who continued to indulge their children's whims, Dorothea was appalled both by what she saw and the fate that apparently lay in store for them. Early in 1927 she visited Gwen Plunket Greene, then living at her son David's and daughter-in-law Babe's house in Knightsbridge. Her sister's bedroom seemed cold and uncomfortable, and Gwen's interests wholly subservient to the frenetic social life of the young people on whom she was quartered. "David and his wife have cocktail luncheons every day from 1:30 to 2:30 & she Gwen is allowed no food until they have finished ... She says the parties are tremendous & noisy ... c. 15 bottles of drink on sideboard." It was all too much for Dorothea's sense of moral and social responsibility. Did these young people ever "come to life"? she wondered. And, in an atmosphere of self-indulgence and irresponsibility, how would they ever grow up?

There are fewer references to Elizabeth in her parents' diaries during 1926. For some of this time she was working as an assistant in a dress shop run by Lady Angela Forbes. Then, in the summer of 1927, she disgraced herself so thoroughly that Arthur and Dorothea were transfixed by shame. Dorothea's diary for June 17 runs simply: "One of the worst days of my life. Poor E oh the pity of it." Arthur was yet more cast down: "The darkest day of the deepest humiliation I have ever had." At a distance of eighty years, and with both diarists ominously silent on detail, it is difficult to establish precisely what Elizabeth had done, but she seems to have been detected in a liaison with a family friend named Craigie. Interestingly, a "Mr. Craigie" and his wife are mentioned among the guests at the Impersonation Party, held a few weeks later, where Elizabeth was photographed dressed as Iris Tree for the *Tatler*. A handwritten letter to Dolly survives from late June:

> *I am writing to tell you how frightfully sorry I am for hurting you +*
> *father. From nobody's fault I have had to make my own life—I may*
> *not have made it very well—but there it is—but whatever I may*
> *think or do, the last thing I ever wished to do was to hurt you so*
> *much.*
>
> *I may be treading a road that leads nowhere—but perhaps it is*
> *better than scratching about in a desert.*
>
> *Try to forgive me.*
> *Ever your loving*
> *Elizabeth*

Whatever the exact circumstances of the affair, and its exposure, it is clear that Arthur and Dorothea imagined some moral line to have been crossed and that its aftermath plunged them into the deepest mental anguish. Comparing her daughter with her more biddable son early in 1928, Dorothea judged that "it is simply chance that M has not gone to the dogs as E has. As A says it would be thought exaggerated if what we have gone through in these last 10 months had been written in a book. It is unbelievable that one can go on." Arthur continued to search for hints of better behavior, noting when Elizabeth paid a visit to Shulbrede that "I cannot quite abandon hope for her. She is now 27 and there is something poignantly pathetic as well as repulsive in seeing her pretty little face in the country sunlight smeared with coloured dirt." The following year, though, brought little change to the prevailing pattern. "E seems to live in another world," he wrote in January 1928. Back from a holiday in Mallorca in the early autumn, she seemed "very well and cheerful and full of amazing stories of her experience." There was so much good in her, Arthur lamented. "I wish she could find a decent man." Early in the New Year, with a general election imminent, father and daughter were invited to make a broadcast talk at the BBC on the extension of the vote to women over the age of twenty-one. The recording went well ("The BBC people said it was the best conversation they had had") but Arthur was depressed by their preliminary dinner: "Her outlook, her manner and appearance upset me."

A symbolic demonstration of the life Elizabeth led, and the kind of people with whom she led it, had been offered to the Ponsonbys only a month before. Early in January she had announced her intention of asking a party of friends down to Shulbrede for the weekend. Arthur was plunged into gloom. "I am not looking forward to it," he noted on the preceding Friday. "I am not *au courant* with the latest obscenities and obscenity is the keynote of these young people, sex the obsession." Arthur had been browsing in Aldous Huxley's *Point Counter Point*, whose themes seemed all too redolent of the world Elizabeth inhabited. "I cannot believe that this wearisome reiteration of sex and cohabitation is either clever interesting or amusing. However it is little use either objecting protesting or even discussing it." Moody and distressed, Arthur found himself comparing wife to daughter. The difference between Dorothea and Elizabeth was that "D is always there E is never there. By there I mean not only physical and actual but moral intellectual and spiritual there—in fact reality."

Seventy-two hours later, amid a landscape of strewn glasses and empty bottles, the air heavy with the reek of stale tobacco smoke, Arthur sat down to consider his weekend: "The party is over. They have gone. It was worse than we expected. In fact a scene was only just avoided." Elizabeth had arrived on the Saturday, along with Babe Plunket Greene—regarded with some suspicion by the Ponsonbys after her recent divorce from their nephew—Eddie Gathorne-Hardy and an

American writer named Harcourt Wesson Bull. They were joined on the Sunday by Count Anthony Bosdari and four other guests, a woman known only as "Little Monica," apparently a prostitute rescued from the streets of Piccadilly, and her young male companion "Pansy," David Greene's homosexual chum Paddy Brodie and a cinema actor named Kim Peacock. Arthur's account of the Bright Young People in action is worth quoting at length:

> E arrived with her very close friend of 21 Babe Greene (daughter of Mrs. Bendir the prominent booky's wife) who recently divorced David Greene: then a heavily painted very common dissipated girl. Eddie Gathorne-Hardy a young pervert with rather pretentious literary leanings and an innocent young American. Drinking began an hour after they arrived. We had provided what would be usual but it proved utterly inadequate. They did not stay up as late as we expected. They went to bed soon after two. They had brought some more drink with them.
>
> On Sunday a further contingent was expected at luncheon but owing to ice on the roads they did not turn up until 3 . . . They consisted of a girl who seemed to have been picked up very late at night off Piccadilly. A shiny cinema actor, a bogus Sicilian Duke and two other anaemic undistinguished looking young men. At 5 brandy was called for by the girls as the sherry which had been going on during the afternoon had given out. Owing to the weather some decided to stay the night in Haslemere. So M went to make arrangements, bringing back 4 more bottles. At this point my patience broke down . . .

While Matthew was decanting the first bottle of brandy, a furious Arthur attempted to hide the other three in the toolshed. There followed a bruising row between father and son: Matthew urging the dictates of hospitality; Arthur coming dangerously close to repudiating his daughter altogether. "He argued with me that I ought to have known what I was in for and as host I ought not to frustrate them. I told him outright that I could not stand E and this party was only a concession to her to prevent having a permanent break." In the end, a crisis was narrowly averted. Arthur "gave in and brought back the bottles." Dinner ("the usual shallow jokes and utterly feeble talk") proceeded without incident. By mid–Monday morning the party had broken up, leaving glasses and cigarette ends strewn all over the floor of the Prior's Chamber, Shulbrede's twelfth-century core. Wide-eyed, Arthur compiled an inventory of the empty containers. "They consumed 1 dozen bottles of Brandy Sherry and Whisky, several bottles of beer and a good deal of wine. The Piccadilly prostitute carried off half a bottle of brandy with her in the car to help her through the night."

Washing up the dirty glasses and repairing the damage to their reeking establishment, both Ponsonbys were darkly aware that some kind of climacteric had been reached. Dorothea's diary entries are acidly laconic. Babe Plunket Greene, she decided, resembled "a procuress of 40. She is hideous—& very unresponsive." Eddie "with his long hair & his horn spectacles—& his weak mouth does not attract me at all." Seldom, she thought, had she seen "such a rabble." The exception was the young American, Harcourt Wesson Bull, "really nicely brought up—& refined—& with charming manners. I wish I could rescue him from this set." Dorothea's account of the party's climax on the Sunday is one of her finest condemnations of her daughter's lifestyle. After Arthur had hidden the bottles in the toolshed,

> Matthew furious said if we invited people of this sort to the house we must behave decently & give them their drink (bought by Babe). He said he had thought of not coming down—& it was our faults for having such people & that we must have known perfectly well that they would drink unceasingly. A. & I protested, that we had known they would have sherry before dinner—but had no conception that the drinking of Sherry—Brandy & Whisky would never cease. He appeared to think that we ought never to have consented to have E.'s friends & that it was all our own fault. A. got very angry about E. & I tried to explain to M. that having seen nothing like it— & it was impossible to realise what these sort of people were

& how they would behave—after all E. Gathorne-Hardy—wretched creature is a gentleman.

At dinner I sat between the young American Wesson Bull and a classe moyen man Paddy Brodie. The Italian held forth & was amusing—I did not join them after dinner. The Harlot unspeakable creature went off with 3 men at 11:30 to the Georgian Hotel. The rest of the party didn't go to bed until 1:30 but it was impossible to go to sleep as Matthew appeared to be taking so many journeys down the passage. This turned out to be for Babe—who required supper—& then her fire made up by Matthew. She sits sipping Sherry & Brandy—& begins to wake up (naturally) about midnight. Then she is lively & hungry, as a result of lateness & soaking—Poor girl what will she become.

Impressed by Wesson Bull's politeness and enthusiasm ("He told me all about his life & talks a great deal & well in tete-a-tete"), Dorothea warned her daughter that "she must not ruin him." Arthur, meanwhile, had made a number of private resolutions. "We are no doubt old-fashioned and the new generation may be very fine," he concluded, "but E is not going to have another party in this house." Though "determined" to avoid a break, he was also keen to remove her from 40 Smith Street, the Ponsonbys' London home. None of this, though, would solve the more fundamental problem. Arthur knew that while he could stop Elizabeth having dissolute parties under his own roof, and possibly even bar the doors of his London establishment to her, neither measure would have the least effect on her mode of life. "The taste of the whole business is disagreeable," he reflected, "and will add now to those dark revolving night thoughts of which E is the centre."

Eighteen months before, in the aftermath of the Craigie affair, Arthur had composed a long, meditative diary entry that considered both his difficulties with Elizabeth and the wider generational divide they so miserably reflected. The passage is hugely characteristic of Arthur's view of the kind of life he led and the obligations he imagined it to impose: rueful, self-questioning, conscious of his own inadequacies, at the same time sharply aware of wider social changes that he was pow-

THE FREAK-MERCHANTS; OR, THE BRIGHT YOUNG PEOPLE.

THEY USED TO THINK THAT THE DEAR OLD BOTTLE-AND-PYJAMA PARTY WAS QUITE ORIGINAL -

TILL THEY WENT ONE BETTER WITH THE BATHING SUPPER-PARTY -

e Bath and Bottle Party, as seen by *Punch* (Courtesy of *Punch* archive)

Oxford University Dramatic Society fancy dress party, 1924: Maurice Bowra (middle of back row), with Patrick Balfour on his right (Courtesy of Deidre Levi)

Oxford Hypocrites Club fancy dress party, March 1924. Back row: Harold Acton, in cap and mask. Second row: Anthony Powell, in helmet with sword; Robert Byron, in top hat with stick (Courtesy of Powell family archive)

old Acton and Evelyn Waugh at Oxford
(...rtesy of James Knox)

Bright Young Impresario: Anthony Powell at
Duckworth (Courtesy of Powell family archive)

...y Sackville-West
...rtesy of Jonathan
...orne-Hardy)

Robert Byron (Courtesy of James Knox)

Gavin Henderson (Courtesy of Selena Hastings)

ABOVE Diana Guinness (center) and Bryan Guinness (far right) electioneering at Newmarket for Bryan's father, Colonel Walter Guinness M.P., 1929
(Courtesy of *Illustrated London News* Picture Library)

LEFT Zita Jungman as Romeo
(Courtesy of *Illustrated London News* Picture Library)

RIGHT Bryan and Diana Guinness on honeymoon in Taormina, 1929 (Courtesy of *Illustrated London News* Picture Library)

BELOW "The type of behaviour that leads to Communism": Rosemary Sanders (standing, in light dress) welcomes her guests to the Second Childhood Party, 1929. (Courtesy of *Illustrated London News* Picture Library)

LEFT He-Evelyn and She-Evelyn at the
Tropical Party, 1929
(Courtesy of *Illustrated London News* Picture Library)

ABOVE Tom Driberg, "The Dragoman"
(Courtesy of Francis Wheen, *Tom Driberg: His
Life and Indiscretions*)

LEFT Leslie A. Hutchinson, "Hutch"
(Courtesy of Ponsonby family archive)

ABOVE The Impersonation Party, 1927. Back row:
Elizabeth Ponsonby, in wig as Iris Tree, with Cecil Beato
on her right. Seated from left: Stephen Tennant, as
Queen Marie of Romania; George Sitwell, with false
nose; Inez Holden; Harold Acton. Foreground:
Tallulah Bankhead, as Jean Borotra
(Courtesy of Ponsonby family archive)

LEFT Cecil and Elizabeth at David Plunket Greene's part
1927 (Courtesy of Ponsonby family archive)

erless to alter. Looking back he saw mistakes, "but not how they could have been avoided." Relative poverty and dislike of ostentation had combined to cut them off from the society to which they naturally belonged. Not that this meant conditions at Shulbrede had become disagreeably austere. In bringing up their children, Arthur thought that he and Dorothea had "adopted no scheme." The problem was that the moral lessons inculcated in the home had failed to have an impact on what were almost genetic yearnings. "We did not sufficiently take into account the luxurious aristocratic heredity on both sides, and although we were not surprised at any reaction against our ethical views and opinions, we somehow expected that the home atmosphere and instinct of self-discipline would tell in the long run."

All this, Arthur acknowledged, had been compounded by the unique conditions of the 1920s. When "the wave which has upset modern youth" broke upon the postwar shore, the average parent, however mindful of his responsibilities, was powerless to resist it. "The situation crystallised without any drastic action on our part." Unconsciously adopting the role of spokesperson for a generation of aggrieved and dispossessed parents, Arthur admitted that he had no answer.

I still do not know what drastic action would have been possible. Unless there is inward conviction and a readiness to accept advice enforced exterior discipline is useless. All the same it may be possible to put up iron railings round the bogs and precipices. We did not do this. What parents do? Some perhaps. But the temperament of the child and not the strength of the railings is the factor that matters.

The child, meanwhile, was twenty-eight, back in London and about to take the starring role in a series of lurid newspaper headlines. The "mock wedding," apparently Elizabeth's original idea, and one of the most famous escapades of the era, took place late in January 1929. Robert Byron, who played a major part in the proceedings, advertised the prank in a letter to his mother: "I am supposed to be going to a fancy dress lunch at the Trocadero," he explained, "a bogus wedding in Trocadero clothes ie 1921." Dressed in a bowler hat and sporting a button-hole and a waxed mustache, Byron—as best man—featured in a party that included Elizabeth, resplendent as the bride, John Rayner as her husband, Oliver Messel as an usher and Babe Plunket Greene as "the undesirable relation"—an all-too-accurate comment on her status in the Ponsonby family. Seated at a special table in the center of the restaurant, this unlikely entourage caused a sensation. No aspect of the imposture was ignored. Messel proposed a toast, to which Byron replied. An unsuspecting clergyman was encouraged to join in and pronounce a blessing on the happy couple, who departed under a shower of rose petals. MOCK MARRIAGE LUNCHEON—OUR BRIGHT YOUNG PEOPLE—PARSON HOAXED, ran one of the following morning's headlines. MOCK WEDDING ANTICS—'BEST MAN' IN OLD BOWLER AND FROCK COAT, chorused another. The coverage stirred a thrill of horror in respectable London drawing rooms. The parents of those responsible hastened to assure their children that they were mixing in the wrong circles. "I had another more horrible paper sent me about that mock wedding," Mrs. Byron protested from Vienna. "I do call it third-rate & can't think how you can let yourself be dragged into that sort of thing with that girl in it too—you are doing yourself harm by that sort of publicity—disgusting . . . you have got some friends of the wrong sort dear boy & I wish you'd drop them." Arthur, trying to concentrate on the impending general election, noted on January 24 that "E again advertised in the papers in some absurd sort of party. It never stops." Four days later the newspapers were still "full of E's pranks."

What was to be done? Even Elizabeth seems to have thought that a dignified retirement from the world of press photographers and parental angst might have its advantages. A week after the mock wedding she departed, together with Babe Plunket Greene, for a cottage at Cranleigh in Surrey, where for a few weeks the two women busied themselves with a short-lived scheme to breed dogs. "I have had too much publicity since you left England, through a harmless joke," she wrote to Clive Bell, early in February, "+ am glad to get away from the black stream of pressmen that throng Smith Street + also from my furious parents." However, even remote cottages in the Surrey hinterland were prey to Bright Young People disruption. "It was nearly wrecked the first weekend," Elizabeth explained in the same letter, "as Eddie + Brian + two other of 'the boys' came down + put all the owner's African ornaments on the fire 'To see what they'd look like burning.'"

For years Arthur had lived in the hope that a suitable husband—wealthy, reliable and staid—might emerge to carry off his wayward daughter to a life of seemly domestic retirement. Suddenly, out of the blue, the "decent man" of Arthur's decade-long imaginings looked as if he might finally have declared himself. The announcement was entirely typical of the way in which Elizabeth dealt with her parents, left to a third party and conveyed with maximum offhandedness. Matthew Ponsonby arrived at Shulbrede late on March 24 "and after dining quite casually as if he were telling us it froze last night he gave us the amazing information that E is engaged to be married." How had this come about? Arthur's diary account of the background to the engagement turns almost telegraphic in its excitement. "She only met him a fortnight ago! He is in a gramophone shop. We know so little about it as yet. But she is to bring him to Shulbrede next week." Initially bewildered by the news, Arthur decided that there were grounds for cautious optimism ("I'm glad he is not a rich, dissolute aristocrat"). On the other hand, he noted grimly, "the money question may be serious."

The fiancé was called Denis Pelly. "I've got the most extraordinary young man attached to me, not bogus, just raving + impossible," Elizabeth had written from Cranleigh to Clive Bell six weeks before, which may or may not be a reference to him. He was certainly at large on the Bright Young People circuit. Ed Burra met him for the first time early in March 1929 at the Eiffel Tower restaurant in the company of Paddy Brodie and Tom Driberg; the young artist found him "rather twee." Photographs, invariably taken at Elizabeth's side, show a tall young man with brushed-back hair, a prognathous jaw and a slightly puzzled expression—as if the business of standing next to his bride-to-be at fancy dress parties was already rather a strain. While over the next few weeks the society magazines offered routine information about his background—his father was the late Major W. F. H. Pelly, he was related to a certain Sir Harold Pelly, he was lately back from Kenya—nothing could disguise the incorrigible dimness of his prospects. Dorothea, pumping her son for details—Matthew had been to see him in the Bond Street gramophone shop where he worked as an assistant—could only extract the vaguest personal characteristics. Matthew pronounced that "he was very tall. Thought he was a gentleman—though he had on rather a bad suit. He had a nice smile & on the whole M liked him."

Further storms of publicity immediately blew over the young couple's heads. "It will not be a mock wedding this time," Elizabeth informed the press. Arthur, in the meantime, rushed up to London to find out exactly what was going on. The first person he saw was his daughter. ("She was very happy and determined said she had always declared she must marry a rich man so it showed she was carried off her feet. She is pushing things forward and rather revelling in all the publicity.") A party at Lady Vita Russell's, which he attended that night, brought instant evidence of the fashionable world's absorption in this unexpected union: "E's engagement was the subject of the evening." Then, on the following day, Denis arrived to lunch with his prospective father-in-law at the House of Commons. Arthur's first sight of him was, on the whole, favorable. "I liked him he is good looking nice minded and very much in

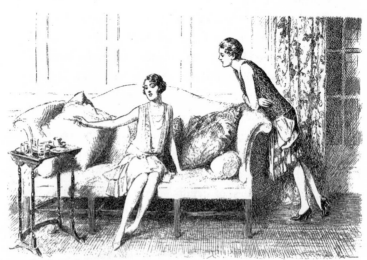

First Maiden. "Do you know young Penderby?"
Second Maiden. "I daresay I do. But you have to know a man terribly well to know his surname."

love." On the other hand, "he has no money and no profession to speak of." There was another, rather ominous, judgment: "I doubt if he has enough grit for the adventure." However, intensely relieved that his daughter seemed to have found her "decent man," Arthur resolved that "we must help all we can."

The preparations for Elizabeth's wedding had to take their place among a riot of other pressing obligations. Dorothea was ill again and, on her doctor's advice, had been temporarily removed to a nursing home. The cook was giving trouble. Among more exalted concerns, Labour was expected to do well in the election and there was even talk, Arthur learned from the visiting Egyptian politician Hamel Mahmoud, of his being considered for the post of foreign secretary should Baldwin's Conservative government fall. Matthew, meanwhile, had announced his own engagement to a girl named Bess Bigham. Moving distractedly from marriage-planning sessions to political meetings by way of consultations with his solicitor, Arthur managed to be present at Shulbrede on March 29 to welcome Denis on his first visit to the family home. Again he believed, or affected to believe, that he was favorably impressed ("There is a certain quiet reserve about the young man which I like"), certain, moreover, that he detected the steadying influence for which he had long yearned ("E too behaves very differently to what she has with other young men. Already she seems to have a certain sense of responsibility"). However, he acknowledged that the young couple's prospects were "exceedingly precarious" and that "the prudent father would certainly not allow it."

But the prudent father was not being given any choice. Over the next few weeks Arthur and Dolly, singly and jointly, considered the question of their future son-in-law's attainments and character with an almost neurotic regularity. Amiable, easy to talk to, good-looking, quiet, modest, athletic, well mannered, Arthur noted approvingly at the end of his first stay at Shulbrede. Already, though, both Ponsonbys had fastened on what they imagined to be Denis's chief shortcoming: a want of that vital ingredient in the Victorian moral stew, character. "I do *not* think he has a strong character," Arthur worried after a day or two in Denis's company, "and it is not to his credit that at 27 he has not got either a suitable or a permanent job." Dorothea had commissioned Matthew to make discreet inquiries among the social circles in which Denis moved. While some of the results were mildly encouraging, "it is admitted that he is a bad man at his job . . . & not a strong enough character—one doesn't know." Weak, diffident, well-meaning but without personal force, Denis lacked several of the qualities his prospective in-laws thought essential for their daughter's maintenance, but they were prepared to give him the benefit of the doubt. Elizabeth, Arthur noted, was amused by her fiancé's reception, "saying he was the first one of her friends we had not detested." The money part of the business, he confirmed, was going to be "exceedingly difficult."

What the young couple might live on—or whom, to put the matter bluntly, they might live off—tended to take second place to the wave of publicity that threatened to engulf the proceedings. Barely a fortnight after Elizabeth's bombshell, Arthur foresaw difficulties, "as E is so much bent on turning everything into a circus." Three days later the *Bystander* gave the engagement a lavish write-up. "Miss Elizabeth Ponsonby," the compiler of "The Passing Hour" column reminded her readers, "the only daughter of Mr. Arthur Ponsonby MP and Mrs. Ponsonby . . . is one of the Bright Young People whose latest rag was a mock Wedding Breakfast." The announcement had been greeted with a "lingering surprise," the report went on. "It came as such untoward news that one who had so often defied conventionality, by the originality of her amusements, should so suddenly capitulate to the most conventional of sentiments." There followed a checklist of Elizabeth's accomplishments over the past five years ("Miss Ponsonby as an actress, Miss Ponsonby as a mannequin, Miss Ponsonby's bottle and bathing party, Miss Ponsonby as a mock bride"), trailed—the *Bystander* had no love for upper-class socialists—with the happy thought that voters might be puzzled by the jarring incongruity of father's and daughter's outlook on life: "As Mr. Ponsonby became a Socialist politician, so his daughter has become a social Socialist, though not, perhaps, without pangs in the paternal heart. Political opponents are so unscrupulous in their attacks, and some of the Labour member's constituents might be led to misinterpret his daughter's escapades."

As for the "circus," Dorothea's diaries are full of the gravest forebodings. There was an early clash of swords when Elizabeth proposed her cousin David's recently divorced wife, Babe, as a bridesmaid. The inadvisability of this choice having been pointed out, and accepted, Dolly turned her attention to the ceremony itself. Brian Howard, already taken on board by Elizabeth to help with the arrangements, had plans for an elaborate spectacle involving twenty-five ushers "& the whole thing like a dress show or a night-club in church." This Dolly envisaged "with horror." The Ponsonbys were not religious people, but they had a strong sense of propriety, and the obligations due to the customs and traditions in which they had been raised. These were further outraged by the knowledge that they were footing the bill. Had Elizabeth possessed any religious beliefs, Dorothea would not have minded. In their absence, she feared the whole thing would degenerate into another Bright Young People's rag: ". . . they will all mock at the clergy & talk at the tops of their voices—as they none of them believe in anything & have no reverence one does not know how they will behave—& A and I have to sanction it by our presence—& I am drawing on our capital for the purpose."

The Ponsonbys' £1,200 or so a year—a comfortable income from the angle of the average shopkeeper or bank clerk—was woefully inadequate for people of their social standing. Elizabeth's upkeep had already placed a serious strain on their resources: now some kind of permanent settlement would have to be made. Distracted by the coming election, and the day-to-day business of the House of Commons, Arthur spent most of April hard at work on his daughter's behalf, closeted himself for long hours with his solicitor ("Outlook very bad for E's affairs. I simply don't see where the money is to come from") and toward the end of the month, milking a connection with his friend Vaughan Nash, even managed to procure his future son-in-law a job, with a firm named County Industries. Unlike the Bond Street gramophone shop, this was a position suitable for a gentleman ("a start anyhow") and with emoluments to match. Denis's salary, added to Elizabeth's settlement, would give the couple an income of £650 a year and they could expect to save money by living for the moment in the Ponsonbys' London house in Smith Street.

The groom's connections, meanwhile, were found to consist of an indulgent but realistic mother. "She is devoted to Denis, but realizes he is weak," Arthur reported. Dolly, alternatively, greeted the spectacle of Mrs. Pelly with gusts of patrician disdain: "a sort of second rate daughter of the regiment ease of manner," she sadly pronounced. "Of course it's pathetic—she lives in a sort of boarding house in Cromwell Road—& I'm afraid she'll be rather a pest." Thankfully Elizabeth had made a hit with her future mother-in-law. Their first meeting went off very well, she reported back to Shulbrede, "which was lucky, as she was prepared to loathe me, having liked his last fiancée very much—but she now adores me, so all is well."

The general election was over. Arthur, returned for Brightside with a thumping 10,000-vote majority over his Tory opponent, was squeezed out of a cabinet job in the minority Labour administration that took office and found himself forced to settle for an undersecretaryship in the Colonial and Dominions Office: like the *Bystander*, Ramsay Macdonald was wary of high-minded aristocratic socialists. The wedding was set for July 5 at the ultra-fashionable St. Margaret's Westminster. As the day approached, Arthur, often prey to unexpected moods and fancies, was struck by a curious note of optimism, convinced at last that his relationship with Elizabeth had turned a corner—that, contrary to the expectations of the previous ten years, all might now be well. "I am profoundly thankful that E has found such a nice man," he wrote late in April. "I have got this pleasant feeling of satisfaction in my heart with E whom I have disapproved of so deeply and yet for whose drift toward the mud I kept on feeling myself responsible." Dolly, on the other hand, had been offered stark evidence of the kind of life Denis and Elizabeth were bent on living. During one of their weekend visits to Shulbrede, she woke in the small hours to hear the two of them talking loudly in the corridor. In the haggard morning light the Prior's Chamber, an antique reception room on the first floor, was "like a scene by Hogarth—cards scattered—cigarette ash on the chairs—tumblers half full of whisky—empty bottles and syphons [*sic*]—crumpled cushions—& a stink of smoke—when one is tired this sort of thing finishes one." Over the next few years, Elizabeth's life would turn more Hogarthian still.

CHAPTER FIVE

THE REVOLT INTO STYLE

"How's London?" said Pringle.

Atwater said: "Pretty empty."

"No parties?"

"No. No parties."

"Any scandal?"

"I haven't heard any."

— ANTHONY POWELL, *Afternoon Men*

By the middle of 1928 the Bright Young People were a recognizable social phenomenon: at once a distinctive part of society and something that was capable of existing beyond the outermost limit of society's margins. Social columnists watched eagerly each spring and autumn for Bright Young parties to "break out." There were Bright Young People advertisements, Bright Young People jokes, Bright Young People novels—the first, Beverley Nichols's *Crazy Pavements*, had already appeared the year before—and established Bright Young People's venues. Across England, and beyond it, the most disparate social arrangements involving the well-off under-thirties acknowledged its presiding spirit and imitated its language. Even the returning expatriates joining the liner at Colombo in George Orwell's projected novella "A Smoking Room Story," set in 1927, have a "Younger Set, the acknowledged arbiters of fashion and elegance," who squeal at one another in "high, silly" voices. Simultaneously, the Bright Young People's activities and peculiarities were monitored across society as a whole: an absorption that extended to the very highest levels. Bryan Guinness, introduced to King George V at a country house party at around this time, was immediately asked why he was not wearing a brown suit—this being the idiosyncrasy attributed to him by "The Dragoman" of the *Daily Express*. A Bright Young People's culture had come into existence, whose key elements, and in particular its communal language, had an impact far beyond the social crucible in which they were forged.

What was Bright Young People style? The most obvious feature of the average Bright Young Person's daily round, contemporary chroniclers agreed, was the frenetic pace at which it was lived. According to Bryan Guinness's novel *Singing out of Tune* (1933), daily routine consisted of waking up late, meeting people for lunch, bringing the lunch party home for tea, moving on to cocktails and dinner—the one solitary event of the day—and ending up with a communal trek around the fashionable restaurants of the West End. One assumes that this is an accurate résumé of the life that he and his wife, Diana, lived on Buckingham Street in the late 1920s. In *Society Racket*, Patrick Balfour noted that the social patterns of the late 1920s had grown ever more hectic:

> Every year the London season becomes more energetic. People must rush from one party or restaurant to another, to a third and fourth in the course of one evening, and finish up with an early morning bathing-party, transported at 60 m.p.h. to the swimming-pools of Eton through the dawn. On the river, a languid evening in a punt is not enough. There must be dancing as well at Datchet or at Bray, and a breakneck race down the Great West Road afterwards.
>
> The next day there is no question of resting in preparation for the evening's exertions. Appointments all the morning, with hair-dressers or commission agents or committees; cocktails at the Ritz before lunch, luncheon parties; tennis afterwards or golf at Swinley, or bridge; charity rehearsal teas, then cocktail parties, a rush home to change for an early dinner and the theater or ballet, after which the whole cycle begins all over again.
>
> Once the week-ends were a rest from all this feverish activity; but now they are more strenuous than the week itself—all its pleasures crammed together into a third of the time, with

large, riotous bright young house-parties, a dozen people motoring down for the day on Sunday, everyone rushing around
the countryside in fast cars, and at night bridge and backgam-
mon and truth games and practical jokes till all hours of the
morning.

This, essentially, is the tone of *Vile Bodies* and of Elizabeth Ponsonby's
routines as glimpsed through the pages of her parents' diaries: a world
of whistle-stop journeys through Home Counties back lanes, frenzied
telephone calling and constant changes of plan, all-day drinking and
physical exhaustion, dominated by the search for novelty; the latest
fashionable restaurant, the newest Thames-side resort. Society magazines competed with each other to produce yet more enticing destinations. The *Bystander* reader of July 1929 who looked up from the
rhapsodic accounts of the Kindersley-Guinness wedding and the Watteau Party held on the *Cytherea* at Charing Cross Pier would have found
a sumptuous black-and-white illustration of the interior of the new
Hungaria River Club at Maidenhead ("The new riverside club is packed
with Society and Bohemia every weekend"). Returning to London in
1931, at the end of the journey that produced his travel book *Remote
People*, Evelyn Waugh made an instant beeline for his spiritual home: "I
was back at the center of the Empire, and in the spot where, at the moment, 'everyone' was going. Next day the gossip-writers would chronicle
who were assembled in that rowdy cellar, hotter than Zanzibar, noisier
than the market at Harar, more reckless of the decencies of hospitality than the taverns of Kabalo or Tabora."

The focus for nearly all this activity was, inevitably, the party. This
was where the Bright Young Person looked to be seen, and where—
equally important—he or she was reported as being seen. The twenties
party assumed a myriad of different forms, some of them wholly distinct, others shading effortlessly into contending versions of the same
thing, yet all, survivors insisted, producing variations on the same powerful scent. To distinguish the twenties party from other kinds of entertainment on offer in succeeding decades wasn't easy, Anthony Powell
suggested. All the same, there was something distinctive about them:

a distinction, moreover, that extended to each of the different rungs of the social ladder on which they were held. At the top came the somewhat rarified world of the debutante dance, staged at a substantial private house in Mayfair or Belgravia, not necessarily exclusive, as the postwar shortage of men had produced a democratizing of the guest lists, but hedged about with the regimentation of dance cards, servants and chaperones. Powell remembered that, with rare exceptions, he tended to meet the girls he knew at dances only at dances. At a similar level to the Grosvenor Square ball came "smart" parties of the kind given by Lady Cunard, Mrs. Harry Brown, Mrs. Corrigan, Mrs. Keigwin or one of the other half-dozen or so fashionable London hostesses. Bright Young People would certainly be seen at these gatherings, but they did not predominate. Neither did they form a majority at another very common type of twenties entertainment, the publishing-literary party. This could take place anywhere between South Kensington and Hampstead, Powell noted, and like Lady Cunard's soirées, did not have the twenties party's authenticating spoor, "though some of the people might be seen at either, or the 'real thing.'"

So what made a classic twenties party? It was on the lower rungs of Bloomsbury—a party held somewhere to the north of Holborn, attended by a smattering of artists and writers with perhaps a couple of guardsmen picked up by one of the guests en route—that, Powell believed, "the true Twenties party comes into sight." Even more authentic and genre-defining were the parties given by Augustus John in his studio at Mallord Street, Chelsea: vast affairs, Brenda Dean Paul remembered, beginning at teatime and continuing long into the small hours, with music provided by bands of accordion-playing Gypsies. To Powell, what gave John's parties their defining period sheen was the sheer multifariousness of the guests: "old friends, rich patrons, tribes of girls answering to the loose description of 'model.'" In James Laver's *Love's Progress, or the Education of Araminta*, a verse satire in faux-Augustan rhyming couplets from 1929, a suburban girl from Kingston, picked up and befriended by a Chelsea painter called—extraordinarily—John, is inveigled into attending one of his "at homes."

That night arrived, and through the studio door
Came Creatures she had never seen before
And whom—a single glance had made it plain —
She never, never wished to see again
One woman wore a dress of crimson lace
And yellow ochre smeared upon her face.
One who was sixty, or a trifle older
Brought a pet monkey perched upon her shoulder.

Other guests include scantily clad women, a man in a bathing dress and an assortment of lesbians and homosexuals. Araminta, who has passed her formative years in "grim, Suburban night," is deeply bewildered by what seems to her a kind of freak show ("She knew not of, nor could she e'er have guessed / That these were what the gossip-writers call / 'All Chelsea's smartest Intellectuals'"). Like their guests, the hosts and hostesses of these entertainments belonged to no distinct social category, although the scale on which the entertainment was done generally demanded a reasonable income. Well-to-do lesbians and male homosex-

uals abounded. Artistic affiliations—painting, photography, ballet—
were proudly displayed. Frequently the random elements brought together in this way created a social melting pot in which the socially
exalted rubbed shoulders with the downright nefarious. This was particularly true of the parties staged on the *Friendship*, a pleasure boat
moored near Charing Cross Pier. According to Anthony Powell:

> At one end of the scale there'd be quite smart people, Diana
> Cooperish sort of figures and so on. At the other there'd always
> be a lot of these girls who were sort of living on the margin—
> you know, they'd do a little modeling; at the same time they
> were not quite tarts but they were being half kept. And then it
> would tail off into the queer, almost criminal world—lesbians
> dressed as admirals, that sort of thing.

However polyglot and socially indiscriminate they might become at
their lower levels, such events also possessed their own protocols in the
field of dress, style and mannerism. Beverley Nichols left a forensic account of his twenty-something younger self proudly arraying himself
for an evening on the town:

> tails by Lesley and Roberts in Hanover Square, waistcoat by
> Hawes and Curtis of the Piccadilly Arcade, silk hat by Locke in
> St. James's Street, monk shoes by Fortnum and Mason of Pic-
> cadilly, crystal and diamond links by Boucheron of the Rue de
> la Paix, gold cigarette case by Asprey of Bond Street, a drop of
> rose geranium on my handkerchief from the ancient shop
> of Floris in Jermyn Street. And on the dressing-table, waiting
> to be sipped, an ice-cold "sidecar," complete with its crimson
> cherry.

Nichols, it should be pointed out, is operating at the top of the range:
most of his fellow partygoers would have been much less sumptuously
attired. Many, too, would have abstained from evening dress altogether.
The twenties was the great age of the fancy dress party, an obsession

with glad rags and bizarre finery that went far beyond the relatively enclosed world of the Bright Young People. Anthony Powell remembered that the mania for dressing up extended even to the dances given by his Territorial Army unit, with middle-aged colonels pinning colored lapels to their tailcoats in a gesture straight out of the Chelsea basements. *Singing out of Tune* contains an embarrassing but authentic-sounding scene in which the host's crippled aunt is assaulted on the grounds that she resembles a cross-dressing journalist. Aspiring partygoers, bent on an evening's pleasure but not always sure where they might end up, often took changes of clothing with them: Alan Pryce-Jones recalled traveling around London with a matelot suit, "the quickest and simplest form of fancy dress." Photographs of Bright Young People parties reflect this mélange of styles: exotic costumes flanked by black ties, white ties and casual wear. At the bohemian end of the circuit, the wearing of formal dress was a sign that one had misjudged the ambience. At one of the parties in *Afternoon Men*, for example, "Some of the guests were in fancy dress and several were in evening dress. A few of those who came in evening dress stood about and looked surprised . . ." For most partygoers, as Beverley Nichols put it, "any excuse was good enough for putting on a wig and painting one's face and roaring round the town."

As to what went on at these "Urban Dionysias," these Bath and Bottle and Mass Impersonation parties, boisterousness, often extending to outright riot, was the order of the day. Survivors who looked back were keen to congratulate themselves on the extent of their dissipation. "Good manners were not at all respected in the late twenties; not at any rate in the particular rowdy little set which I mainly frequented," Evelyn Waugh proudly remembered. "The test of a young man's worth was the insolence which he could carry off without mishap." Nancy Mitford thought that the young people of the 1960s were "sobriety itself" compared to the pleasure seekers of her own hot youth. Unpoliced and chaotically organized, their doors often open to gatecrashers or even passersby invited in off the street, Bright Young People's parties frequently degenerated into drunken violence and outrageous practical jokes. To Alannah Harper, the twenties party, seen in retrospect, was "a Jerome Bosch hell." Fights could be indiscriminate, with girls as well as

men a target for assault. At a cocktail party given by the photographer
Olivia Wyndham in 1929, the hostess lost her temper with a guest
named George Goodenough and punched him in the face. According to
Ed Burra, who was present at the time, "not to be outdone Goodenough
let out such a biff that O was layed out everyone rushed & held the com-
battants back and the language *ma chère fidone* nothing has been heard
like it since the general strike." Brenda Dean Paul's reminiscences are
full of horseplay turning unexpectedly dangerous: the "Earl's sister"—
Brenda was always coy about names—who revenged herself on a hostess who had been slandering her by rubbing a lobster mayonnaise into
her hair as she lay comatose on a divan and trussing her up beneath the
supper table (the victim nearly died); the "well-known journalist"
found unconscious at the foot of a staircase and bundled into a taxi,
whose driver was ordered to deliver him to a randomly chosen address in
Notting Hill Gate.

As well as providing opportunities for licensed raucousness of this
kind, Bright Young People parties were popularly supposed to consist of
orgies of drug taking and sex. These reports are exaggerated. Drugs had
been part of the West End scene since the Great War: the actress Billie
Carleton had perished of a cocaine overdose on Armistice Night. Coroner's court proceedings from the period contain several accounts of drug
fatalities; there were celebrated Soho dealers such as "Brilliant" Chang,
an expatriate Chinese who formed a tacit alliance with Mrs. Meyrick,
whose clubs he frequented, until his arrest and deportation in 1924. But
such figures tended to belong to the subterranean fringes of the Bright
Young People world, the twilit landscapes of the Soho basement where
nightclub hostessing shaded into outright prostitution. "Drug" references in Bright Young People reportage are usually lighthearted, bound
up in a rather naïve desire to shock or deliberately mislead. Traveling in
the Mediterranean, on the journey that produced *Labels*, Evelyn Waugh
decided to amuse himself with a Greek fellow Oxonian by assuring him
that there was "a terrible outbreak of drug-taking at the university."
Nancy Mitford, staying with her friend Mary Milnes-Gaskell in Scotland and finding the company dull, reported that "Mary and I are going
to try and shock them by pretending that we drug." The twenty-two-

year-old Miss Mitford, it is safe to say, had never sampled anything stronger than an aspirin.

Although several Bright Young People would at later stages in their careers dramatically succumb to heroin addiction, the real drug casualties here in the late 1920s tended to be visiting Americans or veteran bohemians who had acquired their interest in narcotics on the Continent. Beverley Nichols remembered a lurid night out in Paris in the company of the American farceur Avery Hopwood. His companion having collapsed in the gutter, Nichols tried to put him to bed. Dropping the packet that held his cocaine supply, Hopwood flung himself on the carpet in an attempt to ingest the scattered flakes. Among homegrown figures who operated on the Bright Young People's fringe, Mary Butts was an opium addict and the author of "Fumier," a semifictional account of the mechanics of opium use. None of this is to deny the fact that drugs, especially cocaine, known as "uppies" and generally imported from Paris, were frequently on offer at Bright Young parties or that prominent Bright Young People dabbled in them: Diana Mosley later accused Elizabeth Ponsonby—on no particular evidence—of promoting cocaine use.

Whatever the prevalence of drugs, surviving descriptions of drug use are generally recounted in tones of shocked disapproval. Brian Howard, seeing a cocaine addict for the first time in a Berlin restaurant in 1927, assumed that the man was engaged in "deep breathing exercises." To think, Howard piously reflected, watching him return to the table occupied by his wife and children, "that tucked away in one of those capacious pockets lay a little folded slip of paper, or a little bottle, containing all the sugars of hell." *Crazy Pavements* contains a terrific account of the debauched Lord William Motley practicing his vice: "It all happened in a second. A little packet of blue paper was in his hand. It was opened and his fingers dipped into the white powder. With a clumsy gesture he stuffed the powder into his nostrils and sniffed— once, twice." Brian Elme, Nichols's juvenile hero, feels sick: "As Lord William took it, his whole being seemed charged with the melancholy of the damned." Undoubtedly Nichols had seen something like this take place at a Mayfair party or in the private room of a West End restaurant, but the melodrama brought to the scene suggests that it was an exception rather than a commonplace of social life. Equally significant, perhaps, is a prefatory passage in which Nichols suggests that the observant reader, having followed Brian's progress through upmarket London, will have noticed an obvious omission in the list of vices on display. "No single whiff of cocaine has blown across these pages, nor have we heard even the rattle of a miniature hypodermic syringe." Drug-taking, Nichols implies, is one of the dissipations that detached observers *expect* to find in novels about Mayfair, whether it exists or not.

It was the same, up to a point, with sex. Disapproving elders might imagine that the younger generation swam from one partner to another through a sea of unbridled sexual license, but the reality was often sharply different. The debutante world was tightly policed. The heterosexual experience of Bright Young Men of the Waugh-Powell vintage—homosexuality was a different matter—seems to have been rather limited, confined to prostitutes (often encountered abroad) or older, not necessarily Bright Young, women. Anthony Powell, for example, conducted a brief relationship with the painter Nina Hamnett, a long-term ornament of the Soho ateliers. Waugh's diaries show him going through a promiscuous early-thirties patch, but his targets were mostly society women. On the female side, while there were notorious femmes fatales lickerishly at large in the Mayfair jungles, Nancy Mitford's account of herself and her boyfriend Hamish Erskine decorating their half-naked bodies in preparation for a fancy dress party are almost painfully innocuous: jolly good fun rather than the prelude to debauchery.

As with drug-taking, public assumptions of licentiousness often arose out of the mischievous desire to shock: the "Mayfair lovely" remembered by Douglas Goldring who enlivened a party by reading from the volumes of Krafft-Ebing and Havelock Ellis discovered in her grandfather's library. Much was made of the "bachelor girl," with her latchkey and her unsupervised visits to the homes of gentlemen friends—Alec Waugh's 1920s fiction is obsessed with her—but the bachelor girl could usually look after herself. "A Stitch in Time, or Pride Prevents a Fall," another of James Laver's verse satires, stars virginal Belinda, whose virtue is preserved by her unwillingness to let a potential suitor glimpse the green chemise that she has hastily darned with pink thread. Laver's point is that Belinda, a society girl who goes to bed at dawn, is entertained by young men in their flats and is generally thought to be free with her favors, is actually chaste:

> *Though life moves faster than it moved of yore,*
> *And primrose paths are all asphalted o'er,*
> *Though pleasure bears an e'er increasing load,*
> *And broader still is broad Destruction's road,*
> *Not yet is every pillion in the land*
> *Bound straight for BRIGHTON and the PAPHIAN strand,*
> *And nymphs there are, like several I have known,*
> *Who sup at two, but always sleep alone,*
> *As chaste as those who with the Family dine,*
> *And kiss papa, and go to bed at nine.*
> *And such was she, one of that fairy band . . .*

Much more conspicuous was the private language that the Bright Young People constructed for themselves. Like Bright Young People's parties, this wasn't immediately distinguishable from the other varieties of esoteric diction on display, in particular the "smart" language of the pleasure-seeking upper classes. Clipped, terse and wisecracking—Harold Acton maintained that it was specifically designed to carry over the noise of the gramophone—this depended for its effect on exaggeration, the freight of meaningless adjectives such as "divine," "wonderful" and "extraordinary." Nancy Mitford's account of a dance-floor conversation, written up for her column in *The Lady*, perfectly conveys this kind of peacock-hued overstatement:

"My dear, the floor! It's a sort of morass. Have you noticed? Not just ordinary sticky, but *deep*. I mean, almost reaching to the ankle."

"Yes, and full of pot-holes, too."

"Oh, the ghastliness of that band. Do let's go somewhere else, shall we?"

"Of course, this hock-cup simply tastes like bad sweets melted in tooth-water—that's *all*."

"Who are all these revolting people?"

"The entire population of Wormwood Scrubs, I should think, if you ask me."

"Do let's get out of this soon."

Beverley Nichols offers a similar account of the specimen Bright Young Person's reaction to a newly minted copy of the *Tatler*, all twittering emphasis and ghostly italics: "My dear, look what Cecil's done to Edith Sitwell this week. He's sketched her flat on the *floor*, my dear." Or of the ubiquitous pictures of Baba and Nancy: "He's surrounded them with *balloons*, my dear, and hung a lot of delicious *cellophane* round their necks, and lit them from *behind*, and they look *too* ravishing, my dear, and I can't wait to be done myself."

Brian Howard and Eddie Gathorne-Hardy, all the evidence insists, really did talk like this. ("My dear," Howard is supposed to have admonished his boyfriend Sam in a Paris *parfumerie* just after the war when the latter began spraying himself with samples, "you're not putting out a *fire*.") Bright Young People's refinements to this template took several forms. On the one hand they specialized in telegraphic truncations: Waugh, for example, referring to his books *Remote People* and *Black Mischief* as "Remoters" and "Blackers" (the Lygons' country house at Madresfield was similarly transformed into "Madders"). There were American imports such as "sock a dinner to a pal," meaning treat a friend to a meal. But most flagrantly they brought to it elements of the nursery such as diminutives and whimsy words. Evelyn Gardner, although she sincerely admired *À la Recherche du Temps Perdu*, referred to its author as "Proustie-Woustie." Her prospective father-in-law, Arthur Waugh, was "a complete Pinkle-Wonk." In much the same way the characters in Nancy Mitford's *Highland Fling* are apostrophized as "My sweetie bo," "What a poodle-pie" and so forth. A second garnish was the remark of jaw-dropping incongruity. Brian Howard, invited to inspect Bryan and Diana Guinness's son Jonathan as he lay in his cradle, is supposed to have remarked, "My dear, it is so *modern* looking," to the astonishment of the nurse. A third was the emergence of words with exclusive, coterie meanings—"bogus" (i.e., artificial, false), "climbing" (arriviste, opportunistic), "sick-making"—of the kind codified by Evelyn Waugh in *Vile Bodies*. At one point Miss Runcible's friends commiserate with her on her ordeal at the hands of the Customs and Excise: "'*Well*,' they said. '*Well!* How too, too shaming, Agatha, darling,' they said. 'How devastating, how unpoliceman-like, how goat-like, how sick-making, how too, too awful.'"

In some cases these neologisms could be traced back to a particular incident or representation. *Vile Bodies*, for example, makes inspired use of the adjective "sheepish," as in "a perfectly sheepish house." This arose from a conversation between Waugh and the twelve-year-old Jessica Mitford, whose pet lamb he had promised to include somewhere in the novel. *Vile Bodies* offers a striking example of the way in which in-jokes coined by a tiny handful of people could move rapidly outward from their original orbit to colonize a much wider sector of society. Alec Waugh, given the finished manuscript to read shortly before Christmas 1929, asked his brother if the hitherto unheard-of expressions "drunk-making" and "shy-making" were his own invention. No, Waugh assured him, the young Guinness set was using them.

By the early New Year, a few days before publication, Alec noticed that these usages had jumped social ship to reemerge in circles not necessarily connected with the Guinnesses. The day after *Vile Bodies* went on sale, "every conversation" was peppered with "poor-makings," "drunk-makings" and "rich-makings." The social range of these neologisms was not limited to upper-class London: three decades later Loelia Ponsonby noted that it still surprised her when she heard a bus conductor remark that he couldn't care less, "smart" usage from the era of the General Strike. Waugh's sensitivity to Bright Young People argot followed him into other books. In *Labels* he visits a Parisian nightclub called Brick-Top's. The eponymous hostess comes to sit at his table. "She seemed to be the least bogus person in Paris." Traveling in the Holy Land, and mindful of his friend Tom Driberg's job on the *Express*, he refers to the tour guide as a "dragoman."

Linguistic exclusiveness, however rapidly diffused, was balanced by a cosmopolitan—sometimes exaggeratedly cosmopolitan—outlook. This was particularly evident in the Bright Young People's fascination with black American culture, or rather with the highly stylized versions of black American culture brought to England in the mid-1920s. Florence Mills and her Blackbird troupe, who first appeared in London in 1926, the singer-pianist "Hutch"—Leslie A. Hutchinson—and before him the actor Paul Robeson were all fixtures on the West End party circuit. "It's not a party. There won't be a black man," Evelyn Waugh would say, when issuing some minor invitation, acknowledging this ubiquity. Waugh's diaries give a good idea of the multiracial nature of many Bright Young entertainments. An entry from February 1927 reports a lunch date with Olivia Plunket Greene and her mother, at which the former "could talk of nothing but black men . . . Later to the Blackbirds and called on other niggers and negresses in their dressing rooms. Then to a night club called Victor's to see another nigger—Leslie Hutchinson." At around the same time, Waugh dined at a party given by the art dealer and historian Langton Douglas, whose illegitimate daughter Zena Naylor lived with Hutch.

As Waugh's casually racist language demonstrates, Bright Young attitudes to black American entertainers differed wildly from individual to individual. To some they were no more than exotic curiosities, encouraged more for their novelty value than to satisfy any deep-seated artistic urge. To give Waugh his due, the comic portrait of "Chokey," who escorts Mrs. Beste-Chetwynde to the Llanabba sports in *Decline and Fall*, is quite as much a joke about Mayfair socialites who patronized black actors as a mark of Waugh's conviction that black people are funny, especially when they presume to know about English culture and dilate upon their souls. The same point can be made of Lady Courtenay's remark about the evening-suited Emperor Seth in *Black Mischief*: "Got up as though he were going to sing spirituals at a party." But many Bright Young People, among them Brian Howard, Elizabeth Ponsonby and Brenda Dean Paul, were genuinely moved and exalted by these byproducts of the Harlem Renaissance—something that Waugh himself was happy to concede. In *Brideshead Revisited* he allows Howard, in the guise of his alter ego Anthony Blanche, to defend the Blackbirds to a suspicious Boy Mulcaster: "No, they are not animals in a *zoo*, Mulcaster, to be *goggled at*. They are great *artists*, my dear, very great artists, to be *revered*."

With a very few Bright Young People, or those on their margin, this absorption took on an ardent, ideological focus. Nancy Cunard, for example, who scandalized her mother and much of polite society by living openly with the black actor Henry Crowder ("What is it now, Maud?" Margot Asquith is supposed to have inquired. "Drink, drugs or niggers?"), later compiled a groundbreaking anthology of Negro culture for the Communist publishers Lawrence & Wishart. But the realities of interracial sex, of which Nancy's *mésalliance* was the most prominent example, are unquantifiable. Hutch, for instance, was famous as a womanizer; undoubtedly some of his conquests were white society girls; one of them may even have been Babe Plunket Greene. On the other side of the coin, what Douglas Goldring calls the *"femme de joie"* could frequently make a nuisance of herself with happily married black actors, few of whom, Goldring thought, "had any particular desire to be taken up by London's Bright Young People." Goldring's sympathies were with the black American artists, "who behaved much better than their hosts."

Not all the overseas visitors welcomed to West End fancy dress balls were black. Touring American writers and artists were often temporarily accommodated beneath the Bright Young People's roofs, not always with successful results. One of the guests at Stephen Tennant's literary party at Wilsford in June 1927 was the poet Elinor Wylie. Vain and impressionable, accompanied to Wiltshire by a baggage trunk containing countless changes of clothing, Wylie rapidly became a focus for practical joking. The highlight of the gathering was a midsummer night's trip to Stonehenge. Here Wylie, dressed in a silver lamé gown, was hauled up on to one of the stones and mock-worshipped by such attendants as Beaton, Rosamond Lehmann, Sacheverell Sitwell, Rex Whistler and Zita Jungman. Encouraged by this reception, Wylie began to recite some of her poetry in the rich accents of New Jersey. Then, divining that she was being made fun of, she burst into tears and demanded to be taken straight back to London. And if the cultural tourists eager to see what all the fuss was about sometimes imagined themselves to have been patronized and condescended to, neither was the atmosphere they had come to admire necessarily exportable. That Bright Young People's humor might not be capable of wholesale transfer across the Atlantic was demonstrated by the publisher George Doran's attempt, early in 1928, to install Beverley Nichols as editor of the *American Sketch*. Ferried to New York along with his furniture and manservant, and with a brief to transfer a somewhat staid and down-market periodical into something that might compete with *The New Yorker*, Nichols found himself in command of a single editorial assistant and a magazine filled with advertisements about dogs. Despite commissioning drawings from George Grosz and printing Beaton's photographs, he lasted only a few months before returning to England.

These embarrassments served to emphasize the essential character, and also some of the limitations, of the Bright Young People. At heart it was a British, metropolitan phenomenon. Detached from its breeding ground—effectively a few square miles of West End London—it sickened and died while simultaneously causing grave offense to less sophisticated onlookers. The descent of bands of weekending Bright Young People on Home Counties villages and rural retreats to the suspicion and outrage of the local populace is a feature of early 1930s fiction. In *Afternoon Men*, the artist Pringle introduces a decidedly mixed collection of house guests to his local pub. " 'Arlots," someone murmurs as the women sit down. Later the servant girl Ethel's parents arrive to protest at the laxity of the morals on display ("It isn't the same as in London, Mr. Pringle; in a little place folks talk and what one says the other repeats, and we've got to look after our girl."). It is this disregard for provincial sensitivities that scuppers Basil Seal's chances of standing for Parliament for an out-of-town constituency in *Black Mischief*. ("He does seem to have behaved rather oddly at the Conservative ball . . . and then he and Alastair Trumpington and Peter Pastmaster and some others had a five-day party up there and left a lot of blank checks behind and had a motor accident and got run in—you know what Basil's parties are. I mean, that sort of thing is all right in London, but you know what provincial towns are.") The reality of Bright Young excursions was often only a little different from this, as Ed Burra reported to his friend Billy Chappell from Springfield, near Rye, in summer 1929:

> Such merry times have been going on at Thornsdale what with dashing nude into the river and Brenda Dean Paul walking about in Lido trowsers the whole village is an uproar . . . when bonny Brenda tripped down to the river for a splash she discovered a young man sitting by the stream so she said Oh-er-do you mind me bathing without a bathing dress so the young man said no & in went B meanwhile the young man who had been having a lovely time peeping through the osiers rushed out & said he'd summons her then Jerry swept down just as Farmer Jones wife and daughter were rowing over the ferry & out rushed farmer J & threatened to fight Jerry . . .

To do one or two of the Bright Young People justice, they were sharply aware of the contrast between their own lives and those lived beyond the London party circuit. Some of the most interesting Bright Young relationships of the period were those conducted between metropolitan gossip mongers and friends temporarily detached from the loop. Anthony Powell and Henry Yorke (the novelist Henry Green), Eton contemporaries and Oxford neighbors, found themselves separated for the first time in 1927–28, with Powell working at Duckworth while Yorke was dispatched to the Birmingham plant of Pontifex, the family manufacturing firm: this experience informs Yorke's second novel, *Living* (1929). The letters they exchanged at this time are oddly revealing: Powell reporting on the progress of his social life and the activities of mutual friends; Yorke increasingly conscious of his detachment. Beneath the surface of shared interests and professional solidarity—each had literary ambitions and Yorke had already published his first book—ran a widening emotional fissure. Several of Powell's letters touch on the Biddulph sisters, Mary and Adelaide ("Dig"), to whom both were romantically attracted. "The more one sees of the Biddulphs," Powell wrote in 1928, "the more one learns. I'm at a loss to know why they tolerate one at all.

Mary, describing a dinner party at the Russells at which we had both been present said with extraordinary venom: 'and they talked about *Oxford* the whole time and all the *books* everyone had written there.' "

The faint air of coldness that infected their relationship when Henry married Dig in 1929 had two sources. On the one hand Powell felt that his own rejection could be traced back to his inferior social status: the army officer's son losing out to the wealthy manufacturer. On the other, he felt that Yorke had behaved disingenuously. But Henry, as Powell knew, was an odd character altogether ("There always existed deep and secret recesses in Yorke's mind that were never revealed"), intimately connected to the intellectual, book-writing end of the Bright Young People world inhabited by Powell, Waugh and Robert Byron, but never ceasing to complain about it. In fact, Yorke's letters from the late 1920s are full of complaints: a Bright Young People party to which Robert Byron had taken him ("You must promise never to let me in for anything like that . . . again. Arty high life is not my line"); Byron's travelogue *The Station* ("without exception the worst book I've ever read," he told Powell); a visit to the Yorkes' country house at Forthampton made by Byron and the newly married Waughs ("Evelyn + his wife are coming for the weekend next week, so is Robert. I loathe Robert for his absolutely incredible vulgarity . . . Mrs. Waugh is a very silly piece").

Much of what Powell and Yorke had to say to each other was on the lightest imaginable level. An undated letter from 1927 from Powell offers a résumé of a society ball:

Actually I am recovering from getting very drunk last night, and if I do nothing I feel everyone in the office is looking at me, so I have to write letters as there is nothing on at the moment. The scene of the debauch was the Rothschilds' dance. Matthew [Ponsonby], Anthony, Richard Greene etc. were all present in varying degrees of liquor . . . Altogether it was rather a funny evening. When I say "*drunk*," of course, I do *not* mean "drunk" in the Oxford sense, but it's extraordinary how awful one feels the next day when out of practice, even if one's only drunk half a glass of port.

There was also an exchange of informed gossip on one of the key Bright Young People texts, Waugh's *Decline and Fall*. Shortly after publication in the autumn of 1928, Powell wrote "to thank you for the unspeakably funny information about Brian identifying himself with Captain Grimes. Surely someone has drawn his attention to the fact that he has none of the latter's endearing qualities." But Yorke, hard at work on his novel of factory life, had begun to show an awareness of the world beyond the spangled palisades inhabited by most of his Eton and Oxford contemporaries. "Things look very bad just now in the industrial districts," he wrote to Powell in August 1928.

> All the motor bicycle and most of the motor trades seem to be going smash. This means that the h.p. + the petrol tax will have to be taken off + it will then be the moment for Mr. Ford, even now building a huge factory on the other side of the Thames. Unemployment is getting very bad in Birmingham + walking through the streets one finds everywhere an extraordinary atmosphere . . . of sullenness and ill-will. How people like Robert can still go on touring Europe (he is now in Czechoslovakia) with all these exciting things going on at home, I can't understand.

Over a decade later, in *Party Going* (1939), Yorke would produce perhaps the most dazzling critique of the London society world ever written. For the moment, though, he was anxious to make up for lost time. Early in 1929 he moved south to work in Pontifex's London office, became engaged to Dig and began to attend some of the social events he had previously only heard about from Powell. The transformation was noted by Evelyn Waugh, who swiftly came up with a nickname for the newly married novelist and his bride that would be wholly in keeping with the life they now led: "The Bright Young Yorkes."

ELIZABETH IN PARTIES

One of the most absorbing artifacts to surface from the Ponsonby archive is a rectangular brown-and-beige photograph album that, to judge from the pencil marks on the inside back cover, cost its owner all of 31s. 6d. at around the time of the General Strike. Here, between about 1927 and 1933, Elizabeth preserved the mementos of her extensive social life. The first page or two houses pictures of a trip that she and her father took to America (a tough-looking lady well-wisher draped in a banner reading NO MORE WAR presents Arthur with a bunch of roses), the back end carries rows of desultory holiday snaps but the rest is simply a succession of parties. Impersonation Parties and Theatrical Parties, American Parties and Court Parties—a thronged and picturesque pageant of outré costumes, beaming faces, and always in their very center the small woman with the charged glass and the unfeigned smile.

The faces, by and large, are familiar. At the Impersonation Party, Stephen Tennant sits languidly to one side, the flowing court dress necessary for his portrayal of Queen Marie of Romania tumbling like a miniature cataract over the photograph's lower margin. Cecil is at Elizabeth's side, her hand, fingers still clutching a half-smoked cigarette, curled round his waist. At the Plunket Greene bash of summer 1927 the two of them pose decorously by the front door, Elizabeth in what might be a pair of silk pajamas, Cecil in white ducks, shirt and velvet tunic, hair a Harlowed expanse of platinum. At "Heather Pilkington's Party" in the same London season, Cecil, in what looks like a two-piece made out of aluminum foil, cozies up to Brian Howard, the latter clad in a star-patterned frock and hung around with chiffon scarves. Elsewhere, Elizabeth is embraced by her hostess while a middle-aged gentleman in a pleated kilt and kneesocks, who would clearly be much better off at home with his wife and children, frolics on the sofa.

In the end, curiously enough, most of the faces fade away: the supporting cast, the scene swellers, accessories to the main event. What remains, the thing that the eye instinctively seeks out, is Elizabeth, the glass borne in the left hand, the head tilted at an angle, the gaze practically seraphic. Tennant and Beaton are preening themselves, there to be seen, wondering whether the destiny of this particular snap will be the *Tatler* or the *Sketch*. Elizabeth, on the other hand, is simply enjoying herself. Her rapture is not that of the narcissist (Stephen) or the social opportunist (Cecil), who foresees a gratifying late breakfast in front of next morning's papers, merely the kick of the honest pleasure seeker. Looking at her, as she stands next to Cecil in her pageboy wig, supposedly representing Iris Tree, you see exactly what she meant when she told her parents, to their considerable disgust, that social life, this kind of social life, with these kind of people, was the only form of existence she cared to lead. You see, too, what little chance Arthur, Dorothea or anyone else had of stopping her leading it.

Denis first turns up in the album perched on a carousel with his wife and Brian Howard in a picture taken at the 1929 Theatrical Garden Party, then in his Circus Party getup of acrobat's costume, cape and prick-ear cap (Elizabeth, at his side, wearing the same gear, is enveloped in the cape). He looks, well, progressively less tolerant of the circumstances in which he finds himself. On the carousel he ventures a slightly nervous smile: Elizabeth and Brian are having all the fun. At the American Party, with Elizabeth in boater, bow tie and horn-rims, he settles for a kind of off-duty quarterback look of open-necked shirt with the letter *P* engraved on it: rueful, downcast, gaze way off camera, fixed firmly on a patch of floorboard away to the left of the lens. There is a rather telling shot of him taken in April 1930, tieless, drink in hand, Elizabeth draped solicitously over him, clearly feeling the strain. A second woman, whom the *Tatler* caption writer identifies as Lady Mercy Dean, smiles at him from the adjoining bar stool. Denis isn't responding. He looks mournful, resigned, wondering just how all this is going to turn out. His final appearance is at the Court Party of March 1931, uncertain and faintly confused in guardsman's uniform complete with teetering busby. Next to him an extraordinary drag queen—or rather, to judge from her appurtenances, Drag Queen—reclines across the sofa. Elizabeth, meanwhile, also in uniform, hands clasped across her sword hilt, beaming at the camera, is plainly having the time of her life.

CHAPTER SIX

PARTYGOING: 1929

The sad truth to me is that these young people are not getting the best out of life—that they are wasting precious time—& may perhaps one day regret it pitifully. The perversion & lack of purpose & reverence for anything is to me most terrible—psychological failure & a lack of spirituality is so much more pre-occupying than poverty & the material state of the poor. I wonder hopelessly how one can make the present generation see.

— DOROTHEA PONSONBY, Diary, October 24, 1929

The Bright Young People came popping all together, out of someone's electric brougham like a litter of pigs, and ran squealing up the steps. Some "gate-crashers" who had made the mistake of coming in Victorian fancy dress were detected and repulsed. They hurried home to change for a second assault. No one wanted to miss Mrs. Ape's *debut*.

— EVELYN WAUGH, *Vile Bodies*

B y the time Henry Yorke arrived in London at the beginning of 1929, the society world that he had monitored for the past two years from the aerie of the Pontifex works in Birmingham had begun to change. Never entirely coherent, its ties of friendship and association sometimes gossamer-thin, the Bright Young People community was more than usually susceptible to the processes of breakup and renewal that affect any social group. The movement's inner core had been in existence for upwards of four years. Its original members were getting married—the society papers of January 1929 were full of Zita Jungman's engagement to a guardee named Arthur James—taking jobs or forming relationships that took them out of the Bright Young Person's orbit. In all kinds of ways, and with all kinds of attendant publicity, all kinds of people were moving on. Cecil Beaton was in New York excitedly furthering his career. Stephen Tennant was on the Continent for the good of his health. Evelyn Waugh and his wife spent the first half of 1929 on a Mediterranean cruise. Again, the excuse was the shoring up of a frail constitution. She-Evelyn had been ill during the autumn: the trip would allow her to recuperate while her husband collected material for an upcoming travel book. In their absence, the group's alignment underwent a substantial shift, becoming at once more exclusive and more "artistic," more image-conscious and more disparaged. Above all, it came to be dominated by what the newspapers had already begun to refer to as the "Guinness Set."

Bryan Guinness, the eldest son of Colonel Walter Guinness, minister of agriculture in Stanley Baldwin's Conservative government, was a tall, good-looking and immensely wealthy scion of the famous brewing family. A friend once reported that he received a twelfth of a penny for each bottle sold. Literary-minded—Duckworth had been persuaded to publish a volume of his poetry on commission—he already operated at the heart of the Bright Young People's world, had known Byron, Howard and Acton since Eton days and had been inducted into the Mitford household by Nancy. According to Byron's account, his friend first set eyes on Nancy's younger sister Diana at a fancy dress ball at the family home when she was barely sixteen: "I seem to remember her faraway dreamy look as she danced or sat out with the sophisticated Brian Howard," the intoxicated swain recalled. Even in her mid-teens, Diana was the acknowledged beauty of the Mitford sisters. Given her youth, and the disquiet bred up in Lord and Lady Redesdale's breasts by her elder sister's antics, she took some time to figure in those areas of London society beyond the ballroom. Alec Waugh, a reliable gazetteer of female talent, thought that he first encountered her at his brother's housewarming at Canonbury Square in November 1928. By this time Diana's immediate future was already sealed. Six months earlier Robert Byron had recorded traveling down to Swinbrook with Bryan and thinking his friend "grotesquely in love with Diana Mitford." Those close to the couple expressed surprise. Bryan, informed observers maintained, possessed little of his future wife's inner steeliness. "The more I see of Bryan the more it surprises me that Diana should be in love with him," Nancy shrewdly pronounced, "but I think he's very nice." The adjective haunted Bryan throughout his career. He proposed in July 1928, shortly after Diana's eighteenth birthday, overcame a certain amount of opposition from his prospective in-laws—Lady Redesdale's puritan conscience was shocked by the thought that a girl barely out of the schoolroom should marry one of the richest young men in England—and finally took his bride to the altar at St. Margaret's Westminster on July 30, 1929.

All the mechanisms of a grand society wedding ground inexorably into gear. The Earl of Rosse was best man. The *Daily Mail* and the *Daily Express* ran admiring photo spreads. A portrait of the bridal group reproduced in the *Sketch* shows no fewer than eleven bridesmaids: bevies of Mitfords and Guinnesses, Diana Churchill—Winston Churchill was a cousin of the bride—Nancy standing soberly at Diana's elbow, Unity, pigtailed and Valkyrie-like, flanking her on the farther side. Three weeks later the *Sketch* secured a "delightful honeymoon snapshot" of the young couple in Taormina. Bryan looks serious and reflective; Diana, gravely beautiful, seems miles away. Returned to London the newlyweds moved into a substantial town house at 10 Buckingham Street, extensively refurbished by Bryan's doting parents during their absence, which would become a focus for Bright Young People activity throughout 1929. If not artistic patrons in the quattrocento sense, the young couple were enthusiastic sponsors of art and artists, eagerly disseminating books by friends and offering material help if they thought it was needed. John Banting, for example, was commissioned to paint an enormous six-feet-by-four-feet portrait of Diana. At Christmas 1929, the young couple sent copies of *Living* as presents. Evelyn Waugh, on whom Guinness hospitality was lavished in the later part of the year, responded with the dedication of *Vile Bodies*. Already, though, tensions were beginning to declare themselves. Diana both enjoyed the social whirl into which she was thrown and made intellectual friends among the Bloomsbury notables with whom the Guinnesses' artistic interests brought her into contact. Bryan, less keen on entertaining, wanted to give up London altogether. "Let's go to the north of Scotland," friends remembered him fruitlessly proposing.

Young, wealthy—their annual income was put at £20,000—beloved of the society columnists and with a large and well-appointed house at their disposal, the Guinnesses played a conspicuous role in the party world of 1929. This, most observers agreed, was reaching its apex: a riot of "freak" entertainments in which successive waves of hosts battled to outdo their predecessors in the matter of theme, costume and behavior. Come late February, "Corisande" of the *Evening Standard*'s "Woman's World" column could be found informing her readers that "some of the smartest and prettiest women in London have been searching for a dress appropriate for a Wild West Party, and cowboy costumes are at a premium." Fifteen bachelors would be entertaining their friends at Harold Acton's house in Lancaster Gate, the paper reported. According to the *Sketch*, which provided a double-page portrait gallery of the guests, the event was "voted as one of the 'best' and most original parties of the winter. Splendid costumes were worn, 'everyone' was there, and the atmosphere of the wild and woolly west was achieved by such notices as 'Anyone shooting the pianist will be severely censured.'"

Not to be outdone by his Eton and Oxford contemporary, Brian Howard was already hatching plans for an extravaganza to celebrate his twenty-fourth birthday on April 4. Advertised as the "Great Urban Dionysia," featuring an invitation card sixteen inches high and consisting of parallel columns headed *J'accuse* and *J'adore*, this, like many gatherings of the period, involved the most elaborate preparations. Guests were encouraged to visit the British Museum in search of suitable costume designs. Howard became obsessed by choreography and décor, insisting that new arrivals should at first be introduced to Olivia Wyndham, impersonating Minerva: "You'll be dressed in something beautiful, my dear, and enter in on a bull." Hotly anticipated, its attractions endlessly canvassed in the preceding weeks, the Great Urban Dionysia was in the end adjudged to have fallen rather flat. Unimpressed by John Banting as Mercury à la Cocteau, wearing a winged engine driver's hat, Ernest Thesiger as Medusa and Mary Butts as a caryatid in high headdress and blue wig, "Domino" of the *Evening Standard* found the proceedings "definitely suburban" in their lack of excitement.

June came in a blaze of invitation cards. Alec Waugh, among others, remembered the "general heightening" of the social tempo in summer 1929, a process he thought speeded up by the presence in London of several rich Americans who "helped to set the pace." A new kind of entertainment, too, had made its way across the Atlantic. This, Cecil Beaton told "Johanna" of *The Lady* when they met at Mrs. Keigwin's "Catalan Ball" early in June, was going to be a "whoopee party." "Johanna" was suitably impressed, not only by the Moorish decorations but also by "Miss 'Baby' Jungman, who had not dressed up, but came in an ordinary red frock," Alannah Harper in white evening dress and Nancy Beaton "in quite the most successful frock of the evening with an enormously long train covered in hundreds of flowers." Three weeks later the Guinnesses held an 1860s party at Buckingham Street, coinciding with the "Watteau Party" on the *Friendship* at Charing Cross Pier. All these entertainments, however, were put in the shade by the "Circus Party," convened a week later by the young couturier Norman Hartnell at a hired house in Bruton Street. On this, perhaps the most elaborate freak party of the 1920s, so much reporters' ink was expended that, as "Johanna" rather desperately put it, "You will have heard so much about this that I do not think there can be anything left for me to tell." Here guests discovered that the premises had been decorated in the style of a fairground. The booths displayed live animals, including a dancing bear, a seal and a Siberian wolf. There was dancing to a circus orchestra, a jazz band and an Italian accordion quartet, while the guests included Lady Dean Paul and her daughter, dressed by the designer Willie Clarkson as, respectively, a Lyons waitress and a female wrestler, Olivia Wyndham with a pair of live snakes coiled round her neck and Diana Guinness in an immense crinoline, looking, as Brenda put it, like a Sèvres shepherdess.

The Circus Party extended deep into the small hours of July 2. Three days later two of its star guests found themselves walking together up the aisle of St. Margaret's Westminster. Like the Guinness-Mitford wedding of a few months before, Elizabeth Ponsonby's marriage to Denis Pelly was a press sensation. Invitations were at a premium. Mary Butts wrote rather forlornly to Eddie Gathorne-Hardy from Paris to say that she would have loved to come, had anyone asked her. Both Ponsonby parents left detailed accounts of the spectacle: loving, optimistic and attempting to portray the union in terms of fresh starts and roseate futures. Arthur, flustered by "an atmosphere of excitement with the telephone going, presents arriving, dresses and photographers," soothed his nerves by going twice to the nearby Crosby Hall, where the reception was being held, to make himself useful to Nelly, the Ponsonbys' harassed maid. The ceremony itself stirred all his protective feelings toward his wayward daughter:

> The gown was very pretty and although her make-up was too much for my taste, she had mitigated it. My first thrill came when I saw her in perspective sitting in the large car like a bride in a fairy story without an expression of blasé assurance but real simplicity and a touch of nervousness. Both of us being undemonstrative I contented myself by just kissing her hand. At St. Margaret's we walked straight in and slowly up the aisle. I felt that was all right—a ceremony not entirely meaningless either to her or to me. The building and the music, the sight of my four brothers and sisters and my friends were very moving and as I stood by them I could not help remembering the many sleepless nights and the hideous revolting thoughts when the mud and the slime seemed so near. A look at Denis was a refreshment.

Dolly's account is more detailed, small things and large things mixed: Elizabeth's dress (by Hartnell) "of silk net on tulle covered over with satin leaves and pearls," the tiny bridesmaids, anxieties for the future. As Denis and Elizabeth walked down the aisle together, the sun burst dramatically through the windows, drenching the couple in coruscating light. "Oh may they be happy and good," Dolly wished. She approved of the service: "It all seemed to me reverent & much less worldly than any London weddings I have been to—and the fact that Denis and Eliz. are so happy & devoted gave it the right atmosphere." Subsequently, some of Dolly's habitual sharpness returned. Mrs. Pelly, whom Arthur had in tow, she considered "certainly the ugliest woman I've ever seen." The reception was adjudged "a huge success," beginning formally with the greeting of family and friends, ending up as a variation on a Bright Young People's party. Hutch played the piano. Finally, as the *Tatler* put it, "Mrs. Denis Pelly . . . sprang into the arms of Mr. Brian Howard, whose white velvet tie needs no further advertisement, and opened the ball." Dolly went happily home to Smith Square, delighted by her last glimpse of "E. standing up in the gallery" and looking "wonderful with her high crown."

The London season, with which most Bright Young happenings were synchronized, was nearly over. There was just time, three weeks later, for one of the era's most memorable practical jokes. Taking place under Guinness supervision, and hatched at Bryan and Diana's house, it involved the fabrication of an entire art exhibition as well as the impersonation of a spurious artist. The idea, according to Bryan Guinness, was Brian Howard's, possibly influenced by a well-advertised stunt in which Lady Harris's landscape paintings had been exhibited pseudonymously, and the rationale nothing more than "an excuse for a party." The objets d'art, hastily knocked up by Howard with assistance from John Banting, painted on cork boards and framed with lengths of rope, were modernist pastiches in the style of Braque and Picasso. *The Adoration of the Magi*, for instance, depicts three matchsticklike shapes, one of them three-headed, abasing themselves before a geometrid representation of Mary, who bears a small circle in her hands. Evelyn Waugh produced an accompanying piece of art criticism and selected guests, including journalists, were invited to an "at home" at Buckingham Street to view an exhibition of "Pictures and Sculptures by Bruno Hat." A catalogue blurb offered details of the artist's origins and affiliations. He was represented as a thirty-one-year-old native of Lübeck, now resident in Clymping, Sussex (where the Guinnesses had a summer cottage), and engaged in running a general store with his stepmother. Self-taught and unambitious, he had never previously exhibited a picture. "A month ago, however, several examples of his work were taken to Paris, and the opinion there was so immediately favorable that successful arrangements have been made for an exhibition." Visitors to Buckingham Street discovered, in addition to the paintings, a morose and mostly silent man with a luxuriant mustache and dark glasses who, seated in a wheelchair, grumbled in a marked German accent about the color of the walls and the publicity he was receiving. This was Diana's brother, Tom.

Who, if anyone, was taken in? Margot, Lady Oxford and Asquith, treated a reporter to some erudite remarks on the abstract in art. Winston Churchill, asked what he thought of *Christ Meeting the Disciples Coming from Emmaus* (in black knitting wool stretched between black-headed hatpins), commented, "A lot of bloody rubbish!" Lytton Strachey, who arrived at the exhibition with Violet Tree, bought two of the paintings in a spirit of mild amusement. Tom Driberg in the *Daily Express*, to whom full details had been given, tried to give his readers the impression that he was exposing a sensational imposture:

AMAZING HOAX ON ART EXPERTS
UNKNOWN ARTIST WITH FALSE MOUSTACHE
'MR. BRUNO HAT'

"The Dragoman" also noticed Maurice Bowra's attempt to enliven the atmosphere by greeting the artist in his native tongue. Tom Mitford was equal to the tease, remarking that he was a naturalized Englishman and did not care to be reminded that he spoke German. What remained after the columns of newsprint had been filed away was a private joke that had lost its privacy. Bryan Guinness, in particular, was anxious to play down its significance. "It all made quite an amusing excuse for an iced coffee party to which people came and went after looking at the pictures," he laconically pronounced, a charade rather than a hoax as everyone was in on the secret. If there was a casualty it was Brian Howard, who, Diana maintained, believed that he would be hailed as a precocious new talent by the critics.

Rising from the torrent of newspaper coverage that accompanied the Bruno Hat exhibition and other similar entertainments can be heard the faint—and sometimes not-so-faint—bark of criticism, occasionally extending to outright hostility. Five days after Elizabeth Ponsonby's wedding, many of the people who attended it could be found at

Rosemary Sanders's house in Rutland Gate for what became known as the "Second Childhood Party." Here the guests, many of whom arrived in prams and baby carriages, were supplied with dolls, bottles and comforters, and ordered drinks at a bar set up in a playpen. The press disapproved: "The type of behaviour that leads to Communism," one onlooker suggested. *The Lady* reported that an organized attempt had been made to break the party up. The thought that Bright Young People's gatherings were now no more than straightforward displays of bad behavior occurred to even sympathetic observers. "Has the freak party reached the point at which it becomes both an absurdity and a nuisance?" "Johanna" worried in mid-July. Some parties were degenerating into "such a display of 'high spirits,'" she deposed, "that they have become a source of annoyance to the young."

They were also becoming a source of annoyance to the old. *Punch*, which had first regarded the Bright Young People with a certain amount of quizzical amusement, was now turning nasty. Shortly after the Great Urban Dionysia, the magazine produced a rather labored parody titled "The Dull Young People." Here *Punch*'s correspondent is escorted by "Lady Gaga" to an entertainment hosted by "the Honorable Batsin Belfry" and her husband, "Bobo." Arriving at "a little house in Bloomsbury" ablaze with light, the couple fight their way to the dining room, over whose door hangs a sign reading WE'RE ALONE. RUN IN FOR YOUR RUM. Here Bobo, in maritime gear, dispenses drinks to "a perspiring mob of boys and girls in rather too elaborate fancy-dress, most of the latter showing a curiously unoriginal preference for trousers." On the counter sits "a massive maiden in a cavalry officer's mess-kit, whom everybody addressed as 'Colonel,' and next her a fresh-faced lad dressed as a bride, complete with veil and orange-blossom." The latter, just down from university, is already a promising dress designer whose creations in satin pajamas are "simply *super*."

For all its heavy-handedness, this is a rather accurate take on the Bright Young People's ambience. In particular, it reproduces the heterodox nature of most late-1920s parties: a certain amount of upper-class luster ("a youthful absentee member of the Upper House")—the titled host—descending into a raffish collection of lesbians and cross-dressing young men. Its criticisms are those traditionally leveled at Bright Young People: that they were neither bright nor young, neither brilliant nor original; that what imagined itself to be shocking was merely tired and affected: "The old familiar features of din and drink, of mild dare-devilry and self-conscious dissipation were such as may be met with in many quite middle-class haunts." Losing sight of Lady Gaga for half an hour, the interloper eventually finds her with her arm round the waist of "a young heavy-weight in horn-rims dressed as a baby" listening to a hollow-eyed girl in a tutu and an opera hat who is singing a song with the refrain "It's *ter*ribly thrilling to be wicked." He leaves in disgust. "Frankly, I had discovered nothing conspicuously bright or youthful at this much-advertised party. I didn't even observe any particular 'stunt.' It was just rather dull, artificially raffish and altogether too self-conscious."

These criticisms would continue to be raised against freak parties for the rest of the year. *Punch* returned to the attack in the week of the Bruno Hat furor with a squib titled "She Whoops to Conquer." Here, "Rachel," having discussed the variety of entertainments available to the modern partygoer, notes that "the latest idea among the givers of these tasteful assemblies" is to throw what one London hostess calls "a Whoopee." Tea, Brahms and cucumber sandwiches are now perceived to be "bourgeois," along with coffee, gentlefolk, ices and a band on the lawn. "Nay, then, they are suburban. My grateful thanks to the Whoopee lady, and we will all try to be Brighter Young People, lest we drop out of society, and are no more seen." There follows a list of suggested variations on the "Whoopee" template: a "Zippee" ("Dancing till five o'clock, when we shall change into evening dress and have breakfast, at which liver and bacon and liqueurs will be served"), a "Speakeasy," at which guests will be invited to bootleg their own drinks, and a "Snowball," whose invitation card advertises "Dancing and Drugs" ("At midnight Chinese attendants will offer cocaine, heroin, veronal, morphine and leaf-opium on beautiful lacquered trays . . . At four o'clock in the morning a fleet of real ambulances will arrive, decorated with my racing colors, and will convey those who are by that time remotely portable to their homes").

Much of this is conventional middle-class resentment of the idea of young people enjoying themselves, and—more important—being seen to enjoy themselves in public. Simultaneously, many of these complaints are mirrored in the attitudes of more reflective Bright Young People, who combined an absolute determination to please themselves, to grasp whatever amenities happened to be available, with a growing awareness that the milieu in which they moved would turn out to be wholly destructive. Evelyn Waugh's first two novels, for example, written between 1927 and 1929, convey, to begin with, a deep-rooted fascination with "smart" metropolitan life, balanced and eventually overrun by a profound sense of disgust and futility, the whole characterized by the reader's awareness that Waugh is so bound up in the environment he surveys as fatally to compromise whatever judgments are being made. Significantly, these ambiguities—and their eventual resolution—are intimately connected to the progress of his marriage, and in particular the crisis into which it was plunged in the summer of 1929.

The Waughs' Mediterranean cruise had not been a success. Unwell when they set out, She-Evelyn fell seriously ill with a combination of pneumonia and pleurisy, had to be taken off the boat at Port Said and nearly died. Her recovery was slow, the trip correspondingly prolonged. By the time the couple arrived back in England in June, they were deeply in debt. He-Evelyn resolved to sequester himself in the country to write journalism and get on with the novel that was to become *Vile Bodies*, while his wife, wanting to make up for lost time, and in the company of suitable male chaperons, enjoyed herself in London. Before this separation they spent a week or two at Canonbury Square and, among other excursions, attended a dinner party given by Tom Balston, Anthony Powell's boss at Duckworth, who had published Waugh's biography of Rossetti and commissioned an account of the Mediterranean trip. Balston, a neurotic bachelor and no expert on human relationships, remarked to Powell that he thought the marriage, still less than a year old, was showing signs of strain. Powell, who knew all the parties involved, to the extent of being on holiday with one of them when the storm broke, left the most informed account of what subsequently took place. Among She-Evelyn's escorts on the London dance floors was John Heygate, an easygoing baronet's heir who worked as an announcer at the BBC. Both Heygate and She-Evelyn, together with Powell, were guests at a second dinner party given by Balston at the end of June. Powell and Heygate had attended the Watteau Party on the *Friendship* the night before: Powell remembered that Heygate, overcome with fatigue, went to sleep between courses. In the same week Powell and his friend the musician Constant Lambert threw a cocktail party at Powell's basement flat in Tavistock Square. The Waughs arrived separately; neither stayed long. On July 9, She-Evelyn informed her husband, by then back at his country hideaway in Beckley, that she was in love with Heygate. Powell, at this point still wholly ignorant of what had come to pass, was by then traveling in Germany with the third part of the triangle. At Munich, a week or so later, he received the immortal telegram INSTRUCT HEYGATE RETURN IMMEDIATELY WAUGH.

Strenuous efforts were made to save the marriage. The telegram turned out to have been sent in the middle of a fortnight's attempt at reconciliation. During this time the Evelyns were photographed—the male half looking distinctly uneasy—at the "Tropical Party" on board the *Friendship*, cohosted by Alec's friend Vyvyan Holland. ("The author of *Decline and Fall* looks somewhat scared, although there were no fierce Zulus on board," the *Bystander* noted.) Subsequently, She-Evelyn, ordered by her mother to Venice to think things over, returned to move herself and her belongings from Canonbury Square to Heygate's South Kensington flat. Waugh was devastated by the betrayal. "I did not know it was possible to be so miserable & live," he told Harold Acton. He was sustained by his friends, notably the Guinnesses, who invited him first to Pool Place, then to the family castle at Knockmaroon and finally to Paris. Here, at the Ritz, late in October, in the company of Bryan, Diana and Nancy, he celebrated his twenty-sixth birthday. Back in London his petition for divorce on the grounds of his wife's adultery was working its way through the courts. ("Well," She-Evelyn is supposed to have remarked, when the solicitor's letter arrived early in September, "you can't call life dull.")

The manuscript of *Vile Bodies*, meanwhile, perhaps a quarter of which had been written during Waugh's time at Beckley, had come to a grinding halt in mid-July. Then, in the more congenial company of the Guinnesses, he resumed work, conscious of the drawbacks of writing a supposedly comic novel in the aftermath of emotional breakdown. There may have been a short stay at the Spread Eagle at Thame, for an undated letter sent to John Fothergill at around this time from Waugh's parents' home in North End Road asks, "Could you let me have a room for a week or ten days from this Thursday? I want to try and write a book." Beneath his signature Waugh has written, "In case you have not read it I've a surprise to tell you now that my wife made a cuckold of me so I am living here." As for the writing itself, it had been "infinitely difficult," he told Henry Yorke. "It all seems to shrivel up & rot internally and I am relying on a sort of cumulative futility for any effect it may have." However, a first draft was finished before he set off on his Paris trip.

Several critics have noted the dramatic change of mood that sweeps over *Vile Bodies* at the beginning of its seventh chapter. This was the point at which Waugh broke off work to attend to the crisis in his domestic affairs. Within three pages of its resumption there is an aside about "cocktail parties given in basement flats by spotty announcers from the BBC"—a clear reference to Heygate's livelihood. For some time afterward Waugh referred to Heygate as "the basement boy." The upping of the tempo, from light comedy to something far more caustic, is undeniable and understandable, yet Waugh's change of direction in the two-year stretch that realized *Decline and Fall* and *Vile Bodies* is less marked than it seems. Substantially about the same people, exploring the same themes, reaching more or less the same conclusions, they differ only in their perspective. The Waugh who wrote *Decline and Fall* in the second half of 1927, shortly after giving up his inglorious career as a schoolteacher, viewed the smart metropolitan world of West End partygoing from its margins: Anthony Powell thought most of the background was picked up from gossip columns. The Waugh who began *Vile Bodies* in the early summer of 1929 and resumed it in the early autumn was an insider, using language and real-life models that he had listened to and observed at firsthand.

And like its successor, *Decline and Fall* has its own change of tack. This happens at the point where Paul Pennyfeather leaves Llanabba

Castle for the blandishments of Mrs. Beste-Chetwynde, by whom he is seduced and ultimately betrayed. Of each of the novel's three sections, in fact, only the opening part—a kind of pantomime burlesque of Waugh's time in Denbighshire—has any tethering in the realities of his life to date. Powell, significantly, thought that these opening chapters were some of the best his friend ever wrote. However detached Waugh may have been from the epicenter of the Bright Young People's world when he conceived it, the novel is still deeply indebted to their milieu. There are Captain Grimes's remarks about the war. Even more important, perhaps, is the sustained mockery of middle-class culture. As an undergraduate at "Scone College Oxford" prior to his humiliation at the hands of the Bollinger Club, Paul reads *The Forsyte Saga* before going to bed. A few pages later, drummed out of Oxford after losing his trousers at the hands of the Christ Church bloods, he hears his guardian's daughter's gramophone "playing Gilbert and Sullivan in her little pink boudoir at the top of the stairs." These are aesthetic marker flags, in which characters betray their inadequacy through the second-rateness of their cultural tastes. In much the same way, Jasper Fosdick in *From a View to a Death* offers to lend someone the family copy of J. B. Priestley's *The Good Companions*. The implication is clear: Jasper and his kind are hopeless middlebrow drones.

The Bright Young People themselves are first glimpsed at Mrs. Beste-Chetwynde's weekend party at King's Thursday: "The first to come were the Hon. Miles Malpractice and David Lennox, the photographer. They emerged with little shrieks from an Edwardian electric brougham and made straight for the nearest looking glass." "David Lennox," celebrated for a picture of the back of Mrs. Beste-Chetwynde's head, is clearly Cecil Beaton. The reference to "Miles Malpractice" and his Edwardian brougham suggests a nod toward Stephen Tennant, and Tennant made the identification himself. In fact, "Miles Malpractice" is a refinement of later editions. His original, cast aside after complaints, was "The Hon. Martin Gathorne-Brodie," a composite of three notoriously flamboyant ornaments of the scene, Martin Wilson, Eddie Gathorne-Hardy and Paddy Brodie. Certainly Miles's vocal style—when a game of cards is suggested on a Sunday night, he observes, "Wouldn't that be rather *fast?* It is Sunday. I think cards are divine, particularly the kings. Such *naughty* old faces. But if I start playing for money, I always lose my temper and cry"—seems closest to Gathorne-Hardy.

Cut from the same sexually ambiguous cloth is "Lord Parakeet," who arrives at King's Thursday in the small hours having "just escaped less than one second ago" from Alastair Digby-Vane-Trumpington's twenty-first birthday party: "Parakeet walked round bird-like and gay, pointing his thin white nose and making rude little jokes at everyone in turn in a shrill, emasculate voice." Again "Lord Parakeet" is a substitute. Early printings have "The Hon. Kevin Saunderson"—rather too close, as Waugh acknowledged, to its original, the Honorable Gavin Henderson, and altered after representations from mutual friends ("letter from Robert [Byron] *very* cross about Gavin Henderson and Kevin Saunderson," runs an entry in Waugh's diary from October 1928). The Bright Young People may be incidental to the staging of *Decline and Fall*— bizarre scene swellers brought in to amuse with their fluting dialogue— but they are unmistakably an element in the oppressive social forces at whose hands Paul receives such an unequivocal defeat. There is a significant moment in the novel's closing chapter when Paul, back at Scone College and completing his theological studies, is visited by Peter Pastmaster, Mrs. Beste-Chetwynd's son, in the aftermath of a Bollinger dinner: "You know, Paul," Pastmaster drunkenly pronounces, "I think it was a mistake you ever got mixed up with us; don't you? We're different somehow."

Vile Bodies preaches exactly the same lesson: the perils of involvement with people beyond one's own social and moral compass. In this case, though, the critic operating offstage is, in fact, Waugh himself. The complaints that he levels against the Bright Young People are essentially those leveled by every other disparager of the day: naïveté, callousness, insensitivity, insincerity, flippancy, a fundamental lack of seriousness and moral equilibrium that sours every relationship and endeavor they are involved in. What gives them their conviction is the sense of a world seen from within, whose chronicler, more to the point, is aware of his own proximity to its core. The novel's most famous passage, endlessly quoted in social histories of the 1920s, panoramically defines the scope of the Bright Young Person's world:

Masked parties, Savage parties, Victorian parties, Greek parties, Russian parties, Circus parties, parties where one had to dress as somebody else, almost naked parties in St. John's Wood, parties in flats and studios and houses and ships and hotels and night clubs, in windmills and swimming-baths, tea parties at school where one ate muffins and meringues and tinned crab, parties at Oxford where one drank brown sherry and smoked Turkish cigarettes, dull dances in London and comic dances in Scotland and disgusting dances in Paris—all the succession and repetition of massed humanity . . . Those vile bodies . . .

Like *Decline and Fall*, the novel comes crammed with projections of real-life acquaintances. The "Hon. Agatha Runcible, who protests of her ordeal at the hands of the Customs officials, 'My dear, I can't *tell* you the *things* that have been happening to me in there. The way they looked . . . too, too shaming. Positively surgical my dear, and *such* wicked old women, just like *Dowagers*, my dear,'" can be readily identified with Elizabeth Ponsonby. Equally clearly, "Johnnie Hoop," admired for his highbrow party invitations ("'Wasn't the invitation clever? Johnnie Hoop wrote it.' 'Well, yes, I suppose it was. And you know, was it dreadful of me, I hadn't heard of any of the names'"), is Brian Howard. "Miles Malpractice" ("Darling, your face—eau de Nil") again seems closest to the mannerisms of Eddie Gathorne-Hardy. The encounter of the "Marquess of Vanbrugh" with his fellow gossip writer "Lord Balcairn" at a high-profile social event is Waugh poking fun at Viscount Castlerosse and the Honorable Patrick Balfour, the *Daily Sketch*'s "Mr. Gossip." *Vile Bodies* is full of these private jokes, glimpses of linguistic plumage interpretable only by a tiny handful of readers ("Miss Runcible said that kippers were not very drunk-making and that the whole club seemed bogus to her"), tongue-in-cheek references in some cases put there to amuse an audience of two, the book's dedicatees.*

---

* *Bright Young People in-jokes recur in Waugh's 1930s novels. On Tony Last's first meeting with the explorer Dr. Messenger in* A Handful of Dust, *Messenger asks if he knows "a Nicaraguan calling himself alternately Ponsonby and Fitzclarence" who has just robbed him of £200 and some machine guns.*

Thus Waugh remarks of one party: "The real aristocracy, the younger members of the two or three great brewing families which rule London, had done nothing about it. They had come on from a dance and stood in a little group by themselves, aloof, amused, but not amusing." This conveys very well the gulf that existed between the Guinnesses and the Bright Young People's more raffish bohemian fringe. Again, like *Decline and Fall*, the novel advertises a smart, upper-class and essentially metropolitan society next to which all other social groups and locations are irretrievably jejune. When Adam, Nina and Ginger are invited to a party held on board an airship, the exodus from known haunts immediately dampens the collective spirit: "The long drive in Ginger's car to the degraded suburb where the airship was moored

chilled and depressed them." In one of the funniest scenes, demure and impressionable Miss Brown invites a gang of partygoers back to her parents' house for a late-night shindig ("To think that all these brilliant people, whom she had heard so much about, with what envy, from Miss Mouse, should be here in papa's dining room calling her 'my dear' and 'darling'"). Chez Brown, it turns out, is 10 Downing Street, whose inhabitants read of the night's events ("The brightest party the Bright Young People have yet given") in the morning paper over their breakfast table. Significantly, the Browns are represented as thoroughly middle-class, their son working in a motor shop to which he "had had to get off early," the children enjoined to talk to their prime ministerial father at breakfast time. ("He was quite hurt yesterday. He feels out of things. It's so easy to bring him into the conversation if you take a little trouble . . .")

Here, you feel, Waugh is rather on the Bright Young People's side. He aspires to a smart metropolitan life from whose vantage point the idea of anyone working in the motor trade is deeply funny. When the novel, rather unexpectedly, acquires a moral focus it does so by commenting—however obliquely—on standard Bright Young People's attitudes such as indifference to the war or dislike of "conventional" society. At one point, for example, Adam sets off to extract a check from Nina's father. The date is November 11: "It was Armistice Day and they were selling artificial poppies in the street. As he reached the station it struck eleven and for two minutes all over the country everyone was quiet and serious. Then he went to Aylesbury, reading on the way Balcairn's account of Archie Schwert's party." After a day spent in a modern version of *Alice's Adventures in Wonderland*, Adam returns to London at the point when the legion of commuters are boarding their trains: "They were still wearing their poppies." The contrast with flippant, rootless Adam, anxious to wheedle money out of his bride-to-be's father so that they can afford to conduct a relationship which neither of them takes with the least seriousness, is rather obvious.

Striking much the same note is a long passage in which Waugh describes a party given by Lady Anchorage at Anchorage House. As his account of the guests makes clear, this is an entertainment at which no self-respecting Bright Young Person would be seen dead:

a great concourse of pious and honorable people (many of whom made the Anchorage House reception the one outing of the year), their women-folk well gowned in rich and durable stuffs, their men-folk ablaze with orders; people who had represented their country in foreign places and sent their sons to die for her in battle, people of decent and temperate life, uncultured, unaffected, unembarrassed, unassuming, unambitious people, of independent judgment and marked eccentricities, kind people who cared for animals and the deserving poor, brave and rather unreasonable people, that fine phalanx of the passing order, approaching, as one day at the Last Trump they hoped to meet their Maker, with decorous and frank cordiality to shake Lady Anchorage by the hand at the top of her staircase.

Lady Circumference, another veteran of *Decline and Fall*, sees all this and "sniffed the exhalation of her own herd," shaking her head at Mrs. Hoop's inquiry: has she "seen the ghosts"? Johnnie's mother, on the other hand, ascends the staircase "step by step in a confused but very glorious dream of eighteenth-century elegance."

In an essay on Waugh, left unfinished at his death, George Orwell defines this as an "irrelevant outburst" in favor of people who still harbor a sense of obligation and fixed standards of behavior. "The note of affection and esteem, out of tune with most of the rest of the book, is unmistakable," Orwell concludes; the Bright Young People are damned by their exclusion from it. The same oddly sympathetic gaze can be found trained on another social category: ordinary middle-class people caught up in the generational war. *Vile Bodies* is full of mock-serious pronouncements on "The Topic of the Younger Generation." Many of them are formulated at Lady Anchorage's party. Here Lord Metroland remarks, "I don't understand them, and I don't want to. They had a chance after the war that no generation has ever had. There was a whole civilization to be saved and remade—and all they seem to do is to play the fool." The intriguing Jesuit Father Rothschild, on the other hand, canvasses the idea of "an almost fatal hunger for permanence" among the young. Neither of these statements, you suspect, should be taken at all seriously. Much more pointed, and again much less relevant to the storyline, is a page or two of reportage in which Adam sits in a railway carriage listening to a pair of middle-class housewives, "and they, too, were talking about the Younger Generation." One of the women complains that her son won't settle to his job, gets on badly with his father, has undesirable friends and won't show any interest in the nice girl his mother wants him to marry. The other worries about her manicurist daughter, who has taken up with a man old enough to be her father, "and, anyway, I *hope* there's no harm in it . . ." Played absolutely straight, and no doubt deriving from an exchange that the author himself had overheard in similar circumstances, this seems to show Waugh sympathizing with another social group forced to deal with a collapse in traditional values, of which the Bright Young People were an all-too-conspicuous symbol.

The short-lived union between Adam and Nina in *Vile Bodies* founders on the rock of Nina's infidelity. The implications, though, run deeper than this. Waugh's fundamental point is that the world of the Bright Young People, its incessant partygoing, late-night carousings and high-speed excursions to nowhere in particular, was calculated to undermine any settled relationship, or, rather, that a settled relationship was impossible to achieve within its orbit. Meanwhile, two other young people, both of whom would have read the novel with great interest, were experiencing their first few months of married life. Elizabeth and Denis made several visits to Shulbrede in the second half of 1929. On each occasion the elder Ponsonbys were favorably impressed. "E and Denis to tea," Arthur noted in mid-July. "Both very well, she looking charming and both touchingly affectionate." Arthur was convinced that marriage had brought a marked improvement in his daughter's character. Recording another visit, made a fortnight later, he claimed to have noticed "three or four notable moments of restraint, consideration and kindness on her part. This is what I lay awake thinking of now in place of the old dark thoughts. It is wonderful." There were plans for the Pellys to move out of Smith Street into their own small house or flat, with attendance to be provided by Nelly, the family's faithful domestic. Another advantage of having Nelly on whichever premises to which the couple might relocate was, as Dolly's diary tacitly admits, her willingness to supply details of Denis and Elizabeth's social life.

It was a quiet autumn. The various Bright Young People who had combined to stage the Bruno Hat exhibition were now dispersed across Europe. The Guinnesses were away in Ireland and then in Paris. Waugh was finishing his novel. Brian Howard and John Banting had retreated to La Napoule in the south of France, ostensibly to work. It was not until the end of October that *The Lady* could announce that "Bright Young People parties have begun." There was only one certainty about them, "Johanna" declared: "As a rule you can sit down beforehand and make a list of practically everyone you are likely to meet, and, as far as Miss Olivia Wyndham's party of last week was concerned, I could have written before the event, for I knew that, as people were invited to come 'as you would like to be,' most of the women would dress as men or boys and many of the men arrive in feminine attire." The guests included Brenda's younger brother Brian and Sir Francis Laking. The hostess "wore one of her favorite sailor-suits, and so did Mrs. Denis Pelly, whose husband wore the acrobat's costume in which he came to the famous circus party."

The Pellys were at this point about to relocate from Smith Street to a flat in Sussex Place. Late in October, Dolly accompanied Nelly there in a taxi with the last of Elizabeth's things. She thought the flat too small to be convenient, but approved the drawing room with its cream varnished walls, "her nice china & glass and comfortable chairs." However, Dolly's intelligence network had turned up some disquieting information. On the day after her visit to Sussex Place, a family friend, John Strachey, came to lunch to recount his exploits at a party given by one of Elizabeth and Denis's set, which sounds very like the "as you would like to be" event. At any rate, Dolly found the details deeply distressing:

He said he had never seen so much drink consumed in his life— that every woman was painted & most of the men—especially a young boy Hugh Wade (I have heard of him from E) who had a painted luscious mouth. He never saw such a "naughty boy" or so many "naughty boys" or so many people drunk. They carried on till 4.

Eventually Dolly found herself locked in an argument over the cause of these excesses. Disagreeing with her suggestion that "you could have quite good parties without being drunk," Strachey put the blame on Joynson-Hicks: "it was all the taboos and restrictions that the older generation had put on the young that made them act as they do." Reflecting on the example of the Plunket Greene children, who had never had the slightest restriction put on them, Dolly thought this absurd. But she was also inclined to reproach herself. "The sad fact is that it is my children who take him to these parties," she mused, "& who have introduced him to paint & make-up—which he now says he prefers to people not made up." What depressed her most, alternatively, was the inescapable fact that Elizabeth and Denis were "going on exactly as they always did." Denis in particular, the faithful Nelly confirmed, habitually stayed up drinking until four in the morning: "Consequently he looks ghastly." Dolly suspected ennui: "It is a good deal that they are bored with Life & feel sapped—drink rouses them & makes them feel cheerful once more. Their talk is mostly noise & laughter—& the more noise they make the more successful they feel it is."

Dolly's diaries from late 1929 have another subtext. Compared to the company the Pellys had kept before their marriage, they were now moving in somewhat loucher circles. This preference for seedier acquaintances than those entertained at, say, Buckingham Street would set them apart from the Bright Young People's upper echelons. The young Guinnesses enjoyed the society of bohemian artists and well-connected homosexuals, but they would probably have balked at entertaining Hugh Wade, an epicene young man who earned his living playing the piano at the Blue Lantern in Ham Yard. There was also the problem of squaring this relentless social life with the humbler obligations of paid employment. The first indication that affable, easygoing Denis might be lurching toward disaster came at the end of November, when Arthur received an urgent message from Vaughan Nash, who had got Denis his job six months before: "Serious irregularities have occurred in the accounts of County Industries and Denis is suspected." Arthur hurried round to see his daughter and son-in-law and found the former "in a state of splendid fury at Denis's being accused of all this." Anguished yet circumspect, Arthur tried to balance the glaring discrepancies in County Industries' petty cash with what he knew of Denis's character. Denis was "casual, happy go lucky and too easy but I do not yet believe he is dishonest." Believing the company's accounting systems to be unsatisfactory and the irregularities the result of structural flaws rather than fraud, Arthur advised him to "fight every inch."

Vaughan Nash had been commissioned to investigate the case. Arthur looked anxiously on. As ever, his distinguished parliamentary career proceeded alongside. Ramsay Macdonald's suggestion, eventually accepted, that he should exchange his Sheffield constituency for a seat in the House of Lords can have brought scant consolation. Early in December Nash presented his report. The findings were unambiguous. "Denis has been guilty of culpable negligence and irregularities amounting to dishonesty," Arthur lamented. "He has been habitually taking money from the petty cash. He is dismissed . . . What on earth can we do with him? Poor unfortunate E." Starkly aware that had Nash not been involved, the outcome would have been a court case and imprisonment, Lord Ponsonby of Shulbrede, as he was about to be gazetted, tried to put a faint, mitigating gloss on this disaster. "It is not intentional and conscious calculated dishonesty," he maintained. "It is a sloppy casual irresponsible view which he inherits from an impossible mother."

What was to be done? Arthur spent the rest of December balancing his ministerial responsibilities with an attempt to bring some kind of order to the mounting chaos of Denis and Elizabeth's life. Not only did the sense of personal responsibility weigh him down, what irked him even more was their complete refusal, as he saw it, to confront the realities of the mess in which they found themselves. A diary entry from mid-December confirms the absolute stranglehold which Elizabeth's failings now held on his life:

Elizabeth and Denis's affairs must necessarily darken everything and oppress us although it seems to have very little effect on them as we hear of them going about much as usual. I cannot see any way out at the moment. E wont [*sic*] face the facts or make any sacrifice. They will gradually drain us. The House of Lords luckily acts as comic relief to ease the tension.

The disillusioned father who mused over the past year's glut of diary entries in the first days of 1930 would have been disagreeably conscious of the gap between his glittering hopes and their drab fulfilment. A few months before, as preparations for the wedding gathered pace, he had fancied himself reconciled to his wayward daughter, gratified that she seemed to be making something of her life in partnership with a man she loved. Now her only distinction was her notoriety: "famous," he miserably concluded, "for her extravagant pranks in a wastrel society."

ON THE MARGIN: INEZ

Even more than Beaton's photo of the Wilsford fête champêtre, the group portrait taken outside Captain Neil McEachran's house in Brook Street in July 1927 in the wake of the Impersonation Party is a kind of Bright Young People's symposium. Here, dazzlingly arrayed, are the scene's long-term ornaments and conductors (Stephen, Cecil, Elizabeth), their proud attendants (Harold Acton, Georgia Sitwell), exotic passage migrants such as Tallulah Bankhead, resplendent as Jean Borotra, the tennis player. In the very middle of the throng sits a small, gamine and rather fragile-looking girl with a quizzical expression on her face: Inez Holden.

Several of Anthony Powell's recollections of his hot twenties youth take in girls, glimpsed in or around the Bright Young People's world, who existed, as he put it, "on the margin," snatching precarious livings from a variety of sources. These included handouts from men, whose relationships with them could vary from taking a friendly interest to more or less "keeping" them. Girls of this sort belonged to no obvious social category. They ranged from upmarket shop assistants who made a little money by modeling on the side to penurious gentlewomen scratching a few shillings a week out of society journalism while also including fully fledged "adventuresses" in the Doris Delavigne mold over whose background, income and emoluments lay a permanent blanket of fog. No one, not even her closer friends, could say with any certainty to which of these categories Inez Holden may have belonged. Both Waugh and Powell met her for the first time in the summer of 1927, Waugh in the offices of the *Daily Express*, where she was briefly employed, shortly before he himself was sacked; Powell in Waugh's company on the way to lunch at the Gargoyle.

Immensely pretty in the approved twenties style, an accomplished mimic and torrential talker, Inez was also a wholly mysterious figure. The hard-up daughter of an equally hard-up cavalry officer, she lived, as Powell phrases it, "fairly dangerously in a rich world of a distinctly older generation." Looking back on her time at the *Express*, she recalled that "there was a period in my life when I knew only millionaires . . . They were always asking me to arrange for them to buy the paper for a halfpenny instead of a penny." This makes her sound like the *poule de luxe* of the St. John's Wood villa and the rich man's checkbook. Powell wasn't sure. There was no way of knowing, he decided, what physical shape, if any, these shadowy relationships took.

Still more mystery hung over Inez's elevation to the world of light literature. In 1929, Duckworth, ever reliable sponsors of the Bright Young author, published her first novel, *Sweet Charlatan*, but it was no doing of Powell's ("unconvinced of its merits") or Waugh's. In fact, Inez had come across Duckworth's junior partner, Thomas Balston, somewhere and brought pressure to bear of a kind to which this unmarried and somewhat nervous middle-aged man was altogether unused. According to Powell, an interested observer, "she made hay of him." Duckworth published a second, much better, novel, *Born Old, Died Young*, two years later.

All this has a resonant echo in Powell's own fiction. *What's Become of Waring* (1939), his fifth novel, is an elaborate projection of Powell's time at Duckworth a decade before, turning on the career of T. T. Waring, a best-selling yet enigmatic travel writer whose death sparks off a quest to establish his true identity. Duckworth is reinvented as the firm of Judkins & Judkins, whose senior and junior partner, Bernard and Hugh Judkins, bear striking resemblances to Balston and his superior Gerald Duckworth. Yet the roman à clef element goes further than this. *Waring*'s female lead, Roberta Payne, who among other accomplishments is T. T.'s former fiancée, is clearly based on Inez: "The little articles she wrote were often amusing, but they could not possibly have kept her alive. She was usually so well housed and dressed that it was generally supposed that obscure rich men, too dull to be allowed to appear, contributed something to her upkeep."

Like her real-life equivalent, Roberta makes hay of Hugh Judkins, persuading him to publish a collection of her newspaper journalism ("Hugh knew as well as I did that a book of Roberta's collected newspaper articles would not sell a dozen copies") and being escorted by him on a Scandinavian cruise, from which Judkins returns in a state of nervous collapse. "Roberta was a charming creature," the novel's anonymous narrator concludes, "though you could rarely believe all she told you."

CHAPTER SEVEN

SUCCESS AND FAILURE: TWO PORTRAITS

It is no *good* trying to make me a journalist. I would rather kill myself. Fortunately, I am the kind of writer who will make money.

— BRIAN HOWARD, letter to his mother, 1930

Success will come.

— from the same letter

The Bright Young People phenomenon offered almost limitless opportunities for social and professional advancement. In nearly every line of sophisticated employment—the arts, upmarket interior decorating, the fledgling BBC—influential sponsors stood by, happy to pipe the specimen Bright Young Person on board. Everywhere one looked, it seemed—in newspaper gossip columns, in publishers' offices, in the anterooms of great hostesses—there were other Bright Young People to hand, ready to wave the neophyte on his way with an approving paragraph, a contract or an invitation. In an environment where the younger generation was news merely for being itself, Bright Young writers and artists broke into print and onto gallery walls with almost indecent haste. Evelyn Waugh and Harold Acton published their first novels at the age of twenty-four (Acton had already brought out two collections of poetry before he left Oxford). Henry Green's *Blindness* appeared in sight of its author's twenty-first birthday. Anthony Powell published his first novel—literally, as it was brought out by Duckworth, where he worked—at twenty-five. Publishing *Highland Fling* in 1931 at the advanced age of twenty-six, Nancy Mitford would have considered herself a late starter, darkly aware that most of her Bright Young compatriots were several yards down the track.

Elsewhere in the arts, Ed Burra staged his first exhibition, at the Leicester Galleries—"Mr. Burra's pictures created a distinctly favorable impression," the *Tatler* enthused—a month or two after his twentieth birthday; Constant Lambert and William Walton had begun to make names for themselves as, respectively, composer and arranger when scarcely out of their teens. Not since the days of the Romantic poets, it seemed, had upper-brow arts-world employment been so hospitable to anyone under thirty. All one needed, Bright Young contemporaries lined up to affirm, was talent, application and enthusiasm. Failing this it was possible—as the careers of several Bright Young People roundly demonstrated—to get by on sheer persistence.

By the standards of the day, both Robert Byron and Brian Howard were uniquely placed to exploit this set of circumstances. The links between them were not only generational—they were born within a few weeks of each other in the spring of 1905—and professional (each fancied himself a writer from a very early age), they were also personal. By the late 1920s each had known the other for nearly half his life: at Eton, where they had both been members of the legendary Eton Society of the Arts; again at Oxford; finally in their admittedly very different post-university careers.

Socially—to start with fundamentals—neither conformed to the standard upper-class Etonian pattern. Howard's background was mysterious, three-quarters American, wholly exotic. Byron, like Anthony Powell, was the son of middle-class parents who thought the £300 a year required to send a boy to Eton a sound investment. As if to confirm this detachment from conventional patterns of behavior, both were flamboyant homosexuals. Their distinctiveness as personalities, both at Oxford and in the world after it, undoubtedly had something to do with sexual orientation, while moving several stages beyond it. Much of this separateness was physical—Howard tall, pale, with dark, receding hair; Byron of medium height, plump, with waxy skin and popping blue eyes—but at least as great a part was temperamental. Even the world-

lier Oxford undergraduates of the mid-1920s thought Howard an extraordinary figure: sophisticated, knowledgeable, aloof. Maurice Richardson
remembered a first sighting in Oxford High Street in the autumn of
1925: "He looked so tall and distinguished with his huge brown eyes and
long lashes, I thought he must be foreign. He was smoking an exceptionally fat Turkish cigarette. Two black Spaniel puppies were padding along
at his heels."

Trying to come to grips with Byron's character several decades after
his early death, Anthony Powell diagnosed a mid-Victorian throwback,
furious and uncompromising, his path through life characterized by "an
absolute determination to stop at nothing." Certainly neither Byron nor
Howard cared in the least for the sensitivities of the people they rubbed
against, worried about giving offense or thought it necessary to adopt a
conciliatory tone. Howard's twenties career, in particular, is a riot of malicious practical jokes, no-holds-barred verbal assaults on conversation-
alists who were manifestly not up to his fighting weight, a kind of
terminal faroucheness that stretched the Bright Young People's trademark tolerance of eccentricity to its limit. Even Stephen Tennant, cut
from the same aesthetic pattern, complained to his friend Edith Oliver
that Brian was "notorious and *not liked.*"

Quick-witted, sharp-tongued and rebarbative, the pair were also
intensely ambitious. Ominously, Byron was the more focused of the
two, already launched in his early twenties on the architectural-cum-
anthropological inquiries that formed the subject matter of his early books;
Howard was content to work leisurely at his poems, confident of a "genius" that he preferred to "mature slowly." Each, too, had already lined
up an impressive gallery of Bright Young sponsors keen to offer advice,
introductions and publicity. Byron's letters from the late 1920s are full of
references to well-placed wire pullers: Patrick Balfour, whose first major
appointment was celebrated in a note to his mother ("Patrick has now
got the *Daily Sketch* gossip and £1,100 a year for doing it!"), Beverley
Nichols, whom he consulted about transatlantic publicity in Nichols's
brief period at the *American Sketch*. Howard, too, knew exactly how to
make the world of the 1920s gossip column work to his advantage, featuring constantly in the pages of the *Tatler* and *Bystander* and getting

his friend Lady Eleanor Smith to cover events in which he had a particular interest in her column in the *Weekly Dispatch*. Above all, given the
penury to which they were occasionally reduced, each had wealthy
friends ready to offer material support. Byron's early trips around the
Near East were substantially underwritten by Old Etonian *convives*;
Howard, who survived on handouts from his mother, frequently found
himself relying on the patronage of his friend Eddie Gathorne-Hardy.

All these were substantial advantages. Many an aspiring writer from
the age of Stanley Baldwin and Ramsay Macdonald got by on markedly
less money, influence and connection. They were underscored by a genuine mutual esteem, the result, it seems fair to say, of each party examining the other and finding in him something that he either detected in
himself and responded to, or lacked and regretted. Byron had only been
desultorily aware of Howard's presence at Oxford. Launched on his
metropolitan career, he found himself telling Henry Yorke, "It is perhaps curious to you but I must say that throughout my sojourn in London, I have found Brian intellectually far the most sympathetic person.
He does not sneer when one is serious." There were disagreements over
religion—"I have a God and you do not," Byron told his new friend—
but a united front over what Byron termed their "instinct for the vital."
Come 1927 this unanimity of purpose looked as if it might bear serious
fruit, with a project that—on paper, at any rate—had the potential to
become one of the great Bright Young endeavors of the era. This was
a book—strictly speaking, a symposium—titled *Values* or possibly
Value, which Brian and Robert would edit and use as a showcase for the
talents of their Oxford generation. Though entirely serious in conception—"Value," as defined by the editors, stood for "the pursuit of the
real" or "that essence of true satisfaction" which is humankind's goal—
the material advantages of the project loomed large in both editorial
minds. According to Byron, "Its primary intent is to convert literary as-
piration into income. It is a form of literary advertising, and as such best
undertaken on a cooperative basis."

To this end, the most elaborate plans and outlines were discussed
throughout the latter part of 1927. Robert and Brian were to provide
the "prefatory affirmations." Other contributions, divided into three

sections, "Material," "Transcendental" and "Aesthetic," would include a short story by Henry Green ("The Factory"), a poem by Tom Driberg ("Restaurant") and a drawing of God by Evelyn Waugh consisting entirely of abstract form "yet in some measure coherent and having perhaps some slight relation to the Revelations of St. John the Divine." There were also plans for a photographic still life, its paraphernalia to be assembled by the editors, representing "the Impression recorded by the term 'World' on the mind of an English bourgeois." Thus framed, *Values* sounds like an exceptionally upmarket undergraduate magazine—indeed, most of those involved were only a year or two out of university—yet there was sufficient interest from Chapman and Hall to prompt the dispatch of synopses to potential contributors. All that remains, however, is Robert's hypothetical contents list and a page or so of Brian's thoughts on the nonexistence of truth. Given that when Byron wanted a thing done, he generally achieved it, what went wrong? Why did the book not appear, on the same publisher's list as *Decline and Fall*, in the autumn of 1928? The answer lies in the chronic inanition of the second editor: an inability to engage himself with the business of life which, in the end, realized a career that existed largely in the subjunctive.

Robert Byron's parents—remote connections of the poet—set up home in 1903 on £150 a year and the proceeds of an engineering practice. There were "expectations," in the shape of a wealthy grandparent, but in the end the old gentleman opted to divide his fortune among the family as a whole. With his Eton and Oxford education, the milieu in which their son operated was not unlike that of Anthony Powell, involving grand friends and grander affiliations but at its economic level unrepentantly middle-class. The intimate of such Etonian grandees as Lord Clonmore, later the eighth Earl of Wicklow, and Michael Rosse, Byron was eternally conscious that he had his own way to make in the world. Even at nineteen he could be found telling his mother, in response to an inquiry about job prospects, "*I* think the *Daily Mail*. My object is not to make a success as a writer for the next five years—or try to—but to adopt that form of journalism which will give me most experience and

make me travel." Like Howard—another eerie parallel—Byron vener-
ated his mother ("The Mum's boy to end all Mum's boys," Anthony
Powell thought) while ignoring his nonintellectual father. Both parents
were happy to entertain their son's friends at Savernake Lodge, the family house in the Wiltshire forests bought with Grandpa Byron's legacy.
Convenient for the Guinnesses' country home at Biddesden and within
striking distance of such London-based friends as the Yorkes, this later
became an out-of-town Bright Young People's retreat to rank with
Cullen Castle or the Mitford residence at Swinbrook, Oxfordshire.

At Oxford Byron was known for his ardent neo-Victorianism, a university craze whose manifestations encompassed everything from
Harold Acton's luxuriant side-whiskers to an attempt to stage a period
ballet in which Robert would assume the role of Queen Victoria. Anthony Powell left a vivid account of him seated at the rickety piano of
the Hypocrites Club, loudly intoning Victorian ballads of the most vis-
cid sentimentality.

> Rose a nurse of ninety years
> Set his child upon her knee —
> (*f*) Like summer tempests came her tears—
>   (*fff*) Like summer tempests came her tears
> —(*ppp*) "Sweet my child, I live for thee."

Down from Oxford with a third in modern history in the summer of
1925, his notebook already bulging with literary schemes, Byron immediately set off on a jaunt around Europe with his friends Alfred Duggan
and Gavin Henderson, rich young men (Duggan was the stepson of the
Marquess of Curzon, Henderson the heir to his grandfather, Lord Faringdon) who would effectively subsidize the excursion and whose preference for staying in grand hotels soon exhausted the £60 that Byron
had raised for the trip. The tour, accomplished in Henderson's car, took
in Hamburg, Berlin, Salzburg, Italy and Constantinople and a visit to
Athens, where the trio linked up with Henderson's old friend Leonard
Bower, honorary attaché at the British embassy and a long-term attendant on the Bright Young People's scene.

Having accumulated sufficient material for a travel book, Byron returned to Oxford intending to occupy the extra term's residence that would allow him to obtain his degree by editing the *Cherwell*, the undergraduate newspaper, and promoting himself to potential employers. Hauled up before the proctors for the ninth time after he and Henry Yorke had harangued from the window of the Liberal Club a mob of undergraduates assembled in the Cornmarket on Guy Fawkes night, he was ordered to leave the university directly the term had ended. By January 1926 he was in London, living in rooms at Montagu Street and, as he had promised his mother a year before, working as a trainee reporter on the *Mail*. The distinguishing feature of Byron's trajectory at this, and indeed at every other, stage of his career was its hardheadedness. Keen on smart social life and with Henderson, now working at the Mayfair decorators Turner, Lord & Co., on hand to support him, he continued to combine the generally frivolous demands of his day job with after-hours labor on what was to become *Europe in the Looking Glass*. The *Mail*, for whose benefit he divulged the recipe of the Yolanda cocktail presented to him by M. Aletto of the Ritz, and reported on the wildfire spread of the Charleston, eventually sacked him at the end of February. Simultaneously, *Europe in the Looking Glass* was accepted by Routledge. He had just turned twenty-one.

The book would not be published until the autumn, but by now the patterns of Byron's twenties career were in place: hard work, extensive foreign travel and high-powered socializing, each of them sustained and encouraged by a range of contacts in the Bright Young People's world. Needing the money to fund further researches in Greece, for example, he applied to Miss Todd, the editor of *Vogue*, using Elizabeth Ponsonby—whose brother, Matthew, he had known at Oxford—as a go-between. The book, inspired by this second journey to the Near East which culminated in a trip to Mount Athos, would be published by Duckworth, where Anthony Powell was now installed. Each step in Byron's path, in fact, seemed to benefit from these affiliations. Back in England in the autumn of 1926 he set off with Henderson to stay with Nina Seafield at Cullen, where, deprived of the traditional amenities of the West End, guests re-created the atmosphere of the cocktail hour by drinking martinis from gigantic wineglasses. Returned to London and another set of rooms in Montagu Street, he oversaw publication of *Europe in the Looking Glass*—there was an approving review from Patrick Balfour, then working on the *Glasgow Herald*—and was introduced to the Blackbirds, whose art, he believed, "throbbed to the savage beat of the dark continent." The spring and summer of 1927 found him firmly ensconced in the upper reaches of the Bright Young world, holidaying with Michael Rosse at his seat at Birr Castle in Ireland before returning to a round of partygoing: the Impersonation Party; the Sailor Party, where Lytton Strachey came as an admiral; an Episcopal Party, where everyone dressed as a bishop; and a gathering involving "some new variation on the theme of the pirate king."

Byron's was an original if idiosyncratic mind: among several self-conscious quirks, he disliked Shakespeare and pronounced *Hamlet* an "emotional hoax." In the context of the middle-class young men on the make in whom twenties London abounded, he is a pattern demonstration of his circle's ability to combine a thoroughgoing seriousness in one's intellectual pursuits with an incurably frivolous social life. In Byron's case this meant cultivating a reputation as a Byzantinist—his next book for Routledge would be a scholarly compendium titled *The Byzantine Achievement*—while simultaneously impersonating Queen Victoria at drunken parties attended by some of the silliest people in London. Undoubtedly, Byron saw no incongruity in these juxtapositions. His friends, after all, were his friends. The homosexual circles in which he moved, despite the regrets of such fervent admirers as Nancy Mitford, were louche to a degree. What separated him, on the other hand, from the majority of the people he came up against was a sense of resolve that was as much moral as personal. He believed in good causes, rights and wrongs, battles that ought to be fought. With his incessant traveling through Europe and his sharp eye for detail, he was capable of grasping the implications of developments in Continental politics long before they occurred to his friends. In Wiener Neustadt in October 1928, for example, he witnessed rival demonstrations by social democrats and fascists in which thousands of troops had been mobilized to prevent trouble. Inspecting the market square, Byron saw "a tremendous procession in the Ring with banners blazoned 'Heil Hitler.'"

The anti-Nazism which occupied him increasingly during the 1930s was at this point years ahead of its time. Alert to the currents of national and international politics, he was also notably shrewd about people. Watching the spectacle of his friend Bryan Guinness "frantic with love" for Diana Mitford, he noted:

> As a matter of fact, I think Diana Mitford is particularly charming, very pretty & amusing in a way which one seldom meets & which is not at all that of the ordinary debutante trying to charm . . . The truth of it all is of course that Bryan is still monstrously young . . . What he little knows is that he has fallen in love with a girl who will soon be much older than he can be.

In the light of Diana's later adventures, this is uncannily prophetic. At the Guinness wedding in January 1929 he figured as chief usher. Patrick Balfour informed readers of the *Daily Sketch* that "Mr. Byron has designed an original wedding present . . . It is a book plate and bears the legend 'Stolen from Bryan and Diana Guinness.'"

All this made Byron a considerable figure, never to be discounted in any list of Bright Young achievements and eccentricities. *The Station*, his account of the Athos trip, attracted a chorus of praise on publication in July 1928. D. H. Lawrence's review in *Vogue* began: "Athos is an old place, and Mr. Byron is a young man. The combination for once is *really* happy." But the constant references in Balfour's column to "Mr. Robert Byron, the clever young writer and authority on all things Byzantine" had their downside. Like many another Bright Young Person with artistic aspirations, the baggage of his social life was always liable to spill over into consideration of his "serious" work, to the point where the latter would seem to be compromised by the former. *The Byzantine Achievement*, published four weeks after Byron's twenty-fourth birthday, was widely and favorably reviewed, yet his last sustained appearance in print had been as the best man at Elizabeth Ponsonby's mock wedding party. If Byron saw no contradiction between the Ritz bar and the Byzantine study, serious-minded friends had their doubts. Henry Yorke's disapproval—possibly the source of their disintegrating friendship—focused on Byron's "vulgarity." Ominously enough, these complaints extended to the literary work. Byron's mild criticisms of the proposed title of Yorke's new novel, *Living* (1929), produced a furious spat. "I didn't really see as you had told me so often how disgusting you thought 'The Station' & how even more disgusting, shoddy in fact its contents—I didn't see why I might not say I preferred one of yr titles to the other," Byron protested with an altogether uncharacteristic meekness. "I didn't think that would offend." Yorke naturally had his own affiliations in "arty high life": at the same time his books remained in a separate part of his existence, far away from the social circles in which he trod. Byron, much less well-off and far more socially inclined, could never make this separation.

On the other hand, the opportunities available to him in 1929, as the Bright Young People's collective star reached its zenith, showed just how far he had come in the four short years since he had left Oxford. In April he stayed with Balfour in Yeoman's Row, teaming up with Mark Ogilvie-Grant, who did the illustrations, to produce light social pieces for *Vogue*. Come the summer, Gavin Henderson, now living in Calcutta, proposed a joint excursion to Sikkim in the Himalayas. Once again, subsidy was required for the outward journey. Once again, highly placed friends came good, in the shape of Daphne Weymouth, who introduced him to Lord Beaverbrook. Happily, the proprietor of the *Daily Express* was about to launch a campaign in support of Empire free trade. The paper agreed to pay for his air ticket to Karachi—£126—in return for articles describing the flight. On July 27, shortly after Henry Yorke's wedding, Byron left England for the East.

Byron's was an exceptional case. There were other Bright Young People, equally well connected and ambitious, whose careers proved much less amenable to this kind of management.

Not long before his death, in the spring of 1966, Evelyn Waugh doubtfully inquired of Nancy Mitford if she knew of "a Mrs. Lancaster, who gives you as reference in soliciting help in writing a treatise on Brian Howard." Intrigued by the project ("I can't believe he will be the subject of many biographies"), Waugh was also anxious that a man with whom he had enjoyed deeply equivocal relations should be given his due. "It would be a pity," he pronounced, "if some hack who didn't know him or see his point should take him in hand." Calmed by Nancy's assurances, Waugh suggested to Mrs. Lancaster that she make use of the brief details supplied in his own recently published autobiography, *A Little Learning*. Mrs. Lancaster's *Portrait of a Failure*, which eventually became a compendium by many hands rather than a standard biography, consequently reproduces Waugh's somewhat lapidary judgment. Significantly, the person to whom Howard is immediately compared is Byron. "At the age of nineteen he had dash and insolence, a gift of invective and repartee far more brilliant than Robert's . . . Mad, bad and dangerous to know."

Brian Howard's was a chaotic, frustrating and, in the end, for all its high-octane attachments, rather solitary life. Lived out for the most part in that exotic never-never land where the Ritz bar meets the out-of-season Continental resort, it was also hedged about with a disappointment of which its subject remained defiantly aware. Launched into the world as a precocious teenage poet, his only lasting achievement was the coeditorship of a glorified school magazine. Expected, not least by himself, to write novels that would out-Firbank Firbank in their orchidaceous subtleties, he ended up as a tragicomic turn in works by other people. The success was eternally deferred, the glory all secondhand, and the piece of writing that most accurately perpetuates his memory is a pastiche by Cyril Connolly ("Where Engels Fears to Tread") that, however indulgent its tone, holds nearly everything he did or believed in up to ridicule.

At the heart of this thirty-year chronicle of waste, torment and dereliction lay what his Eton contemporary Anthony Powell would certainly have diagnosed as a question of upbringing. He was born into an almost Jamesian world of mid-Atlantic shades and splendors. Howard senior was a freewheeling international art dealer who enjoyed setting his cap at the celebrities who patronized his exhibitions. His mother, Lura, the daughter of an American Civil War veteran, apparently discovered the existence of the "other woman" midway through her honeymoon. There was plenty of money—at one stage the Howards maintained an establishment in Bryanston Square and a sixteen-bedroom country house in Sussex—and some exalted family connections (Brian's godparents included Prince Christian of Schleswig-Holstein and the novelist George Meredith) but also a sense of something having gone wrong, of dramatic frets and fractures beneath the surface, disagreeable roots imperfectly covered up. Even the family surname, pleasantly redolent of the Howard dukes of Norfolk, was a fraud. The original patronym, abandoned by the socially ambitious Mr. Howard, turned out to be Gassaway, and one of the last poems Brian ever published was an evocation of his lost American grandfather.

To obscure origins and Francis Howard's intermittently roving eye could be added the substantial problem of Brian himself. Ever perceptive where his own inadequacies were concerned, he defined his claustrophobic relationship with Lura Howard as "an absolutely *boringly* classical textbook case—sissy son, Oedipus and everything." Exasperated by his son's homosexuality, Howard senior eventually ordered his wife to choose between the two of them. Unhappily, her choice of Brian made things worse. Doting, solicitous, obstinate about money, at times practically vampiric in her attentions, Lura still managed to convey a faint impression that her real affection lay elsewhere. As well as leaving Brian, as one friend put it, "on the outside of his own family," these maternal shacklings also drove him into a kind of emotional cul-de-sac. Deep into middle age he noted shrewdly that "if I *make a success* I leave her. If I continue as a failure, I naturally remain." Staying put, he provided a continual testimony not only to his own inanition but to art's fatal inability to pay the rent.

None of this perhaps gives a proper idea of the person Brian Howard was, the kind of career he led—or failed to lead—and the curious mixture of frivolity and idealism that characterized his life. At Eton he combined jaw-dropping precocity in the arts ("Who is this Proust? Huxley was talking about him? Perhaps I ought to read him") with a fanatic determination to please himself. "It has seldom been my experience, in many years of work among boys, to come upon one so entirely self-centered and egotistical," a housemaster wrote anxiously back to Bryanston Square. "As far as his moral nature is concerned I cannot find what standards he has other than those of pure selfishness." Still in sight of his sixteenth birthday, he had a poem accepted by Orage's *New Age* and was "discovered" by Edith Sitwell ("I see more remarkable talent and promise in your work than of any other poet under twenty with the exception of my brother Sacheverell"), who published his "Barouches Noires," a nineties-ish fantasia about drowned lovers, in her anthology *Wheels*.

Not everyone was convinced by these displays of intellectual fireworks. Anthony Powell, among several early detractors, "never liked him, nor thought, even at Eton, that he had a vestige of any real talent in any of the arts. All he seemed to me interested in was self-advancement and forms of exhibitionism that brought him into disrepute." It is the eternal anti-dandy complaint about showing off, but even Powell had to admit that without Howard's administrative zeal, the *Eton Candle*, coedited with Harold Acton, would have perished on the drawing board. Published in the spring of 1922, priced half a crown, dedicated to "the illustrious memory of Algernon Charles Swinburne" and, with the exception of an Old Etonian supplement, mostly written by the editors, the *Candle* whipped up a terrific storm, despite the refusal of the poet laureate, Robert Bridges, to contribute. "Amazing how some people will throw away their opportunities, isn't it?" Howard commented to Acton, on receiving the letter.

His own contributions included "The New Poetry"—a spirited defence of Eliot-era vers libre—and a poetic salute to "The Young Writers and Artists Killed in the War":

And you went out and got murdered—magnificently —
Went out and got murdered ... because a parcel of damned old men

Wanted some fun, or some power, or something.
Something so despicable in comparison to your young lives ...

Already, though, there were signs that his talent, if that is what it was, had passed its sell-by date. Having scraped into Oxford ("a sort of passionate party all the time—one rushes from one amusement to another until one's sense of proportion and self-control gradually vanishes ..."), where harder-headed contemporaries like Acton were already forging careers for themselves, he spent his time in well-bred socializing. Maurice Bowra recalled a dinner party of such blue-blooded exclusivity that Howard was able to address the company—a meaningful glance at Bowra, who sat beside him—as "My Lords and gentleman." Coming down from the university without a degree, he progressed by easy stages into the role of Bright Young People's impresario. As "Johnnie Hoop" he wanders aimlessly through *Vile Bodies*, devising elaborate costumes for fancy dress balls and designing outsize party invitations. "These had two columns of close print: in one was a list of all the things Johnnie hated, and in the other all the things he thought he liked. Most of the parties which Miss Mouse financed had invitations written by Johnnie Hoop."

This is a direct reference to the sixteen-inch-high invitation sent out in advance of the Great Urban Dionysia, held in celebration of Brian's twenty-fourth birthday in April 1929. Barbed, too, as Johnnie only "thinks" he likes the things he likes. Waugh's implication is clear: Brian was merely trying to impress less sophisticated friends with his upmarket name-dropping. In fact, Brian's list of likes and dislikes, featured under the headings of *J'accuse* and *J'adore*, is uncannily representative both of his own foibles and the way in which the Bright Young People liked to position themselves aesthetically. *J'accuse*'s principles are more or less democratic. The items listed included "Chic," "Ladies and Gentlemen," "Public Schools," "English 'Society,'" "Those incredibly 'Private' Dances," "The *Tatler* and the *Sketch*," "People who find themselves out of place in a full third-class carriage anywhere in the world," "People who think that a title is of the slightest importance" and, inevitably, "The Bright Young People." Under *J'adore*, on the other hand, are filed "Men and Women," "Elegance," "Wood and Stone," "Russian films," "D. H. Lawrence," "Wild Flowers" and "A Field-mouse in a Bonnet." The list ends with a passionate declaration of humanist intent:

> The sort of people who enjoy life just as much, if not more, after they have realized that they have not got immortal souls, who are proud and not distressed to feel that they are of the earth earthy, who do not regard their body as mortal coils, and who are not anticipating after death, any rubbishy reunion, apotheosis, fulfilment or ANY THING.

In the light of Brian's lifestyle, social circles and stated ambitions, much of this is horribly misleading. No one, it might be said, made more of his status as a Bright Young Person, or hankered more zealously after the society of grand friends who cared very much whether their names were prefixed with "The Honourable" on envelopes. There were times, associates thought, when he almost convinced himself that he belonged to the aristocratic class in which he moved. Waugh remembered an Oxford party brimful of luster and éclat that was broken up by hearties. "We shall tell our fathers to raise your rents and evict you," Howard threatened the mob. "At such moments I think he really believed that Gassaway was a Whig magnate," Waugh thought. In much the same way, the sworn enemy of the *Tatler* and the *Sketch* enjoyed bragging about his appearances in their pages, while the disparager of "tell-tale-tits, slit-tongues, lickspittles and all social snippet writers" owed most of his notoriety to the sponsoring pen of his friend Tom Driberg on the *Express*.

As ever in these representations of gilded youth, the reality of Brian's life in the late 1920s was sharply at odds with its public projection. Friends remembered him as a slightly lost figure, unrequitedly in love, angling for literary work that failed to arrive, "bemused" by his status among the Bright Young People, convinced that if he bided his time and marshaled his material, dazzling opportunities would land at his feet. Meanwhile, there were constant trials of strength with his mother: Lura, suspicious of his bohemian friends, determined to keep him as short of money as possible; Brian perpetually hard up but aware that for all her intransigence Mrs. Howard had a point. "Whenever I feel how silly and unkind it is of you to leave me in this condition, in which, to be frank, I can scarcely eat, I immediately say to myself that, viewed from your angle, what else can you do?" runs a letter from this period. Worried about her son's homosexuality, Lura had already dispatched him to Germany in 1927 for psychoanalysis. The late 1920s were full of attractive-sounding schemes: flats loaned from friends in which, once comfortably established, he would sit down to write "saleable stuff"; some kind of film work fixed up by Count Anthony Bosdari ("He is quite consistent about ultimately making me a supervisor of the settings for First International Pictures, which the new company is being called"). But the jobs never materialized, the foolscap pages were never filled. Most of Brian's considerable energies were expended on trivia: planning his parties, researching costumes at the British Museum, deviously reconnoitering social events where he wanted to cut a figure: getting wind of Norman Hartnell's Circus Party in July 1929, he first approached the host with a list of desirable guests and then had several invitations professionally forged.

Still there were occasional poems stacking up in his manuscript book: bright, mannered and strident, nearly always to do with himself, his childhood and its memories, the whole densely romanticized, drenched in an ominous, profligate scent. "Self," written in 1929, evokes some characteristic images of solitude amid bright landscapes:

Wait, you whom I love, if you will
until the sunset picks the last rose, slowly, and goes.
It will leave, now, only black and white
and I shall be the stranger on this rock.

The summer and early autumn of 1929 found him staying with John Banting at La Napoule in the south of France, where it was thought that a frugal existence away from the fleshpots of Cannes would encourage some serious hard work. Here Brian wrote several of the poems that appeared in his only collection, *God Save the King*, published by his friend Nancy Cunard at the Hours Press two years later. One poem that he would certainly have had with him in France, though it was written a year or so earlier, was the title piece, a four-page evocation of early life lived out at the same time as a war that, the poet implies, would radically inform that life's scope. "This begins about my private school— goes on about the last War, with me in it (imaginatively) and dying spiritually before reaching fulfilment" was Brian's explanation. From its ironic title down, "God Save the King" is full of archetypal Bright Young People's preoccupations: doomed youth, the "madness" of being young, childhood ruined by the news from Flanders:

> *But, as dirt gets between the teeth and sweat creeps between the*
> *   piano keys*
> *worms into everyone, nails into a cross*
> *so Mars, the loud newspaper boy, rode across our roses*
> *and trampled our teacups into the lawn.*
> *No storm destroyed our pastoral symphony, no grand tempest, but*
> *   instead*
> *as dirt gets into the teeth, the newspaper got in at the garden gate*
> *and we were all filled with hate . . .*

The closing stanzas carry a dramatic image of war's human consequences, "My brother," who has "lain down to rest a moment / to blow a tired, red bubble in the mud. / I have lived. I am now dead before I am dead."

Like much of Brian's poetry, "God Save the King" is full of arresting lines that, taken together, fail to maintain their initial momentum. The penultimate section, on the other hand, ignores these projections of a battle in which the poet himself had not taken part, for a pointed, and ultimately personal, vision of "Englishness":

> *. . . England, my green house, England, my green thought*
> *in my green shade, yellow sand, emerald isle, silver sea, hearts*
> *   of oak*

white walls, rule Britannia, Britannia rules the waves, never
  waives the rules, but
the thunder's got into the milk, my darling, and the shorthorn's
  got T.B.
and what, we soon begin to say, is going to become of me?

As Brian knew by this stage in his life, it was a good question: one that would be asked more urgently in the 1930s and all the trackless years that lay beyond.

THE MEANING OF GOSSIP

One of the funniest episodes in *Vile Bodies* takes in Adam Fenwick-Symes's appointment as "Mr. Chatterbox," gossip columnist on the *Daily Excess*. Adam's accession is not without its difficulties. His predecessor, Balcairn, has committed suicide, having filed a valedictory column of such staggering invention that it attracts more than sixty libel writs. The consequent blacklist devised by Lord Monomark, the *Excess*'s proprietor, prohibits the mention of practically any well-known name. But Adam is not downcast. He begins his new career in a modest way with a series of "Notable Invalids," before moving on to a *galère* of "Titled Eccentrics," in which earls given to dressing up in costumes of the Napoleonic era and insane peers sidetracked by comparative religion are given their brief moment of media glory.

Encouraged by the reception afforded to these little-known but indisputably real people, Adam ups his game and invents a roster of wholly imaginary subjects: "Provna," the rising young sculptor; a personable young attaché at the Italian embassy named "Count Cincinatti"; "Captain Angus Stuart-Kerr," the celebrated big-game hunter. Inexplicably these phantoms catch on, are seen elsewhere by rival columnists, become public property to the extent that Adam grows almost proprietorial about them, issues brusque rebuffs to other papers that purport to chronicle their movements. The most inspired of these creations is "Imogen Quest," "a byword for social inaccessibility," as Waugh puts it, and a hostess of such vertiginous chic that no one seems ever to have been invited to one of her parties. The illusion of Mrs. Quest's existence is sustained by fictitious means—Provna, no friend to female beauty, declares that she "justifies the century"—until the moment when Lord Monomark asks Adam to effect an introduction. That very day the Quests set sail for Jamaica.

Another of Adam's innovations lies in the field of male dress styles. Single-handedly he creates a craze for black suede shoes for evening wear. Sporting gentlemen, meanwhile, are seen at point-to-points in the ultra-modish bottle green bowler hat. In the end, as the days pass, Mr. Chatterbox's column becomes "almost wholly misleading." Obscure temperance hotels in Bloomsbury are represented as the haunt of fashionable London and the buffet at Sloane Square advertised as the center of "the most modern artistic coterie." Then Lord Monomark, hitherto content to swallow everything Adam has thrown at him, orders that there shall be no more mention of Count Cincinatti, of whom the Italian ambassador has never heard, or the bottle green bowler hat, which no one has ever been seen wearing. Nina, taking on the column for the day on which Adam is off visiting her father, flaunts both these ukases and gets her fiancé the sack.

All this raises a much more fundamental question. For whom was the gossip of the late-twenties society column written? And what function was it supposed to fulfill? Lord Monomark's commendation of Adam's efforts is triple-pronged. "I like your page. It's peppy; it's got plenty of new names in it and it's got the intimate touch I like." At bedrock level such accretions of personal detail and quasi-bizarre behavior had two audiences: the people being written about, who could recognize themselves and each other; and the far larger number of people not being written about, for whom the column was a kind of raree-show of remote and efflorescent exotica. But what about the winnowing process that provided Mr. Chatterbox and his real-life equivalents with their final cast?

On the one hand proprietors, editors and, presumably, readers wanted novelty, the shock of the socially new and the frisson of the behaviorally unfamiliar. On the other hand they also wanted assurance, known characteristics, a recognizable landscape they could take or leave at will. Hence the "tags" with which gossip column habitués were always invested: the fashionable novelist Mr. X, the highly accomplished daughter of Earl Y, Lady Mary Z, the innovative young artist whose work will shortly . . . Readers needed to keep tabs, to maintain their perspective, not to lose sight of their quarry in ever more densely populated undergrowth. If novelty and familiarity could be welded together, then so much the better. The ideal subject for "The Dragoman" or "Mr. Gossip" was someone—preferably a woman—with a long-term public reputation who went on behaving outrageously. Elizabeth Ponsonby combined these characteristics in excelsis: a quintessential establishment figure, whose father had been page of honor to Queen Victoria, but also the dashing and erratic representative of a whole new mode of young persons' existence.

At the same time these tags neither instructed nor edified: they were simply there to authenticate. They had no real meaning. From the angle of the reader—Priestley's Mr. Smeeth, say, chewing his pipe on the bus into town—the fashionable novelist and the highly accomplished Lady Mary Z are barely distinguishable from one another. The reader's curiosity, in fact, was almost bovine. It went only so far. It wanted, above all, to be reassured that the grass it ate was grass, that the people presented for its inspection, whoever they might be, were worth reading about. By extension, the scale of values on offer is quite arbitrary. The distinctions of wealth, prestige and talent are immaterial. What matters is the exposure, with each new manifestation of celebrity a link in a chain that in some cases extends back to the subject's birth. Contemporary gossip fanciers would have been able to contextualize Elizabeth Ponsonby's rackety progress through the twenties by way of a galleryful of existing portraits: mannequin, party giver, mock-wedding impresario; real-life bride . . . The ultimate effect is oddly mythological: a weird, outwardly innocuous but in the end faintly sinister frieze, in which quiddity is reduced to idiosyncrasy, life is a continual twitch upon the thread of past nonachievement—a triumph of form over content.

CHAPTER EIGHT

DECLINE AND FALL: 1930–31

"Do you think one of these days everything will come right?"
"No."

— ANTHONY POWELL, *Afternoon Men*

It's no go the gossip column, it's no go the ceilidh,
All we want is a mother's help and a sugar-stick for the baby.
— LOUIS MACNEICE, "Bagpipe Music"

I n April 1930 the Bloomsbury diarist Frances Marshall and her partner Ralph Partridge were guests at Knole, the country house in Sussex inhabited by Harold Nicolson and his wife, Vita Sackville-West.
Here Eddie Gathorne-Hardy and Nancy Morris, with Alix Strachey and
Brian Howard in attendance, had combined to throw what was billed as
a "Hermaphrodite Party." Beginning at eleven on a sweltering late-
spring night and continuing into the small hours, the gathering was determinedly homosexual in spirit. Most of the young men present were
weighed down with pearl necklaces and makeup. The atmosphere was
stifling and the buzz of chatter so loud that the music from the vast
gramophone horn swiftly became inaudible. The cross-dressers included Eddie Gathorne-Hardy, reduced almost to tears after a good-
looking German guest declined to dance with him. "I've been simply
*mis*erable about my costume, my dear," he confided to Frances. "I've had
a *good* cry about it." As the young man hove into view he commanded
her: "Now, *do*, my dear, just *take* him by the hand and *throw* him into
my arms." Frances did her best, but it was no good. The German boy

turned out to be more interested in her than in the Earl of Cranbrook's younger son.

Heterosexual and serious-minded, Frances and Ralph were conscious of their detachment from this kind of stylized debauchery. Neither of their costumes was in the least convincing: Ralph wore a red wig and Spanish shawl over his trousers but failed, as his companion acknowledged, "to look in any way feminine." Frances confined herself to a yellow silk Empire dress, a bowler hat and an ersatz moustache. As ever, her eye for social detail was much in evidence. There was a vogue for this kind of entertainment, she rather disdainfully noted: "All the creative energy of the participants goes on their dress, and there is none of the elaborate performance of earlier parties. Personally I think this is a sad come-down, a sign of decadence."

By this stage in the Bright Young People's trajectory, this kind of complaint was increasingly common. Veterans of the partygoing scene were turning jaded. The original spark had gone out, long-term observers lamented, and spontaneity had been replaced by calculation. Ever larger sums were being spent on outlandish entertainments which, however elaborate their effect, lacked charm, wit or genuine ebullience. Looking back on the stunt parties of 1929, Patrick Balfour detected the scent of ulterior, and even commercial, motive: Norman Hartnell's Circus Party was "given to advertise a firm of dressmakers," he sniffed. Well-publicized events like the Second Childhood Party and the Wild West Party were pale imitations of the trail-blazing gatherings of the mid-1920s. "They lacked the imaginative spirit which animated the entertainments of Mr. Tennant, Mr. Howard and Co., for the Bright Young People made a genuine art of party-going." Now, apparently, that art had become debased. Those involved had grown bored with their own creations. Cyril Connolly's journal for 1929, for example, contains a barbed little spoof titled "Round the Table." Here Connolly pastiches the newspaper gossip columns: "A sponge and barnacle party in which guests compete to see who can stay the longest is the latest amusement of the Bright Young People—'We had to invent it,' said Miss Cetera Etcetera, 'to keep out gate-crashers, who are mostly poor people and sooner or later have to return to their work.' The winners of this competition are a young married couple. 'It solves our house-warming,' Mrs. Waugh said."

What had gone wrong? At the most basic level of personnel, the Bright Young People's original elements had continued to disperse. Beaton's horizons were now firmly cosmopolitan, his professional gaze fixed squarely on America. Stephen Tennant, in poorish health, spent most of his time abroad. Some Bright Young People were claimed by marriage and children, or the necessity of earning a living. There were conscious, or semiconscious, sloughings-off of a lifestyle that was becoming irksome. Connolly married an heiress, Jean Bakewell, in February 1930 and rented a house near Toulon. "If you hate both diehards and bright young people, you have . . . to go and live abroad." Harold Acton, disenchanted by his lack of literary success, would soon depart, via America, to China, where he remained until 1939. Other scene swellers from the twenties shivaree found their paths leading inexorably elsewhere. Mrs. Meyrick, released from prison after fifteen months' hard labor, retreated to Monte Carlo, where she was offered a stake in a new club. "Monte Carlo is chiefly inhabited by older people and therefore you must cater for them," she explained. "I know all my good old British clients will stand by me if I start up here." By this stage, too, the movement had begun to sustain its first casualties: Sir Francis Laking, for example, the friend and admirer of Tallulah Bankhead (to whom he bequeathed a phantom collection of motorcars), was already dead at twenty-six from a surfeit of yellow chartreuse.

These individual destinies were only the symptoms of a wider malaise. What fatally injured the Bright Young People in the end was the thing that had helped to create them: publicity. Large-scale press attention, Patrick Balfour thought, transformed what at first had been only the diversions of a few friends into something significant, important, a full-fledged "movement" whose slightest extension or retreat would be instantly analyzed by the gossip columnists. What had been a subconscious impulse became "a self-conscious crusade." Bohemianism, most histories of bohemian societies insist, can stay true to its authenticating spirit only by not trying too hard. Here, spontaneity had become a series of stunts. At the heart of this decline, and further diluting the

Very Young Flapper. "JOLLY FINE, ISN'T IT?"
Mature Ditto. "H'M, THINK SO? YOU SHOULD HAVE SEEN THE COCKTAIL-PARTIES IN THE DEAR OLD 'TWENTIES."

movement's original spirit merely by their presence, came a new breed of partygoers, less well-off, less well connected, but determined to emulate what they had read in the papers. Baronet's daughter that she was, Brenda Dean Paul identified a bad case of "social blood poisoning":

> And by the latter I mean that, lacking in social discrimination, a lot of new blood was introduced, gate-crashers of little social or artistic merit, outsiders in fact, who in turn introduced their friends, so that the parties became more and more frequent, more and more lacking in originality and amusement, until they became merely massed drinking orgies, attended by a few bleary-eyed, demoralized bright young pioneers, too tired, too much in a groove to break away.

It was a far cry from the "Men and Women" of Brian Howard's *J'adore* lists and the "People who find themselves out of place in a full third-class carriage anywhere in the world" of his *J'accuse.*

This transformation—from an original style to a mass-market imitation of it—was not without its ironies. In particular, the man who, more than anyone else, had exposed the Bright Young People to public gaze was now, for the first time in his life, able to set up as a bona fide Bright Young Person. Newly divorced, luxuriating in the success of *Vile Bodies* and the highly paid journalism that followed in its wake, Evelyn Waugh reemerged into the West End world of the early 1930s as a bachelor-about-town, conducting affairs with married women and attending every kind of socially upmarket entertainment. Waugh's diary, which resumes in 1930, is full of references to the Bright Young People's old guard. With the turmoil of the past few months behind him, he was determined to make up for lost time. On June 6, for instance, he gave "what should have been an amusing luncheon party at the Ritz but there was a horse-race that day and everybody chucked." Mass absenteeism notwithstanding, the guest list still included Eleanor Smith, Sacheverell and Georgia Sitwell, the Guinnesses, Nancy Mitford, Frank Pakenham, William Acton and Elizabeth Pelly, née Ponsonby. Nine days later he set off for Oxford with Harold Acton and Zena Naylor and dined at the George with the Pakenhams: "Elizabeth Pelly and John Betjeman joined us in the car." A month later he was at a party given by Lord Donegall, where "I sat downstairs most of the time with Zena Naylor and Elizabeth Ponsonby."

The references to Elizabeth—three in six weeks—are significant. Some Bright Young People might be moving on into less artificial environments; new recruits to the movement might be frantically sampling the pleasures they assumed had been denied them for too long; the Pellys, on the other hand, were cheerfully carrying on regardless. Watching from the margins of this extended chronicle of dissipation were, as ever, the anxious figures of Arthur and Dorothea. Late in January 1930, Dolly recorded a long conversation with Nelly, who continued to divide her time between Smith Street and the Pelly domicile in Sussex Place: "At least she poured out to me about how hopeless it was & that she was always going on at them." With Denis still out of a job, the couple's besetting sin was extravagance: enormous laundry bills which they made no effort to settle, nightly parties over which Nelly despaired. Miss Elizabeth did listen to her remonstrances, Nelly maintained, "but Mr. Pelly never." As for the scale of this entertaining, according to Nelly, "They had 20 people in the evening usually with Syphons [sic] & beer &

bacon & eggs—'& I've told them they can't go on like this.'" Noting that her servant seemed "really worried," Dolly added her own depressing gloss: "I fully realize that nothing can ever be done with Denis & that nothing goes home. It's a perfect impasse." Lady Ponsonby's suspicions were reinforced a week later when a copy of *Vile Bodies* fell into her hands. "Think I cannot have the same wit as modern people as I can't see the amusement of this book," she pronounced. "I actually have to skip pages." The novel's excellent reviews bewildered her. "But these sort of things are said about it. 'The funniest book for years'—funny, richly & roaringly funny & so on. I believe to some people indecency is synonymous with wit. Evelyn Waugh's impropriety is to be scruffy . . ."

Arthur, meanwhile, was trying to solve the couple's pressing financial difficulties. There was a chance that Denis might get a job in the Gaslight and Coke Company, but would he be up to it? his father-in-law wondered. "I told him he would not and that I had no confidence in him but I much wanted him to prove me wrong." Their situation, Arthur slowly divined, had an ominous circularity. To stabilize their lives, Elizabeth and Denis needed an income that could be guaranteed only by Denis's acquiring a full-time job. Should he acquire it, on the other hand, his wife would find the new responsibilities merely tedious and a drag on her own freedom. "Will E help him? This I doubt most of all—she will be thoroughly bored of his having to go off so early. That is the trouble with her. Her vision of life is all wrong. Founded on a small society of rich idle people on whom she sponges." In fact, Arthur's view of the Pellys' social circles was slightly inaccurate. The new friends that the couple made, here in the twilight of the Bright Young People's era, were more seedy than glamorous. Hugh Wade worked in a nightclub. John Ludovic Ford, invariably known as "Ludy" and a significant figure in Elizabeth's life over the next few years, owned a garage. Early in April Dolly had to attend to another of Nelly's monologues on the subject of "E & D's lives & the lives of their friends—she didn't know how they stood [it], she knew she couldn't." On the previous evening, Nelly confided, she had stayed up until 5 a.m. "because D & E had gone to a party & she knew she would never get up in the morning." The Pellys returned at four bringing sixteen people with them "& sat around doing nothing she said just talking." Denis, it turned out, had got into the habit of asking everyone he met at parties to dinner and bridge, an excess of hospitality that led to some bizarre telephone conversations. On the previous day, Nelly reported, Eddie Gathorne-Hardy had rung up to ask if he were expected to dinner. No, certainly not, Nelly told him. "But Nelly," Eddie had protested. "I wasn't drunk when Mr. Pelly asked me." "You probably were," Nelly shot back.

Though eventually taken on by the Gaslight and Coke Company, Denis had done nothing to alter his routines. Arthur, always keen to find chinks of light amid the enveloping murk yet darkly conscious of the underlying tensions of his family life, made further assessments of the young man's character. In mid-May both Ponsonby children and their respective spouses arrived at Shulbrede for the weekend. "We all got on very well together," Arthur reported, although he noted the growing antagonism between his wife and her son-in-law. "He is frightened of her and she has too low an opinion of him to take any trouble with him." Returning to the subject a week later, Arthur decided that Denis had gone up slightly in his estimation: "His athletic proficiency is attractive and he seems so far to be sticking to his job." But he continued to deplore his daughter's frivolity: "She is slow in awakening to any possible serious view of life."

The Pellys continued to spend almost every evening in perpetual transit around the West End—and occasionally further afield—in search of diversion. On the night of which Nelly had complained, they turned out to have been at parties in Green Street and Park Lane before ending up at Tallulah Bankhead's house in Farm Street, from which most of the guests were finally evicted at breakfasttime. Despite press disapproval, the stunt party continued to eat up space in the society weeklies: the American Party—Elizabeth in horn-rim glasses and false mustache; the Court Party, where Denis appeared in guardsman's uniform with busby. It was still possible, in the hands of an imaginative host with plenty of money to spend, for these entertainments to preserve something of the spirit of the decade that had passed. Guinness entertainments continued to be respectfully reported: the hospitality on offer to the visiting American writer Carl Van Vechten in June 1930 included a cocktail party at which Diana "received with a baby at her breast and an Irish wolfhound as big as a colt at her feet . . ." Meanwhile, David Tennant's Mozart Party, staged on April 29, 1930, and commemorating the composer's visit to London in 1764, was remembered as perhaps the most sumptuous gathering of the era. Brenda Dean Paul, for whom the memory of it "stood out forever," reckoned that it had cost nearly £3,000. Throughout its eight-hour progress, the meticulous eye for detail brought to the décor of the Gargoyle Club was sharply in evidence. Guests—more than five hundred of them—were greeted at the ground floor of the New Burlington Street Galleries by flunkies dressed as eighteenth-century runners. Lift operators and pageboys then conducted them into a room decorated with antique silver, china and crystal, where they were entertained first by a frock-coated and periwigged orchestra and then by a jazz band. The ball was preceded by a select dinner, attended by perhaps a tenth of the guests, whose menu had been taken from a royal cookbook owned by Louis XVI and whose setting reproduced a fête staged at the Tuileries a century and a half before. Here society columnists were able to admire the host, masquerading as Don Giovanni, his wife (allowed a certain amount of period license on account of her advanced pregnancy and dressed in a crinoline) and Harry Melville got up as Beau Brummel in a plum-colored suit and carrying Brummel's original silver-topped cane.

The press was enraptured: "Never in recent years can there have been such efflorescence of cotton-wool wigs in a London ballroom," "The Dragoman" enthused. "For loveliness of costume and imagination in the details there has surely been no more remarkable party for years," another encomiast pronounced. "Eve" of the *Tatler* acclaimed "one of the very best parties of the year . . . Nearly everyone came in eighteenth-century white wigs, full skirts, flowered waistcoats, embroidered coats and buckled shoes, and the effect was really lovely, for they seemed at the same time to have assumed some of the dignity and grace of the eighteenth century." In its closing stages this array of bygone dress styles provided one of the most dramatic images of the Bright Young People, a juxtaposition of stylized otherworldliness and the realities of interwar British life that has all the starkness of a medieval morality play. Debouching into Piccadilly in the small hours, still dressed in the fashions of the 1760s, some of Tennant's guests came upon a gang of workmen digging up a gas pipe in the street and had themselves photographed alongside. Several figures are clearly identifiable. Patrick Balfour stands atop a mound of rubble with his arm round a startled laborer. Cyril Connolly inspects the scene through an eyeglass. Cecil Beaton, with Denis and Elizabeth at his elbow, wields a borrowed pneumatic drill with all the stricken confidence of a child at large with a chainsaw.

Meanwhile, there was more damaging gossip floating back from chez Pelly. A fortnight after the Mozart Party, Dolly had dinner with Matthew and his wife, Bess: "Both full of the fantastic, & to me dreadful doings in Sussex Place." Denis's latest exploit, they revealed, carried out in Elizabeth's absence, had been to pick up a female entertainer known as the "male impersonator" in a nightclub, bring her back to the flat and encourage her to give a party in his sitting room ("She brought 20 men") until one o'clock in the morning. ("The woman who apparently had nowhere to sleep was accommodated by Denis in the dressing room . . .") Dolly felt "utterly depressed & wretched by the life led by these 2 Denis and Elizabeth." Come the summer there was another opportunity to observe Elizabeth and her friends in action when the Pellys arrived at Shulbrede for tea. On her own turf, and with real people before her rather than the wraiths of Nelly's reportage, Dolly was able to moderate the contempt and offer several wonderfully acerbic portraits of the couple's hangers-on. Hutch was expected but failed to show. Other guests included Barbara Ker-Seymer, Olivia Wyndham ("a cross picturesque woman") and John Banting. As with Brian Howard some years before, Dolly could hardly bear to take her eyes from Banting: her account of him—"one of the most evil-looking people I've ever set eyes on"—oozes fascinated repulsion:

He sets out to look evil & like a very modern picture of the Tahitian school. The effect is entirely that of a desperate convict of whom you say that man ought to be shut up. His head is shaven—his eyes are very small—his lips very thick and sensual

& with a sardonic expression—he has a moustache which caused argument among us at dinner—as to how it was done—plucked or shaved—only a long line of close hair, like an eyebrow. His coloring is dun or gray—like the people in Augustus John's early pictures—& his figure & shape likewise—not charmingly angular like John Strachey but ugly. He said he could play tennis a little—& I thought he was being modest—but it was the most amazing exhibition ever seen—he didn't know where to stand & when the ball came at him—whirled round & round waving his arms like a windmill & sometimes got the ball & drove it to the furthest corner of the orchard.

Determined to get him to talk about art, and to know what he thought of John Strachey's paintings, Dolly opened with a modish phrase picked up from Roger Fry: "Is your art based on equivoque or ellipsis?" Banting gave as good as he got, but Dolly could not separate the art from what she assumed was the personality of the artist: "The man is perverted, I feel sure. I gauge him too by the company he keeps living with Brian Howard the whole winter in a villa in France." Returning the next morning with Elizabeth and Denis, Banting seemed more disagreeable still: "The repellent friend has crowned his appearance of criminology with a burglar's cap. He was so repellent—I felt I couldn't look at him. He wears a rather dirty white shirt & under it a striped bathing costume!"

In no way stretched by his government responsibilities—Macdonald had appointed him to an undersecretaryship at the Ministry of Transport—Arthur had plenty of time to brood over the paralyzing question of his daughter and his daughter's marriage. Gradually, as the winter and spring of 1931, he became aware that her difficulties were not merely those of improvidence. In late November he had noted a "crisis approaching over E and Denis's debts," but by April there were "distressing reports" of fractures in the relationship itself. John Strachey had talked of the couple's "continual quarrelling and bickering." Arthur "hoped to goodness" they were not drifting apart. Emotionally, he detected a complete impasse: "He is shallow and weak and she is shallow and strong and no help to him whatever." There was, increasingly, a suspicion that much of the blame for the couple's frenetic lifestyle could be pinned on Elizabeth. John Strachey, visiting Shulbrede in early May, took Denis's side, Arthur noted, "as he thinks he is genuinely keen on his work and is fed up with the manikins and night club round which E insists on." "Manikins" is presumably Arthur's way of stigmatizing the gang of epicene if not openly homosexual young men in whose company Elizabeth was photographed for the society weeklies. That a financial crisis was looming—a lesser evil in Arthur's and Dolly's eyes—seems clear from the Pellys' removal in April from their flat in Sussex Place to the Ponsonby headquarters in Smith Street.

In the midst of these agonizings over the couple's profligacy, the Ponsonbys were uneasily conscious of their inability to act. Elizabeth, they knew, would go on spending money and someone would eventually have to foot the bill. In May Arthur and Dolly "talked over the Elizabeth problem," agreeing that it had now assumed "proportions which are serious, baffling and seemingly beyond our control." A fortnight later, to his intense annoyance, Arthur discovered that Elizabeth was being sued by Peter Jones for the substantial sum of £82. He took what he hoped was decisive action: settled the debt, forbade the shop to open any new account and only to allow transactions in cash. In furtherance of this credit squeeze, Nelly was told to tell Elizabeth that accounts opened at other shops would be stopped and that delays in settling weekly bills must be reported home. Elizabeth's letter to her mother about the affair sounds faintly disingenuous: "I can't tell you how sorry I am about the Peter Jones business—it was really rather taken out of my hands, I had no idea Fiby [a pet name for her father] thought of paying off the whole amount + I did not realize it was nearly so much." Dolly would also not have been impressed by the codicil, which placed social life firmly above filial obligation: "Don't come + see me tomorrow—as I've suddenly remembered it is the Theatrical Garden Party + I have promised to go with someone . . ."

The "someone" is unidentifiable but it was certainly not Denis. Although there is no documentary evidence of his opinions on any subject, beyond a stray reference or two in Arthur's diaries, it seems clear that his son-in-law was reaching the end of his tether, that his wife's so-cial round grated on his nerves and hindered him from functioning effectively at his job. By this time much of Elizabeth's partygoing seems to have been undertaken on her own, with Denis amusing himself or staying behind in Smith Street. Though kept in the dark over certain aspects of his daughter's behavior, Arthur scented worse trouble. Sidelights from a dinner with family friends who knew something of Elizabeth's goings-on "showed me E's life an absolute nightmare." At some point around this time he wrote what he later termed "an appeal" begging her to mend her ways. Then on July 5 he noted, "E and D. Touch and go. At any moment a break up and in any case continual bills and debts to pay."

The stage was set for Elizabeth's starring performance in what informed judges were to rate as the most notorious gathering of the whole Bright Young People's era: the White Party. Like Second Childhood and Bathing Parties, White Parties, in which furniture, décor and occasionally even food matched the white suits and ball gowns of the guests, had enjoyed a mild vogue: Elizabeth had given one herself with Babe Plunket Greene, now remarried and relaunched into society as the Countess Bosdari. This particular variant, hosted by the flamboyant Old Etonian Sandy Baird at his mother's house near Faversham on a Saturday night in early July, ended in tragedy. Elizabeth went down on her own, or rather in the company of two more or less disreputable friends, "Ludy" Ford and Gordon Russell, a minor actor, who shared a nearby property called Goodtrees. Though the exact nature of this three-way relationship is lost in time, it seems clear that both men had designs on Elizabeth and that this emotional collision had already provoked several quarrels. Elizabeth and her escorts arrived at Town Place sometime before midnight and decided to leave it at around 5 a.m. The events of the next twenty minutes were conveyed to Arthur early on the following day when, arriving at Haslemere station on his way to Shulbrede, he and Dolly were confronted by the news "in all the papers that E driving from a party early Sunday morning had had an accident outside Maidstone in which the driver her friend Gordon Russell was killed while she escaped with only bruises . . . Russell's friend Ford had had a quarrel and fight with him and had been arrested for being drunk in charge of a lorry."

After a day of telephoning and seeing his solicitor, Arthur drove down to Kent with Denis. Here he found Elizabeth "shaken and upset and binging herself up with drink." A coroner's inquest, held the next day at Bexley and lavishly covered by the newspapers (5 A.M. CAR PURSUIT FOLLOWS DANCE FIGHT, CRASH ON HILL, PEER'S DAUGHTER CLIMBS OUT OF WINDOW, etc.), bore out Arthur's summary. Elizabeth, the principal witness, confirmed that there had been a blazing row or, as the coroner, Mr. Neve, put it, "some disagreement" between her escorts as they prepared to set out. Russell had told her he had quarreled with Ford and would not take him home.

"But it was Mr. Ford's car?"

"Yes."

"Did you know there was an assault?"

"No."

"You elected to go with Mr. Russell?"

"Yes."

"You did not see Mr. Ford to tell him you were going?"

"No."

Elizabeth's explanation of the crash was that neither she nor Russell knew the country between Faversham and Maidstone and kept stopping to look at signposts. At one of these halts, Russell—perfectly sober, she maintained, but known for his erratic driving—skidded the car across the road. The next thing she knew the car was upside down. With difficulty she climbed out of a half-open window and discovered Russell three-quarters inside the car with the whole weight of it lying on his chest. Mr. Neve then turned his attention to Ludy Ford, arrested shortly afterward, though some distance away, for being drunk in charge of a motor vehicle.

"Did you know they were going without you?"

"I saw them start."

"Was it with or without your sanction that they went without you?"

"I was not asked."

"The car was taken without your sanction?"

"Yes."

"You had quarreled with the dead man?"

"Yes."

"Were blows exchanged between you?"

"Yes."

Representing himself as "rather dazed," having been tripped up by Russell in the course of the fight, Ford was then asked: Was he pursuing him? There was a pause. "I was in pursuit of Russell, but I think he did not know it."

Mr. Neve approached his summing-up with all the caution appropriate to a case involving the daughter of the Labour leader of the House of Lords. He was "not using these words in any sinister sense, but Russell and Mrs. Pelly did in fact take the car without the sanction of the owner." As to whether Ford might have been in pursuit of Russell, "I am not concerned to say Yes or No, but the fact that Mr. Russell was 10 minutes ahead of Mr. Ford and both were going over the same road was probably in Mr. Russell's mind. He probably thought that he had gone away with the car and the lady, and Mr. Ford would be coming along the same road." If anyone was to blame, it was Russell for driving carelessly. "The whole story is not a particularly pleasant one," he concluded, "but I am glad that the little altercation between friends had nothing to do with the cause of death."

As they could hardly fail to do in these circumstances, the jury returned a verdict of accidental death. Arthur provided his own bitter summary of the affair in his diary. Russell, he decided, "was a drunken pervert with suicidal mania. He was in love with E. Ford lived with him and is a nervous unbalanced stuttering young pervert too. The whole thing is a sordid discreditable business and E who would naturally be master of herself in such circumstances is completely overwhelmed and demoralized." This, he grimly reflected, was her answer to the appeal of a fortnight before. If there was a shred of comfort, it could be found in Denis's behavior, his refusal to go to the party, his apparent attempts to "behave decently." On the other hand, "clearly their relations together are on very unstable foundations. They seem always to misunderstand one another. She is no help to him, he no companion to her." In the meantime, the repercussions of the White Party still had some way to go. The wave of publicity had already brought abusive and anonymous letters. Worse, Elizabeth was clearly feeling both the physical and psychological effects of the crash. Three days after the inquest Arthur returned to Shulbrede after a meeting of the East Africa Committee to find his daughter on the premises and asking to see the family doctor. She was found to have fractured a rib and put to bed for a week. Reassured by having her under his roof and in a state of near immobility, Arthur thought that this was "a good start" for whatever plans he might now cook up for the Pellys' salvation. "Now Denis who it seems has been going on anyhow at Smith Street has got to be tackled. We can only make plans from week to week."

There was, as Arthur might have foreseen, one substantial impediment to his schemes. With Elizabeth "in bed and fairly reasonable," he found that he was able to have what he called a "pretty straight talk" with Denis. However, a week later Arthur noted "things going badly."

Judicious representations to the authorities might, he fancied, have kept his daughter out of Ford's trial at Maidstone Quarter Sessions on a charge of driving a motor vehicle under the influence of drink. Elizabeth, on the other hand, was bent on attending and being called as a witness. Not for the first time, Arthur found himself having to reverse his opinions. A fortnight before he had wondered whether Denis was the better behaved of the two. Now he was inclining to his daughter's side. Several family friends had spoken to her. In London with her parents she seemed "quite reasonable and affectionate." She had also found some kind of job. Meanwhile, Denis's behavior was "less satisfactory, bad symptoms."

It was in this atmosphere of heightened marital tension that Elizabeth made her appearance at Ludy Ford's trial. Cross-questioned in the witness box, she maintained that Ford was quite sober at the party but that she had seen him and Russell fight several times. This admission led to some pointed exchanges with the prosecuting counsel, Mr. Singles.

Q: Are you accustomed to seeing your gentlemen friends fighting?

A: I know people do fight occasionally.

Q: The idea of those two young gentlemen having a stand-up fight does not occur to you as strange?

A: It did not on that particular occasion.

Q: There was no special reason for it, was there?

A: There was a reason from the point of view that Mr. Russell had been in a bad temper with Mr. Ford for the past few weeks, and was working up to a quarrel. I have seen Mr. Russell fight before. He was frightfully quick-tempered.

Q: He must have been an unpleasant person to have much to do with?

A: I did not find him an unpleasant person.

Several other witnesses who had seen Ford before his arrest also denied he was drunk. The erratic behavior that had caused him to be taken into custody was, they rationalized, the result of shock at hearing of his friend's death. At this point the case was stopped by the judge and Ford found not guilty. From the Ponsonbys' angle, everything had turned out as well as could have been expected. Arthur's diary, however, is ominously silent about the cross-examination. By his reckoning his daughter, having abandoned her husband to attend a disreputable party, had been fought over by two equally disreputable men, one of whom had killed himself through careless driving with the other in vengeful pursuit. For Elizabeth, alternatively, press reporting of the case had a particular significance. For the first time in a seven-year rampage through the public imagination her notoriety was represented in the past tense. "As Miss Elizabeth Ponsonby," ran an account of "Mrs. Denis Pelly's" appearance at the inquest, "she was one of the Bright Young People." Mysteriously, and without those involved even appearing to notice the fact of its dissolution, a whole age had come to an end.

THE BOOKS BRIAN NEVER WROTE

The books Brian Howard never wrote would fill a decent-sized shelf. It takes only a few moments' immersion in the mass of letters and diaries he left behind him to disclose the presence of a phantom library, a literary life lived almost entirely in the subjunctive, where practically everything is provisional, unfinished or merely inchoate. Everywhere he looked, his contemporaries—the friends he had known at Eton, the blue-blooded young men he had stalked at Oxford—were bursting into print, but Brian stayed silent. Or not so much silent as quietly optimistic, certain that in the end the creative juice would flow, the pen—for once—not fall instinctively from his hand, the words pour out to deflower the virgin page. It was all a matter of time, inspiration, the perfect subject, the appropriate treatment, of finding the space, in a world where one did nothing at all, to create the something that would authenticate that world and give it meaning.

The first faltering steps amid the foothills of this imaginary Parnassus were taken in Oxford days. "I have been writing a vast amount of rather better stuff lately," he told his friend Bryan Guinness in 1926, "and expect to get out a book of poetry in the winter." As if this versifying zeal weren't enough, he was also writing a novel, "and actually getting on with it. Only a couple of chapters so far, though, but for once, I enjoy writing prose, and have every idea of finishing it." In Berlin a year later, undergoing analysis at the hands of Dr. Prinzhorn, his letters home are awash with literary schemes. A German diary was abandoned in favor of "a treatise which I have been planning since I visited Heidelberg. It is to be a sort of philosophical speculation on the nature of the contemporary gentleman." Almost on the instant, though, this promising line of inquiry was thrown over, or perhaps only reimagined, and Lura Howard was briskly informed that Prinzhorn "is helping me very much with my new book . . . This is the story, roughly speaking, of a young Indian Maharajah who makes it the object of his life to become an English gentleman, and gradually comes to the conclusion that this is the worst thing in the world worth being." The working title was *The Cow Jumps over the Moon*—the cow to symbolize the maharajah, India, Nietzsche and the *élan vital*, the moon representing English gentility, Christianity and materialism. "I am very excited about it and feel confident of writing a book that will put me at the head of *my* generation."

But his generation was already speeding away beyond him, effortlessly unburdening itself of those novels, travelogues and slim volumes of verse that Brian knew he could write if only . . . If only what? Evelyn's first novel was in the press. Harold Acton had already produced two books of poems, not to mention the baroque fantasia *Cornelian*, whose appearance, early in 1928, Brian regarded as horribly premature. ("I don't think he should have published it, do you?" he suggested to Acton's brother William, for this was "essentially the clever young man's first novel—that thing that no one ought to publish.") In these circumstances Brian's silence could be regarded as deliberate. Acton and Byron might be rushing headlong into print. There were others who sensibly preferred to let their juvenilia remain in their notebooks. "I don't want to be handicapped, in the future, by a mass of bad early stuff," he proudly rationalized. "I know I have genius, of a kind, and I prefer to let it mature slowly. Meanwhile I educate myself."

Yet how slowly was slowly? And was this leisurely ascent to stardom compatible with the lack of maternal subsidy? Couldn't he have just a little more freedom, he petitioned Lura Howard in 1929, "now that I'm *really* serious, *really* trying to get a book done." Now, he feared, he would have "to write a quick, bad, *succès de scandale*." But there was no scandal or indeed success. What did emerge, on the other hand, was a no-nonsense aesthetic template, an emphatic how-to guide, which would bring the aspiring novelist instantly up to scratch:

THE NOVEL. 45,000 words. 5,000 words per week. The descriptive parts must be poetry, rather in the manner of Virginia Woolf. The dialogue, of which there must be a lot, very realistic. The tone of the novel must be light and humorous, without being in the least satirically so, like Firbank. Serious childishness, rather. No "wit" and, of course, no epigrams. *There must be a supernatural flavor*, about ordinary incidents. It must be outspoken, conveying the impression that it could not be anything else.

Descriptions *à la* Woolf, serious childishness, Firbank's ghost and a supernatural flavor, and all in 45,000 words. Was this the project mentioned in the course of a letter to his mother from 1930 ("I have written four thousand words of a novel which I intend to continue daily until it is done")? We shall never know, as the publishers' lists for 1931 contained only his solitary volume of poems, *God Save the King*, its appearance somewhat overshadowed by the absentmindedness of its sponsor, Nancy Cunard, who forgot to send out any review copies.

This by now chronic inability to produce anything was, as even Brian began to realize, becoming a problem. A second book of poems, the notionally titled *Splendours and Decorations of Bavaria*, somehow failed to materialize. Perhaps, when it came down to basics, one was still searching for a suitable medium. At last, he triumphantly informed his mother in 1931, he had found his prose style. "I have long strived to combine force and naturalness in prose, and I had to do it before starting my novel." Which novel would that be? In any case, the next letter home that touches on literary schemes hares off along an entirely different track. "My new plan at the moment is neither essays nor a novel," he wrote from Athens a year later, "but a kind of travel book. Simple but original." And, of course, unwritten.

By this time, ominously enough, the neurosis about not writing anything had reached such a pitch that it began to produce pieces of writing about not writing. "About Writing," a sketch from this period, finds a nonwriter called "Russell" explaining to a friend that he has just downed a glass of brandy "because of the terror of trying to write." Everything, Russell gravely explains, from money, the consciousness of not keeping up one's position as a clever young man and the necessity of not disappointing one's father, is driving him to write a book. But what kind of a book? Travel? Every young man writes a travel book and the result, young men being what they are, is simply a list of his irritations. So why not write a better one, the friend encourages, stand opposite the pyramids and *deal* with them? No, Russell ripostes. He is "haunted by a preference for trying to make a work of art. Not a Bright Young Baedeker." Well, a novel, then, the friend persists. "A novel! Heavens. A novel is a story. I can't make up a story. I can't live other people's lives. I can't live my own." And so incriminatingly on.

But there were only so many glasses of brandy one could drink. Faced with the "appalling bullying ghost" that is art, what was one to do? Perhaps, in the end—a common enough solution here in the collusive thirties—it was better to join forces, pool the inspiration and share the work. "Did I tell you that Wystan Auden asked me to collaborate on a book with him?" he told Lura Howard, some time in 1937. "I consider this a great feather in my cap from the most famous young poet of England." Where MacNeice had trodden perhaps Brian could tread too? The publishers Robert Hale had offered an advance of £6 a week for two months, and while doubtful about taking the money Brian decided, "I do want to do the book. I suddenly feel I can." An ambitious-sounding work titled *The Divorce of Heaven and Hell*—how wonderful Brian's titles always are!—a series of studies in English character and behavior, this was intended to explore "the great final division" in life: "between the Body and the Mind, to use the jargon of contemporary philosophy, Intellect and Intuition." An elaborate two-part synopsis survives. But no book.

Postwar, deep into the arid 1940s, a note of optimism still breaks occasionally above the routine murmurs of drift and foreign wanderings. In 1946 there was talk—but only talk—of a biography of Norman Douglas that he might write for the publishers Home & Van Thal. It was still possible, of course, to persuade oneself—or rather one's acquaintances—that this lifetime of lying fallow presumed a steely sense of interior purpose. "How wise you were to wait," Stephen Spender encouragingly remarked sometime in the early 1950s. ("Well, he didn't know that it was less shrewdness than sloth," the subject of this encomium conceded.) By this time Brian had another theory. What had kept him from writing, he declared a month before his fiftieth birthday, was "first—too much self-criticism, perfectionism. Second a swelling guilt." However, against all the odds, against all the gargantuan counterweights of habit and inanition, the creative flame still flickered faintly. He was "going to buy a big thick book tomorrow morning," Mrs. Howard learned in 1953, "and start, at least, keeping a journal. Baba [his pet name from infancy] has got to stop being Baba and start being Brian." And finally there was a fail-safe standby, the thing that would redeem all previous absences and hesitations, that triumphant validation of past time, however lackadaisically spent: the memoirs. "I want to ask your advice about a publisher for my autobiography," he addressed Cyril Connolly in 1956. "I seem to have got really started on them now, though they won't be finished for another year and that will only be Vol. 1 because I digress a great deal—I feel, Cyril, even if I 'say it myself,' that I shall probably be able to choose my publisher without fear of refusal, so which publisher shall it be?" What Connolly wrote in reply has not been preserved. Needless to say, no manuscript was ever found.

CHAPTER NINE

CELEBRITY CULTURE

The social column should not be scorned. It sheds revealing sidelights on the life of our times for the benefit of our grandchildren. In any case it is indispensable to the analysis of the epoch.

— PATRICK BALFOUR, *Society Racket*

"I can't think of what to say," said Lord Vanbrugh. "My editress said she was tired of seeing the same names over and over again—and here they are again, all of them. There's Nina Blount's engagement being broken off, but she's not got any publicity value to speak of. Agatha Runcible's usually worth a couple of paragraphs, but they're featuring her as a front-page news story tomorrow over this Customs House business."

— EVELYN WAUGH, *Vile Bodies*

More so than any youth cult that had preceded them, the Bright Young People were a creation of the media. The celebrity of the original treasure hunters and scavengers of the mid-1920s was the result of newspapers taking up the movement, defining its characteristics, burnishing its leading personalities and exporting the whole—increasingly detached from its roots—to the world beyond. The relationship—close, intense and with spectacular fallings-out on both sides—was wholly reciprocal. Editors wanted newsworthy stories which, in a frivolous age, this collection of predominantly upper-class pleasure seekers, many of them the children of famous parents, seemed uniquely qualified to provide. As their activities gathered pace, the Bright Young People wanted attention drawn to themselves and their goings-on presented in a more or less favorable light. Beverley Nichols's remark that the partygoers of the late 1920s disported themselves all the more fiercely "because we knew that the press was watching—and watching with a very disapproving eye" is faintly disingenuous. *Punch* might lampoon "the dull young people" or *The Times* condemn the gate-crasher with no sense of obligation to his host, but middle-market newspapers, eager then as now to appeal to younger readerships, were nearly always disposed to mild indulgence. Lord Monomark's enthusiasm for Adam's column in the *Daily Excess* ("Now see here Symes, I like your page. It's peppy, it's got plenty of new names in it and it's got that intimate touch") perfectly conveys the kind of editorial landscape in which the Bright Young People took root and prospered.

At the same time there was more to this connection than mutual need. On the one hand it turned the activities of the Bright Young People into self-consciously public events, which would not have happened—or, rather, would not have happened in quite the same way—without the presence of the press. On the other, the lines that separated its individual elements—those written about and those doing the writing—became increasingly blurred. Several Bright Young People worked on newspapers themselves or were in a position to supply editors with leads, gossip or pieces of freelance journalism. If the atmosphere of the late-twenties gossip column occasionally seems rather stifling—the Guinness-Mitford wedding in all its blue-blooded glory, the Honorable Mrs. Pelly spotted once again at the Café de Paris—it is because the world of society journalism had been so successfully colonized by the Bright Young People that they were able to influence a significant part of its agenda.

In their rush to emblazon themselves across the pages of the *Tatler*, the *Bystander* and the *Sketch*, the *Mail* and the *Express* and half a dozen other newspapers besides, the Bright Young People were also taking advantage of some of the profound changes that had begun to affect society journalism since the war. These had less to do with newfangled subject matter—newspapers had always been interested in "youth," high society and eccentric entertainments—than with changes in personnel. There had always been gossip columns, even in the starchiest days of the Victorian era, but the social status of the people who wrote them had not been high. Thackeray's complaint against the muckraking journalist Edmund Yates in the famous "Garrick Club Affair" of the late 1850s was that of ungentlemanly conduct: Yates, he maintained, had printed details about him that could have been picked up only from private conversations eavesdropped on at the club of which they were both members. Seventy years later the idea of the deferential satellite had begun to develop into something far more complex. In *Society Racket* Patrick Balfour, himself a key beneficiary of the change, offered a survey of what seemed to him to be a radical transformation of the form. The pre-1914 "paragraph writer" had generally been a woman with journalistic connections, employed by a society hostess as a kind of press secretary. In this guise she would supply details of her mistress's entertainments, movements ("Lady X has lately departed to Biarritz") and couture, express "general regret" when she was ill and "general satisfaction" when she recovered. Photographs of Lady X at Ascot, Lady X at Cowes and Lady X accompanying her husband to the Eton-Harrow match at Lord's could be offered to news desks, along with occasional items that might have the effect of embarrassing Lady X's rivals in the field.

In the less hidebound atmosphere of the postwar era, newspapers began to recruit from within, employing society people themselves to write their social news. Percy Sewell, the original "Dragoman" of the *Express*, was, Balfour believed, one of the first columnists to know the world he wrote about rather than having its details conveyed to him indirectly or being told what to write by his titled employer. However, Colonel Sewell's daily descent on the *Express* office—where, as his subordinate Tom Driberg remembered, he might contrive to introduce the names of his friends Lady Maureen Stanley, Sir Horace Rumbold and Lady Sybil Grant onto the page—was in no way revolutionary. His forte was elderly aristocratic ladies and aged clubmen. It was not until 1926 that the *Sunday Express* introduced the first signed social column, Lord Castlerosse's "Londoners' Log." But other editors took their cue, and within a year Fleet Street was full of well-connected and correspondingly well-informed society columnists who either admitted their identities at the foot of the page or did not scruple to reveal them to their friends. Lady Eleanor Smith began contributing sightings from her

"Window in Mayfair" to the *Sunday Dispatch* in 1927. Lord Donegall appeared in the soon to be defunct *Sunday News*. Balfour began his career on the *Evening Standard* before graduating to an influential job on the *Daily Sketch*. Naturally, there were distinctions to be made—Castlerosse was the middle-aged man about town, Donegall a younger, "modern" version—but the cumulative effect was the same: social columns that were better informed, more smartly written and included confidential details that would have been unthought of before the war.

The new style of society journalism, and the behavior of society journalists, did not go unremarked. In certain quarters it and they were received with furious hostility. *The Times*, in particular, fought a long rearguard action against what it called "the social columnist." To this end it printed a letter from "A London Hostess" complaining about the "sneak guest." What had at one time been "mere idle and comparatively harmless chatter," this lady alleged, had developed into "a regular system of spying, fueled by the publication of the most deplorable hints and insinuations." Such protests were quickly extinguished. There was a particular irony in *The Times* mounting an attack on the publicizing of social events: as several rival journals gleefully pointed out, its "Court and Social" page was the only medium in the United Kingdom in which people paid to advertise their social gatherings. The gossip column, Balfour declared, was an institution in which *all* parties—host and hostess, partygoer and press cameraman—gamely colluded. People who led public lives were fair game, he insisted: "Hostesses who invite the Press to their parties for the purposes of advertisement must today consider themselves in the same position as dramatists who invite the Press to their first nights." Evelyn Waugh took the same no-nonsense line. Hard words were said about the "selling of one's friends" by those who were never sold, he told readers of *Passing Show* early in 1929. The truth was that society secretly adored its publicity. "Once it becomes known that you are 'Mr. Chit-Chat of the Daily Excess' your social popularity is ensured and invitations from total strangers cover your chimney-piece."

Inevitably, there were occupational hazards. Not everyone appreciated the links that were proposed for them with London's smart younger set, much less the venues in which these entertainments took place. "As a Member of Parliament and a man holding responsible positions in the City of London and elsewhere, Major Kindersley strongly resents the publicity you have given his name in association with the Gargoyle Club and the apparently unusual fancy dress dance to be held under its auspices," ran a letter of complaint to Balfour's office. What really irked the specimen Mayfair hostess, it might be said, was the sight of the gossip-monger's craft being practiced by stealth: amateur freelancers subsidizing their social life with late-night telephone calls and surreptitious head counting. But the newly liberated palisades of the social column were ripe for infiltration by the Bright Young People. Several of them—Balfour, Driberg and half a dozen lesser fry—were gossip columnists themselves, grateful for tips, happy to supply publicity, permanently on hand to puff their friends and their friends' activities. Others used their connections with society magazines to bring in much-needed pocket money. Nancy Mitford, for example, who began her career supplying anonymous paragraphs, once underwrote a trip to Cullen by arranging to photograph the party for the *Tatler*. By the early thirties Nancy had graduated to signed columns in *The Lady*, humorous reflections on such topics as "In the Witness Box," "The Art of Being Photographed," "The Long Weekend Party" and "The Fourth of June." Bright Young People who had established their reputations, on the other hand, tended to use particular gossip-writing friends as conduits to the wider world. Robert Byron shamelessly employed Balfour to publicize his books and his foreign jaunts. Waugh, alternatively, used Driberg's column in the *Express* as a kind of message board, encouraging his old school contemporary to announce his conversion to Catholicism in 1930, the row he conducted with the editor of *The Tablet* over *Black Mischief* in 1932 and, as late as 1936, his engagement to Laura Herbert.

There were rare occasions when proximity to the gossip world could be a hindrance rather than a help: Alan Pryce-Jones's chances of marrying the daughter of a senior Conservative MP in the teeth of parental opposition were extinguished by sympathetic paragraphs to the effect that "love will find a way." In his own case, love was told to absent itself and find a proper job. But in general Bright Young People were effective conspirators in the backstairs world of late-twenties gossip broking, creating an environment in which certain Bright Young entertainments, and their impresarios, could be guaranteed more or less favorable coverage.

Understandably, this engagement existed on several levels. More reflective Bright Young People had occasional doubts about the value of the world they had involved themselves with, worried that friends busily at large in it were selling themselves short or that they themselves would be tainted by the association. Cyril Connolly's late-twenties journals offer characteristic agonizings on this theme. An arriviste to his bones, Connolly was hugely attracted by the "smart" world that gossip columnists fed off and fascinated by the spectacle of his friend Balfour in action ("Patrick was telephoning; and waited ten minutes to speak to Princess Bismarck"). From another angle the man who settled himself in Yeoman's Row in September 1927 wondered if sharing a house with a society columnist was good enough for the serious image he was cultivating for himself: "No man likes to admit that he is about to live with a fool." Before long, however, Connolly had joined the trade himself, selling his own snippets to magazine editors and presumably making use of such crumbs as fell from Balfour's table. Rather like Waugh, Connolly's fascination with smart society could often tip over into outright contempt. His diaries, consequently, combine a good deal of snobbish delight in the company he kept with bitter—and rather heavy-handed—satires of Balfour's professional beat:

The Café Anglais Leicester Square. Ting a ling. Ting a ling thrill. Your usual table Mr. Balfour, room please for Mr. Tossoff of the Daily Squirt. Close up of a young man of an extreme elegance, pouting, receding, wherever possible, except at his waist which is slightly pot bellied. "Waiter this caviar is cold—bring me the temperature of the room." "O Darling, O I'd adore to—O can't we all go somewhere sometime and do something—O Darling, I'd adore to, Why there's—and there's"—"He's the dragoman"—"He's ipecacuanha Smith"—"He's our lives from day to day."

There was to be plenty more of this—Mr. "Poke" Balfour sitting with the lovely Diana Brassiere and Lady Priscilla Piprag—none of it quite salving Connolly's deep unease over the time he spent in Yeoman's Row and the conflicting emotions it aroused in his ever-sensitive breast.

There were dozens more Connollys: young, well-connected men who in another age, satisfied with their lots, would have proceeded into the world of the professions or Parliament but who now, fetched up in a less congenial environment, were marking time, sticking with the people they had grown up with and using them to promote what careers they had—Connolly at this stage was making his name as a *New Statesman* reviewer—and being used in their turn. Singly and collectively, helped by sensation-seeking editors and a sensation-seeking press, they had by the end of the 1920s created an early form of celebrity culture whose impact could be felt at practically every level of society. The Bright Young People themselves judged their social success by weight of press cuttings. In *Basil Seal Rides Again* (1963), Evelyn Waugh's late-period return to the world of his youth, Waugh notes of Sonia Trumpington that, "like most of her generation," she had when young "filled large volumes with press-cuttings and photographs of herself and her friends." Yet these continual appearances in the media could not have been kept up without support from further down the social scale. Gossip columns, in other words, both fulfilled a need and supplied a market. Had they not done so, editors would not have printed them. In *Vile Bodies* the Honorable Agatha Runcible and her satellites take up residence in a house owned by Lord Throbbing, Miles Malpractice's elder brother. At first the caretakers resent this invasion. Then, as Miss Runcible explains, "We gave them drinks and things, and now they're simply thrilled to the marrow about it and spend all their time cutting out 'bits,' my dear, from the papers about our goings on."

As a media phenomenon, consequently, the Bright Young People's allure worked on several levels. Editors were interested not merely in "names" but in the juxtaposition of celebrated parents and the hedonistic antics of their children: Elizabeth Ponsonby setting up as a mannequin while her father labored in committee rooms with J. H. Thomas and Ramsay Macdonald; the Mitford girls outraging the otherwise placid atmosphere of the Swinbrook breakfast table. (Lady Redesdale once complained that whenever she saw a newspaper headline beginning "Peer's daughter in . . ." she knew instinctively that it was one of her children.) To the thousands of readers who existed on subsidiary rungs of the social ladder, the goal was aspirational: one had attended a nightclub mentioned by "The Dragoman"; one had been at school with the cross-dressing adornment of the latest charity pageant. Peripheral associations of this kind acted as a powerful spur: the journalistic equivalent of the twenties hit song "I've Danced with a Man Who's Danced with a Girl Who's Danced with the Prince of Wales." Further down the ladder, middle-class readers of papers such as the *Express* and the *Mail* looked on with a combination of puritanical disapproval and fascinated prurience. All this had an incremental effect in focusing public attention on the Bright Young People, in establishing the protocols by which they got written about, characterizing the type of people they were and selecting their leading personalities for comment and exposure.

Naturally the process could not have succeeded without its orchestrators, media impresarios who understood both the nature of the world they were reporting and the aspects of it that would interest their readers. The most important of these columnists were Balfour and Driberg—the latter the most important of all, as he wrote for Beaverbrook's mass-circulation *Express*, the most influential middle-market paper of the day. In the context of early-twentieth-century social history, Driberg's career is a striking example of the extremely circuitous route by which talented young men could introduce themselves to the public gaze—and also of the deceits which occasionally had to be practiced while this introduction was taking place. Despite his public school and Oxford background, Driberg, as a card-carrying Communist and a predatory homosexual, was exactly the kind of person of whom Lord Beaverbrook might have been expected to disapprove. For all these disabilities, Driberg's credentials for the kind of job he pursued were impeccable. At Oxford he had known Acton, Howard and Bryan Guinness, and written vers libre in the approved sub-Eliot style. Intending on a literary career, he rented a room in Frith Street at 12s. 6d. a week, raising additional funds by pawning his valuables and even resorting to casual prostitution. When the money ran out, he took a job as general factotum in a café for 5s. a week plus bed and board. A great one for lowlife and downmarket companions, Driberg always maintained that he was perfectly happy at this time and enjoyed his daily routines. Like other Bright Young People, though, he had influential sponsors. Edith Sitwell, who admired his poems, lobbied on his behalf. Her brother Osbert was sent to petition Beverley Baxter, Beaverbrook's editor on the *Express*, and shortly before Christmas 1927 Driberg was summoned to an interview with the features editor. Hired on the strength of a piece on London nightlife, at a salary of £3 a week, he found himself filling the trainee reporter's berth lately vacated by his old Lancing friend Evelyn Waugh.

Tall, saturnine and vaguely clerical in appearance, Driberg and his gravity went down well with senior members of the *Express*'s staff. He was a ceremonious young man who once rebuked his younger colleague Osbert Lancaster for failing to stand up when the editor came into the room. To enhance his position, however, he needed a scoop. Significantly, each of his first exclusives for the paper came courtesy of the social networks he had developed at Oxford. The first covered the arrival in Oxford of the American evangelist Dr. Frank Buchman and his attempts to recruit among the undergraduates (REVIVAL SCENES AT OXFORD, STRANGE NEW SECT, PRAYER MEETING IN A COLLEGE). The second was his telephoned report from the Bath and Bottle Party at St. George's Swimming Baths. Realizing that in Driberg they possessed one of the few people in Fleet Street who could write about Bright Young entertainments as an insider, the *Express* appointed him assistant to Colonel Sewell, whose column "The Talk of London" was signed "The Dragoman," a Turkish word meaning guide or conductor. At this point in their history the Dragoman's musings consisted of innocuous gossip about Sewell's aristocratic friends. Almost immediately the contrasting styles of the two compilers became apparent: Sewell hymning the accomplishments of Sir Horace and Lady Maureen, Driberg supplying paragraphs that contained "mostly the names of my school and Oxford generation, people of a younger generation than Sewell's, many of them not rich or aristocratic, some of them writers and artists."

There was no overnight revolution. Colonel Sewell continued to purvey anodyne scraps of information gleaned from friends' luncheon tables. Driberg, meanwhile, was introducing the names of Nancy Mitford and Evelyn Waugh to the *Express*'s readership—Christopher Sykes remembered Driberg bringing a copy of *Decline and Fall* to a nursing home where Sykes was recovering from an operation in September 1928—commending frivolous new novels and exhibitions and in general reducing the median age of the column's cast by two or three decades. In later years, as the former stalwart of the two-person University of Oxford Communist Party—the other member was A. J. P. Taylor—Driberg professed a certain guilt at the Dragoman's apparent lack of political awareness. Happily, justification lay to hand. Under Driberg

the tone of the column, so far as I could influence it, became more and more satiric. I described in detail the absurdities and extravagances of the ruling class in a way calculated to annoy any working-class or unemployed people who might chance to read the column; at a time of mass unemployment I felt I was doing something not without value to the Communist Party, to which I was still connected.

From the vantage point of Driberg's late-twenties lifestyle, this is horribly unconvincing. The number of unemployed people who chanced upon the Dragoman's reporting of the Wild West Party and the Great Urban Dionysia could have been counted in small handfuls, and those readers would have struggled to find very much political awareness in the portraits of Brian Howard, Babe Plunket Greene, Harold Acton, John Betjeman and Peter Quennell with which Driberg filled his columns, or such entertainments as the Greek Party, whose invitation instructed: "Extraordinarily beautiful dresses, which are not expensive to make, may be copied from the Greek vases in the British Museum." In the 1930s, Driberg did manage to smuggle the odd reference to hunger marches and unemployment into his dispatches from the Mayfair front line, but in his late-1920s heyday his stance was essentially that of the

Bright Young Person reporting a social event from which he had himself returned home earlier that morning.

There were occasional rows with Beaverbrook, who favored "profiling" rather than paragraphs of gossip, but in general Driberg was a success, sought after by hostesses and a proven contributor to the *Express*'s dominant role in the marketplace. In 1933 he mutated into "William Hickey," a Fleet Street institution that continues to this day. But Driberg was a sharp operator, an astute performer on the high-wire act of the twenties social column who knew exactly how far he could go while maintaining apparent detachment. Other Bright Young People whose reputations had been forged in the 1920s—a process in which they had cheerfully conspired—were unable to stop the cavalcade they had set in motion.

For all the incidental drama of her career, Brenda Dean Paul's was a rather typical Bright Young Person background, combining grandeur, exoticism and lack of money, the whole bound up with a scent of racketiness that eventually enveloped practically everything she touched. Her mother, Irene Wieniawski, the youngest daughter of a celebrated Polish violinist and composer, had met her husband, Sir Aubrey Dean Paul, on a visit to England as the guest of Nellie Melba. By her own account Brenda, born in 1907, grew up "a solemn, pensive baby . . . a curiously purposeful child. Early on I sensed a goal, some state and condition of beauty and truth, and sent out feelers, groping blindly in my child's perplexity." The infant Brenda demanded to go to boarding school ("Knowing with a curious foresight that suffering was inevitable with a nature such as mine, I determined of my own accord, and long before my teens, to submerge my sensitive instincts to the best of my capacity"). A number of convents having cheerfully welcomed and eagerly bidden farewell to her—*"Ah, c'est toujours la même chose avec Brenda,"* one exasperated Reverend Mother remarked: wartime taxation, two residences and school fees precipitated a domestic crisis, her mother's departure for America and the breakup of the family home.

Zealously at large upon the margins of London society, where their friends included Noël Coward, Mrs. Benjamin Guinness and her daughters and the Jungman sisters, Brenda and her mother were increasingly strapped for cash. By May 1923, when Brenda was attending her first evening parties, they were living in furnished rooms in Ebury Street, Lady Dean Paul working in Baroness d'Erlanger's dress shop while her daughter put in appearances at Nancy Prior's school of acting in Westminster. Subsequently they removed to a tiny flat in a mews behind the baroness's house in Piccadilly. Like Elizabeth Ponsonby, with whom she had probably come into contact at this point, Brenda was convinced that her talents were best suited to the stage. At Easter 1924, adding three years to her age, she walked into the office of a theatrical agent and was offered the role of ingénue in a northern touring company.

There were to be other dramatic performances, both on and off the stage. Lady Dean Paul, meanwhile, had set up as a society dressmaker, operating out of a studio in Yeoman's Row and numbering among her clientele Queen Mary and the Prince of Wales. For a while, abetted by well-placed sponsors, the business looked as if it might prosper—Mrs. Guinness arranged a dress show of her models in which a dozen debutantes paraded them before a select audience at Carlton House Terrace—but the running expenses and the late hours were too much for Lady Dean Paul's pocket and health. Brenda, by this time, had determined to separate herself from her mother, largely to pursue a relationship with Harry Walker, David Tennant's associate in the running of the Gargoyle Club. "W," as Brenda cryptically referred to him in print, was ten years older than his mistress, "but in knowledge of life and understanding of human nature he was as old as the mountains and the seas." There were endless rows and quarrels, "but invariably I forgave him, for I realized that he was too important an element in my life, and my affection was not of the clinging physical womanly kind, but a far deeper union of the spirit, bound by a telepathy and understanding both natural and spontaneous." The affair was over by the end of 1927 and Brenda, already established as the society It girl of her day, looked out for fresh opportunities.

By this stage—she was still barely twenty—the main stanchions of her character were firmly established. They included an eagerness to take part in any social event that happened to be on offer, a fatal attraction for the wrong type of man and a deep-rooted emotional frailty that led her to embark on the most madcap schemes—these were usually connected to her acting ambitions—at the drop of a hat. Taken to the Chelsea Arts Ball at Christmas 1927, she struck up a conversation with an attaché at the British embassy in Berlin, who offered introductions to the city's film world. Nothing loath, Brenda set out across the Continent by train. En route to Berlin, again by chance, she fell into conversation with a film producer, who offered her a screen test. Introduced to Berlin nightlife, then at the height of its Weimar-era decadence, Brenda was unimpressed. "Curiously enough, amidst all this atmosphere of 'degeneracy,' which it is called in this country, there was nothing squalid in their behavior . . . There was nothing really deeply shocking when one regarded these people from the standpoint of interesting phenomena . . . sincere and serious." Sadly, visit, screen test and burgeoning movie career alike were curtailed by a bout of appendicitis: Brenda went back to England.

Rather like Iris Storm, the peripatetic heroine of Michael Arlen's *The Green Hat* (1924), Brenda was constantly restless. Desperate to leave her London base once more ("I could never remain in England"), she next set off for Paris. Here at a party she met a man named "Leo" who retired into a room with what looked like a box of Eno's fruit salts and returned "reborn." The box turned out to contain powdered heroin. Squired around Paris by her new friend, Brenda was induced to sample the drug. As with the Berlin transvestites, the effect was disappointing. Concealing the fact that this was her first experience of narcotics, she took a pinch and held it to her nose in the approved Parisian manner. "The result was hardly what I expected, no exhilaration was mine, no re-born revitality, just the feeling that the top of my head had been suddenly and neatly decapitated like that of a boiled egg." She woke from a drug-induced stupor to a blazing argument with Leo, who attacked her with a hot poker.

Back in London, in the hot summer of 1928, Brenda became an acute observer of the development of the Bright Young People's party. A scene sweller from the earliest days, she remembered the pioneering enthusiasm that had produced parties "outstanding" in their originality, had been taught dance steps by Florence Mills ("If anyone, Brenda, will learn to be a dancer, a colored dancer, you will. You have it in you. Why, one would think you were born in Harlem," Miss Mills enthused) and attended every gathering of the day from David Tennant's Edwardian extravaganza to the Bath and Bottle Party. At David Tennant's Greek Party, for which the host hired a restaurant in Marylebone High Street for the night, decorating the interior as an Attic temple, she had herself wound into yards of white chiffon and lacquered her hair into golden ringlets. "It was a mad, crazy party with many beautiful dresses." The American Party, staged at a West End gallery, she marked down as "by far the wildest and most enjoyable" she ever attended. "Never have I seen people let themselves go the extent they did that night, for the band had been specially imported from Harlem, and the rhythms intoxicating without the additional stimulus of alcohol."

No dowager viewed the degeneration of late-twenties social life with more disdain than Brenda. Hot for genuine bohemianism—she liked the socially indiscriminate crowd of Mayfair habitués and stage folk who illumined the American Party and was a friend of Ed Burra— she was appalled by the new wave of outsiders who began to colonize Bright Young People's territory at the end of the 1920s. But there was also the looming question of herself: what she intended to do with her life, where this breathless round of partygoing, country weekends and foreign trips might eventually take her. Stick thin, ever effervescent, always exquisitely got up, her likeness survives in an endless stream of press photographs: posing, glass aloft, with elaborately marceled hair; pouting over her shoulder while dancing with the painter Stephen Hill at the Mozart Party. Now romantically involved with David Tennant ("Mr. David Tennant is an eager student of Philosophy," Eleanor Smith informed readers of the *Sunday Dispatch*. "One of the greatest triumphs of his philosophy is that he has persuaded the laziest girl of my acquaintance to rise at eight o'clock each day to join him in his researches"), she decamped to Canada with him, only to fall out with her escort, who cabled for his wife and daughter to replace her.

As the Bright Young People's movement moved closer to its death throes, Brenda's path through the Mayfair throng became yet more erratic. By this time her reputation was practically a guarantee of trouble at any social gathering she attended. Greeting John Strachey on a teatime visit to Shulbrede in December 1930, Dorothea was alarmed to note that the young man had "a wound on his nose":

> He told me about it—a party given by a man in Glebe Place. David Tennant went up to Brenda Dean Paul & called her a whore—which she is—only one doesn't say these things in public. He then proceeded to have a fight with some man who took her part & they got to sprawling on the floor, John went to pull David Tennant away & was belabored by Hermione his wife who burned J's nose with a cigarette.

By late 1930 Brenda was traveling abroad with "Gerald." The itinerary included New York, California and Tahiti. Impressed by the "gentleness, sympathy and intelligence" of the Harlem partygoers, she caused a sensation at the New York Stock Exchange, where she was mistaken for the Hollywood actress Clara Bow; a police escort was required to extract her from the crowd. A second trip to America produced a recipe for what Manhattan christened the "Brenda cocktail," a terrifying concoction made up of equal parts French white wine and gin with a dash of grapefruit juice. But the storm clouds were gathering. "Gerald," who had asked her to marry him, was respectfully turned down. Brenda was keener on a new admirer, known as "the romantic interest." Back in England and holidaying with her fast friend Anthea Carew ("one of the staunchest friends I've ever had"), a crisis presented itself: Brenda thought she might be pregnant. The "romantic interest," tracked down to New York and at first supportive, eventually telephoned to plead poverty brought about by the Wall Street crash.

The effect on Brenda's frail constitution was decisive. After some serious drinking, she fell dangerously ill and was given morphine to prevent what the doctors feared would be a fatal hemorrhage. To add to her difficulties, Lady Dean Paul was also seriously unwell. Her daughter, meanwhile, without herself being aware of the fact, was turning into a heroin addict. "Whether it was owing to my devitalized condition, I do not know, but my system had become so acclimatized to the regular administration of morphine during the past weeks, that I sought the immediate advice of a doctor, genuinely unaware of what the true malady from which I felt myself suffering turned out to be." Dispatched to a nursing home, she was given hyoscine, which sent her into convulsions. Instructed to convalesce but still relying on a private morphine supply, she tried to commit suicide by slashing her wrists with a piece of broken tooth glass. With one prescription allowed her by the doctor who was supervising her recovery, Brenda then acquired a second from a medical man who was booked to operate on her for a gynecological condition. This was illegal, and in November 1931 she received seven summonses for offenses against the Dangerous Drugs Act. Clive Bell, a friend of Lady Dean Paul, agreed to stand bail. Arraigned at Marlborough Street Magistrates Court, Brenda was eventually given probation for three years and sent to a nursing home.

Prison, Brenda's friends agreed, had been avoided only by a hairsbreadth. More alarming, though, was her physical condition. Gwen Plunket Greene, who had become involved in the case through her daughter Olivia's friendship with Brenda, provided an eyewitness account of her first appearance in court to her sister:

> We got B off by the skin of her teeth. The magistrate seemed till the very last moment inflexible—sitting staring at Brenda like a juggernaut . . . Brenda looks dying—she is so utterly changed that Olivia says she can't make out *who* she is . . . If you could see her! It's too terrible. One of the solicitors said to me that he cd not look at her. I sat immediately behind her . . . + her shaking body and sobs were intolerably painful. Every policeman's face was a study in pity and concern.

Her weight, by this stage, had fallen to barely eighty-six pounds. As she fell into her friend's arms after the verdict was pronounced, Gwen thought that a hearth rug weighed more. "It is pitiful."

As far as Brenda's health and happiness were concerned, this was the end of any attempt to lead a normal life. It also marked the heightening of her relationship with the press. This was a curious alliance in which each side may be said to have exploited the other: Brenda alternately welcoming and reproving the reporters who dogged her steps and making money from articles written in her name; newspapers offering dramatic bulletins on her periodic collapses. Judged solely by weight of newspaper cuttings, Brenda had, by the early 1930s, attained a degree of celebrity that far outstripped Elizabeth Ponsonby, or indeed any other of the Bright Young People, and extended well beyond middle-class newspapers such as the *Mail* and the *Express* into the world of the Sunday tabloids. Notorious, drug-ridden and now motherless—Lady Dean Paul had died in early 1932—she was at this point being helped by a "Mrs. E," possibly a reference to Gwen Plunket Greene. One of this lady's self-imposed tasks was to plot a reconciliation with the romantic interest, whom Brenda had previously attempted to sue "in an endeavor to secure some compensation for the harm I considered he had done me." Desperate for money to settle lawyers' bills and nursing home fees, she eagerly accepted a Sunday newspaper's proposal for a series of articles about her time in Tahiti. Still, though, the funds were running low and the situation compounded by the authorities' insistence that she should live in suitable accommodation with a nurse or chaperone. In the end, neither being procurable, she was given an ultimatum: either find a supervising doctor or face admission to Holloway Prison Infirmary. After some prevarication, an old friend of her mother's found a medical man who was prepared to take her in.

There followed one of Brenda's most memorable exploits, perfectly illustrative of both the almost random impulses that governed her life and her underlying dependence on drugs. "Doctor Z," in whose care she reposed, decided to assist her recovery by administering morphine in small doses. Several factors now conspired to disturb his patient's equilibrium. Shortly afterward, all ties with the romantic interest having been severed, she announced her engagement to "a certain young stockbroker," met at a cocktail party, "whose genuine sympathy and apparent admiration had been clear for all to see." There was also hope, advertised by "a certain young Frenchman connected with the Fox Film Company in Paris," of film work abroad. In August 1932, on a whim and a weekend ticket but with no passport, Brenda absconded to France.

It was a disaster on all counts. Predictably, there was no sign of "M. Duprès," the Fox Film Company's gallant emissary. Worse, Brenda quickly ran out of morphine. Her predicament might have been soluble had not Paris been deserted for the Feast of the Assumption and most of the pharmacies closed. As it was she collapsed in a cheap hotel, begging the doctor who was eventually summoned: "*Morphine . . . Je suis morphiniste.*"

Almost from the moment of her admission, Brenda's stay in the British Hertford Hospital became a press sensation. The switchboard was jammed by inquiring reporters. Back in England, posters proclaiming BRENDA'S LATEST ESCAPADE appeared on every street corner. Her fiancé, meanwhile, determined to leave London to rescue her. His progress was monitored by the radio news on an almost step-by-step basis: "Brenda's fiancé leaves for Croydon . . . He has reached Croydon and boarded the air liner . . . He is over the Channel . . . He passes Etaples . . . He is at Le Bourget . . . He is in a car . . . He reaches Paris . . . HE IS AT THE HOSPITAL." He arrived to find the telephone lines at the Hertford still jammed and a crowd of French journalists—the local media having woken up to Brenda's newsworthiness—camped outside in the street. Returning by air to England, they were pursued to Doctor Z's house by a convoy of newspapermen: "The street outside was like Paris, lined with reporters and camera-men. They filled the hall; some were even half-way up the stairs." Exhausted, ill and thoroughly exasperated, Brenda greeted the interrogative throng who trailed her up the staircase by throwing her suitcases at them.

The fiancé, who no doubt had his reasons, seems to have chosen this moment to quit the scene. By the early autumn, still in lowish water, Brenda found herself in further trouble with the authorities. Keen to get hold of extra morphine, she persuaded a friend—also a regular user—to send it up by train from the country to Waterloo. This, too, was illegal and Brenda, her progress around the capital now being monitored by the police, was arrested outside the station parcels office. While arrangements were being made for her trial, she was dispatched to Holloway Infirmary and placed in the observation ward. ("Never had I seen such a bed! It was an iniquitous creation of iron and straw, and seemed about fifteen inches wide, with coarse unbleached calico sheets the color of cheese.") Remanded for six months, she was transferred to the care of a Dr. Frederick Stewart at his residence in Beckenham, with instructions to report back in four weeks' time. There followed another nine days of hyoscine, administered by a Dr. Given. However, by this time Brenda's system was so habituated to hyoscine "cures" that "the quantity sufficient to knock me out was sufficient to kill ten men." There were additional problems: her kidneys were affected; an inflamed tooth needed a cocaine injection. Having missed the court appearance, she was sentenced in her absence to six months' imprisonment.

Brenda, in fact, was seriously ill—so ill that the police doctor who examined her at Dr. Stewart's residence refused to sanction her removal. Friends made representations in the highest quarters—the Home Secretary himself was approached—but authority declined to yield: Brenda was returned to Holloway. Here "Prisoner 54086's" condition deteriorated rapidly. Stomach spasms made her unable to keep down food. "As the day of my appeal drew nearer, I became a burning mass of alternating hope and despair." Happily, the appeal succeeded and she was sent to a nursing home at Chobham, the fees met by a subscription levied by Gwen Plunket Greene. This produced £500. Its beneficiary, on the other hand, was left in near solitude. "Perhaps too this was a kind of prison?" she mused. Escaping from the Chobham establishment, she was quickly recaptured and went into a further decline. At one point her weight fell to a little over seventy pounds. The only palliative, her doctors discovered—though they declined to reveal the treatment—was to administer further small doses of morphine.

Irrespective of its effect on Brenda's health, all this presented an interesting legal problem. The funds raised by Mrs. Plunket Greene had all disappeared. At court, to which Brenda was subsequently returned, there was great doubt as to what could or should be done. In the end the magistrate adjourned the case for a week "to find out what my powers are in a position like this." The press, meanwhile, was rallying round. DRUGS OR MADNESS AND DEATH, flared one headline. UNLESS SHE RECEIVES EVER-INCREASING DOSES OF DRUGS, BRENDA WILL GO MAD AND DIE, ran another. SOCIETY GIRL LIVES FOUR WEEKS IN HOLLOWAY

WITHOUT DOPE BUT WOULD DIE WITHOUT IT IN LUXURY NURSING HOME, suggested a third. With neither medicine nor the legal process apparently able to help her, Brenda reached her lowest ebb: "I was done, utterly done. The horror of it, the foul distorted sensationalism of those headlines." Help was at hand, however, in the person of Lord Dawson of Penn, the king's surgeon, who told the court that she was quite capable of looking after herself if she could recuperate quietly in the country. "You are quite mad, you know," this gentleman is supposed to have remarked, "but you are a young and foolish girl and you can and should be saved." In funds again, after pocketing £50 for another newspaper article, Brenda retired to what she imagined would be the tranquil anonymity of Devon. Alas, her reputation had gone before her, "and I soon realized to what terrible extent of harm and damage all the publicity of my case had wrought. A wretched libel had been circulated there, through a certain section of the press, of my supposed drug smuggling activities in Devonshire, and I found every door closed to me." A sailor she knew had been dismissed from his ship for supposedly trafficking on her behalf and the locals cut her dead.

Again the funds were running low. Once more, though, a Sunday paper was on hand to offer money for a series of articles recounting her plight, which could then be turned into a book. While welcoming the offer, Brenda discovered that her notoriety had reached the stage at which it was impossible to lead any kind of even semipublic life. She hired a hotel room to begin work on her life story, only to be asked to leave when the manager discovered who she was. A well-known actress studiously ignored her in a cocktail bar. These slights, and the strain of having her experiences committed to paper, produced a relapse and she retired once more to the Beckenham nursing home. What was to be done? Mallorca looked a safe bet, but the barrage of press publicity had traveled as far as the Balearics and the authorities announced that they had no accommodation for "mental cases." Brenda would not be allowed to land. Finally, Elizabeth Ponsonby mentioned the secluded cottage at Cranleigh in Surrey which she had once rented with Babe Bosdari. Here Brenda and her brother Brian arrived in June 1933, determined to complete the manuscript that would disclose the truth of her misfortunes to the world. They were pursued by numberless messages of support from the newspaper-reading public, including one from a widower in India who offered his hand in marriage. Six months later, refreshed by country air—photographs show a still painfully gaunt young woman self-consciously disporting herself in the cottage garden—Brenda wrote, or dictated, what were to be the concluding words of her autobiography: "I am in a 'limbo,' a place of hazy peace, that I dare not think to shatter, and where I shall halt until it is decided by the gods whether now, at the end of my first life, 'To be continued,' or 'Finis' shall be written."

CHAPTER TEN

GAY YOUNG PEOPLE

How is one to find the perfect young man, either they seem to be half-witted, or half-baked, or absolute sinks of vice or else actively dirty . . . All *very* difficult.

— NANCY MITFORD, letter to her brother, Tom, June 1928

TUES. FEB 1	Tea Babe
	Dine Beverley
THUR. FEB 3	Dine Paddy
FRI. FEB 4	Lunch Brian
SAT. FEB 5	David's Party
FRI. FEB 11	Boulestin 7:30 Harry Melville
TUES. FEB 15	Tony dinner, Gargoyle 7:30

— EDDIE GATHORNE-HARDY'S diary, 1927

Homosexuality was as characteristic of the Bright Young People as a cloche hat or an outsize party invitation. No English youth movement, it is safe to say, has ever contained such a high proportion of homosexuals or—in an age when these activities were still illegal—been so indulgent of their behavior. There were several reasons for the irretrievable air of campness with which the average Bright Young entertainment of the 1920s was riotously invested, symbolized, perhaps, by the unwritten law of the Oxford Hypocrites Club that "gentlemen may prance but not dance." On the one hand the movement's constituency extended deep into the bohemian subworld in which homosexuality had immemorially flourished. On the other, most male Bright Young People were recruited from English public schools, where homosexuality, if not tolerated by vigilant headmasters, was endemically present among the pupils. Looking back on her teenage years, Jessica Mitford noted that "nearly every English boy I knew had a terrific exposure to homosexuality . . . Some stuck to it, some didn't, but nobody paid much attention either way, as I recall . . ."

To this already charged atmosphere could be added the tendency of many of the era's young men to pass through a homosexual "stage" before settling down into heterosexual marriage. Evelyn Waugh, for example, went through a violent gay phase at Oxford before setting his cap, unsuccessfully, at Olivia Plunket Greene. Even Brian Howard, than whom no other homosexual Bright Young Person was more notorious, assumed until at least his late thirties that his eventual destiny was the altar steps and joked with his mother about prospective grandchildren. Wider cultural factors tended to magnify these confusions. As we have seen, newspaper columnists worried endlessly about the new breed of young man—epicene, nonathletic, defiantly "cultured"—who had grown up since the war. The members of Oxford rowing eights who lost to Cambridge in the annual university boat race were routinely stigmatized as "decadent"—rather as if, as Anthony Powell protested, the oars were wielded by Harold Acton and his friends. In these circumstances it was not always easy to distinguish period flamboyance from what contemporary newspapers regarded as deep-dyed inversion: many society hostesses were prepared to treat Stephen Tennant as a mannered eccentric rather than a potential corrupter of youth.

Bright Young People's homosexuality, consequently, took in a variety of forms: predatory career homosexuals; nervously experimental young men; Wilde-era survivors; and many more besides. At its core lay a group of orchidaceous Etonians—Eton was perhaps the most openly gay school of the era—with an insider's knowledge of each other's characteristics and peccadilloes. When Tom Mitford tried to warn his sister Nancy off Hamish Erskine, it was because he himself had had an affair with Erskine at Eton and knew his unreliability firsthand. Into this Etonian category fell such ornaments of the scene as Brian Howard, Eddie Gathorne-Hardy, Gavin Henderson and Sandy Baird. Socially distinct from this grouping, but often associated with them, was a rougher band of artistic bohemians such as John Banting, of whom even indulgent patrons frequently despaired. "It's a pity he thinks of nothing but drinking and fucking because I think he has talent," Eddy Sackville-West lamented of a man whom at other times he found "congenial, interesting, good + beautiful"; Sackville-West also figured as Banting's patron, having him to stay at the family house at Knole and commissioning him to decorate his sitting room. Then came groups of older men, many of whom had been at large in London society before the Great War or even in the late-Victorian twilight, onlooker-participants such as the Honorable Evan Morgan, later Lord Tredegar, at one time a friend of Firbank—Firbank's nickname for him was "Heaven Organ"—regarded with grave suspicion by the stiffer kind of interwar parent. Alan Pryce-Jones remembered his echt Victorian father warning him that he was "old enough to know there exists a man named Evan Morgan." Should he ever find himself in the same room as Morgan, Pryce-Jones senior advised, he should leave it immediately.

Beneath these separate but interconnected groups came a category of rather nervous young men, groping their way—in some cases literally—to an understanding of their sexuality: Cecil Beaton's journals from the early twenties are a characteristic mixture of fascination and repulsion, an intense desire for the society of homosexual sophisticates coupled with faint alarm at the thought of the likely physical consequences. In one frank conversation with his younger friend, Beverley Nichols bragged of his sexual conquests, implied that he had slept with, among other celebrities, Oliver Messel, Somerset Maugham and Noël Coward, and declared that were he to be castrated, there would be nothing left to live for. Beaton was understandably startled. As Beaton's timorousness in the company of a well-known predator like Nichols demonstrates, each of these gay coteries was likely to be strongly suspicious of the other's intentions. Confronted by the standard-bearers of an earlier homosexual generation, Etonian aesthetes tended to be faintly contemptuous of something they regarded as overly louche and chronologically fusty. Brian Howard, for example, complained loudly about a *Vogue* portrait that showed him standing next to Evan Morgan: "The ravishing beauty of my face and my figure rendered my proximity to this old starfish most suspicious to the ignorant." Even Howard balked at the kind of entertainment offered by this breed of host. The same letter—to William Acton—records a visit to "the most horrible party given by Evan Morgan, which began at the Eiffel Tower and ended at somebody's bedroom at Prince's Hotel in Jermyn Street." In the end, Howard rushed out into the street "clutching my remaining bits of virtue—bundled them into a taxi and trundled home. I've never seen anything so stupendously naughty, even in Oxford!"

At the other end of the scale, inexperienced middle-class boys making their first forays into Howard–Gathorne-Hardy circles were frequently wary of the enticements on display. Beaton, taken up by the Mayfair "smart set" in 1927, believed that it was a "mistake" to see too much of Howard and the latter's friend Paddy Brodie. Nonetheless, he agreed to join the pair at dinner at the Gargoyle, where the party included Eddie Gathorne-Hardy and Charles Fry, later a successful publisher and in this capacity memorably described by John Betjeman as "a phallus with a business sense." All four declared their intention to "find a man" and brought out powder puffs. Torn between a fear of getting out of his depth and a lurking attraction to Eddie, Beaton eventually put on makeup himself. Despite a row with Howard, Beaton found himself "falling for Eddie—so quiet and cold and unreal; his body looking as though it were made from pieces of Meccano . . . his eyes like boiled eggs." In the end he was bundled into a cupboard, "where most exciting thrilling things happened," and accompanied home in a taxi. Here, however, Beaton panicked and denied his new friend entry to the house. A full-blown affair followed, whose correspondence was used by Eddie as a lure to younger acolytes. "If you come to bed with me, my dear, I'll show you all Cecil Beaton's love-letters to me, my dear," he told a young man named Robin McDouall at about this time. McDouall kept his distance.

All sections of this burgeoning community were keen to take advantage of another characteristic figure from the period: the slightly older—in some cases very much older—woman, whose interest in younger, sexually ambiguous men was occasionally artistic, sometimes unrequitedly romantic, at others almost quasi-maternal. Beverley Nichols, who made great play of his matinee-idol good looks, was plagued by elderly female admirers who invited him to dinner and privately regretted the disparity in their ages. "I lunched with Mary Ridgely Carter at 41 Portman Square . . . a tiresome American who ought to have been cast as a housemaid and makes a very bad heiress. In love with me, apparently," runs a diary entry from early 1934. Mary Butts happily attached herself to the late-twenties partygoing circuit in the role of confidante and costumier. Gay young people were always keen to exchange details of these patrons. "My dear Tom," Mark Ogilvie-Grant instructed his friend Tom Driberg from Sicily late in 1929, "when in Palermo, do not neglect to ring up Princess Niscemi, who lives at the Villa Niscemi . . . She is a sweet American." Driberg would have taken the hint.

There were other hints, far more ominous than Baedeker-style hostess reports from abroad, that needed to be kept in mind. Reading Beaton's and Howard's accounts of the debauched parties they attended, it is rather easy to forget that homosexuality was illegal, regarded with horror by press and public alike, that known homosexuals were cruelly stigmatized and subject to the most punitive penalties. In most parts of interwar society, proof of inversion was enough to end a career. Bright Young People, on the other hand, managed to emerge relatively unscathed from the repressive legal regime administered by Sir William Joynson-Hicks at the Home Office. There were several explanations for this absence of scandal. One was the high degree of influence and connection wielded by Bright Young homosexuals. Driberg, for example, brought up in 1935 on a charge of indecently assaulting one of the two unemployed Scottish miners he had invited to spend the night at his flat, benefited both from the status of his socially exalted character witnesses and the decisive interference of Lord Beaverbrook, who ensured that no Fleet Street newspaper reported the case. As the stepson of a former foreign secretary, Stephen Tennant was, if not untouchable, then always liable to have his antics marked down as youthful eccentricity. A highly discreet bush telegraph, with satellite offices, offered advice on possible police activity, canvassing occasions on which it might be prudent to lie low. Thus, Mary Butts, recently relocated to Paris in the

summer of 1929, wrote to Eddie Gathorne-Hardy with some "rather disquieting" London news:

> A young "literary gent" called here about my "works." We
> went to the Bouef, & a drink having loosened his tongue—he
> told me (he had just left London) that he had heard through
> Raymond Mortimer something which he understood to be a po-
> lice "push" in the offing, directed against certain "moeurs" of
> our time & of all times, & that you *personally* stood in some im-
> minent danger of their attention. This at third hand may be
> nothing; I hardly know either the young man or Mr. Mortimer
> (& the latter I suspect to be liable to panic). On the other hand,
> England is *not* France. This may be worth nothing. On the other
> hand, I cocked an attentive ear . . .

How was it, amid an atmosphere of official vigilance and Home Office
crackdowns, that Eddie—who made no bones about advertising the fact
of his homosexuality—managed to stay out of prison? The most obvious explanation is that on the one hand he was the younger son of an
earl and that, on the other, he confined his activities either to his immediate social circle, who knew what to expect, or to working-class rent
boys, often soldiers from the Guards regiments stationed in London,
who were being paid for their silence. It was when homosexuals strayed
beyond these traditional catchment areas and, like Driberg, preyed on
members of the public that trouble was likely to arise.

"England is *not* France," Mary Butts had reminded her London-
based friends. Neither was England Berlin or some of the remoter quarters of southern Italy, where what Brian Howard later called the
"amenities" of complaisant local youths could be surreptitiously and
cheaply enjoyed. For the more circumspect Bright Young homosexual,
prudence often dictated excursions beyond London in search of sex.
Country weekends, with the exception of well-known bohemian destinations such as Winchelsea and Rye, were generally not far enough
afield to escape prying eyes and censorious talk. Even Eddie, whose

father owned the surrounding estate, found shouts of "Cissy" pursuing
him around the back lanes of Glenham, Suffolk ("Lady Cissie to you,"
he invariably shouted back). Foreign capitals, or out-of-the-way parts
of the French Riviera, were consequently a much better bet. Eddy
Sackville-West, an exact Eton contemporary of Eddie's, spent Christmas 1927 with Harold Nicolson in Berlin, reporting back to his friend
E. M. Forster that

> I was dragged about at night from one homosexual bar to an-
> other. The behavior is perfectly open. There are even large
> dance places for inverts. And some of the people one sees—
> huge men with breasts like women and faces like Ottoline
> [Lady Ottoline Morrell], dressed as female Spanish dancers—
> are really quite unintelligible . . . They just moon about like
> great question marks . . . I spent a pleasant & interesting night
> with a Lithuanian peasant of 20, covered with mother of pearl
> buttons, very beautiful creature.

Again, early in 1930, Sackville-West found himself among a motley collection of gay young—and not so young—bohemians living in a house
a few miles west of Cannes. These included the Bloomsbury art critic
Clive Bell, John Banting, Roland Penrose and Sandy Baird, a young
Etonian supposedly destined for the diplomatic service, who wore face
powder and was characterized by Harold Nicolson, with whom he had
had a brief affair, as "an absolute little bum boy." A letter home to Raymond Mortimer paints a depressing picture of drunken arguments, quasi-
romantic quarrels over the stream of louche young American visitors
and furtive assignations in Cannes, the whole stoked up by the constant
atmosphere of jealousy and intrigue. Baird, in particular, was outraged
by the presence of an American who preferred Sackville-West's attractions to his own: "Frightful row with Sandy over the young man," Eddy
reported to Mortimer; "though S has ten others, he cannot bear the
thought of my even having one."

The Sackville-Wests and the Bairds were well able to take care of
themselves in these disagreements. The real casualties of gay young bo-

die Gathorne-Hardy

(Courtesy of Jonathan Gathorne-Hardy)

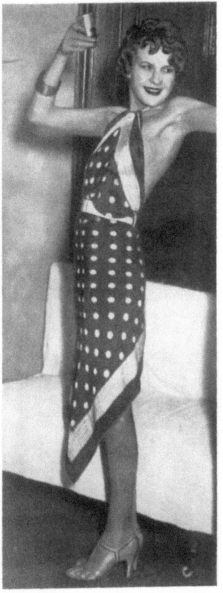

Brenda Dean Paul in the 1920s

(Courtesy of Brenda Dean Paul, *My First Life*)

verley Nichols (Courtesy of Bryan Connor)

Broadcasting for the Flapper vote: Arthur and Elizabeth at the BBC
(Courtesy of Ponsonby family archive)

The Adoration of the Magi by "Bruno Hat"
(Courtesy of Marie-Jaqueline Lancaster, *Brian Howard: Portrait of Failure*)

Rosa Lewis and Mark Ogilvie-Grant at a society wedding, 1930s (Courtesy of Daphne Fielding, *The Duchess of Jermyn Street*)

hn Banting (Courtesy of Marie-Jaqueline Lancaster, *Brian Howard: Portrait of Failure*)

e Court Party, 1931: Denis in uniform, with bearskin (Courtesy of Ponsonby family archive)

Leaving St. Margaret's Westminster,
July 5, 1929

(Courtesy of Ponsonby family archive)

As acrobats at Norman Hartnell's
Circus Party, 1929

(Courtesy of Ponsonby family archive)

The Theatrical Garden Party, 1929,
with Brian Howard (far left)

(Courtesy of Ponsonby family archive)

Brenda returns from Paris.

(Courtesy of Brenda Dean Paul, *My First Life*)

"She only met him a fortnight ago! . . . We
know so little about it as yet." Elizabeth and
Denis announce their engagement, March 1929.
(Courtesy of Ponsonby family archive)

The American
Party, 1931:
Elizabeth (far
left) stands next
to Brian Howard.
(Courtesy of Ponsonby
family archive)

Digging up Piccadilly: Denis (with cigarette), Elizabeth (pearls), Cecil (pneumatic drill), Cyril Connolly (opera glasses), Patrick Balfour (flanked by laborers)
(Courtesy of Patrick Balfour, *Society Racket*)

Weekending at Shulbrede with Arthur and Dorothea (note the expression on Dorothea's face)
(Courtesy of Ponsonby family archive)

Brenda and Stephen Hill take to the
floor at the Mozart Party, 1930.
(Courtesy of Brenda Dean Paul, *My First Life*)

The hosts, David and
Hermione Tennant
(Courtesy of *Illustrated London News*
Picture Library)

hemia, alternatively, were women. Some of them were doting mothers, perpetually alarmed by reports of their sons' behavior, who determined to marry them off to rich and well-born girls. Perhaps the most notorious of these arranged marriages was that between Gavin Henderson and Honor Phillips, the daughter of the shipping magnate Baron Kyslant. Other Bright Young People approved of Mrs. Henderson (Evelyn Waugh wrote of a party in summer 1927 that "Gavin was there with his wife, whom, tho' it sounds absurd, I rather liked"). The groom, on the other hand, was aghast at the trap into which he had been led. The engagement was announced in November 1926. On the following day Henderson left for Australia, where he remained for four months. On his return, the atmosphere of premarital tension dominated his relationships with his friends. Robert Byron was present on an evening at the Night Light when Henderson went on the rampage with the young Conservative MP Bob Boothby and smashed up the club. Meanwhile, serial misfortune attended the wedding preparations. Forged invitations were discovered to have been sent out to well-known people. The stag night, convened at a hotel in Henley, ended in disaster when the guests, having ordered up twenty gallons of petrol in advance from a local garage, marched down to the river after dinner and literally set the Thames on fire, scorching the establishment's lawn and burning down an adjoining row of chestnut trees. At the wedding itself, held at St. Margaret's Westminster, society notables were put out to find themselves mingling with a group of young black women, the groom having invited Florence Mills and her troupe as a way of annoying his mother. Evelyn Waugh's account of the newly married couple at a party was a rare sighting, as the marriage lasted only a few weeks. Henderson was rumored to have spent his wedding night with a sailor picked up earlier in the evening.

Left even more wretched than worried mothers were Bright Young Women who attached themselves to homosexual men in the hope of "reforming" them. Nancy Mitford spent four years in pursuit of Hamish St. Clair Erskine before being thrown over by him more or less in public. Yet Hamish, as every memoir of the period insists, was as unlikely— when hard decisions about his future had to be made—to settle down to marriage as Gavin Henderson. How could Nancy not have known? A younger sister thought that she simply did not understand: "I don't think she knew he was queer . . . because otherwise why should she have said that she was engaged to him?" If this sounds far-fetched, even by the standards of the 1920s, then there were women much older and worldlier than Nancy Mitford who failed to comprehend the truth of the relationships in which they were involved. In the legendary early-thirties scandal in which Earl Beauchamp—the bisexual father of six children—was threatened with exposure by his overbearing brother-in-law the Duke of Westminster and forced to leave the country, his wife had to have the nature of her husband's "weaknesses" explained to her, and even then apparently remained ignorant of his real reason for living abroad.

Against this backdrop of ignorance and denial, Nancy's pious hope that Hamish might in the end be persuaded to settle down to a faux-heterosexual marriage is excusable. There was also the fact that the distinction between an out-and-out gay and an ambiguous young man evolving by degrees into a potential husband was sometimes difficult for an inexperienced observer to grasp. Cyril Connolly's early instincts, for example, were firmly homosexual, a change of direction taking place only when he came down from Oxford. Abetting this confusion was the tendency of Bright Young homosexual life—like many other aspects of the wider environment—to be conducted in an atmosphere of signature remarks and in-jokes, an argot that was sometimes not fully comprehensible even to the people who used it. "I've just been lunching with your mama," Nancy Mitford informed Mark Ogilvie-Grant in 1930, "& inadvertently gave her a letter of yours to read in which a lift boy is described as a Driberg's delight." Naturally the allusion was lost on Mrs. Ogilvie-Grant: "What *is* a Driberg's delight? Dear Mark has such an amusing gift for describing people." Did Nancy know herself? Or, rather, was she aware of the surface manifestations of the homosexual world in which many of her male friends moved, without wondering what went on beneath them? Whatever the precise nature of Nancy's understanding, the resentments bred up in her by the attitudes she witnessed extended over several decades. She later admitted to her sister

Jessica that she would have liked to marry Robert Byron, "but he was a total pederast [Nancy's word for "homosexual"] . . . This wretched pederasty falsifies all feelings & yet one is supposed to revere it." Gavin Henderson, too, remained forever on her private blacklist: "I can't like Gavin even for old's sake," she told Harold Acton in the 1950s, "I frankly think he is a Beast."

In the end nearly all these trails lead back in the same direction: to the willowy, epicene and impossibly languid figure of Eddie Gathorne-Hardy. Nearly eighty years on from his late-twenties heyday, Eddie's idiosyncrasies—most of them surviving only in anecdote—are not easy to pin down. But it would be accurate to say that he combined erudition, companionability and personal loyalty with outrageous flippancy, unswerving sexual promiscuity and—gathering all these things up into their slipstream—an undeviating determination to please himself at whatever private or communal cost. Slightly older than some of his Bright Young contemporaries (he was born in 1901), educated, inevitably, at Eton and Christ Church—where he knew and had supposedly been propositioned by Anthony Eden—he was a younger son, perennially hard up and forced to make his own way in the world. Having failed for the diplomatic service, that traditional resort of younger sons, he ended up working for the antiquarian bookseller Elkin Matthews, where his tall, drooping figure became a magnet both for gossiping acquaintances and for customers seriously interested in books. Cecil Beaton's diary account captures something of his supremely odd appearance: "uncommonly tall, vellum complexion, tortoiseshell glasses, long hair, a bemused expression about his eyes and mouth." The apparition had "a deep, crumbling voice" and "talked about seductions and affairs." At a time when even out-and-out homosexuals could be chary about admitting their sexual preferences, Eddie, while enjoying the company of Elizabeth Ponsonby and her friends ("He is badly trained by these cocktail women," Dorothea thought), made no secret of his particular interests. Among his grandmother's servants was a timorous, nonpracticing homosexual butler named Maslin. "Do you know what

I'm going to do tomorrow, Maslin?" Eddie is supposed to have inquired of this retainer. "I'm going to go up to London, Maslin, and I'm going to pick up a nice, *very* good-looking guardsman, take him back to my flat and I'm going to *have* him, Maslin." "You're a very lucky young gentleman, Mr. Eddie," Maslin is supposed gloomily to have replied.

There were various Gathorne-Hardy domiciles at this time, each of them venues for a certain kind of gay young society: an establishment in Queen Square; a famously sleazy flat shared with Brian Howard at 39 Maddox Street, where fungus grew on the staircase, haunted by John Banting, whom John Betjeman remembered "throwing knives when in the mood." The loucheness of the Maddox Street ménage was noted even by its cotenant. "Really Eddie," Brian wrote from Austria early in 1931, "I do think you ought to have a lock put on the red door at the bottom of our stairs. It would be so easy to have it done + the flat would then be *safe*, which at present it is not. If you think it over, it is impossible to live in a place where one *finds people waiting*, where a number of people know they can get in all day."

The problem is that so little of it is reconstitutable, simply a matter of eye-catching reportage: Eddie seeking diversion in a railway carriage by setting fire to a fellow passenger's copy of *The Times* and, when asked his name, replying "Violet, Duchess of Rutland. What's yours?"; Eddie urinating into Rosamond Lehmann's handbag during the screening of an avant-garde film, possibly Buñuel's *Un Chien Andalou*. (Was she very cross? his nephew wondered. "Not very, my dear. Perhaps she thought it was all part of a surrealist ambience, my dear.") Evelyn Waugh, a shrewd observer of Eddie's goings-on in the late twenties, inserted a paragraph into *Vile Bodies* in which Miles Malpractice, having camped out, as it were, in Lord Throbbing's house in Hertford Square, finally quits the premises on his brother's return from abroad. Subsequently, Throbbing suffers from "the successive discoveries by his secretaries of curious and compromising things in all parts of the house." The butler has to be taken away in a van. However, Miles's real legacy is longer-lasting: "Long after these immediate causes of distress had been removed, the life of Throbbing's secretaries was periodically disturbed by ambiguous telephone calls and the visits of menacing young men who wanted new suits or tickets to America or a fiver to be going on with."

Eddie's friends noted his taste for rough company. "I do hope that *Ike Baker* is not being really dangerous," Brian wrote, again from the Austrian trip. "He might be, easily. He is not, for instance, in the least afraid of going to prison, having been there frequently, and he is a professional burglar."

At the heart of all this, though—the menacing young men, the affected chatter, the grapplings with Beaton—lay a paradox, or perhaps only an evasion. It would have been easy to write off the Eddie seen sashaying along Charlotte Street to an accompaniment of wolf whistles as an irredeemable period buffoon. Nothing, on the other hand, exceeded, say, Brian Howard's respect for Eddie's opinion of his poetry (forwarding him a draft of "Self" in 1929, he admitted to "*much* misgiving . . . I'm risking a *lot* in sending it *you*—you terrify me"). As an antiquarian bookseller, Eddie acquired a knowledge of seventeenth-century bookmaking that was more or less unequaled. As a friend, in a notoriously impecunious age, his generosity exceeded all reasonable bounds: it was all very well for Lura Howard to assume that his friends would eventually abandon him financially, Brian once suggested, "but Eddie says he never will." And yet the erudition, the generosity and the loyalty combined to produce only a desert of nonachievement, a fatal disinclination to engage with the wider environment at any serious level. In the end, you suspect, Eddie was simply scared of the business of living: the commitments it demanded, the terrible obligation it imposed to do something other than please oneself. All this was highly amusing for a time. To set against it, the accounts of Eddie's later years, after the London party circuit had broken up, do not make edifying reading. Like his friend Elizabeth Ponsonby, he was someone who flourished only in a particular environment and among a particular group of like-minded friends. The 1930s would leave him stranded, a piece of unclassifiable period jetsam thrown up on an ever more inhospitable beach.

. . .

There were few Bright Young relationships in which the question of milieu failed to loom uncomfortably large. With its enthusiasm for gay novelists—Ronald Firbank was an especial favorite—its reliance on classical themes for its parties and entertainments ("Greek" had been synonymous with "homosexual" since the early Victorian era), substantial parts of the Bright Young People's world could, as Nancy Mitford noted, be thought to be actively proselytizing on homosexuality's behalf. Simultaneously, there were other kinds of men attached to the scene who, while homosexual themselves, disapproved of the Bright Young People's world on moral grounds, writhed with fastidious curiosity when exposed to it and ultimately left it for good. Nowhere, perhaps, were these tensions more dramatically expressed than in the fraught but—for the time—unusually prolonged relationship between Siegfried Sassoon and Stephen Tennant.

Even to the sophisticated Mayfair partygoers of the late 1920s, nothing could have seemed more incongruous than the coming together of what looked to be diametrical opposites: "Little Lord Fauntleroy and the old Earl," as Edith Sitwell put it. At the time of their first meeting in June 1927, Sassoon, a rugged war hero turned pacifist figurehead, was already in his forties; Tennant—the last word in period aestheticism, frail, androgynous and self-absorbed—was barely out of his teens. From the earliest days Sassoon's feelings for Tennant were undercut by his mounting dislike for the world in which his boyfriend moved. Going down to Wilsford for the first time in the following autumn, he took a wrong turning in the Wiltshire lanes and thought "for two pins I'd go straight back to London. How can I face all those bright young people?" Among the row of photographs in which Sacheverell and Georgia Sitwell and Zita and Baby Jungman parade in their Watteau costumes, Sassoon is a conspicuous absentee. Despite these uncertainties, mutual admiration blossomed. After a late-night trip to Stonehenge, Tennant stayed in his guest's room until dawn, making "the most passionate avowals and intoxicating all my senses." Not long afterward, Tennant arrived at Sassoon's quarters in Campden Hill Square. Taking out his pocket mirror, he combed his hair and inspected his eyelashes while Sassoon played the themes from Rachmaninov's third piano concerto. Their

relationship would have to be kept secret, he explained, to avoid the vigilant eye of his mother, Lady Grey, but he confessed that this new understanding left him "almost swooning with happiness."

Sassoon, meanwhile, though keenly aroused by this wavy-haired
young androgyne, was already disturbed by the company he kept and
the attitudes he struck. In particular, he was upset by Tennant's revelation that he had attended the Impersonation Party that summer dressed
as Queen Marie of Romania and, in this disguise, been kissed by a Nor-
wegian diplomat. Already the attachment was falling into a predictable
pattern: Sassoon trying to separate Tennant from his Bright Young acquaintances; Tennant quietly avoiding the nets thrown out to pinion
him. They spent a symbolic Christmas at Weston, the Northamptonshire home of Sacheverell and Georgia Sitwell, where a party including
Beaton, Elizabeth Ponsonby and Dick Wyndham enlivened the festive
season by cross-dressing, drinking, playing charades, making home
movies and eating extravagantly. Sassoon professed himself appalled by
the litter of lipstick-stained glasses, overflowing ashtrays and other de-
tritus left for the Weston servants to clear away.

Already complicated by Sassoon's disapproval, the relationship was
also threatened by Tennant's poor health. In January he left for the
Bavarian Alps, where it was thought that the air might benefit his suspect lungs. "Oh darling," he wrote back, "what wouldn't I give to find
your arms around me?" A further communication from Paris about
shopping expeditions and a dressing gown patterned with pink leopard-
skin went down less well. Sassoon wondered gloomily whether his
young friend wasn't simply "a glaring example of the behavior of the
rich people I loathe and despise." Back in London for his brother David's
marriage to Hermione Baddeley, Tennant entertained Sassoon with stories of the wedding, its smashed glasses and Gargoyle Club hell-raising.
Sassoon by this stage had determined to cast himself in the role of sav-
ior and moral scourge. Listening to these decadent tales of the Tennant
union, he realized, rather unexpectedly, that he liked hearing about such
people if only to relish the thought of rescuing Stephen from their
clutches.

Sassoon's romanticism and his Puritanism came inextricably mingled.

He began to envisage himself as a knight in armor—less of a metaphorical conceit than it sounds—who would swoop down on the degenerate gatherings by which his beloved was now beguiled and carry him off to . . . well, to what exactly? However much Tennant affected to enjoy Sassoon's company, it was abundantly clear that he liked stunt parties and country house weekends, and that a considerable part of his inner life was projected through their artificial lens. A Stephen who did not sally forth into Mayfair clad in, say, a sailor suit and gold earrings with his face dripping maquillage, promising to return to Campden Hill Square at dawn, would not have been the Stephen in whose company the dogged and party-avoiding Sassoon imagined that he flourished. Notwithstanding reports of another riotous party at the Gargoyle, Sassoon decided that he was "more infatuated with him than ever before." If only Stephen could be pried from his habit of appearing at charity matinées dressed as Shelley (Beaton supporting him as Gainsborough), thereby causing his admirer to pen tart little poems like "Doxology de Luxe," demanding that the rich be "damned for ever more," then all would be well and they would settle down in . . . well, in where exactly?

Never one to shirk what he considered to be his moral duty, Sassoon used the busy summer of 1928 as an opportunity to initiate trials of strength. A request that Stephen should absent himself from the Bath and Bottle Party was flatly declined, as was a similar attempt to stop him from attending David Tennant's rowdy fancy dress party. In the end Sassoon was forced to lurk outside the house, listening furiously as the sounds of drunkenness and fighting rose on the night air. Eventually, Stephen emerged, dressed in a tight pink costume covered in Nottingham lace. "The evening almost made me dislike Stephen," Sassoon decided. But what did Stephen think? Vainglorious and affected, but quite intelligent enough to comprehend the emotional havoc he was wreaking, he liked, above all, to be admired. Increasingly, though, in his attempts to rescue his beloved from a social swamp in which he showed every sign of wanting to become permanently immersed, Sassoon had some valuable allies. Stephen's mother and her husband, Lord Grey, were quite as alarmed by his starring role in the gossip columns; they were also worried—despite Lady Grey's official steeliness on the subject—that

Stephen's homosexuality might cause real trouble. Trouble, that is, beyond the outraged sensibilities of Lady Ellesmere and other London hostesses. In an atmosphere of family intrigue, its communications sometimes channeled through discreet third parties such as Lady Grey's friend Edith Olivier, Sassoon found himself arranging—and paying for—a trip to Italy. The party, which also included Stephen's former nanny and his valet, William, embarked for a guesthouse in the mountains at Untergrainau near Garmisch before heading south and joining the Sitwells at Siena. Apparently required to act as a kind of upmarket factotum, Sassoon noted that "packing and unpacking S's things occupies me a lot—about 30 bottles and cold cream jars to unwrap."

As the excursion moved homeward by way of France, Sassoon brooded about the relationship. *Memoirs of a Fox-Hunting Man*, the first volume of his autobiographical "Sherston" trilogy, had just been published to great acclaim. Stephen, meanwhile, was enjoying himself among the Parisian nightclubs while proclaiming that everything was either "heavenly" or "too grim for words." The whirligig was brought to an abrupt halt by the news that Lady Grey was seriously ill. She died shortly afterward, causing Sassoon to reflect, with a surprising degree of optimism, that "S. will need me now more than ever before."

Once again illness supervened. Fluid extracted from one of Stephen's lungs was tubercular. Come January 1929, patient, valet and nanny— also unwell—departed again for Untergrainau and a treatment involving the collapsing of the affected lung. Sassoon followed shortly afterward, declining to be present at the award of the Hawthornden Prize for *Memoirs* on the grounds that "it is a matter of life and death." In fact, the person nearest death's door was Nannie Trusler, who died only a few days after their return to England in late July. The implications of his relationship with Stephen were brought home to Sassoon when, as the two of them stood together on a London pavement, a woman yelled "You two revolting bits of filth" from the window of a passing car.

With the two people he loved best in the world dead within the space of a year, Stephen should have been ripe for the kind of attention— resolute, exclusive and censorious—that Sassoon yearned to give him.

Yet the scope of the life they began to lead, mostly on the Continent, satisfied neither of them: Sassoon doing his best to fall in with his friend's caprices but secretly disillusioned with Tennant's paralyzing detachment from any kind of ordinary life. In November 1929 they were in Paris again, together with the valet, William, and Stephen's pet parrot, Poll, dining expensively in fashionable restaurants and visiting jewelers' shops, where Sassoon bought his friend an emerald ring (£80) and put in an order for a diamond star (£100). Moving south, they visited Max Beerbohm at Rapallo and then headed for Sicily. There were more scenes: "I alternately cried and screamed and abused him and then wept," Stephen recorded. On Christmas Eve they were in Palermo in circumstances memorialized by Stephen in a letter to Edmund Blunden: he writing letters in one room, Sassoon playing Chopin on the gramophone in the other, but frequently coming in to talk, dance or impregnate the air with pipe smoke. Stephen, alternatively, was absorbed by his new white velvet dressing gown. "I wish you could see it," he informed Blunden, whose shaky finances lurched from one crisis to another. "It is like mother-of-pearl and Devonshire cream—if you could mix them."

As personalities, Tennant and Sassoon remained similarly distinct. Ominously, their disagreements had moved on from the realm of temperament to assume an aesthetic focus. To Syracuse, where they stayed early in 1930, came a copy of Robert Graves's newly published *Goodbye to All That*, which contained disobliging references to Sassoon, and news of the death of D. H. Lawrence, whom Tennant admired. Arguing over Graves, Stephen claimed that Sassoon's work had declined since his war poems, brought down by "too much care and deliberation." Meanwhile, Stephen's health was worsening. In England in early summer, he was prescribed rest and confined to Wilsford. His medical man, Dr. Snowden, who had a sanatorium nearby, observed, "Thank God I wasn't born with a temperament like that." The events of the next two years were an extreme version of the months that had preceded them: Sassoon, possessive and overbearing, trying to keep Tennant to himself; the patient alarmed by this sequestration but, when it came to it, more interested in himself than by the brooding middle-aged man who came to visit. Stephen's friends felt excluded. Osbert Sitwell remarked that he had been much more amusing before he took up with Sassoon. By late September 1930, Sassoon was gone, Tennant having said that he wanted to be alone for ten days. In his absence Stephen luxuriated in his idleness. "I suppose I am completely decadent," he reflected.

The ranks of Bright Young People alarmed at their friend's isolation now had an in-house ally. Nurse May, charged with day-to-day care of the patient, was disgusted by Sassoon's attentions. When Tennant was discovered to have lost weight, she pointedly observed, "Yes, poor boy, he ought to have some visitors." Forbidden the house by Dr. Snowden, Sassoon was forced to rely on the Wilsford gardeners, Beryl and Eileen Hunter, for news, together with mutual friends who were allowed access. Rosamond Lehmann reported Stephen more hysterical and self-absorbed than ever, professing to love Sassoon but claiming that "you exhaust him." This was true, but Stephen's effect on Sassoon was quite as destructive. Still kept from the Wilsford gate, he rented a house nearby, skulked in the lane behind the garden wall to eavesdrop on Stephen talking to Rex Whistler and spent Christmas Day 1930 with the Hunters bewailing his treatment. A Christmas message sent up to the house raised no reply. Early in the New Year the Hunters reported that Stephen was in a bad way. The extracts from Browning's letters which Sassoon had thought might raise his spirits were briskly returned by the nurse ("Mr. Tennant isn't yet up to reading letters"). Arriving at the house, Sassoon saw him through the window and asked news from Stephen's friendly aunt Nan, only to be told that he had suffered a hemorrhage and was still an invalid.

There was a brief swan song in the summer of 1932 when Sassoon was invited to Wilsford for tea and conversation—and also a remonstrance from the Hunters, who begged him not to let his life be wrecked by Stephen for a second time. Again came an example of Tennant's almost inhuman detachment. Sassoon praised the women to Stephen, who remarked, "They are very kind, but they don't know how to look after my bullfrogs." His health somewhat restored after a stay at a clinic in Kent, Stephen now asserted his independence by taking part in local social life and attending dances and fancy dress parties with the Mitfords, Rex Whistler and Cecil Beaton. Ultimately the relationship lapsed into an exhausting standoff in which Stephen wrote letters asking him to come and stay, Sassoon pleaded pressure of work and, relenting, discovered that Stephen would refuse to see him. In spring 1933, Sassoon addressed a long, anguished letter to Wilsford: "O Steenie, I have given you the last four years of my life. I was giving you my life all the time, even when you refused to see me or send me a message. I ask nothing of you now; only that you should be aware of the significance of what I am doing and have done for you . . ."

It was time to cut his losses. In September, Sassoon met the twenty-seven-year-old Hester Gatty. Three months later, after a whirlwind courtship and to the manifest surprise of Sassoon's homosexual friends, they were man and wife. "Have you had an emotional and physical overturn?" E. M. Forster wondered in a letter. "Your news, though I accept it as good news, startles me." Reckoning up the half-decade spent trying to keep Stephen from the milieu he loved while appeasing his spectacular narcissism, Sassoon acknowledged that two things had defeated him: The first was temperament—his own as much as Stephen's. The second, though, seemed equally fundamental: nothing less than the bright, artificial world in which Tennant moved, and through which Sassoon followed obstinately and unsuccessfully in his wake.

THE BYRONIC MANNER

It was Evelyn Waugh who noted the "insolence" that typified his band of late-1920s confrères. It takes a career like Robert Byron's to demonstrate quite how multifarious were the forms that these bad manners could take. Anthony Powell, who observed Byron in action for a quarter of a century, thought him Victorian in his violence, a pop-eyed projection of all those choleric majors who sat furiously in the breakfast rooms of their clubs just itching to wrest the morning newspaper out of the hands of the lackadaisical browser at the next table. "A man of extremes," his friend Christopher Sykes pronounced, which is putting it mildly. Invective, rudeness, determination to stop at absolutely nothing, complete disregard for the consequences of that irresistible forward motion—all these were Byron's stock-in-trade. A railway journey invariably meant a quarrel with the guard or an altercation at the ticket office. On at least one occasion a crowded cinema line meant a night in a police cell when, losing his temper at the sight of people behind him being let in to see the film, he was carted off to Vine Street and fined 19s. 6d. for "insulting behaviour."

No one among Byron's contemporaries knew more about insulting behavior. The sarcastic backhander, the thinly veiled threat, the outrageous verbal mugging—in all these departments he was the star performer of his day. Given the Bright Young People's almost limitless capacity to cause offense, this mastery is rather intriguing. Where had it come from? How was it nurtured? What was it about Byron that, in the last resort, caused him to bristle up with affronted fury at the sight of dour officialdom or turn uncontrollably farouche at the slightest impediment to his schemes? The request to see tickets, the minor editorial intervention, the club bore—all these made Byron seethe with fury, in a way that seems not just unreasonable but almost pathological, a bitter emotional extremism with no place in it for degrees of offense. Examining Byron's response to obstructions of the kind that the average life throws up in the path of the people living it one wonders sometimes just exactly what was going on, what point Byron thought he was making—whether, when it came down to it, the spiritual howitzer trained on anyone who blocked his progress was simply the only way in which he was capable of communicating.

Whatever the root cause of this volcanic temperament, each stage of Byron's career was an epic showcase for his talent for upsetting people. At Eton he was known for his "unrivaled powers of invective"; these at any rate are the words used of "Ben Gore," Byron's alter ego in Henry Green's novel *Blindness*. At Oxford, pictures he didn't like were written off with shouts of "Trash. Muck. Rubbish." Launched on to the London party circuit, he mortally offended the aged Harry Melville by breaking in on one of the veteran raconteur's anecdotes with a cry of "Can't you shut up, you hideous old relic of the Victorian age?" But then Byron, with his popping blue eyes and his unquenchable fury, was a relic of the Victorian age himself. Perhaps it took one to know one.

Work—those scholarly articles for the architectural reviews, those diligent excursions in the Near East, those forays along mountain paths to monasteries glimpsed in the Attic dawn—offered countless opportunities for the spectacular eruptions of temperament in which Byron specialized. Reading the accounts of his bust-ups, one wonders whether the whole thing wasn't physiological: that to lose his temper every so often was as necessary for Byron's health and well-being as Sunday lunch and an afternoon nap is for the harassed forty-something father of three. En route through Albania, according to his traveling companion, he "spent most of the time . . . cursing. He cursed almost everybody who did not speak English, sometimes violently, but more often in a pleasant conversational monotone, as though he were discoursing on the beauty of the countryside." The Albanian monoglots, you suspect, got off fairly lightly. Confronted by Dr. Herzfeld, the celebrated German archaeologist, and his reluctance to allow any of the artifacts at Persepolis to be photographed, Byron informed him tersely that the only way of stopping him was either "1. To show me the warranty of your concession proving that you *have* the right"; or "2. Force."

Herzfeld caved in. People usually did. Aggrieved, frightened, uneasily aware that they could not muster the same degree of antagonism, they looked for ways of saving face, referred the matter elsewhere, made their excuses and left. How one feels, for example, for Upton Jones, editor of the Oxford University Press's *Persian Survey*, who in February 1937 ventured to correspond with Byron over his essay "The Architecture of Afghanistan." Although crisply flamboyant and eye-catchingly opinionated, Byron's contribution was also inaccurate and hastily written. Upton Jones proposed changes. "I warn you quite frankly," Byron shot back, "that if this chapter is altered in any way I don't like after I have passed the final proof, I shall put the matter in the hands of a solicitor." Byron won, of course, when he took the matter to the head of the OUP, whose adjudicator found in his favor. When Upton Jones retaliated with some signed footnotes rejecting the essay's more extravagant claims, Byron picked a quarrel over a trifling sum of money that he might or might not have been owed. Still, Upton Jones was lucky not to receive far worse treatment. The person who once inquired of the younger Byron what he would like best in the world got the answer: "To be an incredibly beautiful prostitute with a sharp sting in my bottom."

CHAPTER ELEVEN

AFTER THE DANCE: 1931–39

For ten years I have been obsessed with the idea of war, and the only really unselfish work I ever did in my life was in the cause of peace. Now all that is shattered, and there is a temptation to think that it is shattered for ever.

— BEVERLEY NICHOLS, September 18, 1939

The Bright Young People of the last decade have been played off the stage by a new and tougher gang, who have found better things to do than advertising face creams.

— DOUGLAS GOLDRING, *Odd Man Out* (1935)

According to Patrick Balfour, the 1930s ended on the morning of Monday, September 21, 1931. This was the day on which, after a weekend of pained deliberation, the government took the decision—momentous in terms of national prestige and tradition—to go off the gold standard. Fiscal trouble had been looming for some time. Back in June the Committee of Finance and Industry had filed a report that prompted the chancellor of the exchequer, Philip Snowden, to call for cross-party unity, so severe were the economic remedies proposed. By mid-August the pressure on sterling was so great that the Bank of England could not support the pound without substantial loans from New York and Paris. In a pre-echo of the IMF's response to the crisis of four and a half decades hence, the foreign banks refused to advance the money until the debtor could present a balanced budget. Solvency, as every member of Ramsay Macdonald's Labour cabinet knew, would demand cuts in public expenditure and in particular a reduction in unemployment benefit.

The stage was set for one of those collisions between labor and capital so characteristic of mid-twentieth-century British political life. To institute the measures, Macdonald and his colleagues needed support from the wider reaches of their party. When this failed to materialize, Macdonald resigned, had his resignation refused by King George V and reemerged as the head of a "national government," whose powers had effectively been handed on a plate to Stanley Baldwin's Conservative opposition. A hastily contrived "economy budget" raised income tax from 4s. 6d. in the pound to 5s., cut the dole and announced a reduction in pay and pensions for the armed forces. Within days the country was plunged into crisis. On September 17, sailors of the North Atlantic Fleet at Invergordon mutinied in response to pay cuts. Three days later the government decided to abandon parity between the pound and its existing gold reserves; the value of a sovereign would no longer be linked to the actual amount of money that the nation possessed. In an age when governments routinely accumulate billions of pounds' worth of public-sector debt, this may sound a poor excuse for political meltdown, but its significance for the average British citizen, raised in an atmosphere of solid Edwardian prosperity, cannot be overstated: what the financial historian David Kynaston has called the "illusions of gold" were finally shattered. As Alec Waugh, then in his early thirties, put it: "For me, and I suppose for most Britons born before 1910, the announcement that Monday morning was the biggest shock that we had known or were to know."

Far more than the twelve-day General Strike of five years before, the retreat from the gold standard was a potent symbol of Britain's postwar unease and its dramatically reduced financial power. A sense of national solidarity prevailed. Wealthy holidaymakers still encamped in Continental resorts took the hint and returned home. The Duke of Connaught, who owned a villa in Cap Ferrat, declared that he would spend the winter in Sidmouth and was interviewed for a news film as he sauntered along the esplanade, wrapped in a heavy coat. It was an autumn, Waugh recollected, of belt-tightening and diminished horizons, stern talk of economies needing to be made and duty needing to be done.

Against a backdrop of high-minded patriotic resolve, a general election was fought on October 27. Harried by a virulently pro-Conservative press, the Labour members who had defied Macdonald and the "Bankers' Ramp" were mostly annihilated. The Tory-dominated national administration emerged from the wreckage with a parliamentary majority of more than five hundred seats. A *Punch* cartoon captioned "The Splendid Sword" showed John Bull by his anvil handing Macdonald a weapon marked "National Majority" and remarking, "The best job I've ever done. I feel sure that you can be trusted to use it well." Clearly this was not a time for demonstrations of unbridled extravagance. Alec Waugh, who had partied with the best of them during the 1920s, immediately sat down to compile a book titled *Thirteen Such Years*, which treated the autumn of 1931 as "the climax of postwar England" and purported to show "the transition of English life from the excitement of the Armistice celebrations to the General Election of 1931." The book ended with an imaginary character sketch of an English resident of the south of France: not some pleasure-seeking Bright Young expatriate but a man of sixty gassed in the First World War living there for the benefit of his lungs. Waugh's exemplar considers it his duty to return home and promptly dies of exposure to the inhospitable climate. Times, emphatically, had changed.

Something of this new austerity-conscious atmosphere can be glimpsed in the public reaction to perhaps the last great entertainment of the Bright Young People's era: the "Red and White Party" of November 21, 1931. Hosted by the art dealer Arthur Jeffries, this took place in a borrowed house in Regent's Park and was in almost every particular a self-conscious throwback to the extravagance of five years before. Amid conditions of tight security—no gate-crashers were allowed and invitations were checked at the door—Mr. Jeffries greeted his guests attired in a costume of white pajamas, white elbow-length kid gloves, ruby and diamond bracelets and a muff of white narcissi. Similar color combinations could be seen around the reception rooms. Evan Morgan came in a scarlet toga, his young gentleman friend in a white ski suit. The cigarettes were colored red and white; the food consisted of such items as lobsters and strawberries. Highlights of the next ten hours—the party was still going strong at seven the following morning—included Brenda Dean Paul gratuitously pulling the hair of a girl named Sunday Wilshin, after which she was borne away by the police on one of their periodic drug busts, and Hugh Wade playing "Body and Soul" on the organ, at which point Maud Allen, the owner of the house, sent a message down from the top floor begging him to desist. Alec Waugh, in hot pursuit of Elizabeth Montagu, spent the evening drifting around the lower floors in a "blissful haze," unaware of the high drama of Brenda's arrest or Maud Allen's complaints. All in all it was a fairly typical Bright Young People's night out of the kind that, even a year before, would have been deferentially reported in the society weeklies. In fact the Red and White Party, whose staging coincided with press reports of a march on London by unemployed workers, found itself roundly criticized on grounds of bad taste. How, the *Bystander* demanded, could people not be expected to turn Communist "when such ill-bred extravagance was flaunted, as hungry men were marching to London to get work"?

There were other, equally symbolic, indications of changing attitudes to youthful excess. One of them was the public reaction to the arrest, in May 1932, of Mrs. Elvira Dolores Barney on the charge of murdering her lover, Scott Stephen, with a single shot from a revolver during a late-night quarrel in her Knightsbridge maisonette. The Barney case became a cause célèbre. The defendant was a wealthy divorcée, the twenty-seven-year-old daughter of the government broker, now run rather to seed ("a melancholy and somewhat depressing figure," according to the defending barrister), and the dead man a dissipated minor attendant on what newspapers were still calling the "Smart Set." The Home Office pathologist Bernard Spilsbury was called in to demonstrate that the alleged murderer had intended to shoot herself and that the weapon had gone off accidentally when Stephen had tried to intervene, and Mrs. Barney was acquitted. She was not, and never had been, a Bright Young Person, but the distinction was not one which the average newspaper reader would have been capable of making. As Osbert Lancaster put it, the acquittal verdict "had already produced a widespread revulsion of feeling that involved . . . circles far distant from those in which that trigger-happy and rather sordid poor little rich girl moved."

Lancaster's first suspicion that something had gone wrong came on a summer night in 1932 when, dressed in white tie and tails and in the company of Nancy Mitford, he arrived at a ball staged by Diana Guinness for her sister Unity at Whistler's old house on Chelsea Embankment. A diverting evening seemed guaranteed, Lancaster thought. The hostess's close connections with Oxford and the Bright Young People would ensure "the presence of some of the more picturesque survivors of the previous decade not usually found at such functions." Anemic shire girls and "beefy young ensigns from the Brigade" would be in the minority. Lancaster's first shock came as he caught sight of the usual crowd of sightseers gathered on the pavement. Bracing himself to conceal the embarrassment invariably induced by "the appreciative cooing which the appearance of the female guests normally provoked," he realized that the smiles had turned unexpectedly sardonic. Instead of shouts of "Coo, ain't she lovely," the guests received "solicitous but ironic inquiries after the health of Mrs. Barney and pious expressions of hope that the lady had not forgotten her gun."

Inside the house, fortified by the sight of the hostess, "glorious as some Nordic corn-goddess wearing a magnificent diamond tiara," some of the guests' composure returned. Nevertheless, as he ascended the stair, Lancaster found that he could not rid himself

> of a presentiment of coming, and probably unwelcome, change, which was almost immediately, and quite unexpectedly, reinforced. Suddenly the queue came to an abrupt halt and drew to one side to make way for two descending footmen carrying between them the inanimate form of Augustus John who, it appeared, had been overcome by the heat rather early in the proceedings . . .

It is important not to exaggerate the impact of a few ironic shouts from the assembled proletariat or the sight of a famous Chelsea drunk being carried downstairs to his taxi (Diana Mosley always maintained that the incident never happened), but Lancaster was a shrewd observer of the contemporary scene and he was aware that a change in public attitudes was looming on the horizon. Watching "that defiantly noble, if temporarily horizontal, figure" being taken out into the night, he "felt more strongly than ever that one epoch was ending and another, markedly less care-free, beginning."

More thoughtful members of the Bright Young People had already begun to take note of these changing circumstances. None of their leading lights was immune to seriousness: in most cases the process of sobering up that distinguished their careers in the 1930s had already begun. In any case, the diaspora of the original mid-twenties core group was in full flow. Evelyn Waugh, now divorced from his first wife and converted to Roman Catholicism, had already embarked on the nomadic seven-year existence of far-flung foreign travel and country house visiting that would end only with his marriage to Laura Herbert in 1937. Henceforth his quarry was "smart society," rather than the more bohemian company he had relished in the 1920s. Harold Acton, discouraged by critical reaction to his books, left England altogether for a more or less ascetic life in China. Balfour, hard at work on *Society Racket*, had ambitions to be a "serious" writer. Beaton was increasingly locating himself somewhere in mid-Atlantic, halfway between his camera portraits of Mayfair notables and high-profile commissions for American *Vogue*. Brenda we know about. Everywhere, too, previously settled relationships were in flux, new livings having to be forged. Nancy Mitford, her long engagement to Hamish Erskine at an end, would soon marry Peter Rodd, a good-looking, lady-killing and erratic young man with a fund of recondite information, known to the other Mitfords as "the Tollgater," owing to his habit of haranguing acquaintances on the peculiarities of this ancient English institution. Her sister Diana was about to throw over Bryan Guinness for the former Labour cabinet minister Sir Oswald Mosley, whose political ambitions would be given a dramatic new framing by the events of 1931.

Nothing could be more narrowly symbolic of the fracture of the Bright Young People's world than the breakup of the Guinness marriage. Diana met Mosley in the spring of 1932, by which time his parliamentary career was finished and his relationship with his wife, the ailing Lady Cynthia, at an equally low ebb. Come the summer both couples were staying in Venice, where few of their fellow holidaymakers could help noticing Diana's and Mosley's invariable absences between lunch and dinner. Back in England in the autumn, a final gathering in the old Bright Young style gave notice of Diana's intentions. This was a fancy dress fête champêtre at Biddesden, where the guests included such reliable camp followers as John Sutro, as a cupid complete with bow, tiny wings and golden hair, and Oliver Messel in a Roman toga. The hostess presided in a Grecian gown. Rosamond Lehmann remembered it as "the most awful evening, Tom [Mosley] in triumph with this dazzling beauty, and Bryan, the host, looking like a shattered white rabbit." Early in the New Year, Diana left her husband to live openly as Mosley's mistress.

Diana's motives were neither frivolous nor even self-interested. It was not merely a case of a bored, rich young woman preferring one man's company to another. As the friends and relatives who advised her at the time noted, she admired Mosley for his ideas as much as his physical attractions. It was this conviction that Mosley was the man to pilot England out of its interwar doldrums that steeled her against the widespread disapproval that followed her departure from Buckingham Street ("You know, back in the sane or insane atmosphere of Swinbrook I feel convinced that you won't be allowed to take this step," Nancy wrote anxiously in November 1932, ". . . everybody you know will band together and somehow stop you"). Other Bright Young People, looking back at their younger selves from the vantage point of old age, were equally keen to emphasize their early commitment to the new seriousness of the 1930s. Beverley Nichols's comment is entirely characteristic: "I could not go on much longer, drinking cocktails and talking nonsense while the clouds were gathering over Europe . . ." Diana's apologists, too, make much of her horror of unemployment, her realization, even as a very young woman, that, to use the expression later popularized by the Prince of Wales, "something must be done."

Naturally, these realignments were relative, and Beverley Nichols drank a great many more cocktails and talked a great deal more nonsense before the 1930s were over. Similarly, an awareness of social deprivation does not seem greatly to have impaired Diana's enjoyment of life on Buckingham Street or her country estate at Biddesden, Hampshire. On the other hand, Nichols was a self-proclaiming young man with a conscience, while even before her first meeting with Mosley, Diana's interest in social problems had been stirred by conversations with her father-in-law, Colonel Walter Guinness, later Lord Moyne, a minister in Baldwin's government of 1924–29. Each pursued wildly different paths: Nichols by way of pacifism and the Oxford Movement, pantheistic Christianity and visits to Glasgow tenements, to Anglo-German Fellowship meetings; Diana via Mosley's British Union of Fascists, whose foundation coincided with her split from Bryan, to meetings with Hitler and a marriage to Mosley conducted in Goebbels's drawing room.

In both cases the impulse, however warped or ultimately destructive, was the same: a belief that postwar English life could not go on as it had been going, that the condition of Europe demanded urgent remedial action. These feelings were echoed across the Bright Young People's community. In most cases the level of social and political awareness in which they took root was absurdly low. For all his early realization of the changing shape of European power politics, the eye that Robert Byron turned on domestic affairs was almost absurdly flippant. Writing for *Vogue* in the run-up to the 1929 general election, he claimed that the outcome largely depended on the looks of the individual candidates: Oliver Baldwin was tipped for his "classical profile and buttercup tresses," while Lord Emley's blue eyes, he maintained, had "won all Norfolk with their mute denial of Liberal decline." Ten years later, alternatively, Byron could—justifiably—claim, "One spends one's life trying to save things—Jews, buildings [a reference to his work with the Georgian society] not to mention the world as a whole."

The forced march away from twenties decadence led into some odd corners of the 1930s political landscape. Many of the legendary figures associated with twenties excess had drifted away: Mrs. Meyrick, the nightclub queen who had married two of her daughters into the peerage, died in 1933, apparently from a mixture of world-weariness and pneumonia, leaving only £58. History tends to associate politically minded Bright Young People with fascism in general and Mosley in particular. The reality is a good deal more complex. By the time of the 1931 general election, Mosley had not yet proclaimed himself as an extreme right-wing ideologue. At this stage in his career, as a former Labour cabinet minister who had quarreled with Macdonald over his radical economic proposals, he was much more likely to attract support from the left. Mosley's "New Party," which fought the 1931 election on what was called the "Mosley Manifesto" and failed to win a single seat, had several Bright Young sympathizers: contributors to its house journal, *Action*, included Raymond Mortimer, Osbert Sitwell and Alan Pryce-Jones. However, dissolving the New Party in 1932—at almost the exact time that he began his affair with Diana Guinness—and taking the first steps to establish a full-blown fascist movement, Mosley took very few of his original left-inclined supporters with him.

The Bright Young People's relationship with the Blackshirts of the British Union of Fascists is more equivocal than it might look. Nancy Mitford put her appearances at Mosley's rallies down to youthful naïveté: "Prodd [her nickname for her husband] looked very pretty in a black shirt but we were younger & high spirited then and didn't know about Buchenwald." The Rodds apparently parted company with the BUF after the violent Olympia rally of June 1934, where the treatment of protesters by Mosley's stewards stirred widespread criticism, but not before Nancy had written an enthusiastic article for the July 1934 number of the BUF house journal *Vanguard*, acclaiming fascism as a hope for the future:

> We British Fascists [believe] . . . that our leader, Sir Oswald Mosley, has the character, the brains, the courage and the determination to lift this country from the slough of despond in which it has for too long weltered, to a utopia . . . Soon the streets will echo beneath the feet of the black battalions, soon we will show the world that the spirit of our forefathers is yet alive within us, soon we shall be united by the sacred creed striving as one man for the Greater Britain.

Was she serious? Here, as elsewhere in Nancy's writings, it is difficult to separate out belief, disapproval and the eternal Mitford habit of teasing close members of one's family. Nancy's late-thirties letters to Diana, and to her younger sister Unity—by this time resident in Berlin and operating as a kind of Hitler groupie—are full of a desperate unease, sisterly loyalty, brittle high spirits and mounting horror inextricably commingled. "Call me early, Goering, dear, for I'm to be Queen of the May," she wrote once to Unity, on hearing of her involvement in a Nazi festival—chilling on paper, but perhaps the only way in which someone of Nancy's temperament, upbringing and sensibility could respond to the extraordinary destiny that her sister had mapped out for herself.

Diana, meanwhile, continued to insist, albeit quietly, that the Rodds' involvement with the early days of British fascism was possibly more extensive than they cared to admit, that it endured "for sort of a year. I never say that because it seems hardly fair, because she became so anti. And so that was that. But yes, they were." The wider question of Bright Young People's interest in homegrown fascism remains. Officially this was negligible. A trawl through the membership lists of the Right Club, the Nordic League and the various Anglo-German fellowship organizations of the late 1930s discloses only the usual collection of oddballs and anti-Semites: maverick Tory MPs such as the deranged Captain Ramsay, empire loyalists convinced of the imminent abandonment of Britain's overseas possessions. A representative case might be John Amery, eldest son of the Conservative politician Leo Amery. On paper Amery junior's wartime broadcasts on Berlin radio—he was eventually hanged for high treason—look like a classic example of opposed ideologies: the son rising up to confound his father's beliefs at the worst possible moment. Somehow, though, Amery's behavior is all of a piece with his early career as a shady businessman and prostitute chaser, part of a general self-debasement in which the politics seems tacked on almost by default.

Still, though, there lingers a sense of something atmospheric—the thought that, in the end, however firmly repudiated in public, Mosley's message must have at least some spiritual connection with the world of upper-class dissipation and subsidized high living. But these links are mostly symbolic: David Tennant, for example, attempting to publicize the Gargoyle Club by staging an exhibition of fencing at which Mosley, who had represented his country at the sport, officiated as MC. The psychological connection between the Blackshirts and the idle young rich hangs over many a novel of the period. Patrick Hamilton's *Hangover Square* (1941) examines the relationship between Netta, a farouche and intolerable middle-class girl, and the fascist Peter. Netta is "stimulated" by Peter, Hamilton insists, because his political beliefs and their violent prosecution give him a "halo" of "something bloody, brutal and unusual." Simultaneously, Netta understands his "intense, smoldering, revengeful social snobbery." Denied very much access to the upper classes through want of money, Peter doesn't denounce that class but instead subjects it to a process of intense romanticization. Netta, significantly, is keener on the society columns of the *Tatler* and *Vogue*, "but she was all the same . . . at one with him in spirit." Ultimately, Hamilton makes a direct connection between the frivolous, self-absorbed world of the Mayfair partygoer and the lofted torch of the right-wing political rally:

> And to this was added something else—a feeling for something which was abroad in the modern world, something hardly realized and difficult to describe, but which she knew Peter could discern as well as she herself.
>
> This something, which she could not describe, which was probably indescribable, was something to do with those society columns and something to do with blood, cruelty and fascism— a blend of the two.

Netta and Peter, it should be pointed out, are not genuine Bright Young People but aspiring onlookers, convinced that only a capricious fate has prevented them from appearing on the social stage for which their talents have suited them.

Quite as marked as the occasional right-wing conversion was the determination of many individual Bright Young People to declare for the opposing side. Of all the political converts of the early 1930s, by far the most conspicuous were those who "went left." Robert Byron, Brian Howard, Inez Holden, Gavin Henderson and Tom Driberg all, in varying degrees, committed themselves to left-wing causes in the thirties. A certain amount of this engagement involved the formal channels of political life: Henderson, for example, took the Labour whip on succeeding his uncle as Baron Faringdon in 1934 and made the family seat at Buscot Park available as a venue for the party's discussion groups. Far more of it, though, was indirect, promoted through journalism and behind-the-scenes lobbying. As "William Hickey" of the *Daily Express*, Driberg spent a considerable part of his time inserting surreptitious references to hunger marches and unemployment, went to South Wales to interview out-of-work miners and used part of his holiday entitlement to undertake a fact-finding mission to Spain during the civil war. Driberg's sympathies were well known, to his friends if not to the people who read his column: he remained a card-carrying Communist throughout the 1930s. Other Bright Young People were influenced by symbolic moments of revelation when the true nature of Continental politics suddenly became apparent to them. Byron, as we have seen, had been present at Wiener Neustadt in October 1928 to witness the rival demonstrations by social democrats and fascists. According to Brian Howard, it was the laughter that greeted an incautious remark about Hitler, made at a lunch party of Thomas Mann's in Munich in 1931, which persuaded him to study the German situation.

Of all the twenties aesthetes who turned left in the era of Jarrow, Spain and rearmament, Brian was, if not the first, then certainly one of the most vocal: interviewing the Nazi press chief Dr. Hanfstaengl (Hitler eluded him, after a quarrel with the potential conduit, Unity Mitford), helping Nancy Cunard to assemble her combative symposium *Authors Take Sides on the Spanish Civil War* and contributing one of his best poems, "For Those with Investments in Spain 1937" to the pamphlet series *Les Poètes du monde defendent le peuple espagnol*:

> *I ask your pardon, half of them cannot read,*
> *Your forbearance if, for a while, they cannot pay,*
> *Forgive them, it is disgusting to watch them bleed,*
> *I beg you to excuse, they have not time to pray.*
> *Here is a people, you know it as well as he does,*
> *Franco, you can see it as well as they do,*
> *Who are forced to fight for the simplest rights, foes*

Richer, stupider, stronger than you, or I, or they, too.
So while the German bombs burst in their wombs,
And poor Moors are loosed on the unhappy,
And Italian bayonets go through their towns like combs,
Spare a thought, a thought for all these Spanish tombs,
And for a people in danger, shooting from breaking rooms,
For a people in danger, grieving in falling homes.

The "serious" Brian now found his opinions listened to respectfully, especially by a parental generation that had previously thought him incorrigibly frivolous. Arthur Ponsonby's diary* from 1935 refers to "Brian Howard at luncheon, had been in Germany and had some interesting Hitler stories."

At the same time the transition from Bright Young Person to serious left-wing figure required a degree of harmonization that was occasionally rather beyond him. As his friend Ivan Moffat pointed out, this was a problem that the new decade imposed on many people who attempted to swap a life of well-publicized amusement for political engagement. It was no criticism of Brian, Moffat suggested, to say that his left-wing side was mostly an aesthetic reaction against Nazism: "His position was that he had by then drunk too fully of the B.Y.P. cup, and had suddenly and too late become a left wing figure. It didn't always fit."

Brian's problem was far from unique. At bottom the Bright Young socialists found their careers impeded by a failure to cast off social and artistic baggage picked up along the way. Inez Holden's ability to move seamlessly from high bohemia to a political position that may have included membership of the Communist Party was comparatively rare. On the other side of the coin, Beverley Nichols left an amusing account of his visits to Buscot, and the spectacle of "Gavin, still very much the lord of the manor, still very much a connoisseur of good claret, and still fully, and to my mind rightly, appreciative of the good things of this world, playing host to people whose main object in life . . . is to strangle lords of the manor in the nearest ditch." But the incongruity of Lord

* Not to be confused with the Ponsonby friend of the same name.

Faringdon's taste for high living and some of his political convictions occurred to less waspish observers than Nichols. On the only "party" occasion on which Nichols stayed at Buscot, the guests included Lady Hastings and the future cabinet ministers Susan Lawrence and Ellen Wilkinson (the latter quoted as remarking: "The Lady is too expensive a product to maintain in a failing Empire"). No less fascinating to Nichols was the house telephone list, a copy of which lay on every bedside table: "Number 1—His Lordship's Bedroom," "Number 27—Theatre," "Number 28—Swimming Pool."

It was the same with Driberg. Transparently sincere as was Hickey's commitment to the great humanitarian causes of the day, it occasionally sat rather oddly alongside its author's sybaritic attachment to an older world: his delight in the activities of the Wine and Food society, for example, founded in October 1933 by A. J. A. Symons and André Simon, whose membership list reads like a roll call of former Bright Young People. An evening at the Savoy in October 1936, hosted by Dick Wyndham, found Driberg sampling the restaurant's Lucullan cuisine in the company of David Tennant, Peter Quennell, John Heygate and Sacheverell Sitwell. The apparent gap between political affiliation and social life was noted by his employer, Lord Beaverbrook, who included him in an article about "Café Communists" dictated for the *Evening Standard*'s "Londoner's Diary" in May 1938. The Café Communists, Beaverbrook deposed, were a conspicuous product of our modern social life: "They are the gentlemen, often middle-aged, who gather in fashionable restaurants, and while they are eating the very fine food that is served in those restaurants and drinking the finest wines of France and Spain, they are declaring themselves to be of left-wing faith."

Driberg, part of an assembly that included the publisher Victor Gollancz and the left-wing ideologue John Strachey, retorted that he "did not see why he should also be a victim of the malnutrition which is an endemic disease of capitalism" and that "clear-thinking need not imply poor feeding." He also maintained that he had yet to discover a really "fine" Spanish wine anyway. These, it goes without saying, are the "pansy pinks" of Orwell's demonizing—well-fed fellow travelers who combined their leftist opinions with a reluctance to detach themselves from the traditional observances of their class. What really irks, pace Orwell, is not so much the combination of left-wing views with comfortable lifestyles—for the views were indisputably serious—as the terrible uncertainty of tone that these juxtapositions sometimes inspired. Nancy Mitford's letter to Mark Ogilvie-Grant, written shortly before the general election of 1935, is a case in point:

> I hear that Bobo [the Mitfords' pet name for Unity] and Diana are going to stand outside the Polls next polling day & twist people's arms to prevent their voting, so I have invented (& patented at Gamages) a sham arm which can be screwed on & which makes a noise like Hitler making a speech when twisted so that, mesmerized they will drop it & automatically spring to salute. I expect to make quite a lot of money out of this . . .

Members of a close-knit family, its communal life awash with pet names and private jokes, the younger Mitfords could only express their disapproval of each other by way of slightly hysterical teasing. The satirical passages about Mosley in Nancy's third novel, *Wigs on the Green* (1935), characterized as "Captain Jack" of the "Union Jack-shirts," which caused grave offense to Diana and Unity, strike a similar note: a sensibility that, finding a grotesque and sinister political movement on its own doorstep, so to speak, simply does not know how to react, and can only take refuge in a kind of nursery in-joking.

All this—the well-bred private joke, the leisurely progress from a leftover 1890s aestheticism to an awareness of some of the political realities of the 1930s—furnished the raw material for perhaps the most devastating critique of the Bright Young People, and one Bright Young Person in particular, ever committed to print. Cyril Connolly's "Where Engels Fears to Tread" (1938), subtitled "From Oscar to Stalin: A Progress," is transparently a comment on Brian Howard: the subject is called "Christian de Clavering," which is a whisker away from Howard's middle names. Simultaneously, as Anthony Powell pointed out, it is also to some extent an exposé of Connolly's own pretensions in this field. A keen supporter of the good brave causes, he was also, as his widow put it, "very far from being immune to glamour and *luxe* . . . It was lovely being lion-hunted by rich, smart hostesses, and patted, and told how clever one was . . ." A spoof notice of Christian de Clavering's autobiography, "Engels" is merely a collection of extracts from the work supposedly under review, beginning with a dedication "TO THE BALD YOUNG PEOPLE." There follows an excerpt from the self-justifying introduction, perfectly reproducing the cadences of Brian's vocal tone:

> Why am I doing this, my dears? Because I happen to be the one person who can do it. My dears, I'm on your side! I've come to get you out of the wretched tangle of individualism that you've made for yourselves and show you just how you can be of some use in the world. Stop wondering whether he loves you or not; stop wondering how you will ever make any money. Never mind whether the trousers of your new suit turn up at the bottom; leave off trying to annoy Pa. We're onto something rather big. The Workers' Revolution for the Classless Society through the Dictatorship of the Proletariat! Yes! It's a bit of a mouthful, isn't it? We're used to words of one syllable, words like Freud, Death, War, Peace, Love, Sex, Glands, and, above all, to Damn, Damn, Damn! Well, all that's going to be changed. Morning's at seven, and you've got a new matron.

There follows a vista of de Clavering's early life: home ("My mother an angel. My father a bookie!"); Eton ("An impression, above all, of arches, my dears, each with its handsome couple, and study fireplaces always full of stubs of Balkan Sobranie"); Oxford, where he meets Evelyn Waugh, John Betjeman and Robert Byron, and hobnobs with the great and good ("Now I want all the Guinnesses and Astors to go into the next room and get a charade ready") and finally "London at last. The 'Twenties. Parties. Parties. And behind them all an aching feeling. —Was it all worth it? What is it all for? Futility . . ." Like many Bright Young novelists of the day, Connolly is careful to disguise what he writes in a fashionable acrostic, cross-referencing names and allusions decipherable only by a tiny fragment of his audience. Thus Christian swaps badinage with Beverley Nichols at smart parties ("Beverley, my dear, such a gaffe! I've just gone up to the old Dowager of Buck-and-Cham and mistaken her for the old Dowager of Ham-and-Bran!"), instructs Evelyn Waugh to "of *course*, put me into it," issues an invitation to T. S. Eliot and, when the room grows overfull, instructs his guests to create more space: "Patrick [Balfour], help me spread Elizabeth [Ponsonby] somewhere else. Ronald [Firbank], come out from under the sofa, you're hunching the springs. Fallen out of the window, you say, with Brenda [Dean Paul]? Never mind, for the moment. I want to be alone."

Without warning tragedy looms. Christian's father loses his money. Consigned to Continental exile and genteel English poverty, his son wanders into a bookshop near Red Lion Square and finds the shelves full of slim volumes by unfamiliar names. Who, he wonders, are "Stephen [Spender]," "Wystan [Auden]," "Cecil [Day-Lewis]" and "Christopher [Isherwood]"? But the books are "not at all bad." One quatrain, in particular, haunts him:

> *M is for Marx*
> *and Movement of Masses*
> *and Massing of Arses*
> *and Clashing of Classes*

"It was new. It was vigorous. It was chic." Renaming himself "Chris Clay" Christian joins his first protest march along St. James's Street into the heart of London clubland. In the window of White's, he is surprised to see not only his old aristocratic chums from Oxford but "Peter [Quennell]," "Robert [Byron]" and "Evelyn [Waugh]." "Engels" ends with a warning to its reviewers, who had "better be careful. They'd better be very careful indeed," and a vision of "Commissar Chris Clay" lining up fence sitters for the machine gun. "Remember, my dears, a line is being drawn. Tatatat. See you at the Mass Observatory."

> *Something is going to go, baby,*
> *And it won't be your stamp-collection.*
> *Boom!*

By this time—the era of mass unemployment, the Abdication and the road to Munich—the Bright Young People had become almost wholly mythologized by the press: legendary, fantastic, not quite real. Any remotely exotic social event, and some that were drab beyond measure, drew instant comparison with the entertainments of the previous decade. Ex–Bright Young People who could be run to earth, or found to possess some mild eccentricity, were still seized upon by the gossip columns, but the tone was that of the museum guide proudly displaying some venerable exhibit under dim, antediluvian light. In May 1937, for example, the *Daily Express* ran a report of current reptile prices in a specialist publication called *The Aquarist and Pond-Keeper*. Among certain subscribers who were thought to have oversubscribed was "the Hon. Stephen Tennant," out of pocket to the tune of 3s. 6d. Described as tall, dark and thirty-one years old, Tennant "paints, writes and rated as one of the bright young people back in 1926 . . ."

Occasionally the connection became altogether bizarre. Nancy Mitford would have been surprised to find one of the bridge parties hosted by the Rodds at their tiny house in Chiswick hailed by the *Evening Standard*'s diarist as "a gay, light-hearted affair of the cheerful kind that hasn't happened much since the days of the fabulous past when there were those Bright Young People about." The "fabulous past" was only three or four years distant. Worse, such comparisons were scarcely justified by the realities of entertaining in the Rodds' riverside dolls' house, with furniture pushed back against the wall, cider cup to drink and the card tables crammed into the solitary bedroom. Barely a half-decade on from its late-twenties heyday, the world of white carpets laid out among the Kentish orchards seemed as remote as a classical frieze.

Or perhaps not quite. Here and there among the debris a handful of survivors were still attempting to preserve their lifestyles in a much less hospitable environment. "One may still see at inferior parties debauched and malicious middle-aged hags who were 'bright' enough and 'young' enough in 1923," Douglas Goldring wrote acidly in 1935. Though never seen at "inferior parties," Stephen Tennant was a classic example of the Bright Young Person who made almost no attempt to acclimatize himself to the world of Hitler and Chamberlain. Sequestered at Wilsford Manor and surrounding himself with a choice collection of objets d'art, he published a single book, *Leaves from a Missionary's Notebook* (1937), a Firbankian conceit thoroughly imbued with the spirit of the twenties. Press comment was similarly backward-looking. It was a long time since much had been seen of Stephen Tennant, "one of the more bizarre figures of the nineteen-twenties," the *Evening Standard* commented. Now Mr. Tennant had "come back" with a "precious and limited" book of drawings, illustrating the downfall of "an ingenuous missionary and the demoralization, in a tropical atmosphere, of his female helpmates . . ." Like the *Express*, the *Standard* seemed more interested in Stephen's collection of lizards and snakes. It was 1937, the year of *Authors Take Sides on the Spanish War*. The book, whose publication had in any case been subsidized by its author, did not sell well. Only Cyril Connolly acclaimed this tropical escapism as "a poetic vision of a better world." Tennant himself seemed entirely disengaged from the landscapes around him. Beaton, visiting him a year later as Germany threatened Czechoslovakia, found "someone quite unmoved by the events of the week. Stephen has not even read the papers—he said he liked Hitler's mysticism—the way he parted his hair—the mad starry look in his eyes—Stephen is only interested in himself & his health & now he was particularly occupied as he must enter a clinic tomorrow for a slight operation on his nose."

Down at Shulbrede Priory, meanwhile, everything was going on much as before. Arthur Ponsonby's diary in the months following the White Party makes melancholy reading. Ill, alternately at loggerheads with Denis, plotting to leave him or abruptly changing her mind, Elizabeth, like Stephen Tennant, made no concessions to a changing world:

13 NOVEMBER 1931   E in nursing home. Situation between her and Denis desperate.

2 DECEMBER 1931   E's affairs utterly hopeless. I hear she will not leave Denis and the old round is going to begin again.

26 MARCH 1932   E arrives. In one breath: "I asked _____
                  and _____ to come and stay here
                  tomorrow night and (an afterthought)
                  I am going to divorce Denis."

The grounds were adultery. Denis, in his wife's absence, had spent the night at Sussex Place with a woman and been detected in this lapse by Nelly. Yet Arthur was uneasily aware that Denis's departure from the scene was unlikely to solve any of his daughter's problems. To the cost of court proceedings, and Elizabeth's continuing extravagance, could be added the question of Denis's replacement. Mindful of the emotional triangle that brought about Gordon Russell's death after the White Party, Arthur wondered whether Ludy Ford was being groomed for the role. After observing him in Elizabeth's company, Arthur set down his impressions. He did not dislike the young man but doubted whether he would act as a restraining influence: "Tall good looking, younger than her, has charm but a certain temper . . . hard working, well off. She throws herself at him too much. In all this there is little chance that her habit of life and outlook will change much."

Barely three years had elapsed since the wedding at St. Margaret's Westminster. Concerned as he was for his daughter's happiness, Arthur was also conscious that he could not keep her, either divorced or married, in the style to which she had become habituated. By June 1932 he was noting, "E debt business weighing on us." More exasperating even than the stream of unpaid bills was Elizabeth's apparent obliviousness to the trouble she was causing. Another entry from the same month records a visit to Shulbrede: "She always presents insoluble problems and no one is less aware of it or determined to be less aware of it than herself." Still, amid the divorce preliminaries and the constant demands on his purse, Arthur retained sufficient objectivity to be amused by his daughter's pronouncements, in particular a conversation in which she claimed that by the standards of the social circle in which she moved, her excesses were comparatively mild: "You may complain of my goings on, but you ought to consider yourselves lucky that I am not like many of the others: I don't forge, I don't drug, I don't shoot, I don't steal."

Over the following months, Arthur continued to veer between exasperation at his daughter's self-centeredness and a curious admiration for her honesty. Having made the decision to divorce Denis—the decree nisi was eventually pronounced in 1933—she immediately lost all interest in the proceedings ("She is incapable of pretending anything," Arthur noted). Meanwhile he continued to monitor Ludy Ford. "He puzzles me," runs a diary entry from December 1932. "He is good looking, rather a serious sad look, stammers badly, has a good deal in him but is weak and has been easily led, no grip of himself, could fall into the worst excesses . . ." This sounds very like the accounts of his previous son-in-law, but Arthur believed "there is far more there than in Denis's case." The problem, as Arthur defined it, lay with Elizabeth: "She will look after him if he is ill or unfortunate but if he is well she will only lead him to those senseless parties, drink and dissipation."

Another difficulty—in contrast to Denis's ardent expressions of his regard—lay in establishing Ludy's intentions. Did he, when it came down to it, really have any? In the aftermath of the White Party, after all, Arthur had described him as a "pervert," the Ponsonby code word for "homosexual." The months went by, with little sign of progress. By May 1933, apparently unable to extract precise information either from his daughter or her friend, Arthur arranged to have dinner with Ludy's business partner. Whatever confidences were exchanged deeply upset him. "I cannot write it all down, but the situation appears to me utterly and entirely hopeless." Brooding about his children's lives—Matthew, happily married, was rarely seen at Shulbrede—Arthur was for once reduced to something like anger. He and Dolly had two children, he wrote: one had gone right, the other had gone wrong. "The one who has gone wrong is immediately, weekly, almost daily on our hands, unavoidably present in season and out of season. The other who might by his presence occasionally mitigate these eternal worries we hardly ever see. He might be living in Timbuctoo."

Two days later came "more evidence of Elizabeth's debts, which seem pretty serious." There was also evidence of Elizabeth's serious displeasure at what she regarded as unjustifiable interference. "Angry letter from E," Arthur noted a week later. In it Elizabeth pointedly canceled a visit home planned for the following weekend.

I am afraid I do not feel like coming home for Whitsun.

The unwarranted interference in my affairs has caused so much trouble, anger and unhappiness, that it will take me some time to get over it.

Why is it necessary to go behind my back? I cannot actually see what business it is of anybody's—but if you must get busy about it, why not come to me? I am still alive and able to answer questions.

Yours Elizabeth

There was a somewhat ironic PS: "Please thank mother for the check." In the end the estrangement lasted only a week. By June 10 she was back at Shulbrede: "E arrived in the evening, not a trace of rancor, charmingly cordial with me. What a puzzle she is." The truce did not last. Six weeks later, with Arthur hard at work on a House of Lords speech, a "telephone message about E's parties and extravagance broke up the morning." He went miserably off to her bank and began making arrangements for an accountant to take charge of her financial affairs.

To talk of "truces" being declared in the relationship between Elizabeth and her parents is perhaps misleading. Each side in the triangle loved and respected the other two. But while appreciating her parents—and exhibiting every sign of distress and remorse when her behavior upset them—Elizabeth was determined not to live the kind of life of which they might be expected to approve or to stop spending their money. Still without visible means of support, she seems to have been kept going on Dolly's handouts, with the larger crises that arose every so often further jeopardizing this hand-to-mouth existence. The "insoluble E question" next raised its head in Arthur's diary shortly before Christmas 1933: "E came, desperate, throwing us in the depths of depression again." Three days later Arthur approached Ludy Ford "as the only person who might help."

What was to be done? No doubt as he pondered the question Arthur would have reflected that it had obsessed him for the best part of a decade. But he would also have acknowledged that times—and Elizabeth—had changed. A mainstay of the London society life of the 1920s, her progress around the West End reported on a weekly basis by the gossip columns, the thirty-something woman who wandered through its 1930s equivalent was a much more vagrant presence. The parties she attended in the mid-thirties twilight were not of a kind reported in society magazines. Denis—the kinsman of General Pelly, let us not forget—would do for the *Tatler*. Ludy Ford, the garage proprietor, would not. There are no more references to her in Evelyn Waugh's journal, no more references anywhere apart from Arthur's increasingly anguished diaries.

15 MARCH 1934	E as usual hard up wanting money. I tried to press for a job. But she is utterly desoeuvre waiting for Ludy.
29 APRIL 1934	Sleepless night thinking of E and consequent deep depression.
17 DECEMBER 1934	Shulbrede, Kensington Square and E impossible on income. E is the worst, she costs 700 a year.

Eventually Elizabeth fades even to the margins of her father's diary, reduced to an occasional lurking presence, periodically rising to offer evidence of her hopelessness with money or to canvass some faintly ludicrous job prospect. In the summer of 1936 she was working at the Santa Monica Club in Staines. From this establishment a letter was dispatched to Arthur complaining about the family lawyer's refusal to advance her money. "Much as I should like to, I can't live on nothing at all, even if I am being kept, at the moment I can't even buy a packet of cigarettes." Dolly was supposed to be paying something into her bank account. In the meantime, "Could you send me some notes in an envelope or put a few pounds in the bank. It really is *urgent*." The job, though demanding ("I've never worked so hard in my life"), was financially unrewarding

("They're going to start paying me sometime soon"). In the early autumn Arthur went down to investigate, remarking only that he "did not
see how the club can be pulled round." The receivers were on the premises and "E very busy and receiving 15/- a week!"

And so it went on, through Spain, the reoccupation of the
Rhineland, Czechoslovakia and Munich:

27 OCTOBER 1936	My daughter has drifted back into the chaos of extravagance.
20–21 NOVEMBER 1936	E at Shulbrede. Undercurrent of trouble.
16 NOVEMBER 1938	E with us here at Kensington Square, quite impossible. Yet again I do not know what in the least to do.
21 JANUARY 1939	Elizabeth is lost. We cannot find her. Telegrams, telephones, inquiries have been no good.
8 FEBRUARY 1939	E draining us as usual and refusing to find a job.

And then, unexpectedly, in the summer of 1939, as the war clouds gathered over Europe, Lord Ponsonby's daughter did acquire some kind of
paid employment: she was appointed manageress of a nightclub in the
Piccadilly area ("E for Sunday. She seems to have some curious club
job"). Two months later Arthur gave Elizabeth and her employer ("a
showy pretty friend who runs her club") tea at the House of Lords. If
the incongruity of the situation—a Labour peer gravely attending
to the wants of a nightclub proprietress and her factotum, while
around them politicians anxiously discussed the fate of Poland—
occurred to him, he did not remark on it.

The slow drift to war produced a variety of responses from erstwhile
Bright Young People. Evelyn Waugh, back from Mexico and the trip

that realized the overtly political *Robbery Under Law: The Mexican Object-Lesson* (1939), was hard at work on the novel that became *Work Suspended*, a project left eternally in limbo by the events of early September. Nancy and her husband, Peter Rodd, meanwhile, had finally discovered a cause with which they could wholeheartedly identify. In January 1939, in the dying days of the Spanish Civil War, half a million Republican refugees had escaped from Catalonia across the Pyrenees to Roussillon. Largely ignored by the French authorities, they were herded into a few enclosures along the coast and left to rot. Volunteering to help the international relief effort, Peter arrived to find the death rate running at four hundred a day. Nancy, who went out to join him in the role of van driver, was commissioned to ferry a group of expectant mothers to the port of Sète for embarkation to Mexico. "The boat sailed at 12 yesterday," she told her mother, "the pathetic little band on board played first God Save the King, for us, then the Marseillaise & then the Spanish National Anthem. Then the poor things gave 3 Vivas for Espana which they will never see again. I don't think there was a single person not crying—I have never cried so much in my life."

Other Bright Young People had been professionally engaged in the fight against fascism for some time. Tom Driberg was forced to leave a fascist meeting at St. Pancras Town Hall early in 1939 with shouts of "Jew" and "Hickeystein" ringing in his ears. Robert Byron, having struck up a connection with Sir Stephen Tallents, the BBC's public relations director and minister designate at the inchoate Ministry of Information, had attended the Nuremberg Parteitag of June 1938 as Unity Mitford's guest, sitting so close to Hitler that he could meet the Führer's eye. In Berlin at Christmas 1938 he visited an exhibition of anti-Jewish propaganda. Byron came away "feeling there can be no compromise with these people [the Nazis]—there is no room in the world for them and me, and one has got to go." Listening to Neville Chamberlain broadcast to the nation in March 1939, he decided that "I could not help feeling that it was the most complete justification of my attitude during the last 3 years that could possibly have been uttered . . . I find that the average conservative has begun to realize that the blood of millions will probably be on his hands in the next few months if not in the next few days."

Many "average conservatives," meanwhile, had hastily retreated from previously entrenched positions. Beverley Nichols's *News of England* (1938) dropped the extreme pacifism of the mid-1930s while—hilariously in retrospect—suggesting Mosley as the man who could unite the nation and prevent the slide to war. As late as September 1938, in furtherance of his work for Lord Mount Temple's Anglo-German Fellowship, he entertained a group of visiting leaders of the Hitler Youth to lunch at the Garrick. Mosley's own policy barely varied from that of the British government until Chamberlain's volte-face over appeasement in March 1939. Diana, who had spent large parts of the later 1930s in Germany as her husband's emissary in a scheme to establish a commercial radio station, lunched with Hitler and her sister Unity at the Bayreuth Wagner festival in early August. The evening's performance was *Götterdämmerung*. "Never had the glorious music sounded so doom-laden," she noted. A month later, hearing news of the declaration of war from the British consulate, Unity walked to the middle of the English Garden in Munich and shot herself in the temple. The bullet, while lodged in her brain, did not kill her and she was eventually sent back to England. Diana and her husband would spend three and a half years of the war interned in Holloway.

Whatever the traumas of approaching war, many of the Bright Young People would have been aware of—some would probably have attended—the opening performances of Terence Rattigan's new play. *After the Dance*, which premiered at the St. James's Theatre on June 21, 1939, is nothing less than an anatomy of the Bright Young People's world, seen from the vantage point of seedy middle age. Here in a Mayfair flat, living on a comfortable private income and stoutly supported by attentive servants, David and Joan, a married couple in their late thirties, are gamely attempting to preserve the spirit of the previous decade: boozing, partygoing, conversing in Bath and Bottle Party–era slang and resolutely declining to take anything seriously. They are assisted in this anachronistic lotus-eating by John, an engaging parasitical friend, who stays permanently in the flat and is thoroughly disapproved of by David's younger cousin Peter—desultorily employed as the former's secretary—and his fiancée, Helen. Further spice is added to these relationships by the gradual awareness that Helen's concern over David's drinking is turning into a full-blown infatuation.

Rattigan was twenty-eight when he wrote *After the Dance*: too young to have been an authentic Bright Young Person, but old enough to remember press coverage of the late-1920s society whirl. Consequently the play examines the Bright Young People phenomenon in lavish detail: offering reminiscences of thinly disguised Bright Young People's extravaganzas, dwelling lavishly on period slang, continually returning to its themes of generational conflict and the enduring legacy of the Great War. Interviewed by journalists, Rattigan claimed that *After the Dance* was intended as an attack on the inanities of a bygone generation, and yet the play itself—full of beguiling complexities and oppositions that are by no means clear-cut—is not quite so straightforward. The opening scene, for example, in which Peter sits typing up the chapters that David has drunkenly dictated to him the previous night, while John and Joan recover from their hangovers, both establishes the generational divide and subtly implicates Peter in its consequences. When Peter explains that he resents being his cousin's secretary "because I believe one ought to work for one's living," John retorts that, by strict definition, both of them are parasites: Peter by way of his blood relationship, the older man by means of "a certain ability to act as a court jester." Joan then joins the conversation, defending Peter but betraying her own empty-headedness:

JOAN: There's nothing wrong with his generation. They're just serious-minded. I think it's very nice.

JOHN: You don't think anything of the sort. You think they're bores, and so do I. Whatever people may have said about us when we were young, they could never have said we were bores.

Meanwhile a scattering of Bright Young People references is being dropped unobtrusively into the text. David, who eventually emerges from the bedroom to address his dependents in tones of world-weary irony, is writing a biography of King Bomba of Naples—a futile, dilettantish pursuit, Rattigan implies, and an all-too-plausible Bright Young Person's project: Harold Acton, for example, had written a study of the similarly benighted later Medici. The general air of a group of social dinosaurs precariously at large in a world altogether beyond their comprehension is heightened by the arrival of David and Joan's old friend Julia, accompanied by a cockney boyfriend whose surname she cannot remember and conversing in exquisitely outdated slang ("Darling, what about a tingy-wingy little dinky-boo?" etc.). To the young people present—Peter, Helen and Helen's medical brother George, whom she wants to pronounce on David's incipient alcoholism—all this is a prompt to the most intense disapproval:

> GEORGE: It was the first time I'd ever seen those sort of people. I'd only read about them before.
>
> PETER: Yes, I know the feeling. Whenever I meet Julia Brown or any of the gang that come running into this flat, I always feel they don't really exist.

Bright Young People nostalgia, meantime, is in full spate, with references to "Moya Lexington," a celebrated society drug addict who sounds remarkably like Brenda Dean Paul, and memories of the entertainments of long ago. "Do you remember the party I gave where everyone came as the characters in history they'd liked to have been?" Julia reminisces. These middle-aged nostalgia brokers, Rattigan implies, are morally delinquent, determined to avoid all mention of the world in which they find themselves. There is a symbolic moment when Joan puts one of her favorite records on the gramophone. "Do you remember when this first came out, and they played it at that party of Arthur Power's without stopping for a whole evening?" she demands of John. The record sticks irrecoverably in its groove. The young, on the other hand, emerge as deeply priggish representatives of a moral outlook that seems quite as suspect. There is a particularly revealing scene in which well-meaning Helen lectures David on what she imagines to be the origins of his, and by implication his generation's, malaise. It is the Great

War, she suggests, that makes him lead such a "fantastic life." What, David wonders, has the war got to do with it? Patiently, Helen explains:

> You see, when you were eighteen, you didn't have anybody of twenty-two or twenty-five or thirty or thirty-five to help you, because they'd been wiped out. And anyone over forty you wouldn't listen to anyway. The spotlight was on you, and you weren't even young men; you were children.

What did they do with this spotlight? David wonders again. "You danced in it," she tells him.

Meanwhile, various realignments are beginning to make themselves felt. David and Helen declare their love for each other shortly before a party that Joan has decided to throw in the flat. The event itself receives mixed reviews from the guests. One Bright Young veteran informs the cohost, "David, this is a heavenly party. It's like old times." "Very old times, I'm afraid," David chips back. Arthur Power is less impressed: "I think it's obscene to see a lot of middle-aged men and women behaving like children at a school treat. It's the bright young people over again, only they never were bright and now they're not even young." Joan, having at first received the news of her abandonment with an exemplary stoicism, later throws herself over the balustrade to her death. The final act, set three months later, sees fresh starts on all sides: Helen bullying David into a drink-free lifestyle far from the London fleshpots; John about to depart for a job cleaning windows in Manchester. However, Peter's arrival at the flat to ask Helen to lunch and borrow money from his cousin is enough to cancel out these new initiatives. In the course of a final argument, John convinces David that Peter, rather than himself, is the person with the greater need for Helen's admiration. The curtain closes with David advising Helen to keep her lunch date and reaching for the decanter. Nothing, we are led to believe, will stop him from drinking himself to death.

Well received by the critics ("almost certain to remain on the boards for months to come," *Cavalcade* predicted), *After the Dance* lasted a bare sixty performances. Bygone jeunesse dorée was not a subject in which a nation preparing for war could be expected to take much interest. In its way it is one of the subtler valedictions pronounced upon the Bright Young People. "I don't think one should ever grudge young people the form of escape they choose, however childish it is," John responds to Arthur's complaint about Joan's party. "I think they are very wise." There are worse epitaphs.

CHAPTER TWELVE

PROJECTIONS

Brilliant these sucklings of the pen may be. And startling, as all infant prodi-
gies are startling. But is there anything solid, anything of permanent value,
under the brilliance? When they cease to startle, will they continue to entertain us?

— GILBERT FRANKAU, 1930

Publicity was the drug for which they chiefly craved and in order to obtain it
they fawned on journalists, flattered young novelists of respectable middle-
class origin and even took to writing novels themselves.

— DOUGLAS GOLDRING, *Odd Man Out* (1935)

From an early stage in their history, even as far back as the era of
motorized treasure hunts and the first stunt parties, the Bright
Young People had begun the process of mythologizing themselves,
of projecting various aspects of their behavior and attitudes beyond the
circles in which they moved or—not quite the same thing, perhaps—
having them projected by other people. Some of these promoters
were well-disposed; others—the *Punch* cartoonists, for example—
emphatically not. Such was the resonance of the materials, though, that
the images contrived for public consumption were remarkably uniform.
By the time of the Bath and Bottle Party of 1928, it is fair to say, the
Bright Young Person with his, or her, tatterdemalion getup, stylized
speech and chronic affectations would have been as instantly recognizable an archetype to the average newspaper reader as the "suffragette" of
twenty years before or the pre-Edwardian "swell" of twenty years
before that. Much of this conceptualizing was necessarily low-level, a
matter of gesture, style, inflexion transferred to gossip columns and

magazine sketches: see again the *Punch* columns of the period. As harder-headed Bright Young Men and Women set about forging, or in some cases extending, their careers in the later 1920s, it began to filter down into literature.

Certainly by the early 1930s, a distinctive group of novelists had come into existence who, if not Bright Young People themselves, were closely associated with the movement's inner core. They included Evelyn Waugh, Harold Acton, Nancy Mitford, Bryan Guinness, Anthony Powell, Beverley Nichols and Henry Green, as Henry Yorke signed himself for literary purposes. These associations were strengthened by the fact that many of them shared the same commercial sponsor: between 1928 and 1933, for example, Duckworth, which employed Anthony Powell, published books by Waugh, Beaton, Powell himself, Inez Holden, Bryan Guinness and Byron. Though the group's members were sometimes concerned to distance themselves from each other, and from the Bright Young People generally, the connections between them and the uniformity of their subject matter were profoundly important, if only for publicity purposes. When Edith Sitwell declared of *Afternoon Men* (1931) that Mr. Powell was by far the most amusing and incisive of "what has been known vulgarly as the 'bright young people,'" the effect was to register Powell in the public imagination in much the same way as an "angry young man" of a quarter-century later.

As for the literary world in which the Bright Young novelist took his or her bow, then as now it was composed of any number of interest groups and alliances, mass-market tastes and specialist preferences. If it was the age of the Times Book Club, the Boots Library and the bestseller—of Hugh Walpole and Warwick Deeping and J. B. Priestley, whose *The Good Companions* sold seventy thousand copies on publication in 1929—then it was also the age of the clique, of Bloomsbury, the Sitwells and the "Squirearchy," the gang of Georgian poets, Sussex ramblers and strict-meter obsessives who congregated around the no-nonsense figure of J. C. Squire at the Fleet Street offices of the *London Mercury*. Bright Young People's attitudes to these congeries varied between outright hostility and an awareness of some of the possibilities for self-advancement that keeping in with them might provide. This meant that feet tended to be kept simultaneously in several camps. Thus while Evelyn Waugh's *Rossetti* (1928) mocked the malign influence of Lytton Strachey on biography ("We have discovered a jollier way of honoring our dead. The corpse has become a marionette") and Connolly's reviews had him apostrophized as "that smartiboots Cyril Connolly" by Virginia Woolf, several Bright Young People had strong Bloomsbury connections: Bryan and Diana Guinness were frequent visitors to the Strachey-Carrington ménage at Ham Spray, Wiltshire, and Lytton Strachey often turned up at Bright Young People's parties. It was the same with even so reactionary a literary proposition as the *London Mercury*. *Decline and Fall* might joke about "Jack Spire of the *London Hercules*," but Waugh had known Squire for years through his father and brother, even to the extent of canvassing for him when Squire stood as a Liberal candidate in the general election campaign of October 1924. A glance through the contributors' lists shows that he, Pryce-Jones and Driberg all placed work there in the 1920s, while Pryce-Jones ended up as the paper's editorial assistant.

The process could work the other way: a senior literary figure, say, conscious of which way the winds of fashion were blowing, unexpectedly aligning himself with the newly modish. In Anthony Powell's *The Acceptance World* (1955), set in the early 1930s, Nick Jenkins is flattered to find the elderly writer St. John Clarke commenting "at least by implication favorably" in an American newspaper on one of his novels. Jenkins assumes that this is simply a case of St. John Clarke discerning merit. His friend Barnby, on the other hand, diagnoses an opportunistic conversion to modernism ("I fear it is all part of a larger design"). This mirrors the fortunes of Powell's first novel *Afternoon Men*, and the "scrap of implied praise" flicked toward it by Hugh Walpole, a writer not hitherto known for his encouragement of young, avant-garde talent.

From the viewpoint of the wider market place, the wave of books, newspaper articles and pronouncements served notice of a definite literary community. Most obviously, contemporary readers, let alone contemporary critics, would have noted that the Bright Young novelists were consciously influenced by each other. *Vile Bodies* (1930) betrays a considerable debt to Nichols's *Crazy Pavements* (1927). Nancy Mitford's

Highland Fling (1931) is, in its turn, influenced by Waugh's novel, to the point where the publishers made her tone down some of the more flagrant resemblances ("Have had to alter the book quite a lot as it is so like Evelyn's in little ways," Nancy confided to Mark Ogilvie-Grant, "*such* a bore"). Possibly as a result of these similarities, Nancy affected not to like *Vile Bodies* ("I was frankly very much disappointed in it I must say"), just as Waugh always enjoyed chronically strained relations with Nichols.* But the links between them were inescapable. In the end, for all the occasional rows and recriminations, movement consanguinity invariably won out.

Throughout the twenties and thirties, Waugh, Byron and their friends gamely conspired to puff each other's books and encourage a reviewing network in which those known to them from school and university could nearly always be sure of a favorable reception. When one of the characters in *Christmas Pudding* (1932) writes a novel, Nancy Mitford notes that the critics, "even those who had neither been at Eton nor at Oxford with him," had praised it extravagantly. This atmosphere of spirited collusion meant that attacks from outside the group produced an instant solidarity, whatever animosities might separate the individual Bright Young People involved. Thus in May 1930, Cecil Beaton produced an article for the *Daily Mail* titled "Good Manners Are in Fashion Again." This was immediately attacked in the same newspaper by Waugh. Shortly afterward, Waugh, Beaton and Nichols were themselves the subject of a violent onslaught by the novelist Gilbert Frankau, who maintained that young men who had never lived in the real world should not make exaggerated pronouncements on how other people should conduct themselves. True to his generation, Waugh immediately began to fill his columns with hostile asides about Frankau.

But the similarities between, say, Waugh, Powell and Green were more than a matter of procedural sheen. Looking back on the fiction of the 1930s, Julian Maclaren-Ross identified a genre which he christened

---

* "There is a poor old journalist named Beverley Nichols on board who cares more about his personal appearance than the vainest of ladies and he has come on to this ship purely in the hope of sun-bathing and acquiring a becoming sun-tan. It has been far too stormy to venture out on deck and he is in tears of disappointment." Letter to Margaret and Harriet Waugh en route to Bermuda, January 1955 (The Letters of Evelyn Waugh, Amory [ed.], p. 437).

the "party novel," its subject matter "the day-to-day doings of a 'Bohemian' group much preoccupied with their love affairs and the impact of their personalities upon each other." Again, this makes the Bright Young Person's novel sound like a sociological offshoot. In fact, the connections go beyond social grounding to take in influence, technique, construction, the whole question—in a literary landscape that took these affiliations very seriously indeed—of aesthetic standpoint.

These influences were not always merely literary. Waugh, Powell and Green, for example, were conscious of the impact of cinema on their work, to the point where their novels often seem to be composed in a kind of filmic shorthand, cutting sharply from scene to scene and put together out of ricocheting one-liner dialogue. Green, in particular, had noted this tendency in his writing at a very early stage. At work on *Living* (1929), he told his friend Nevill Coghill: "I think you will like the book I am on now. It's written in a very condensed kind of way in short paragraphs, hardly ever much longer than 1½ to 2 printed pages and often very much shorter. A kind of very disconnected cinema film." In much the same way, *Vile Bodies*'s action, especially in the wide-scale "party" scenes, swings violently from character to character and room to room, often in no more than the span of a sentence. Powell, too, was an obsessive cinematophile who would later earn a precarious living scripting "quota quickies"—films designed to meet the legal requirement that a certain proportion of the material shown in British cinemas should be homegrown—at a studio in Teddington.

Much more deliberate, though, was the literary context. Here, dominant influences ranged from the commercial mainstream to the fanatically obscure. In the first category lay *The Green Hat*, Michael Arlen's bestseller from 1924. This features Iris Storm, a man-eating heroine of quite deathless allure who is described by herself as "a house of men," by someone else as a combination of "a pagan body and a Chislehurst mind," is the first woman in England to have her hair shingled and whose first husband throws himself out of a hotel window on the first night of their honeymoon "for purity," having apparently discovered that his wife is not a virgin. Coolly mysterious, Iris weaves her enigmatic way through much of the fiction of the ensuing decade. She is transparently the inspiration for "Imogen Quest," the phantom ornament of *Vile Bodies*'s gossip columns. Mrs. Beste-Chetwynde in *Decline and Fall* drives the same make of car, a Hispano-Suiza. Anthony Powell always maintained that, on coming to London in the autumn of 1926, he took rooms in the seedy Mayfair thoroughfare of Shepherd Market simply because it was there that the novel's opening scene—a discreet, late-night seduction—is set. As late as 1937, autographing one of his novels for Constant Lambert and his wife, Powell added the otherwise unintelligible words "For purity" to the flyleaf. Significantly, *The Green Hat* often figured as a symbol of generational struggle. Alan Pryce-Jones, having presented a copy to his father on the strength of the reviews, was summoned to the smoking-room fireplace to watch its incineration.

Even more seductive than Arlen's suggestive dialogue, his one-night stands in Mayfair lodgings, his roguish intimations of clubland naughtiness, were the novels of Ronald Firbank (1886–1926), whose impact on the mainstream writers of the 1920s and 1930s was out of all proportion to their meager sales. Shy, dandyish, homosexual, reclusive and compelled to publish his books at his own expense, Firbank's dozen fictions included, in works such as *Caprice* (1917) and *Prancing Nigger* (1924), some of the high points of early English modernism. Set in fantastic never-never lands or in more familiar environments twisted radically out of kilter, they advertise a wit so delicate that it can scarcely be identified, borne forward by scraps of rococo dialogue, the whole invariably undercut with intimations of deep unease, often extending to outright tragedy. This exchange from *Prancing Nigger*, whose alternative title, *Sorrow in Sunlight*, conveys the essence of the Firbank world, may be taken as representative.

"Do you remember the giant with the beard," she asked, "at the Presidency fete?"

"Do I?"

"And we wondered who he could be!"

"Well?"

"He's the painter of Women's Backs, my dear!"

"The painter of women's *what*?"

"An artist."

"Oh."

"I wanted to know if you'd advise me to sit."

The echoes of this highly stylized dialogue would resonate through English fiction for the next fifteen years. As one, Bright Young People with literary aspirations rushed to acclaim Firbank as their mentor. Evelyn Waugh wrote an enraptured essay for *Life and Letters* (March 1929) in which he suggested that Firbank "achieved a new art form" as a way of "bringing coherence to his own elusive humor." Brian Howard thought *Concerning the Eccentricities of Cardinal Pirelli* (1926), at whose climax the cardinal drops dead while in hot pursuit of an attractive choirboy, "the wittiest book ever written. A triumph of indecent sophistication." Anthony Powell, while working at Duckworth, managed to contrive a posthumous collected edition of his books. One or two of the older generation of Bright Young People had even come across Firbank in the flesh, either at his principal London watering hole, the Café Royal, or in one of his Italian haunts. Invariably the reality undercut the illusion: "He was always drunk," Harold Acton recalled; "Too awful," Beverley Nichols remarked in his diary, after witnessing one of these (non)performances. Raymond Mortimer remembered meeting him three or four times in the early twenties: "squirming, crimson-faced, incapable of communication because of shyness and drink." Though hugely gratified to meet a fan of his work, "he spoke only in strangled and disjointed gasps of rapture, hilarity and dismay." Mortimer could not imagine how he contrived to complete a book or even travel without an attendant. Firbank vis-à-vis might have been a grievous disappointment, but the wider impact remained, and in the years after his premature death (in Rome, attended by the highly appropriate figure of Lord Berners) he became an almost legendary figure in Bright Young People's circles and a decisive influence on Bright Young People's fiction.

If Michael Arlen's impact was general—a matter of haunted silences, quasi-philosophical dialogue, fast cars and atmosphere—Firbank's was specific. As a novelist, it is fair to say that he bequeathed three chief legacies to fiction. The first is his ability to re-create "talking heads," two-, three-, or even four-way conversations in which no speaker is ever named, but where the author's ear for speech patterns enables the reader to distinguish immediately between the contending voices. His second technical advance is the way in which his style, by this time utterly stripped down and composed, manages to convey a tumult of impressions—movement, scene, talk—in a minimum of words. The removal of the Mouth family to Cuna-Cuna in *Prancing Nigger*, for example, is announced in the single sentence: "Little jingly trot trot trot, over the Savannah hey—." At the same time Firbank perfected a trick of advancing the plots of his novels by way of allusive dialogue. In the *Life and Letters* essay Waugh instances the case of the Ritz Hotel versus Lady Something in *The Flower Beneath the Foot* as "typical of the Firbank method." At a dinner party King William of Pisuerga observes, of some piece of news, that he could "not be more astonished if you told me there were fleas at the Ritz." Lady Something mishears: "Who would believe it?" she exclaims. "It's almost too appalling . . . Fleas have been found at the Ritz." The Ritz goes unmentioned for the next forty pages, until a character called the Honorable "Eddy" observes to Lady Something that had he known he was going to be ill, he would have gone to the Ritz. "And you'd have been bitten all over," Lady Something assures him. There is another long silence, broken only by an aside in which "an eloquent and moderately victorious young barrister" is mentioned as "engaged in the approaching suit with the Ritz." A few pages later comes a casual remark that the Ritz is empty save for a solitary guest.

Simply through a few tangential remarks, tiny fragments of stone concealed in a vast mosaic, Firbank has built up a plotline that takes place more or less offstage. As the chain of incident set in motion at the Llanabba school sports in *Decline and Fall* demonstrates, Waugh occasionally used this technique himself. The sequence begins when Mr. Prendergast, drunk in charge of the starting pistol, inadvertently grazes little Lord Tangent's ankle with a stray bullet. Somewhat later in the proceedings a guest asks Lady Circumference how her son has been performing. "My boy has been injured in the foot," she coldly replies. "Dear me! Not badly I hope. Did he twist his ankle in the jumping?" No,

Lady Circumference explains, "he was shot at by one of the assistant masters." Twenty pages later, during the course of an organ lesson, Paul Pennyfeather's pupil Peter Beste-Chetwynde casually remarks that, "Tangent's foot has swollen up and turned black." There is another gap of ten pages, until an account of the bigamous union of Captain Grimes and the headmaster's daughter concludes with a reference to the absence of Lord Tangent, "whose foot was being amputated at a local nursing home." It is the authentic Firbankian note, brought out of the modernist shadows and put into a mainstream comic novel.

Just as Bright Young People conversation often proceeded by way of abstruse insider jargon and vocal tics, so the Bright Young People novel can seem to be written in a kind of code, whose solution would authenticate it in the eye of the Bright Young reader. Sometimes this is merely a matter of incidentals: the dropping in of stray references to Mrs. Meyrick or the latest fashionable cocktail. More deliberate was the cross-referencing of other Bright Young authors. Cyril Connolly's *The Rock Pool* (1936), set among the expatriate bohemian community of the French Riviera, finds its hero, Naylor, talking to a girl named Varna whom he has met in a bar. Each line in their conversation is imagined as a move in a game of chess:

"Have you ever broadcast, Mr. Naylor?"

"No, I've never actually been on the air myself, though most of my friends have."

"Announcing?"

"No, giving talks mostly."

"Oh, yes, Alec Waugh has told me all about the talks at the Gargoyle!" (check)

"He's charming, isn't he, though I've always known his brother Evelyn better!" (discovered check)

"I've just missed meeting him."

"???" (and wins)

While trying to affirm their Bright Young credentials, Naylor and Varna are also jostling for precedence, attempting to find, as Connolly puts it, "their common boasting ground." But Connolly is playing the same trick on the reader, establishing a small private space full of mutually acceptable references and allusions: Alec and Evelyn Waugh; the Gargoyle Club; the friends broadcasting on the BBC. This pattern is endlessly repeated. In Nancy Mitford's "Phoney War" caper, *Pigeon Pie* (1940), the heroine, Sophie, jokes that she has left the Left Book Club because the books are left: "I don't mean because they are left [i.e., left-wing] and I can't get Evelyn Waugh and any of the things I want to read. I mean because they are left lying about the house." In *Christmas Pudding*, alternatively, a minor character is represented as a keen Byzantinist "and, like all such, extremely sensitive on the subject." This, as perhaps a dozen of Nancy's readers would have twigged, was a reference to Robert Byron.

As well as dropping the names of personal friends, or alluding to prominent Bright Young personalities, Bright Young People's fiction was also concerned to cultivate what might be called its own cultural corner, providing up-to-the-moment reports on contemporary fads, preoccupations and obsessions. This was most noticeable in the realm of language. As we have seen, *Vile Bodies* contrived to popularize the badinage of a tiny group of people centered on the Guinnesses' house on Buckingham Street in the space of a few weeks. *Highland Fling* fairly thrums with the latest Mitford slang. Equally important was the mapping out, again by discreet allusion, of a specific cultural territory, more or less highbrow and often taking its cue from literature. Bobby Bobbin, the dissipated Eton boy in *Christmas Pudding*, based on Nancy's boyfriend Hamish Erskine, keeps a set of Firbank's novels in his room. On the other side of the coin, Anthony Powell's early novels are full of surreptitious put-downs of contemporary best sellers. In *From a View to a Death* (1933), Joanna Brandon comes home to find her mother reading her favorite book, Axel Munthe's *The Story of San Michele*. Is it a good book? she wonders. "It's a beautiful book, darling," sofa-bound Mrs. Brandon assures her. "A very beautiful book. It's a book that takes your old mother out of herself." Subsequently Mrs. Brandon wonders aloud: "Why aren't all the books that people write beautiful? Why don't writers only write about the beautiful things in life?" Not only is Powell implicitly damning Mrs. Brandon as a sort of futile halfwit, he is also stating his own claims, in a world where most writers peddled the Brandon line, to the aesthetic high ground.

Cloaked as they are in an atmosphere of unremitting frivolity—parties, failed seductions, pleasure jaunts—the themes of Bright Young People fiction take some time to declare themselves. On one level *Highland Fling* is simply a succession of witless conversations shrieked out by a group of empty-headed idiots who in an ideal world would be summarily dispatched to the nearest employment office and told to find a job. Beneath it, though, lies something much more disquieting. Unsurprisingly, the fundamental concerns of Bright Young People novels turn out to be those of the Bright Young People themselves: generational conflict, doubts about the value of human relationships, the resigned expectation of unpleasant things to come. The future, as conceived by a Powell, a Mitford or a Waugh, is never a rosy blur but something hard, sharp and ominous. "Do you think one of these days everything will come right?" Harriet demands of Atwater in *Afternoon Men*. "No," he assures her.

A sense of futility consequently envelops the social gatherings of which these novels consist like a shroud. *Afternoon Men* ends as it begins with Atwater and his friend Pringle loafing in a bar and exchanging desultory gossip about mutual friends. The intervening chapters introduce a succession of characters, all of them occupying some recognizable niche on the fringes of the Bright Young People's world: Lola, whom Atwater seduces after they meet at a party ("She might have been an art student, perhaps, brought along unexpectedly. Her general tendency was to resemble an early John drawing, but she had adapted this style to the exigencies of the fashion of the moment"); the painter Barlow's girlfriend Sophie ("She was fair and plump, a painter's girl, rather like an Eve by Tintoretto. She had some sort of job in a dress shop"); Susan Nunnery, described as "a bit of a menace" ("Is she still living with Gilbert?" someone asks Barlow. He doesn't know. "I can't keep up with girls like that"). The novel climaxes during the course of a country weekend, when Pringle, crossed in love, tries to commit suicide by drowning himself in the sea, only to be pulled out by some passing fishermen. Even self-destruction, it turns out, is beyond him.

Meanwhile, Powell loads the conversation with uneasy references to personal dissatisfaction, the sense of existing in a world without meaning. "It is at times like this that I often think how little there is ahead of us, young men like you and I," observes Fotheringham, another of Atwater's bar-lounging friends. Later on in the novel, the two discuss friendship. "I'm not a religious chap, I don't know anything about that sort of thing," Fotheringham muses. "But there must be something beyond all this sex business." Here, as elsewhere in his fiction, Powell is pulling off a curious double effect: quietly mocking the character who delivers some clichéd observation on "life"—what could be funnier than bored young men who sit in pubs talking about "this sex business"?—while leaving the sentiment itself hanging suggestively in the air above him.

Highland Fling, published in the same year and both a more frivolous and less accomplished piece of work, betrays exactly the same dissatisfactions: a brittleness of tone and observation that can occasionally become quite overpowering. Powell admitted that the milieu of *Afternoon Men*—parties given by unsuccessful painters and their girls, unsatisfactory love affairs with artists' models, time frittered away in drink and conversation—was closely allied to his own bohemian adventures in the late 1920s. In the same way Mitford's novel draws on her excursions to Banffshire to stay with her friend Nina Seafield. Walter and Sally Monteith are a pair of spendthrift Bright Young People who take their aesthete chum Albert "Memorial" Gates up to Scotland to supervise a shoot taking place on the estate of an absent relative. Almost immediately, each of the defining elements of the Bright Young People's world is wheeled smartly into place. Cocktails are drunk with an almost religious fervor. The Monteiths' London flat is admired by Albert for its quasi-Victorian décor ("Two huge vases of white wax flowers stood on each side of the fireplace; over the mantelpiece hung a Victorian mirror framed in large white shells and red plush"). Inevitably, Walter and Sally are connected with gossip writers, have married in the face of parental opposition and have no idea how to curb their improvident lifestyle ("They struggled as best they could on a joint income of a thousand a year"). As the party moves north to Scotland, where a particularly grim collection of elderly guests is lugubriously assembled, several other Bright Young People's preoccupations fall into place. Albert mocks the aged, Hun-hating, grouse-obliterating General Murgatroyd: "I have always had a great *penchant* for soldiers. It fascinates me to think how brave they must be. Sometimes one sees them marching about in London, all looking so wonderfully brave. I admire that." Brisk exchanges over the dinner table take in the war and the contempt of the young for the old.

For all the fervor of its oppositions, *Highland Fling* is very far from being a defense of youthful irresponsibility. Its distinguishing mark, in fact, is a profound irritation with everyone involved. The old are warmongering reactionaries, narrow-minded and middlebrow (General Murgatroyd condemns himself by admiring a picture of some sheep in a field). The young, on the other hand, are immature, frivolous and motivated by bogus values. "You are divine not to be cross," Sally tells Walter when she is found to be pregnant. She is consumed with anxiety as to how the baby is to be clothed. "I mean babies' clothes are always covered with lace, just like underclothes, they must be frightfully expensive." Their friend Jane, who also accompanies them on the Scottish visit, is criticized for not accepting the advantages of the conventional world that surround her. Affecting to dislike her parents—represented as caring and devoted people with her best interests at heart—she falls in love with Albert, intending to become his mistress. Unexpectedly, Albert announces his intention to marry her ("Albert, don't be so childish," she admonishes him. "Have you *no* modern ideas?"). Assuming that her parents will disapprove of the match, Jane is again surprised to find them perfectly calm about her engagement and taking a shine to her fiancé. Worse, they further decline to fulfill the role Jane has assigned to them by regretting the career in stockbroking Albert has manufactured for himself as a ruse to gain their approval. Someone of Jane's sensibility, they believe, should marry "a man of talent, say a writer or artist."

Highland Fling climaxes with an outrageous Bright Young People's stunt: the purchase of a plot of land at the "London Necropolis" and the staging of a mock funeral. Albert, meanwhile, has managed an exhibition of his avant-garde painting. "Those are the Bright Young People, no doubt," Lady Prague remarks at one point. "How very disgusting." "Did you hear what she called us?" Jasper, the architect of the mock funeral, exclaims. "What a name! Bright Young People! O, how unkind to suggest that we are bright—horrid word—I see nothing bright about a funeral, anyway, do you?" Jasper rushes to telephone the *Daily Runner* to secure maximum press coverage: "We had six photographers and a cinematograph at the graveside, and the light was very good today. Would you like to be photographed among the wreaths, darling? It might give quite a good boost to the exhibition?" The novel ends with a barrage of press reports. One, commenting on the funeral, suggests that "the Bright Young People have had their day . . . their jokes, often in the worst possible taste, should now come to an end." Another acclaims Albert's pictures. Like her parents' placid acceptance of their engagement, Albert's artistic triumph again produces an adverse reaction in Jane. "She saw all her dreams of Albert's struggle for fame, with herself helping and encouraging, of a tiny house in Paris only visited by a few loyal friends, and of final success in about ten years' time largely brought about by her own influence, falling to earth shattered." Piqued and near hysterical ("I couldn't feel more jealous if it were another woman"), she writes breaking off the engagement, only to change her mind abruptly and accept him after all. The happy ending altogether fails to disguise the astringency of what has gone before.

Set down in the pages of fiction, Bright Young People invariably come accompanied by a kind of spiritual leper bell. Not only are they stigmatized for being silly, shallow and morally confused; their influence on people thus far uncontaminated by these failings is bound to be contagious. The message of Beverley Nichols's *Crazy Pavements*, a pioneering Bright Young People novel published as early as February 1927, is that practically every aspect of the Bright Young People's world is liable to debase innocents brought into contact with it. An altogether preposterous and sentimentalized Mayfair romance, *Crazy Pavements* features Brian Elme, a golden-haired twenty-year-old who works as a gossip columnist on a paper called *The Lady's Mail*. Brian lives, idealistically, with a slightly older ex–naval officer named Walter on strict *Boy's Own Paper* terms: "Hullo! B . . . What are you looking so mouldy about?" etc. Having no society connections, and hard pressed to fill his column, Brian resorts to inventing most of his stories. Summoned to apologize to a certain Lady Julia Cressey for having unwittingly traduced her, he falls violently in love. Happily, this passion is reciprocated, and Brian is introduced to Lady Julia's "set," a terrific gang of Mayfair harpies including the diabolical Lord William Motley, his sidekick Maurice Cheyne and the nymphomaniacal Lady Anne Hardcastle, all of whom set out enthusiastically to corrupt him.

There follow some already rather predictable criticisms of "smart" Mayfair life. In particular, Brian begins to "understand the techniques of these people's conversation." Their chief characteristic, he decides, is a peacock exaggeration of commonplace statements: " 'Divine,' 'amazing,' 'shattering,' 'monstrous,' were all employed for the most ordinary feelings and facts." Brian wonders, "What language they would speak if something really awful did happen." Meanwhile, his involvement with Lady Julia's jackals leads him into trouble. Lord William, who owns a collection of masks of his friends' faces, takes him to dine at the "Gaga Club" and announces, "We have been rebelling so long against Victorianism that there is absolutely nothing left to rebel against." Walter, seeing which way the wind is blowing, declares, "I'm a selfish beast. I want to go on living with you until the real thing comes." Alas, the late nights spent dancing attendance on Lady Julia and the endless round of cocktails ("The chink of ice in a shaker began to echo in Brian's nerves like a maddening monotone. Whenever there was a pause in the fun, somebody proposed a cocktail . . .") are ruining his looks and weakening his health. Worse, the world of vice and intrigue in which he is now embroiled encourages him to despise the innocent recreations of his earlier life. The cheery out-of-the-way pubs where once he lingered with Walter are now a source of snobbish horror to him: "That filthy place? Have you come to that?" All this reaches a symbolic height in an atmospheric account of what looks like one of the early Second Childhood parties. The invitations are written on children's notepaper topped with a line of pink woolly lambs. Guests are instructed: "Please tell your nurse to call for you at 4 a.m." As for the evening itself:

> The large studio was packed with men and women of all shapes and ages, dressed as children. Through the smoke-laden atmosphere one could distinguish the forms of immense women wearing "crawlers," old men with paddling drawers and shrimping nets, sophisticated pale-faced girls in pinafores, an occasional young man in long clothes. For the rest, there were quantities of sailor suits, flimsy white shirts and jerseys.

The company foxtrots to the strains of a Negro jazz band dressed in shorts, blue shirts and white straw hats, while making arch remarks along the lines of "My daddy's very *rich*," "My daddy's *richer*" and "But my daddy's *dead*."

Clearly, for one of Brian's sensitive disposition and manly bearing, this kind of thing is not indefinitely sustainable. Walter, disgusted by his friend's apparent complaisance, walks out of the ménage. Fortunately, Brian summons the willpower necessary to resist Lady Anne's blandishments and resumes contact with real life. Heading south of the river to the old pub, he finds Walter and starts to enjoy himself again. Waking up in the flat next morning, he realizes that it is "good to be alive . . . One oughtn't to be lying in bed like this. In a few moments one would get up and put on some flannel trousers and scamper with Walter over the clean-swept streets, into the mists of Hyde Park, and splash with a whirl of white and silver into the Serpentine."

No doubt one would. As well as being a wide-scale condemnation of the Bright Young world, *Crazy Pavements* also clings to its own private code. This is less linguistic, or cultural, than sexual: a gay romance, in fact, got up in heterosexual camouflage. Nichols, reminiscing to his biographer half a century later, admitted as much: "Of course Brian and

Walter were lovers, and Lady Julia was based on one of those predatory young queens who collect conquests like scalp-hunters collect scalps." Much the same agenda—the sense of ulterior and almost personal motive—informs Bryan Guinness's *Singing out of Tune* (1933), one of the more substantial Bright Young People novels of the period and full of fascinating sidelights both on the author's relationship with his wife and the world in which they moved. *Singing out of Tune*'s theme is entirely transparent: "smart" society life is an addictive drug, prolonged exposure to which encourages a set of false values liable to destroy the well-being of anyone ensnared by them.

All this is conveyed through a description of the courtship and eventual marriage of Arthur, a serious and conservatively minded trainee accountant, and Agnes, a flighty and rudderless young woman with a hankering for sophisticated amusement. Agnes, as Guinness swiftly makes clear, is a "new" kind of girl who studies at an LCC art school and dislikes the kind of fusty, sentimental writers such as J. M. Barrie whom Arthur admires. The couple meet in the course of a seaside holiday to which Arthur has escorted his mother. Agnes admires his risible experiments in vers libre and accompanies him to a fancy dress ball disguised as a ghost.

Abruptly the novel changes tack and transforms itself into an engagement in the generational war. A vigilant parent of the old school, Agnes's father objects on the grounds of his prospective son-in-law's lack of means and his daughter's youth. The young couple's courtship reaches crisis point at the Chelsea Arts Ball, the latter graphically described: "There was a mob of people in every variety of disguise and nakedness, seeking to pull to pieces the cardboard constructions which were to form part of the procession . . . The scene was one of desperate gaiety." Having quarreled over the attentions paid to Agnes by a fellow reveler, they determine "to build a less transitory nest."

Already, though, the differences between them are moving sharply into focus. Serious, concerned to do the right thing, Arthur is conscious of his responsibilities. In the hotel to which they elope with a fake wedding ring, caution gets the better of him. There is a further row, after which a short interval is agreed so that wedding preparations can be made. Again, fundamental distinctions in bride's and groom's attitude to life declare themselves. Agnes's attitude to her marriage is matter-of-fact. Arthur, on the other hand, is consumed by excitement, certain that his life is about to be changed out of recognition. Lying in bed on the eve of the wedding, he is unable to sleep: "A realization came upon him that tomorrow was the center, the pivot of his whole life."

Sadly, the honeymoon is a grave disappointment, fraught with evidence of the newly married couple's violently opposed cultural outlooks, symbolized in trips to examine Parisian nightlife. Back home, the world of the Bright Young People starts to impinge on their domestic arrangements. Arthur's expectations of marriage are entirely conventional: "Now that they were returned from their honeymoon, Arthur supposed that he and Agnes would live happily ever afterward." However, a friend brings to the housewarming party at their Chelsea flat a gossip writer known as "Fashionable Philip." Amused by the décor—the flat has been done up on modern lines, including a ship's porthole let into the front door—he writes them up in his column. On the strength of this endorsement, Agnes's photo appears in an illustrated newspaper beneath the headline WE SELECT FOR THE PALACE OF CELEBRITY.

All this is calculated to inflame the tensions which already exist in Arthur and Agnes's relationship. Arthur, hard at work at his accountancy training, has little time and less inclination for the smart social life opened up by Agnes's appearance in print. His wife, alternatively, is caught up in a whirl of cocktails and late-night parties. When Agnes announces that she is pregnant, the conventionally minded Arthur is overjoyed: "He was buoyed up by a new confidence in himself and went about singing." Their happiness apparently renewed, they go to stay in a borrowed cottage in the countryside. Here Arthur composes a song, the "Singing out of Tune" of the title. This is an unexpected smash, the hit of a West End stage show and featured in a film. Yet more gratified when Agnes gives birth to a son, Arthur takes an ecstatic early-morning walk in Hyde Park, finding it "full of rejoicing, of life, of hope." Once more, however, the destructive world of the Bright Young People is fast encroaching. "Fashionable Philip" writes up his success in the pages of the *Daily Sensation* and a reference to Arthur being "a chartered accountant in his spare time" gets him the sack.

Fortunately songwriting turns out to be Arthur's métier. Though he never repeats the success of "Singing out of Tune," subsequent compositions allow him a decent income. Simultaneously, however, his livelihood and happiness are compromised by Agnes's "fast" lifestyle. There are occasional idyllic interludes by the Sussex shore, but Agnes is bored by the country and declines to settle there. In the end Agnes goes off with a member of her circle of friends, the Honorable Peter Blenkinsopp—a man originally stigmatized by her as "pathetic"—leaving a trite note of farewell. Divorce follows, after which Arthur "remembered the winds of the sea, and rejoiced, if only for a moment, in his freedom."

Presented as a portrait of a failed marriage, *Singing out of Tune* is, in effect, an indictment of a way of life. Its points are made by a series of oppositions: seriousness about marriage and children versus an excuse for a party; the idyllic rural hideaway versus the exhausting metropolitan round; the domestic hearth versus late-night racketing. The implication is that the lives lived by upper-class young people, the world of the gossip column, the fancy dress party and the late-night club haunting, are fatally destructive to any proper relationship. From chapter to chapter practically every symbol of the Bright Young People's world, from fashionable hairstyles to the Chelsea Arts Ball, is taken out and denounced in a way that, from time to time, seems oddly personal. In later life Diana often told a story in which, early on in their marriage, she and Bryan wandered endlessly through the woods at Versailles, with Bryan continuing to insist that he knew the way. Eventually Diana sat down under a tree and refused to move until a taxi was fetched. A version of this episode appears in *Singing out of Tune*. In her biography of Diana, Jan Dalley assumes that the novel—begun in late 1929, when the guests at Bryan and Diana's flat included Evelyn Waugh—is "based partly on the break-up of the Waughs' marriage." Undoubtedly there are similarities between Arthur's predicament and that of the author of *Decline and Fall*. All the same, Bryan Guinness was a serious and conservative young man married to a woman who relished smart social life

and declined to live in Sussex. By mid-1932, after all, the Guinnesses'
marriage was in serious trouble. By July 1933, shortly before the novel
was published, Bryan was suing for divorce. *Singing out of Tune* is just as
likely to reflect his own resentments as those of Evelyn Waugh.

Singing out of Tune ends in a truce. There were other novels in which
Bright Young incursions into ordinary life—seen as deeply hostile and
unsettling—were stoutly repulsed. Anthony Powell's *From a View to a
Death* (1933) features a socially ambitious painter at work in hunting
country. Arthur Zouch, a bearded portraitist—the beard alone is enough
to render him suspect to conventional eyes—arrives to stay at Passenger
Court, having made the acquaintance of Mary Passenger, the family's
unmarried daughter, in London. Zouch is not an echt Bright Young Person: rather, he exemplifies the kind of humbly born, nest-feathering opportunist who seethed among the Bright Young People's lower reaches.
Nevertheless he is perfectly representative of one aspect of the kind of
social world by which Powell was fascinated: the world of seedy Continental watering holes and irregular unions.

To Zouch's alarm, Passenger Court turns out to harbor not only a
second ornament of this bohemian landscape but one who knows his
identity and can scent his ambitions. Mary's elder sister Betty, the abandoned wife of a bogus-sounding Italian duke, is herself a veteran of
semi-smart Continental café society. Recognition dawns on both sides.
"I'm sure I've seen you somewhere too," Zouch acknowledges. "Was it
in Paris? The Dome or the Ritz bar or somewhere like that?" Fortunately, Betty declines to blow his cover, some kind of accommodation is
established with the elder Passengers and the latter's annoyance at their
younger daughter's engagement is soothed by an assurance that, contrary to their expectations, Zouch is prepared to go out hunting on his
next visit. Meanwhile, Zouch has taken the opportunity of seducing a
local girl, Joanna Brandon.

Defiantly oblique and, like all Powell's novels, resolutely declining
to yield up its precise significance, *From a View to a Death* is at its
sharpest when contrasting the violently opposed modes of life represented

by Zouch and his hosts, and the degree of mutual incomprehension involved. At one point Zouch inquires of Mary what two local personalities are "like." Mary regards him "half-uncomprehendingly. She had not advanced so far as to know what people were like. Anyway, she had no language in which to describe them to Zouch." One of the funniest scenes finds Zouch, out walking in the fields with Mr. Passenger, startled by the irruption of a gang of hikers, led by a bohemian journalist named Fischbein. "Are you staying with the housekeeper or something like that?" Fischbein wonders while Mr. Passenger's gaze is directed elsewhere. "Or are you having a little game with one of the housemaids? Don't tell me you were asked there by the Passengers?" Again, somehow Zouch manages to maintain his position. However, fate has conspired against him. Coming back to the house in the autumn, and pretending that he knows how to ride a horse, his mount runs away with him and he dies in an accident. Mary marries the son of a local magnate, far more suited to her in temperament, income and mental outlook.

Novels such as *Crazy Pavements*, *Vile Bodies*, *Highland Fling*—which was originally to have been called *Our Vile Age* until preempted by Waugh—and *From a View to a Death* are at one level pieces of reportage: rough guides to a society that had only recently come into existence and whose protocols had sometimes still to be established. One of the most substantial products of the genre, alternatively, was the result of nearly a decade's incubation. Henry Yorke, still managing to combine novel writing with superintendence of the family engineering business, kept up his Bright Young Person's credentials during the 1930s, staying at Knockmaroon with the Guinnesses, holidaying at Toulon with the Connollys, Eddy Sackville-West and Nina Hamnett, acting as Evelyn Waugh's best man at his second marriage in 1937. His new idea for a book, worked on intermittently throughout this period, was a serious comedy about "bohemocracy," a novel that would, as his biographer puts it, "see the bright young things against a shadowy, obliquely-presented backdrop of the darkening socio-political situation of the 1930s." Although *Party Going* was not published until 1939, the novels to which it bears the closest resemblance are *Vile Bodies* and *Afternoon Men*. Here a group of idle young people sit in the fogbound Victoria Station Hotel while the masses seethe below them, waiting to set out on a Continental holiday. All is confusion, missed connections and fragmentary dialogue.

As Jeremy Treglown observes, *Party Going* is the first authentic novel of the Second World War, an allegory of an older world of wealth and prosperity swept aside by doubt and turmoil. Yet, in exactly the same way as his contemporaries a decade before, Green was capable of seeding his narrative with tiny hints and allusions to the social landscape of the period which only a handful of his readers would understand. One of the novel's characters, for example, is called Evelyn Henderson, which lifts Waugh's Christian name and Gavin Henderson's surname. Then there are the frequently recalled exploits of the notorious gate-crasher "Embassy Richard," named after the celebrated nightclub and an embodiment of one of the era's great cause célèbres. All this adds up. *Party Going*'s resistance to interpretation is one of its defining characteristics. But beneath its numberless layers of meaning can be detected a fair amount of amused reportage from the exotic social landscape of which its author, however inscrutably or sardonically, was an essential part.

MISS MITFORD'S TONE

Quite the oddest book Nancy Mitford ever published was her fourth novel, *Pigeon Pie*. The oddity lies in the relationship between date of publication, subject matter and authorial tone. A "phony war" caper about fifth columnists and minor deprivation, written during the winter of 1939–40 when the conflict had scarcely begun, *Pigeon Pie* appeared at precisely the moment when some of war's grimmer realities were becoming sharply apparent: immediately before the fall of France. An authorial note on the title page of a later edition confirms that "it was an early and unimportant casualty of the real war which was just beginning."

None of this, though, quite explains the extravagant flakiness of the book's tone, or Nancy's inability to describe the preparations for international conflict without resorting to that time-honored Mitford "shriek." *Pigeon Pie*'s female lead is Sophia Garfield, a wealthy "Bright Young wife" married to an aging diplomat and clearly left over from the paradisal late 1920s. A characteristic note is struck early on when Sophia confesses to her lover, Rudolph, how hard she finds it to make sense of what is happening. "I suppose it is unreal because we have been expecting it for so long now, and must be got over before we can get on with our lives," she explains. "Like in the night when you want to go to the loo and it is miles away down a freezing cold passage and yet you know you have to go down the passage before you can be happy and sleep again."

There cannot be many novels about the buildup to international conflict that compare the experience to going to the lavatory in the middle of the night. In much the same way, the wretchedness of Sophia's husband when war begins—he is a Cliveden set appeaser—is conveyed in a single sentence: "He really seemed astonished that Herr Hitler should be prepared to risk all those wonderful swimming pools in a major war." Nancy's target here, inevitably, is the light-minded idiot who won't be persuaded of war's terrifying consequences until the bombs start falling on his front lawn. All the same, her approach is horribly compromised by the flippancy—or the feigned flippancy—that lies at its core, the suspicion that Nancy, for whom everything was a tremendous tease, for whom even her sisters' relationship with Hitler was a prompt for faintly hysterical in-joking, simply does not know how to respond to an event of this magnitude. The summary of the international situation in the early autumn of 1939 is still more outlandish:

> Rather soon after the war had been declared, it became obvious that nobody intended to begin it. The belligerent countries were behaving like children in a round-game, picking up sides, and until the sides had been picked up the game could not start.
>
> England picked up France, Germany picked up Italy. England beckoned to Poland, Germany answered with Russia. Then Italy's Nanny said she had fallen down and grazed her knee, running, and mustn't play . . . America, of course, was too much of a baby for such a grown-up game, but she was just longing to see it played. And still it would not begin.
>
> The party looked like being a flop, and everybody was becoming very much bored, especially the Americans who are so fond of blood and entrails.

If the condition of being at war is like a small-hours trip to the lavatory, then its preliminary diplomatic maneuverings resemble a "round-game" or a "party." I wonder if my then eighteen-year-old father, about to volunteer for the RAF, would have found that funny. Or a member of the British Expeditionary Force? These are not quite the false distinctions they sound. Far from being a distant observer of the scene, Nancy was in it up to her neck. Her brother-in-law was leader of the British Union of Fascists; two of her sisters had recently lunched with Hitler at Bayreuth (to do Nancy justice, she did throw family loyalty aside and denounce the Mosleys to the authorities). *Pigeon Pie*, consequently, is less an exercise in detachment than straightforward evasion, an attitude to life forged in that artificial late-twenties crucible, in which the events of a decade later can only raise a kind of forced inanity.

Sophia—as did her creator—ends up staffing a first aid post. "There is a water pipe here which makes a noise exactly like those crickets on the islands at Cannes," she reports. Later, on the other hand, during the course of a training exercise, mock casualties are brought in displaying wounds "of the most lugubrious description." Battle-scarred veteran of the society pages that she was, Nancy clearly had her own.

CHAPTER THIRTEEN

GONE TO REPORT:
1940 AND AFTER

I feel ashamed to have grown up in the 1920s and to have been a young
adult in the 1930s. Thank God that generation is now extinct.

— JAMES LEES-MILNE, Diary, October 18, 1997

Quite frankly, I think the Bright Young People brought a great deal of bright-
ness to a world which was still sadly in need of it.

— BARBARA CARTLAND, *We Danced All Night* (1970)

As Arthur Ponsonby sat over his breakfast table on July 31, 1940,
looking at the morning newspapers, his chief anxiety would
have been the progress of the war. France had fallen the previous month. Only nine days previously Lord Halifax, the British foreign
secretary, had officially rejected German peace proposals. Had Arthur
but known it, the day was one of enormous symbolic importance: it was
then that Hitler and his strategists took the decision, first, to delay plans
for a seaborne invasion of the British mainland until the Luftwaffe had
taken control of the skies, and, second, to concentrate their energies on
the subjugation of Russia. Each of these schemes would have profound
consequences both for the short-term conduct of the war and its eventual outcome. For Arthur such information, even had it been available to
him, would not have offered much solace. To this lifelong pacifist the
war was a tragedy. Before its outbreak he had been a prominent supporter of the Peace Pledge Union. Now, thinking the gesture futile at a
time when Britain was seriously in danger of invasion, he confined himself to advising young men of military age who wished to register as

conscientious objectors. One of these, significantly enough, was his own son, Matthew. Even in the midst of conflagration, however, Arthur was not without hope, believing that "humanity is not destined to continue to degrade itself by fratricidal massacre and that something will arrest the descent into an abyss . . ." Little did Arthur know, but he was about to enter his own private abyss with the receipt of a telegram, signed by a West End doctor, bearing a stark twelve-word message: "Regret to have to inform you that Elizabeth died suddenly this morning."

According to his diary, Arthur had last seen his daughter early in June. The account of their meeting is affectionate: "E came to luncheon with me, full of vitality, down on the old men in power. Going on vigorously with her club business." For some time now she had been living in a furnished flat in Jermyn Street, close to the club's premises, but kept going on occasional £100 remittances from her mother. It was to this address that Arthur now hastened. What he found there he could not bring himself to write about for a year. A diary entry for July 31, 1941, recalls "the astonishingly lovely innocent face as she lay there dead." More painful even than Elizabeth's death, perhaps, was the manner of her passing. She had apparently collapsed at her place of work. According to her death certificate, the culprit was fatty degeneration of the heart and liver caused by "chronic alcoholic poisoning." Elizabeth Ponsonby, the ornament of the 1920s, the most mercurial presence of a lost and legendary age, had died of drink.

Arthur, beside himself with grief, spent a melancholy few days dealing with coroners and undertakers. A note from the manager of the Jermyn Street apartment block, acknowledging the discharge of outstanding debts, testified to Elizabeth's enduring popularity: "We all appreciated Mrs. Pelly here." In a letter to a Mrs. Maisie Thomas, presumably Elizabeth's employer, Arthur reflected, "She lived in a world of which I knew nothing." An inventory of the flat's contents offered several clues as to how Elizabeth had sustained herself during the past few years. In particular there was a large heap of pawn tickets. A teapot and cream jug (£1. 10s.), a gem butterfly brooch (£14), a brace of Purdey shotguns (where had they come from? Left over from the Denis years?) for £50—all these had gone to stanch her ever-diminishing coffers. Hugh

Wade, with whom Elizabeth had kept up until the end, was given her grand piano.

Even in the midst of war, Elizabeth's death attracted widespread coverage. Most of this had to do with her bygone public career. A short obituary paragraph in *The Times* struck a more sober note. In the press references to the death of Elizabeth Pelly, wrote "a friend," there had been several stories of her escapades in the twenties. "But some of her friends knew her more serious side which may have been a matter of surprise to strangers." There followed references to her love of Dickens, the pages of Shakespeare she could recite by heart, the "unexpected knowledge" of such subjects as wildflowers and Greek mythology, which "puzzled her more frivolous associates." But the most outstanding qualities that never failed her, the obituarist concluded, were honesty and loyalty: "She showed fearless decision and presence of mind in any emergency or accident. Undiscriminating help for the down-and-out sometimes led her into difficulties. But as one friend put it: 'It would be Elizabeth an unfortunate would be certain to find waiting for him when he came out of the prison gate.'" The *Times* clipping is pasted into one of Arthur's manuscript books under the heading "Obituary for Elizabeth." There is every indication that Arthur wrote it himself.

For all the obscurity of her circumstances and the precariousness of her livelihood, Elizabeth had kept up with some of her old Bright Young connections. A letter of late 1939 from Evelyn Waugh to Lady Diana Cooper notes her involvement in "Federal Union," a proto-European ginger group fronted by Robert Byron and the Earl of Rosse ("all the old figures of my adolescence in the '20s—Elizabeth Ponsonby, Harold Acton, Brenda Dean Paul etc—they have meetings together and publish a very serious paper under the editorship of John Sutro"). It is not known whether Elizabeth was a subscriber to *Horizon*, the highbrow monthly founded by Cyril Connolly shortly after the war's outbreak. But there is at least a fair chance that she would have read, in the May 1940 number, published a few weeks before her death, an epitaph for the whole era of which she had been a part.

"Gone to Report" is one of Brian Howard's most effective poems—not surprisingly, perhaps, for it dealt with a subject for which he had the most deep-rooted feelings. Its protagonist is a mysterious "he" who for twenty-one years has remained "faithful and lounging" under "the last tree of the charming evening street." His flask was "always full for the unhappy." During this twenty-one years he "remained exactly twenty-one years old." Many people trusted him who trusted no one. Many extremely clever people "will kill themselves unless they find him." Crowds across Europe "are beginning to find they've been left in the lurch." And who is this enigmatic and absconding presence? A final stanza solves the riddle:

> He's abandoned his post because he was the greatest of all
>   informers,
> And now he's gone to report. He never had a moment's leisure
> He was paid by so many powers that one shakes with shame
> To think of them. Time, the Army and Navy, Pain and Blame
> The Police, the family, and Death. No one will escape. He got
>   every name,
> And he wasn't at all what he said he was. Mr. Pleasure.

By the time "Mr. Pleasure" made his appearance in the pages of *Horizon*, many of the Bright Young People had themselves "gone to report." That summer, with France now under enemy occupation and the Battle of Britain about to begin, George Orwell was at work on his famous essay "The Lion and the Unicorn." Though critical of the upper classes and looking forward to a social and political revolution ("It is goodbye to the *Tatler* and the *Bystander*, and farewell to the lady in the Rolls Royce car"), Orwell was also keen to give them their moral due. "One thing that has always shown that the English ruling class are *morally* fairly sound, is that in time of war they are ready enough to get themselves killed. Several dukes, earls and what-not were killed in the recent campaign in Flanders. That could not happen if these people were the cynical scoundrels that they are sometimes declared to be."

By and large the Bright Young People were determined to prove him right. Evelyn Waugh served in a commando unit (why couldn't someone on the left do that? Orwell demanded of Anthony Powell, who had told him the news). Powell himself spent six arduous years in the Welch Regiment and as a military liaison officer. Mark Ogilvie-Grant endured long-term sequestration in a German POW camp. Hamish Erskine was awarded the Military Cross after a daredevil exploit in which he was severely wounded and had to be dragged to safety by an NCO, treating the episode with characteristic sangfroid. ("He denied that he was courageous," James Lees-Milne reported, after a boozy evening in Erskine's company in 1944. "There was no alternative to what he had to do.") Howard and Acton served, in various capacities, in the RAF. Inevitably, there were casualties. Robert Byron died in February 1941 when the ship taking him to Cairo to begin intelligence duties in the Middle East was torpedoed off the north of Scotland. Tom Mitford died in Burma shortly before the war's end.

The wearing of a uniform did not, of course, preclude a fondness for old haunts and leisure activities. James Lees-Milne recalled bumping into Sandy Baird in June 1944 in a somewhat louche establishment called the Music Box, together with a sailor who, while Baird was ordering drinks at the bar, asked for Lees-Milne's name and address while murmuring, "I don't want money; only friendship." All the same, it is not entirely fanciful to see the wartime exploits of this group of by now middle-aged men as the symbolic expiation of a great deal of guilt for bygone pleasures. When, in Waugh's *Put Out More Flags* (1942), Alastair Digby-Vane-Trumpington opts to enlist as a private soldier rather than taking a commission, his wife compares him to T. E. Lawrence. "I believe he thought that perhaps if we hadn't had so much fun there wouldn't have been any war," she rationalizes. Although former Bright Young People were kept apart by wartime restrictions on travel, overseas postings and demanding jobs on the home front, something of their original group mentality was narrowly preserved. In December 1940, for example, Connolly could be found writing to Driberg from the *Horizon* office, declining a poem on the grounds of its Eliot-era obscurity, but "enclosing a copy of our Christmas number and asking if you *can* find a paragraph to give it. It's terribly important that we have a miracle of feeding five thousand with this number."

Other survivors, meanwhile, looked back, already conscious of the trappings of legend that seemed to have enveloped them, carefully preserving friendships in which a sense of a luminous collective past would always cancel out present discomforts. Staying with Stephen Tennant at Wilsford during the Blitz, Cecil Beaton noted that "each time I visit him I feel it is as though I am privileged to know Firbank and Beardsley. For nearly twenty years I have known him—& still one feels like the rebellious bright young things we were." Not all the Bright Young People were quite so reverential of these ancient ties. Shortly before the war's end Brian Howard and his boyfriend Sam dined at the House of Commons. There was plenty of port on offer, as Brian reported to Driberg: "I sailed away . . . in a cloud of calm, wise beneficence. Sam, on the other hand, leered at Cecil Beaton in the tube on the way home, causing him to swoon." Even here, amid the rows of bomb-damaged houses, ration cards and an uncertain future, something of the Bright Young People's animating spirit precariously survived.

It continued to survive for the next half century. Even at the close of the Second World War, the era of Attlee, nationalization and the National Health Service, most of the movement's founding fathers were barely into their forties. Several of them lived for another forty or fifty years. At least one is living still. Collectively they exhibited all the characteristics of a group of talented, well-connected people moving on into middle and old age. Some became famous. Others became notorious. Still more faded into a modest obscurity, revered by their friends as dazzling survivors from a much mythologized world, but one altogether forgotten by the public at large.

There is an odd, elegiac moment in Waugh's *Put Out More Flags* (1942) in which Sonia and Alastair Digby-Vane-Trumpington reflect on the passage of their lives from flamboyant youth to sober middle age:

Ten years on, without any effort or desire on their part, merely by pleasing themselves in their own way, they had lived in the full blaze of fashionable notoriety; today, without regret, without in fact being aware of the change, they formed a forgotten corner, where the wreckage of the roaring twenties, long tossed on the high seas, lay beached, dry and battered, barely worth the attention of the most assiduous beachcomber. Sonia would sometimes remark how odd it was that the papers nowadays never seemed to mention anyone one had heard of; they had been such a bore once, never leaving one alone.

Evelyn Waugh continued to extend his reputation as one of the most successful English novelists of the twentieth century. The exotic contemporaries of his youth remained a source of fascination to him. As he explained to his friend Lord Baldwin in 1958: "There is an aesthetic bugger who sometimes turns up in my novels under various names—that was ⅘ Brian ⅕ Harold Acton. People think it was all Harold, who is a much sweeter & saner man." In *Put Out More Flags*, this amalgam masquerades as Ambrose Silk, editor of a magazine called *Ivory Tower*, whose boyfriend Hans—in a clear reference to Brian's companion Toni—"lay in the horrors of a Nazi concentration camp," and of whose previous life Waugh writes: "Ambrose had always rather specialized in manifestos. He had written one at school; he had written a dozen at the university; once, in the late Twenties, he and his friends Hat and Malpractice had even issued the invitation to a party in the form of a manifesto." It was one of Ambrose's many reasons for shunning communism, Waugh jokes, "that its manifesto had been written for it, once and for all, by somebody else."

But Ambrose is a ghost from another world, a faded aesthete wandering the corridors of a more politically committed world, seeing his pioneering idiosyncrasies of manner held up to mockery: "A habit of dress, an elegant, humorous deportment that had been admired, a swift, epicene felicity of wit. The art of dazzling and discomforting those he despised" is Waugh's summary of deutero-Howard's style. "These had been his, and now they were the current exchanges of comedians." Slinking into one of the few restaurants which he can frequent without fear of ridicule, Ambrose finds himself "surrounded, as though by distorting mirrors, with gross reflections and caricatures of himself."

Anthony Blanche in *Brideshead Revisited*, too, is a mixture of Brian's vocal style and Acton-esque flamboyance, reciting from *The Waste Land*, by megaphone, from a window in Christ Church to the sweatered throng leaving for the river. As late as 1950 a letter sped forth from Piers Court, Stinchcombe, to assure Nancy Mitford that the Wandering Jew in *Helena* was "B. Howard again." Prematurely aged and disillusioned by the modernization of the Catholic Church, Waugh died on Easter Day 1966, shortly after beginning a correspondence with his old friend Diana Mosley, not seen since the early 1930s. "There is nowhere I want to go and nothing I want to do and I am conscious of being an utter bore. The Vatican Council has knocked the guts out of me," he explained.

Anthony Powell spent nearly a quarter of a century writing an immense novel sequence, *A Dance to the Music of Time* (twelve volumes, 1951–75), describing upper-class English life—but with extended bohemian forays—in the period 1920–70. In Somersetshire-bound old age, the opinions of his contemporaries expressed in his four volumes of memoirs grew less guarded. "I quite liked old Harold [Acton]," he told an interviewer shortly before his eighty-ninth birthday. "Howard I never liked." He died in 2000.

Henry Green served in the Auxiliary Fire Service during the war. After publishing *Doting*, his ninth novel, in 1952 he sank into torpor. "Bright Young Henry Yorke I hear is quite decrepit," Evelyn Waugh informed Diana Mosley in March 1966. Green died in 1973.

Bryan Guinness succeeded his father Lord Moyne, remarried and had many children, so many that the younger son of his first marriage remarked, "I wish Bryan would not go on having more children, for the money won't go round at this rate." He died in 1992, having written an elegant memoir, *Potpourri of the 1930s*, disclaiming all affiliations with the Bright Young People.

Harold Acton inherited his father's Italian property, La Pietra, which became one of the great tourist attractions for English visitors to

Florence. Among a range of books, he published *Memoirs of an Aesthete* (1948) and a sequel, *More Memoirs of an Aesthete* (1970). Powell and his wife were dining at La Pietra when Acton's boyfriend Alexander left the room, prompting Acton to confide, "He's not nearly so young as he looks." This, Powell thought, was "a characteristic" remark.

Brian Howard began the war working for MI5. There was a symbolic moment in 1940 when, sequestered in a Soho nightclub with his colleague Guy Burgess, loud hammerings on the door advertised a police raid. Asked for his name and address, Howard produced the legendary reply: "I live in Mayfair. No doubt you come from some dreary suburb." Discharged from the secret services, apparently for an inability to keep his mouth shut, he volunteered—quixotically for a man of thirty-seven in poor health—for the RAF, eventually coming to rest as clerk in the public relations department of Bomber Command.

The war supplied characteristic glimpses of Howard, as it were, in action: weaving alcoholically toward a group of army officers in the Gargoyle Club just after Dunkirk with a murmur of "Hmm. Members of a rather unsuccessful profession, my dears," bringing in the elevenses at Bomber Command with a cry of "Delicious Teazle!" and getting his mother to intercede with the squadron leader over a uniform left behind in a pub toilet. Thereafter the path ran steadily downhill: postwar wanderings in Europe with Toni's successor, Sam; TB cures; an addiction to, among other narcotics, synthetic morphine. There were still flashes— occasionally quite substantial flashes—of the old Brian. The Curzon Street bookseller Heywood Hill reported a flying visit from Paris in September 1955: "He arrived at 11 and stayed till 3. He had taken a room at the Ritz but begged us to let him sleep in the armchair and was incensed when we would not ... The next day he borrowed £50 from the shop and the next day he wanted 30 more, so I gave it him myself and he gave me checks on Swiss banks and today there's a telegram from Mrs. H saying stop cheques." On his last night, arriving late at the airport, he amused himself by mimicking the refined voices of the air hostesses, "and the whole terminal was in tumult with loudspeakers shrieking for him." Peace, quiet and a settled life might have saved him, but the domestic stability promised by Lura Howard's purchase of a house near

Nice was quickly extinguished by Sam's accidental death in early 1958. Brian killed himself with an overdose—thought by John Banting, who was present, to be accidental—four days later. He was fifty-two. The obituarists waxed surprisingly lyrical: "It was part of Brian's tragedy that he should have been so like Baudelaire" (Connolly); "a kind of ferocity of elegance that belonged to the romantic era of a century before our own" (Waugh); "a dangerous, brilliant and seminal nuisance" (V. S. Pritchett).

Tom Driberg was expelled from the Communist Party in 1941, apparently for opposing the Russo-German pact. Late in the following year, after a by-election, he entered Parliament as Independent MP for Malden in Essex, supporting Churchill but criticizing the conduct of the war and alleging that the prime minister was badly served by those around him. After joining the Labour Party shortly before the 1945 general election, he retained the Malden seat for a further ten years, before resigning in 1955. There was a curious and unsuccessful marriage to a Mrs. Ena Binfield. When the bride booked a double bedroom for their wedding night, the groom is alleged to have complained: "She broke her wedding vow. She tried to sleep with me." Evelyn Waugh wrote to assure his old school friend that he would be praying that the church was not struck by lightning.

Despite the loss of his seat, Driberg's political career continued to prosper. He became chairman of the Labour Party in 1957 and in this capacity conducted its annual conference at Scarborough. Among other exploits, he was observed by journalists in a cheap café with a couple of rough young men he had clearly picked up during a break in the conference proceedings. In the previous year he had flown to Moscow on behalf of the *Daily Mail* to conduct a sensational interview with Guy Burgess. In 1959 he returned to the House of Commons, winning the safe East End seat of Barking, which he disliked and visited as little as possible. There were frequent money worries. In the 1960s, a decade in which he appeared to feel very much at home, he became friendly with Mick Jagger, whom he encouraged, unsuccessfully, to stand for Parliament, and regularly attended the bimonthly lunches given by *Private Eye*. Here he would have himself announced as "Mr. Richmond," a disguise assumed in the mistaken belief that he was being monitored by agents of the prime minister, Harold Wilson, and correct the magazine's editor, Richard Ingrams, on abstruse points of syntactical, ecclesiastical and social protocol: "My dear Richard, I am astonished that you don't appear to know the correct way to refer to the younger daughter of a Marquess." Ingrams appointed him founder-compiler of the *Eye*'s fortnightly crossword. He retired from Parliament for a second time and, having been ennobled as Lord Bradwell, died in August 1976, leaving a posthumous memoir, *Ruling Passions*, which described his sexual adventures in clinical detail.

Whatever may have been the exact extent of Inez Holden's dealings with the Communist Party, she later spoke of its methods with distaste. She became a great friend of George Orwell, whose first meeting with Anthony Powell she engineered in 1941. A dinner party involving Orwell and H. G. Wells, in whose shed she once lived, was less successful. Wells afterward sent Orwell a note urging him to "read my early works, you shit." Inez Holden died in 1974.

Like Henry Green, Lord Faringdon, formerly the Honorable Gavin Henderson, spent the war in the Auxiliary Fire Service, while exerting himself politically as treasurer of the National Council for Civil Liberties and as a member of the executive committee of the Fabian Society. Labour's first postwar chancellor, Hugh Dalton, described him as "a pansy pacifist of whose private tendencies it might be slander to speak." Flamboyant of manner, Faringdon once addressed the House of Lords as "my dears" rather than "my lords" and, arriving at Malden to campaign for his friend Driberg in the middle of a downpour, complained to the assembled crowd: "The rain. My dears, it *poured*." Subsequently he chaired the Fabian Colonial Bureau, served as a London County councillor and devoted considerable resources to restoring his eighteenth-century mansion, Buscot Park, making provision for the house and its contents to pass to the National Trust after his death. He died in 1977.

Brenda Dean Paul became a familiar sight in the King's Road, "tottering with her friend Miss Baird to refill her hypodermic syringe," as one onlooker put it. Sitting once in a restaurant, she was observed to top up a syringe containing heroin with water from a nearby vase of flowers. Younger acquaintances professed themselves "scared" by the narcotic and faintly sinister atmosphere she carried around with her. She made another court appearance in 1951, charged with possession of 100 milligrams of pethidine, and was remanded on £100 bail. Still convinced of her star quality, she appeared in a production of Firbank's *The Princess Zoubaroff* at the Irving Theatre Club. She was found dead in her Kensington High Street flat in July 1959, of "coronary occlusion due to atheroma," although an overdose was widely suspected. Miss Baird told reporters, "She really was one of the sweetest people you could ever have known."

Cecil Beaton became an immensely successful portrait photographer and theatrical designer. In these roles he conducted a celebrated sitting with Queen Elizabeth, the wife of George VI, and designed the sets for the film *My Fair Lady*, starring Audrey Hepburn. He remained nervous of his prep-school contemporary Evelyn Waugh, who remarked of a selection of his diaries published in 1961, "Neither in verbal expression nor in literary construction does he show any but the feeblest talent." Beaton died in 1980.

Nancy Mitford retreated to France, where she pursued a long and ultimately fruitless association with Gaston Palewski, de Gaulle's wartime *chef du cabinet*. She wrote several best-selling novels, including *The Pursuit of Love* (1945) and *Love in a Cold Climate* (1949), before turning to equally successful historical biographies. She was divorced from Peter Rodd in 1958. Though continuing to disapprove of "pederasty," she preferred English homosexuals to their French equivalents, remarking to a friend in 1947 that "the pansies here [Paris] are all so pompous in comparison with our darling English ones. Brian came here with a terrible creature called Sam, I thought I would hurt myself with laughing." Nancy died in 1973.

Her sister Diana Mosley spent the greater part of the war interned with her husband in Holloway Prison. On their release the Mosleys initially farmed land in Hampshire before moving to France. Sir Oswald made periodic attempts to reignite his political career, standing at North Kensington in the general election of 1959 and again in 1966, on both occasions with a conspicuous lack of success. Lady Mosley died in 2003, having outlived her husband by nearly a quarter of a century. The adjective generally applied to her memoirs, *A Life of Contrasts* (1977), and subsequent comments on such topics as Hitler, Goebbels and the Jews, was "unrepentant."

Beverley Nichols continued to write prolifically in a variety of forms. The bibliography of his writings lists more than sixty full-length items, including detective novels, books for children, political polemic and descriptions of his garden. Toward the end of his career he grew despondent, claiming that he had missed his vocation as a serious composer, that sex meant nothing to him and that he had, in effect, wasted his life. Shortly before his death in 1983 he complained, "Osbert Sitwell called me the first of the bright young people and I am the last of them."

This was not quite true. After occasional visits to America, Stephen Tennant retired to Wilsford. Here he lived in extreme seclusion, shunning company and writing innumerable drafts of an unpublished novel, *Lascar*. V. S. Naipaul, who lodged for a while on the Wilsford estate, offers fascinated glimpses of the Tennant legend in *The Enigma of Arrival* (1987). An antidote to the Tennant mystique was provided by Lady Caroline Blackwood, who believed that he was "an eccentric gay who didn't really do anything." Tennant died in 1987.

Other Bright Young People survived longer even than this. Having made short-lived and unsuccessful marriages, Zita and Baby Jungman spent over half a century living together. Evelyn Waugh, who visited them in their cottage in 1953, reported to Nancy Mitford, "Their condition of destitution & privation, though serious, has been greatly exaggerated." After inhabiting a flat at a converted country house in Northamptonshire, they moved to Ireland to occupy an annex to the Guinness estate at Leixlip. James Lees-Milne, attending a funeral at Carterton in 1995, came upon them outside the church, seated in their "tiny white car," Zita at the wheel. "They are like two very old dolls, turning their heads this way and that in swift movements and saying 'Yes' and 'No' in unison . . . They laughed as they drove off perilously." Zita died in 2006.

After the years spent editing *Horizon*, Cyril Connolly moved on to become chief literary critic for the *Sunday Times*. Following *The Un-*

quiet Grave, which appeared in 1944, his postwar oeuvre included *Ideas and Places*, a selection of *Horizon* editorials, and *The Modern Movement: One Hundred Key Books from England, France and America, 1880–1950* (1966). Three times married, he died in 1974.

Eddie Gathorne-Hardy left the firm of Elkin Matthews on its collapse and reorganization in 1935. Subsequently he undertook botanical expeditions in the Middle East and moved to Athens, where he worked for the British Council. Later he was employed in the intelligence sections of the British embassies in Cairo and Beirut. The party given for him by Brian Howard in 1957 to mark his retirement from the Foreign Office brought together several old Bright Young connections, including Patrick Balfour, now Lord Kinross, Sacheverell Sitwell and his wife, Georgia, and Tom Driberg. Eddie's last years, divided between his flat in Athens and the family's Suffolk estate, were a decline. Even close friends were inclined to think his continued association with Lura Howard self-interested. Meeting him on holiday in France in the early 1960s, Frances Partridge noted, "He hopes to touch Mrs. Howard, mother of Brian, for a large sum before going to Greece, in spite of busting her car to the tune of £180 last time he visited her." Back in Athens in 1967 he voted the military coup, with its strictly enforced curfews, a great bore: "I had to be in by 7 two nights running." Staying with his sister Anne and her husband in the early seventies, Frances Partridge listened to him planning a solitary lunch at the Savoy: "I think I'll have a *woodcock*, my dear, but it must be hung and cooked exactly right, and then, my dear, perhaps some *raspberries*, if one can still get them." Asked by his brother Anthony—like Eddie, in no great physical shape—to get him a drink while pouring one himself, he replied: "No, I *won't*, my dear, I'm bloody well not going to, my dear. I'm older than you, my dear, and much iller and you must do it yourself, my dear." Nevertheless, he faced a series of unpleasant illnesses, including diabetes and syphilis, with fortitude, at one stage begging his friend Angela Culme-Seymour: "Will you *promise* you won't *pray* for me, my dear?" He died in 1978.

· · ·

Eighty years on from their late-1920s heyday, what can be said about the Bright Young People? Like many a youth movement they began unobtrusively, found themselves seized upon by a grateful media and were rapidly converted into a stylized and decadent version of their original form. Their great days were over by 1929: thereafter the stunts tended to be stage-managed, the entertainments pallid imitations of what had gone before, the territory colonized by younger acolytes. Again, like many another youth movement, the Bright Young People carried with them the cause of their future destruction. Starting out in search of an environment where a few like-minded friends could enjoy each other's company, they—or their descendants—ended up in the pursuit of spectacle for its own sake. Degeneration was inevitable, as were the casualties that followed in its wake. For some people, mostly ambitious young men from middle-class backgrounds, this milieu offered a springboard for international success. Evelyn Waugh and Cecil Beaton, for example, found that the Bright Young People's world that they had (briefly) inhabited offered them both a subject and a range of connections from which they could forge durable careers. Once these careers had begun, they had no need of the social backdrop that encouraged them and could move on to more exalted stages.

For others, alternatively, the status of Bright Young Person became a burden they could never put down, a permanent reminder of an outlook on life that would have been better forgotten. Writing a *Times* obituary of his old friend Hamish Erskine in 1973, Alan Pryce-Jones noted, "Hamish, in his day, was a Bright Young Person and his life for the last thirty years exemplified the difficulty of taking on from there." All Hamish possessed, in fact, was his charm and the memory of a world in which charm had perhaps counted for too much. This legacy could work even against Bright Young People who succeeded in their later lives. To spend very much time in the literary company of Nancy Mitford is to encounter a sensibility preserved in the amber of 1928, which has observed the world passing, the horrors of war and their personal consequences—a sister and a brother dead, another sister interned—but whose response is still largely a matter of shrieks and teases.

There were plenty of other sensibilities stunted by the memory of their antic youth. The terrible fascination of a life like Brian Howard's lies in what *didn't* get written, the creative stasis that overwhelmed each new idea and good intention, and the bitter determinism that ran beneath it. For all the surface deceptions ("Fortunately I am the kind of writer who will make money"), Howard knew very well the kind of life he was leading, where he would end up, what would come of it all. There is, consequently, something altogether dreadful about the oscillations of his letters to his mother, the flights of self-delusion ("When my book is finished and I begin to make a little . . . *Success will come* . . . I shall marry someday") forever brought to ground by an awareness of what really lies ahead ("I'm nearly thirty and you've done just about all anyone could . . . I love you so much and I am such a frightful disappointment to you . . . Love has left me, and the capacity truthfully to imagine—vision—is leaving. I consider myself damned"). In strict literary terms Howard is an example of a rather typical twentieth-century phenomenon, the aesthete whose career is fatally compromised by a reluctance to discard the past: the gaudy and debilitating lumber of parties in swimming baths, peacock conversation, a kind of spiritual gavotte through an endless succession of mirrored rooms. All this, though, is to ignore the human cost of a life lived out of suitcases, where each morning's post brings either a bill or a letter from one's mother, and from beneath the canopy of the writing desk undeflowered sheets of paper stare up in permanent reproach.

Of all those affected in one way or another by the Bright Young People phenomenon, it was Arthur Ponsonby who felt the sharpest hurt. Come the war and the death of his daughter, diary-writing had become impossible for him. On the day before his seventieth birthday, in February 1941, he noted: "An opportunity for reflection and beginning Diary again. I shall do neither." The indefatigable chronicler of his time had fallen silent. On the rare occasions that he picked up the pen, his mind dwelled on a single topic. "Hardly a day passes without my thoughts turning back to E and resulting in self condemnation and desperate sadness."

These feelings became yet more acute on the anniversary of Elizabeth's death: July 31, 1941, brought an immense meditation on the consequences of that summons to Jermyn Street. He had thought, Arthur wrote, that time would help "and that my mind would be less inclined to be so constantly attacked by memories, revivals of lost opportunities and poignant bouts of self condemnation." This had proved to be an illusion: "But the emotional has been stronger than the rational." Above all, Arthur blamed himself for the tragedy of his daughter's life. Why, he wondered, blaming his attitude over the years, did he not "help constructively, guide affectionately, lead convincingly and find the right appeal in real love"? A student of Elizabeth's goings-on might answer that she could not be helped, guided or led. Arthur, on the other hand, was enmired in guilt, accusing himself of "growing neglect," which, over the years, had led to "fatalistic apathy." It was not enough, he thought, "to say I was put off by modern youthful life, that I felt embarrassed in any endeavor to enter into it or that I felt no sympathy or welcome for my interference . . ." Looking back on his fretful relationship with Elizabeth, he believed that "we were very good friends in early days." Like her father in many ways, she differed from him fundamentally—and fatally—in others. "She had joie de vivre and gaiety a sense of humor and wit . . ." And yet she possessed "no social gift except with dissolute friends," shunned anything serious "and was immediately bored if any attempt in that direction was made." Arthur realized that his own gravity was embarrassed by this "rather hysterical craving for fun."

But there were positives. He admired his daughter's "immense courage and presence of mind, conspicuous honesty in all that mattered and unfailing loyalty." Again he reproved himself for assuming that these attitudes would rise to the top: "I ought to have got alongside her, made a habit of seeing her constantly in spite of rebuffs which I am sure now might have been overcome." In the downward spiral of Elizabeth's last years, Arthur had found himself powerless to intervene. "Responsible good friends gradually shunned her," which made her defiant and "plunged her into taking up with and helping the disreputable . . . She took on the coloring of those she associated with which gradually became the dregs." It had been a mistake to allow her to marry Denis, Arthur acknowledged, "but at the time there seemed to be worse dilemmas if she didn't." Denis having been disposed of, she had "the love of her life"—presumably a reference to Ludy Ford. "He made it quite clear to us that it could never come to anything but he very wrongly never broke with her completely, so she went on hoping against hope till finally convinced there was no hope she tumbled headlong into the mud and died of it."

Again, Arthur thought he knew whom to blame. "I, like so many men, pompously thought my 'work'—politics and writing—important (pathetic to think of now in retrospect) and that a child's difficulties would adjust themselves in time without my aid, not seeing that close at hand was a problem with no ready solution but one that wanted my first, my constant and my unremitting attention." But what could he have done? It was useless to reflect that Elizabeth liked her parents and enjoyed their company. ("In later years the proper, to her generation, disregard and contempt for parents was very much mitigated and she seemed genuinely glad to come and see us.") In the closing years of his life "this must stand out among my many failures as far the worst."

There is one further reference to Elizabeth in the few random pages of which the remainder of Arthur's diary consists. On July 31, 1943, the third anniversary of her death, he noted: "I often pass her flat in London. It always brings a stab. But I am thankful she is not alive now." These were among the last words he ever wrote. In September 1943, after a short visit to Matthew and his wife, Bess, in Suffolk, he suffered an incapacitating stroke. He never recovered, dying early in 1946, as the spring flowers blossomed on the Shulbrede lawns.

APPENDIX

"DARLING EDDIE . . . LOVE B"

Throughout the early 1930s, Brian Howard was Eddie Gathorne-Hardy's most indefatigable correspondent. From European cities and English counties the postcards poured in, with their scraps of tourists' lore, their relish of sights and persons seen and their intimations of emotional disquiet. Devon, June 1930: "Last night I was deserted by a _____ *you* know—just when I shouldn't have been . . . I am happy again and have put on my heart." Salzburg, April 1931: "I intend to make FULL ENQUIRIES why I haven't been told about Salzburg. It is the *only* small town in Europe outside Spain." Munich, June 1931: "Munich is delicious—the Unger Bad, where I go every day, particularly so—also there is a sort of small Luna Park, full of the tightest, tiniest *lederhosenchen* . . . I lunch with Thomas Mann tomorrow." Toulon, November 1931: "There is a drama going on here . . . Jean C [Cocteau] in a fearful rage in the hotel alone." Vienna, September 1932: "Vienna a swizz sexually—rather sad."

Sometimes the emotional disquiet needed fuller treatment. "Darling Eddie," opens a four-page penciled letter from an Austrian skiing trip in early 1931, "Thank you so much for your darling letter—it arrived when it was very badly needed indeed. I'm afraid nothing is very much good. He has gone to Munich—in desperation I told him I thought it was monstrous of him to go, but of course nothing could have stopped him—and I am alone." "He" was a young man named Sandy, undoubtedly the Old Etonian Sandy Baird, later host of the White Party, with whom Brian had been conducting a long affair. "If I can get myself in control—all will be well" Eddie was assured. "I am going to make a determined effort."

But this was easier said than done. "My journal is the journal of a lunatic. Rage and despair alternating with crazy attacks on everything. *Several times* I have wondered if I am going dotty, really. I have a thick pile of letters to Sandy of every conceivable kind—some the best I have ever written—which he will never see. Some idiocy seizes me, and I sit up all night writing them, and then start again instantly at crack of dawn. I dream of nothing but him. It seems to me that the more one is capable of love—as the Victorians understood it—the more of a failure one is."

Was he "a sort of innately comic-tragic figure"? Brian wondered, in a peculiarly self-lacerating moment. "The sexual aspect of love I have long since been taught not to press, therefore what is it that *always* makes me repulsive, a failure? Sitting about all over Scotland, Frankfurt, London + Austria with quite genuine tears streaming down my face? With only you to turn to, to belabor with the stick of my invariable failure? I am not a bore. I do not nag with love. I am not hideous. Well, well—"

There were more lighthearted moments, when the spirit of high camp took over. An undated sheet of Gargoyle Club notepaper offers a poetic—and for all its comedy rather shrewd—encapsulation of Brian's early career:

I began it at Eton, but never was beaten
They met my misdeeds with applause
I loathed every game, but they knew, all the same
I was terribly sporting indoors
I was sacked in the spring for the usual thing
So I went up to Oxford, of course
Where they grew rather red, when I laughingly said
That my seat wasn't meant for a horse
So I took no more chances, but gave lots of dances
— And said every goodnight in my bed
Though they all think I'm funny, they're all easy
 money

After six, at the bar of the Troc
So I've no use for hearties, or debutante parties
I can get SO much tighter in tights
I can, shave as I sin, I'm the scourge of Berlin
I'm the boy that was blackballed for White's.

NOTES AND FURTHER READING

UNPUBLISHED SOURCES

The primary source for this book has been the mass of papers accumulated by the Ponsonby family (hereinafter Ponsonby). These include the extensive diaries kept by Arthur and Dorothea, letters sent to them by Elizabeth and the documents and other artifacts discovered in Elizabeth's flat after her death. I have also consulted the papers relating to Eddie Gathorne-Hardy (Gathorne-Hardy) in the possession of his family, in particular the collection of reminiscences assembled by his sister, the late Lady Anne Hill, in the late 1970s under the title "Eddiana." The Driberg papers (Driberg), housed at Christ Church, Oxford, contain many unpublished letters from friends such as Brian Howard, Mark Ogilvie-Grant and Cyril Connolly. I have also made use of a run of (mostly) unpublished letters exchanged between Anthony Powell and Henry Yorke (Henry Green) during the period 1926–29 (Powell/Green).

PROLOGUE. DIONYSIUS IN MAYFAIR

On the Bath and Bottle Party, see the *Daily Express*, July 14, 1928, quoted in Marie-Jaqueline Lancaster, *Brian Howard: Portrait of a Failure* (1968), pp. 264–66, Patrick Balfour, *Society Racket: A Critical Survey of Modern Social Life* (1933), p. 171, and Brenda Dean Paul, *My First Life* (1935), pp. 108–109. "Johanna's" remarks appeared in *The Lady*, July 19, 1928.

For Evelyn Waugh's letter of July 1929 to Henry Yorke, see Mark Amory (ed.), *The Letters of Evelyn Waugh* (1980), pp. 36–37. Alan Jenkins discusses the all-purpose nature of the phrase "Bright Young People" in *The Twenties* (1974), p. 29.

For obituaries of Zita James (Zita Jungman) see *Daily Telegraph*, February 23, 2006, and Philip Hoare, *Independent*, March 4, 2006. On the country weekend at Wilsford in 1927, see Hoare, *Serious Pleasures: The Life of Stephen Tennant* (1990), pp. 92–94.

George Orwell's review of *The Rock Pool* originally appeared in the *New English Weekly*, July 23, 1936, and is reprinted in Peter Davison (ed.), *The Complete Works of George Orwell, X: A Kind of Compulsion, 1903–1936*, pp. 490–91. For John Carey's review of Martin Green's *Children of the Sun* (1976), see his *Original Copy* (1987), pp. 39–44. Julian Symons's remarks about Howard are quoted by Green in *Children of the Sun: A Narrative of "Decadence" in England After 1918*, p. 342. "Bookworm's" *Private Eye* review of *Serious Pleasures* appeared in the issue of June 22, 1990.

"The Youngest Generation," Waugh's editorial in the *Lancing College Magazine*, December 1921, is reprinted in Donat Gallagher (ed.), *The Essays, Articles and Reviews of Evelyn Waugh* (Harmondsworth, 1986), p. 11. The entry in Brian Howard's 1939 diary is reproduced from Lancaster, *Portrait*, p. 401. The "At least I'm a has-been" remark is quoted in Michael Luke, *David Tennant and the Gargoyle Years* (1991), pp. 172–73. For Evelyn Waugh on the idea of "High Bohemia," see his *Spectator* review of Cecil Beaton, *The Wandering Years*, July 21, 1961, which is reprinted in Gallagher (ed.), *Essays, Articles and Reviews*.

I. FIGURES IN A LANDSCAPE

On the *Daily Mail*'s coverage of the "New Society Game," see Balfour, *Society Racket*, pp. 164–65. Lord Northcliffe's remarks are quoted in Robert Graves and Alan Hodge, *The Long Week-end: A Social History of Great Britain 1918–1939* (1940), p. 60.

For the Bright Young People's early days, see Balfour, *Society Racket*, pp. 164–66, Loelia, Duchess of Westminster, *Grace and Favour* (1961), pp. 119–22, 164, Lancaster, *Portrait*, pp. 135–37. John Rothenstein remembered his first meeting with Elizabeth Ponsonby in *Summer's Lease: An Autobiography 1901–1938* (1965), pp. 82–83. Dorothea Ponsonby's account of her daughter's involvement with the "younger set" is taken from a diary entry of December 29, 1923 (Ponsonby).

On the "lost generation," see Alec Waugh, "The University of Mainz: Hugh Kingsmill, Gerard Hopkins, Milton Hayes, J. F. Holms," in *My Brother Evelyn and Other Profiles* (1967), p. 73, and *His Second War* (1944), pp. 171–72. For Evelyn Waugh's letter to Henry Yorke about Diana Guinness, see Amory (ed.), *Letters*, p. 40.

On the Bright Young People as a social entity, see Beverley Nichols, *All I Could Never Be* (1949), pp. 40–41, and Douglas Goldring, *The Nineteen-Twenties* (1945), pp. 225–27. For Loelia Ponsonby on the end of the first phase of Bright Young People activity, *Grace and Favour*, p. 122. The *Daily Express* description of Stephen Tennant (September 14, 1928) is quoted in Hoare, *Serious Pleasures*, p. 100. The quotations from Bryan Guinness are taken from *Potpourri from the Thirties* (Burford, 1982), p. 18. "Johanna's" account of Zita Jungman's wedding appeared in *The Lady*, January 24, 1929. For Diana Mosley on the Bright Young People, see Michael Luke, *Gargoyle Years*, p. 50. Her remarks about the fallibility of press reports are taken from Jan Dalley, *Diana Mosley: A Life* (1999), p. 56. On Bright Young People "opportunism," see Nichols, *All I Could Never Be*, p. 40.

Daphne Fielding's list of leading Bright Young People is reproduced from her *The Duchess of Jermyn Street: The Life and Good Times of Rosa Lewis of the Cavendish Hotel* (1964), p. 106. Brian Howard's letter to his mother about Nancy Cunard, Iris Tree and Diana Cooper is quoted in Lancaster, *Portrait*, p. 284. For Osbert Lancaster's account of Harry Melville, see *With an Eye to the Future* (1967), pp. 88–89. The description of Beverley Nichols is taken from Ethel Mannin, *Confessions and Impressions* (1930), p. 238.

On middle-aged interlopers, see *Punch*, December 14, 1927. Henry Yorke's comment is taken from Jeremy Treglown, *Romancing: The Life and Work of Henry Green* (2000), p. 95. Evelyn Waugh's remarks come from an *Evening Standard* article of January 22, 1929 ("Too Young at Forty: Youth Calls to the Peter Pans of Middle Age Who Block the Way"), reproduced in Gallagher (ed.), *Essays, Articles and Reviews*, pp. 45–47.

On the Bright Young People's connection with early-1920s Oxford, see Humphrey Carpenter, *The Brideshead Generation: Evelyn Waugh and His Friends* (1989). This reproduces the *Isis* account of the Hypocrites Club (p. 78), John Fothergill's memory of the "wake" (p. 116) and the itinerary of the November 1923 Oxford University Railway Club excursion (pp. 121–22).

For Brenda Dean Paul's entrance into "Society," see *My First Life*, pp. 51–53. Nancy Mitford remembered dancing with Lytton Strachey at the Sailor Party in a letter to Heywood Hill, see John Saumarez Smith (ed.), *The Bookshop at 10 Curzon Street: Letters Between Nancy Mitford and Heywood Hill* (2004), p. 148. On Mary Butts, see Nathalie Blondel, *Mary Butts: Scenes from the Life* (New York, 1998). Douglas Goldring's account of the party held at her flat in 1923 is in his *Odd Man Out: The Autobiography of a "Propaganda Novelist"* (1935), pp. 282–83. Boothby is quoted in Robert Rhodes James, *Bob Boothby: A Portrait* (1991), p. 72.

The account of the Lygon sisters' small-hours arrival at 10 Downing Street, after being locked out of their own house, is taken from Jane Mulvagh's obituary of Lady Sibell Rowley, née Lygon, *Independent*, November 10, 2005. On the Prince of Wales in the 1920s, see Jenkins, *The Twenties*, pp. 44–50. Cyril Connolly's account of seeing the prince at a party in 1928 can be found in David Pryce-Jones (ed.), *Cyril Connolly: Journal and Memoir* (1983), pp. 130–31.

Evelyn Waugh's attack on Charles Graves is quoted in Gallagher (ed.), *Essays, Articles and Reviews*, p. 39. For Brian Howard's letter to his mother about the White Party, see Lancaster, *Portrait*, pp. 283–84. For Eddie Gathorne-Hardy's engagement diary for 1927, see Gathorne-Hardy.

2. THE SOCIETY RACKET

Evelyn Waugh's comment on Patrick Balfour's understanding of "smart" social life is taken from Artemis Cooper (ed.), *Mr Wu & Mrs Stitch: The Letters of Evelyn Waugh & Diana Cooper* (1991), p. 35. For Balfour on the "period of change" see *Society Racket*, pp. 59–60. Brenda Dean Paul discusses social change in the 1920s in *My First Life*, pp. 96–97. For the teenaged Evelyn Waugh's view of the "extraordinary boom of youth," see Davie (ed.), *Diaries*, p. 103.

On the background to society in the 1920s, see Balfour, *Society Racket*; Jenkins, *The*

Twenties; Ross McKibbin, *Classes and Cultures: England 1918–1951* (Oxford, 1998), pp. 22–43; Graves and Hodge, *Long Week-end*. The statistics of upper-class incomes are taken from McKibbin, p. 38. For Harold Nicolson's comment on Mrs. Greville, see James Lees-Milne, *Ancestral Voices: Diaries 1942–1943* (1975), p. 127. Evelyn Waugh's comments on Babe McGustie were made in a diary entry of October 19, 1925, Davie (ed.), *Diaries*, p. 228. Patrick Balfour's remarks on social outsiders are taken from *Society Racket*, pp. 132–33.

For the Ellesmere ball controversy, see Balfour, *Society Racket*, pp. 128–32, and Hoare, *Serious Pleasures*, pp. 111–14. Beverley Nichols's conversation with Lady Birkenhead is taken from a diary entry of February 23, 1934, quoted in Bryan Connon, *Beverley Nichols: A Life* (1991), p. 180. For McKibbin on the middle-class press and the "society racket," see *Classes and Cultures*, p. 34. Evelyn Waugh's account of Lady Cunard's dinner party is recorded in a diary entry of July 21, 1930; see Davie (ed.), *Diaries*, pp. 323–24.

On "Jix" and the Defense of the Realm Act, see Graves and Hodge, *Long Week-end*, pp. 119–21. Brenda Dean Paul remembered the police raid on the nightclub where she was sitting with Elizabeth Ponsonby in *My First Life*, p. 166. For Mrs. Meyrick, see Graves and Hodge, op. cit., p. 121, and Andrew Barrow, *Gossip: A History of High Society from 1920 to 1970* (1978), *passim*. Evelyn Waugh's account of a visit to Gerrard Street in January 1925 is in Davie (ed.), *Diaries*, p. 196.

Patrick Balfour discusses the "Modern Girl" in *Society Racket*, pp. 140–52. Diana Mosley's memory of her sister Nancy's income is quoted in Laura Thompson, *Life in a Cold Climate: Nancy Mitford—A Portrait of a Contradictory Woman* (2003), p. 69. For Jessica Mitford's recollections of Nancy's struggles with her parents, ibid., p. 73. For Balfour on Elizabeth Ponsonby's shingle, *Society Racket*, p. 146.

The *Daily Express*'s attack on the "Modern Young Man" is quoted in *Society Racket*, p. 161. The résumé of Alec Douglas-Home's career in the 1920s is taken from D. R. Thorpe, *Alec Douglas-Home* (1996). Balfour discusses the Modern Young Man's plight in *Society Racket*, pp. 153–60. Cyril Connolly's remarks about the "reluctance to settle down" are quoted in Carpenter, *Brideshead Generation*, p. 146.

Evelyn Waugh canvassed his prospects as a spokesman for "youth" in a letter to A. D. Peters of late November 1928, quoted in Gallagher (ed.), p. 35. For his journalism on this subject, see "Too Young at Forty," op.cit., "To an Unknown Old Man," broadcast on the BBC on November 28, 1932, and quoted in Gallagher (ed.), p. 35, and "The War and the Younger Generation," which originally appeared in the *Spectator*, April 13, 1929, and is reprinted in Gallagher, pp. 61–63. For Doris Delavigne, later Viscountess Castlerosse, see Mark Amory, *Lord Berners: The Last Eccentric*, 1998, 143–45.

3. YOUNG MEN ON THE MAKE: LONDON 1924-28

For the most recent and comprehensive account of Waugh's career in the 1920s, see Selina Hastings, *Evelyn Waugh: A Biography* (1994). On Beaton, Hugo Vickers, *Cecil Beaton* (1985). For Anthony Powell on the Beaton-Waugh relationship, see his *Journals, 1982–1986* (1995), p. 203. Waugh's review of Beaton's *The Wandering Years* is reprinted in Gallagher (ed.), pp. 568–70. The remark about being a "scheming snob" is quoted in Vickers, p. 54.

Evelyn Waugh recorded his experiences of Mary Butts's party and his evening at the Savoy in diary entries for September 15 and 20, 1925 (Davie [ed.], *Diaries*, pp. 221 and 222–23). For Beaton's friendship with Alannah Harper and his subsequent troubles with his father, see Vickers, pp. 58–62. For Waugh's first meetings with Elizabeth Ponsonby, *Diaries*, p. 226.

Dorothea Ponsonby's opinion of David Plunket Greene was recorded in a diary entry of March 25, 1924, and her criticisms of Olivia in an entry of July 29, 1924 (Ponsonby). On Matthew's arrest in the Strand, see Arthur Ponsonby, diary entry of April 21, 1925, and Dorothea Ponsonby, diary entry of August 3, 1925 (Ponsonby).

On the ascent of Cleopatra's needle, see Barrow, *Gossip*, p. 27. Loelia Ponsonby distinguishes between "Treasure Hunters, and the friends of my cousin Elizabeth" in *Grace and Favour*, p. 122. For David Tennant's Edwardian party, Brenda Dean Paul, *My First Life*, p. 101. On Mrs. Corrigan's "All Star Theatre," see *Grace and Favour*, p. 115. On the Duchess of Sutherland's fancy dress party, see Barrow, *Gossip*, p. 29. For Beaton's progress in 1926, see Vickers, pp. 71–87. Ed Burra's letter to Barbara Ker-Seymer of December 9, 1927, about Beaton's colonization of *Vogue* is printed in William Chappell (ed.), *Well, Dearie! The Letters of Edward Burra* (1985), p. 40.

John Betjeman evoked the atmosphere of Yeoman's Row in "For Patrick, aetat: LXX," *A Nip in the Air* (1974). On the Gargoyle Club, see Michael Luke, *Gargoyle Years*, passim. Elizabeth Jane Howard's memory of the club's interior is recorded in her memoir *Slipstream* (2002), pp. 112–13. For Burra on the Gargoyle, see Chappell (ed.), *Well, Dearie!*, p. 54. Daphne Fielding's remark appears in *Duchess of Jermyn Street*, p. 126. Constant Lambert is quoted in Powell, *To Keep the Ball Rolling: The Memoirs of Anthony Powell, Volume Two, Messengers of Day* (1978), p. 23.

On the Cavendish Hotel, see Fielding, *Duchess of Jermyn Street*, and Michael Harrison, *Rosa* (1962). Anthony Powell discusses the Cavendish atmosphere in *Messengers of Day*, pp. 49–54. On Alfred Duggan's "night out," see James Knox, *Robert Byron* (2003), p. 120. For Jessica Mitford on Bright Young People visits to Swinbrook, see Dalley, *Diana Mosley*, p. 53. Brian Howard's judgment on Nancy, given to Harold Acton, is quoted in Thompson, *Life in a Cold Climate*, p. 82. For Osbert Lancaster's memories of late-1920s Oxford, see his *With an Eye to the Future*, p. 69. For Nancy's trip to Cullen, see Selina Hastings, *Nancy Mitford* (1985), pp. 62–63.

Alec Waugh remembered the early summer of 1927 in "My Brother Evelyn," *My Brother Evelyn and Other Profiles*, p. 181. For the Impersonation Party, see Lancaster, *Portrait*, pp. 229–30, and Hoare, *Serious Pleasures*, pp. 82–83. Dorothea Ponsonby's opinions of Brian Howard, Eddie Gathorne-Hardy and Patrick Balfour were recorded in diary entries of June 6, 1927; June 4, 1927; and July 17, 1924, respectively (Ponsonby).

For "Lambert Orme," see Harold Nicolson, *Some People* (1929). On Stephen Tennant in 1927 and his relationship with Beaton, see Hoare, *Serious Pleasures*, pp. 80–99. Hoare quotes Driberg's description of him in the *Daily Express*, p. 100. On Evelyn Waugh's early involvement with the Bright Young People, see diary entries of September 22, 1926; February 28, 1927; and March 7, 1927 (Davie [ed.], *Diaries*). The subsequent account of his adventures in London until the autumn of 1927 is taken from the same source. For Powell's encounters with him in the following months, see *Messengers*, pp. 62–66.

For Tennant's social activities in 1928, see Hoare, *Serious Pleasures*, passim. Nancy Mitford's letter to her brother, Tom, about the Pageant of Hyde Park Through the Ages is printed in Charlotte Mosley (ed.), *Love from Nancy: The Letters of Nancy Mitford* (1993), p. 27. For Nancy Mitford on Lady Burghclere's opinion of her daughter's marriage, Saumarez Smith (ed.), *The Bookshop at 10 Curzon Street*, pp. 117–18. On Waugh in the period immediately following his marriage, see Powell, *Messengers*, pp. 97–99.

On Beaton's American trip of late 1928, see Vickers, pp. 109–21. His letter to "Johanna" was printed in *The Lady*, December 20, 1928. Tennant's letter to him about *Decline and Fall* is quoted by Hoare, *Serious Pleasures*, p. 122.

4. PARENTS AND CHILDREN

For Balfour's discussion of the "rebel army," see *Society Racket*, pp. 159–60. Isherwood's reappraisal of *All the Conspirators* is quoted in Valentine Cunningham, *British Writers of the Thirties* (Oxford, 1988), p. 113. The Betjeman couplet is from "For Patrick, aetat: LXX," op. cit. For Dorothea Ponsonby on Balfour, see diary entry of July 17, 1924 (Ponsonby).

On Nancy Mitford's struggles with her parents, see Hastings, *Nancy Mitford*, passim. For the letter about staying with Nina Seafield and the "orgy" at Lady O'Neill's, ibid., pp. 57 and 58. The letter to Tom about Brian Howard is reproduced in Mosley (ed.), *Love from Nancy*, p. 21, as is the letter to Mark Ogilvie-Grant about the family's reaction to *Vile Bodies*, p. 39. For Jessica Mitford's retrospective view of her sister in the 1920s, see her letter to the Duchess of Devonshire of May 14, 1993, reproduced in Peter Y. Sussman (ed.), *Decca: The Letters of Jessica Mitford* (2006), p. 673.

Arthur Waugh's letter to his friend Kenneth McMaster about Evelyn is quoted in Alexander Waugh, *Fathers and Sons: The Autobiography of a Family* (2004), p. 252, as is the letter from Evelyn Gardner outlining her mother's objections to him as a son-in-law, p. 201. Anthony Powell's comment on contemporary attitudes to marriage is in *Messen-*

gers, pp. 30–31. For Dorothea Ponsonby on her sister, Gwen Plunket Greene, see diary entry of July 29, 1924 (Ponsonby).

On the Ponsonby family, see Raymond A. Jones, *Arthur Ponsonby: The Politics of Life* (Bromley, 1989). For Arthur on Elizabeth's acting career and his attempts to write plays for her, see the diary entry of March 24–27, 1922. Further comments on her behavior at this time are recorded in his diary entries of May 14, 1922; September 17, 1922; and February 11, 1923. For Evelyn Waugh's first meetings with Elizabeth, see his *Diaries*, January 26, 1926, p. 244. Driberg's gossip column paean to her, and his mature opinion, are in Lancaster, *Portrait*, p. 266.

The text of Dorothea Ponsonby's letter to Elizabeth appears in her diary, October 1923. See also entries of March 27, 1924, and October 1924. Arthur's comments are taken from a diary entry of April 17, 1924. The letter from Elizabeth describing the fatal accident is undated. Subsequent quotations are from Arthur's diary, August 13, 1924, and Dorothea's diary, May 1926 and January 22, 1927 (all Ponsonby).

Elizabeth's disgrace in the summer of 1927 may be traced in Arthur's diary for June 16, 1927, and Dorothea's for June 17, and in a letter from Elizabeth to her mother dated June 27, 1927. Dorothea's comparison of her two children occurs in a diary entry of March 18, 1928. Subsequent comments from Arthur are taken from diary entries of January 8, 1928; September 15, 1928; and February 4, 1929. On the Bright Young People's visit of early 1929, see entries in Dorothea's diary, January 5, 6 and 7, 1929, and in Arthur's, January 4 and 7, 1929 (all Ponsonby).

Arthur's "meditation" on Elizabeth is dated July 1, 1927 (Ponsonby). For the mock wedding, see Knox, *Robert Byron*, pp. 173–74. Arthur's remark about Elizabeth's "pranks" is taken from a diary entry of January 28, 1929 (Ponsonby).

For Elizabeth's stay at Cranleigh, letter to Clive Bell, February 7, 1929. On the circumstances of Elizabeth's engagement, see Arthur's and Dorothea's diary entries for March 24, 1929, and Arthur's for March 27, March 29, and April 2, 1929. See also Dorothea's diary, April 6, 1927. For Burra on Denis Pelly, Chappell (ed.), *Well, Dearie!*, p. 55. Arthur's comment about the "circus" was made on April 7 (all Ponsonby). The *Bystander* report appeared in the issue of April 10, 1929.

For Dorothea's worries about the marriage ceremony, see her diary for April 6, 1929. Arthur's further comments are reproduced from diary entries of April 11 and 22, 1929. Dorothea recorded her meeting with Mrs. Pelly on June 20, 1929. Elizabeth's letter about her future mother-in-law is undated. For prewedding comments, see Arthur's diary, April 27, 1929, and Dorothea's, June 23, 1929 (all Ponsonby).

5. THE REVOLT INTO STYLE

The fragments of "A Smoking Room Story," left unfinished at Orwell's death, are printed in Peter Davison (ed.), *The Complete Works of George Orwell, XX: Our Job Is to Make Life Worth Living* (1998), pp. 188–200. For Bryan Guinness's meeting with King

George V, see *Potpourri from the Thirties*, p. 13. Balfour's remarks on the hectic social patterns of the 1920s are taken from *Society Racket*, pp. 222–23. Anthony Powell discusses the twenties party in *Messengers*, pp. 32–35. For his comments on the parties staged on the *Friendship*, see Michael Barber, *Anthony Powell: A Life* (London, 2004), p. 57. Beverley Nichols remembered arraying himself for an evening out in *All I Could Never Be*, p. 196. For Alan Pryce-Jones's matelot suit, see his *The Bonus of Laughter* (1988), p. 34.

For retrospective views of twenties boisterousness, see Evelyn Waugh, "Max Beerbohm: A Lesson in Manners," *Sunday Times*, May 27, 1956, reprinted in Gallagher (ed.), *Essays, Articles and Reviews*; Nancy Mitford, quoted in Thompson, *Life in a Cold Climate*, p. 74, and Lancaster, *Portrait*, p. 263. For Ed Burra's description of the fight at Olivia Wyndham's party, see Chappell (ed.), *Well, Dearie!*, p. 55. Brenda Dean Paul's reminiscences of the atmosphere of the twenties party are taken from *My First Life*, pp. 105–106.

Nancy Mitford's letter about "pretending to drug" is quoted in Hastings, *Nancy Mitford*, p. 55. For Nichols and Avery Hopwood, see *All I Could Never Be*, pp. 191–92. Brian Howard's account of the Berlin cocaine addict is in Lancaster, *Portrait*, pp. 237–38. For Goldring on the desire to shock, see *The Nineteen-Twenties*, p. 62.

Selina Hastings reproduces Nancy Mitford's account of a dance floor conversation in *Nancy Mitford*, p. 70. For Beverley Nichols on twenties slang, see *The Sweet and Twenties* (1958), pp. 210–11. On Evelyn Gardner, see Waugh, *Fathers and Sons*, p. 199. For Brian Howard at the Guinnesses' cradle, see Nancy's letter to Mark Ogilvie-Grant in Mosley (ed.), *Love from Nancy*, p. 39. On the transmission of *Vile Bodies* slang, see Alec Waugh, "My Brother Evelyn," op. cit., p. 195, and Loelia, Duchess of Westminster, *Grace and Favour*, p. 118.

On the vogue for black American culture, see Evelyn Waugh, *Diaries*, February 28 and March 10, 1927, and Goldring, *The Nineteen-Twenties*, p. 227. For Elinor Wylie's visit to Wilsford in June 1927, Hoare, *Serious Pleasures*, pp. 78–79. On Beverley Nichols at the *American Sketch*, Connon, *Beverley Nichols*, pp. 135–37. Ed Burra's letter to Billy Chappell is reproduced in Chappell (ed.), *Well, Dearie!*, pp. 69–70.

Anthony Powell's letters to Henry Green are mostly undated. The comments about the Biddulphs were probably written in 1928, the résumé of the Rothschilds' dance in 1927 and the letter about Brian Howard's identification of himself with Captain Grimes in October 1928. Yorke's replies come from letters dated August 23 and October 13, 1928 (Powell/Green). The complaint about "Arty high life" was made in a letter to Robert Byron of February 20, 1928, and is quoted in Treglown, *Romancing*, p. 77.

6. PARTYGOING: 1929

On Bryan Guinness and Diana Mitford and their courtship, see Dalley, *Diana Mosley*, passim; Guinness, *Potpourri from the Thirties*, p. 10; Knox, *Robert Byron*, pp. 162–63; Alec Waugh, "My Brother Evelyn," p. 188; Nancy Mitford, quoted in Dalley, p. 61.

For the freak parties of 1929, see Lancaster, *Portrait*, pp. 267–69. On the "heightened social atmosphere," Alec Waugh, "My Brother Evelyn," pp. 189–90. On the Whoopee Party, "The Lady Looks On," *The Lady*, June 6, 1929. For Norman Hartnell's Circus Party, see "The Lady Looks On," *The Lady*, July 11, 1929, and Brenda Dean Paul, *My First Life*, pp. 106–107.

On the Ponsonby wedding, undated letter from Mary Butts to Eddie Gathorne-Hardy (Gathorne-Hardy), Arthur and Dorothea Ponsonby, diary entries of July 5, 1929 (Ponsonby), Jones, *Arthur Ponsonby*, p. 182.

For the Bruno Hat exhibition, Guinness, *Potpourri from the Thirties*, pp. 16–17; Lancaster, *Portrait*, pp. 273–75; Harrison, *Rosa*, p. 244. On the Second Childhood Party and its aftermath, Barrow, *Gossip*, p. 46, and "The Lady Looks On," *The Lady*, July 18, 1929. "The Dull Young People" appeared in *Punch*, April 24, 1929, and "She Whoops to Conquer" in the issue of July 24, 1929.

On the breakup of Evelyn Waugh's first marriage, see Hastings, *Evelyn Waugh*, pp. 190–99; Powell, *Messengers*, pp. 123–28; letters from Waugh to Harold Acton and Henry Yorke, September 1929, in Amory (ed.), *Letters*, pp. 38 and 39. Evelyn Gardner's comment is taken from Hastings, *Evelyn Waugh*, p. 199. Waugh's undated letter to John Fothergill, private collection.

For Gavin Henderson and "Kevin Saunderson," see Waugh's diary entry for October 8, 1928, Davie (ed.), *Diaries*, p. 297. The typescript of George Orwell's unfinished essay on Waugh is reproduced in Peter Davison (ed.), *George Orwell: The Complete Works, Volume XX: Our Job Is to Make Life Worth Living* (1998), pp. 74–77.

Arthur Ponsonby recorded Denis and Elizabeth's visits to Shulbrede in the summer of 1929 in diary entries of July 18 and 31 (Ponsonby). On Olivia Wyndham's party, "The Lady Looks On," *The Lady*, October 31, 1929. For Dorothea's account of the Pellys' flat and her conversation with John Strachey, see diary entries of October 23 and 24, 1929. Denis's dismissal from his job can be traced through Arthur's diary entries of November 29 and December 2. The comments about Elizabeth's and Denis's affairs "darkening everything" and Elizabeth being famous for her "pranks in a wastrel society" occur in diary entries of December 15, 1929, and January 3, 1930, respectively (all Ponsonby).

7. SUCCESS AND FAILURE: TWO PORTRAITS

For Byron and Howard generally, see Knox, *Robert Byron*, and Lancaster, *Portrait*. Anthony Powell remembered Byron and Howard at Eton in the first volume of his memoirs, *Infants of the Spring* (1976), pp. 109–15. Maurice Richardson's reminiscence of Howard is quoted in *Portrait*, p. 200. Stephen Tennant's complaint about him is taken from Hoare, *Serious Pleasures*, p. 80n.

Byron noted Patrick Balfour's appointment to the *Daily Sketch* in a letter to his mother of November 24, 1928; see Lucy Butler (ed.), Robert Byron, *Letters Home* (1991), p. 109. The letter to Henry Yorke about finding Howard intellectually sympathetic is quoted in Knox, p. 151. For the disagreements over religion, ibid., p. 152. On the *Values* project, see Knox, p. 152, and Lancaster, pp. 251–53.

Byron's letter to his mother about job prospects, written in 1924, is reproduced in *Letters Home*, p. 38. Anthony Powell's remark about "The Mum's boy to end all Mum's boys" is taken from his *Journals 1990–1992* (1997), p. 143. For Byron's performances at the Hypocrites Club, see *Infants*, pp. 156–57. On Byron's career in the mid-1920s, Knox, passim. On Hamlet, the emotional hoax, *Infants*, p. 110. The description of the fascist parades at Wiener Neustadt is quoted in Knox, p. 164, as is his account of Bryan Guinness's courtship of Diana Mitford, p. 163. For his quarrel with Yorke, see Knox, pp. 176–77.

Evelyn Waugh's letter to Nancy Mitford of May 29, 1965, is reproduced in Amory (ed.), *Letters*, p. 631. For his final judgment on Howard, see *A Little Learning* (1964), p. 197. For Howard's comments on his Oedipus complex in a letter to Peter Watson, see Lancaster, *Portrait*, p. 476. The remark about "making a success" is taken from the same letter. "Who is this Proust?," *Portrait*, p. 95. His housemaster's letter and the letter from Edith Sitwell, ibid., pp. 39 and 46–47. For Anthony Powell's criticism, ibid., p. 120, and *Infants*, p. 104. The comment to Acton about Robert Bridges is reproduced in *Portrait*, p. 50.

The description of Oxford, in a letter to William Acton, is from *Portrait*, p. 129. Mrs. Lancaster reproduces the invitation to the Great Urban Dionysia. For Waugh on the Oxford party, see *A Little Learning*, p. 197. The letter to Lura Howard about his lack of money is quoted in *Portrait*, pp. 270–72 and is also the source of the remarks about "saleable stuff" and possible film work. For the letter to Eddie Gathorne-Hardy about "Self," ibid., p. 589.

8. DECLINE AND FALL: 1930-31

On the Hermaphrodite Party, Frances Partridge, *Memories* (1981), p. 178. On signs of "decadence," Patrick Balfour, *Society Racket*, p. 172, and Pryce-Jones, *Cyril Connolly*, p. 227. On Mrs. Meyrick's retreat to Monte Carlo, Barrow, *Gossip*, p. 54; on the death of Sir Francis Laking, ibid., p. 51. For Brenda Dean Paul's views on "social blood poisoning," *My First Life*, p. 97.

Evelyn Waugh's meetings with Elizabeth in 1930 are recorded in diary entries of June 6, June 15 and July 23, Davie (ed.), *Diaries*, pp. 313, 315, 324. For Nelly's complaints to Dorothea, see the latter's diary entry of January 28, 1930. Dorothea recorded her opinion of *Vile Bodies* in a diary entry of February 9, 1930 (Ponsonby). Arthur wrote about the couple's difficulties in a diary entry of March 17, 1930. For Nelly's further complaints about the Pellys' social lives, see Dorothea's diary entry of April 9, 1930.

Arthur's observations on the weekend visit and on Denis generally, diary entries of May 19 and 26 (all Ponsonby).

For the Guinness cocktail party, see Carl Van Vechten, letter to Alfred A. Knopf, Bruce Kellner (ed.), *Letters of Carl Van Vechten* (New York, 1987), p. 115. On the Mozart Party, see Luke, *Gargoyle Years*, pp. 80–83, and Brenda Dean Paul, *My First Life*, p. 102. "Eve's" report appeared in the *Tatler* of May 7, 1930, p. 246. Dorothea's account of her dinner with Matthew and Bess is recorded in a diary entry of April 12. For the visit of Barbara Ker-Seymer, Olivia Wyndham and John Banting to Shulbrede, ibid., August 17 and 18, 1930. Arthur's growing concern is apparent in diary entries of November 29, 1930, and April 26, May 3, and May 21, 1931. For the Peter Jones affair, see his diary entry of June 8, 1931, and an undated letter from Elizabeth to Dorothea. See also Arthur's diary for June 12 and July 5, 1931 (all Ponsonby).

For the White Party and its aftermath, see Lancaster, *Portrait*, p. 283, and Arthur's diary for July 1931, passim, press accounts of inquest and Ludy Ford's trial (Ponsonby).

9. CELEBRITY CULTURE

Beverley Nichols's comment on the "disapproving eye" of the press is taken from *All I Could Never Be*, p. 41. For Balfour on the pre–Great War "paragraph writer," *Society Racket*, pp. 88–89. On the "sneak guest" controversy, ibid., pp. 98–100. Evelyn Waugh's article for *Passing Show* ("Careers for Our Sons: The Complete Journalist: Secrets of Press Success"), January 26, 1929, is reprinted in Gallagher (ed.), *Essays, Articles and Reviews*, pp. 47–49.

Major Guy Kindersley's letter is reproduced in *Society Racket*, p. 117. For the columns by Nancy Mitford listed here, see *The Lady*, March 27, April 10, May 1, and June 11, 1930. Alan Pryce-Jones recalled the effect of press coverage on his abortive love affair in *The Bonus of Laughter*, pp. 82–83. For Connolly on Balfour, see Pryce-Jones, *Cyril Connolly*, pp. 182, 101, 205.

For Driberg, see Francis Wheen, *Tom Driberg: His Life and Indiscretions* (1990), passim, and the portrait in Alan Watkins, *Brief Lives* (1982). Both of these draw heavily on Driberg's own *Ruling Passions* (1977). All quotations from Brenda Dean Paul are taken from *My First Life*. For her relationship with David Tennant, see Luke, *Gargoyle Years*, passim. John Strachey's account of the fight involving David Tennant is recorded in Dorothea Ponsonby's diary, December 16, 1931 (Ponsonby). For the trial of 1973, undated letter from Gwen Plunket Greene to Dorothy Ponsonby (Ponsonby).

10. GAY YOUNG PEOPLE

For Jessica Mitford's comments on English public school boys' "exposure to homosexuality," see letter to Merle Miller of November 3, 1971, in Sussman (ed.), *Decca*, p. 436.

Eddy Sackville-West's complaint about John Banting is quoted in Michael De-la-Noy, *Eddy: The Life of Edward Sackville-West* (1989, reissued 1999), p. 128. The remark about his being "congenial, interesting, good + kind" comes from an undated letter to Duncan Grant, private collection. On Evan Morgan, later Lord Tredegar, see Pryce-Jones, *The Bonus of Laughter*, pp. 30–33 and passim. For Howard's comments about Morgan, made in a letter to William Acton, see Lancaster, *Portrait*, pp. 167 and 168. Bryan Connon discusses Beaton's early relationship with Nichols in *Beverley Nichols: A Life*, pp. 134 and 136–37.

For Beaton's adventures with Howard and his friends, see Vickers, *Cecil Beaton*, p. 90. For Eddie Gathorne-Hardy and younger acolytes, letter from Robin McDouall to Lady Anne Hill (Gathorne-Hardy). Beverley Nichols's diary entry of February 21, 1934, quoted in Connon, *Beverley Nichols*, p. 180. Postcard from Mark Ogilvie-Grant to Tom Driberg, November 1, 1929 (Driberg).

On Driberg's arrest for indecent assault, see Wheen, *Tom Driberg*, pp. 95–99. Mary Butts, letter of July 15, 1929, to Eddie Gathorne-Hardy (Gathorne-Hardy). For Eddy Sackville-West in Berlin, see De-la-Noy, *Eddy*, p. 117. For the Cannes house party, ibid., pp. 129–30.

Evelyn Waugh refers to Mrs. Gavin Henderson in a diary entry of August 23, 1927, *Diaries*, p. 287. On Henderson's engagement and short-lived marriage, see Knox, *Robert Byron*, pp. 126–27. "I don't think she knew he was queer," Deborah Devonshire, quoted in Thompson, *Life in a Cold Climate*, p. 95. Nancy's letter to Mark Ogilvie-Grant, ibid., p. 96. For Nancy's comment to Jessica, see Knox, *Byron*, p. 176. The letter to Harold Acton of January 27, 1952, about Gavin Henderson is reproduced in Mosley (ed.), *Love from Nancy*, p. 289.

On Eddie Gathorne-Hardy, typescript of memoir by Lees Mayall (Gathorne-Hardy), Jonathan Gathorne-Hardy, *Half an Arch* (2004), passim, Dorothea Ponsonby, diary entry of June 4, 1927 (Ponsonby). John Betjeman remembered John Banting's behavior at the flat in a letter to Lady Anne Hill (Gathorne-Hardy). For Brian's comments on the Maddox Street atmosphere, letter of January 30, 1931 (Gathorne-Hardy). For Brian Howard's letter about "Self," see Lancaster, *Portrait*, p. 589. For Stephen Tennant's relationship with Siegfried Sassoon, see Hoare, *Serious Pleasures*; Jean Moorcroft Wilson, *Siegfried Sassoon, The Journey from the Trenches, A Biography 1918–1967* (2003); and, definitively, Max Egremont, *Siegfried Sassoon* (2005). Forster's letter about Sassoon's marriage is quoted in P. N. Furbank, *E. M. Forster: A Life, Volume Two, Polycrates' Ring, 1914–1970*, p. 181.

11. AFTER THE DANCE: 1931–39

On the "end" of the 1920s, see Balfour, *Society Racket*, p. 56, and Alec Waugh, *A Year to Remember: A Reminiscence of 1931* (1975), pp. 149–53 and 156. On *Thirteen Such Years*, ibid., p. 184. For the Red and White Party, see Waugh, ibid., pp. 176–77, and Harrison,

Rosa, p. 245. For an account of the Barney case and its technicalities, see Douglas Browne and E. V. Tullett, *Bernard Spilsbury: His Life and Cases* (1951), pp. 355–60. Osbert Lancaster remembered the Guinnesses' ball for Unity Mitford in *With an Eye to the Future*, pp. 118–19.

On the collapse of the Guinness marriage, see Dalley, *Diana Mosley*, pp. 117–27. Beverley Nichols recalled his new seriousness in *All I Could Never Be*, pp. 197–98. On Diana Mosley's political awakening, see Dalley, p. 124. On Byron's political sketches for *Vogue*, see Knox, *Byron*, p. 179. "One spends one's life trying to save things . . . ," letter to his mother, January 15, 1939, *Letters Home*, p. 295.

Goldring's analysis of the generational fallout is taken from *The Nineteen-Twenties*, p. 225. For Mrs. Meyrick's death, see Barrow, *Gossip*, p. 65. On Mosley's career in the early 1930s, see Dalley, *Diana Mosley*, pp. 104–16, and Martin Pugh, *Hurrah for the Blackshirts!: Fascists and Fascism in Britain Between the Wars* (2005), passim. "Prodd looked very pretty in a black shirt," letter to Evelyn Waugh, quoted in Dalley, p. 190. The *Vanguard* article is quoted by Hastings, *Nancy Mitford*, p. 97. "Call me early, Goering, dear," quoted in Dalley, p. 190.

For John Amery, see David Faber, *Speaking for England* (2005), passim. On *Hangover Square* and the psychology of fascism, P. J. Widdowson, "The Saloon Bar Society: Patrick Hamilton's Fiction in the 1930s," in John Lucas (ed.), *The 1930s: A Challenge to Orthodoxy* (Hassocks, 1978), pp. 131–32.

On Brian Howard in the 1930s, see Lancaster, *Portrait*, passim. Arthur Ponsonby's diary records him lunching at Shulbrede on April 23, 1935 (Ponsonby). For Ivan Moffat's remarks, *Portrait*, p. 392. Beverley Nichols remembered his stays at Buscot in *All I Could Never Be*, pp. 308–12. On Driberg, see Wheen, *Tom Driberg*, pp. 82–104. For Cyril Connolly's susceptibility to "glamour and *luxe*," Deirdre Levi to author. Nancy Mitford's letter to Mark Ogilvie-Grant about the 1935 general election is reproduced in Mosley (ed.), *Love from Nancy*, p. 71.

The *Daily Express* report on subscribers to *The Aquarist and Pond-Keeper* is quoted in Hoare, *Serious Pleasures*, p. 223. The *Evening Standard*'s comment on the Rodds' bridge parties is quoted in Hastings, *Nancy Mitford*, p. 89. For Goldring on "malicious middle-aged hags," *Odd Man Out*, p. 227. On *Leaves from a Missionary's Notebook* and Beaton's visit to Wilsford in 1938, see Hoare, *Serious Pleasures*, pp. 230–31 and 235.

For Elizabeth Ponsonby in the early 1930s, see Arthur's diary entries as quoted. On her financial problems, ibid., June 19 and 23, 1932. "You may complain of my goings on," ibid., September 19, 1932 (all Ponsonby). Further quotations taken from diary entries of October 17, 1932; December 29, 1932; and May 24, 1933. Elizabeth's letter, dispatched from 263 King's Road, was probably sent on June 2, 1933. For the telephone message about her parties and extravagance, Arthur's diary for July 27, 1933. The "insoluble E question," diary entry of November 20, 1933, also entries of December 8 and 11, 1933 (all Ponsonby). Other diary entries as quoted. See also letter from the Santa Monica Club and other sporadic entries throughout late 1930s (Ponsonby).

On the Rodds in Roussillon, see Hastings, *Nancy Mitford*, pp. 116–19. For Driberg at the Fascist meeting, see Wheen, *Tom Driberg*, 110–11. For Byron's comments, see *Letters Home*, pp. 292 and 299. On Nichols's pacifist activities in the late 1930s, see *All I Could Never Be*, pp. 314–21.

12. PROJECTIONS

On Bright Young People's connections with the *London Mercury*, see Patrick Howarth, *Squire: Most Generous of Men* (1963), passim. For Powell on Hugh Walpole, see *To Keep the Ball Rolling, Volume Four: The Strangers Are All Gone* (1982), p. 148. Nancy Mitford's opinion of *Vile Bodies* is taken from a letter to Mark Ogilvie-Grant of March 15, 1931, quoted in Thompson, *Life in a Cold Climate*, p. 88. For the sequence of articles by Beaton, Waugh and Frankau, see Gallagher (ed.), *Essays, Articles and Reviews*, pp. 78–80 (text of Waugh's article "Such Appalling Manners," *Daily Mail*, June 14, 1930), and Waugh's diary entry for June 19, 1930, *Diaries*, p. 316.

Green's letter to Nevill Coghill is quoted in Treglown, *Romancing*, p. 72. For Michael Arlen, see Alec Waugh, "Michael Arlen in Retirement" in *My Brother Evelyn and Other Portraits*, pp. 255–70. Alan Pryce-Jones remembered his father's reaction to *The Green Hat* in *The Bonus of Laughter*, pp. 45–46.

On Ronald Firbank, see Miriam J. Benkovitz, *Ronald Firbank* (1969); Anthony Hobson (ed.), *Ronald Firbank: Letters to His Mother* (Verona, 2001); Anthony Powell, introduction to *The Complete Firbank* (1961); and Evelyn Waugh, "Ronald Firbank," originally published in *Life and Letters*, March 1929, and reprinted in Gallagher (ed.), *Essays, Articles and Reviews*, pp. 56–59. For Bright Young People's opinions of Firbank, Brian Howard's praise of *Concerning the Eccentricities of Cardinal Pirelli* is reproduced in Lancaster, *Portrait*, p. 172, Harold Acton to author, Beverley Nichols, quoted in Connon, *Beverley Nichols*, p. 76. For Raymond Mortimer's recollections, see his review of Miriam Benkovitz's biography, reprinted in *Try Anything Once* (1976), pp. 187–89.

Beverley Nichols's later comments on *Crazy Pavements* are quoted in Connon, p. 127. Jan Dalley discusses the background to *Singing out of Tune* in *Diana Mosley*, p. 68. For the Guinnesses' walk in the woods at Versailles, ibid., p. 123. Jeremy Treglown's remarks on *Party Going* are in *Romancing*, p. 121.

13. GONE TO REPORT: 1940 AND AFTER

Telegram announcing Elizabeth's death, Arthur's diary entries for June 4 and July 31, 1940, death certificate, letter from the manager of the Jermyn Street apartment block, letter to Mrs. Maisie Thomas and pawn tickets (all Ponsonby). Arthur's obituary note appeared in *The Times*, August 6, 1940. Evelyn Waugh's letter to Lady Diana Cooper mentioning Federal Union, sent on Christmas Eve 1939, is reprinted in Artemis Cooper (ed.), *Mr Wu & Mrs Stitch: The Letters of Evelyn Waugh & Diana Cooper*, pp. 101–103.

For "The Lion and the Unicorn: Socialism and the English Genius," see Peter Davison (ed.), *The Complete Works of George Orwell, XII: A Patriot After All*, pp. 391–434. The quoted passages can be found on p. 432 and p. 404 respectively.

On Hamish Erskine's exploits in the war, see James Lees-Milne, *Prophesying Peace* (1977), p. 11. On Lees-Milne's encounter with Sandy Baird, ibid., p. 202. Connolly's letter to Driberg is dated December 5, 1940 (Driberg). For Beaton's visit to Stephen Tennant during the Blitz, see Hoare, *Serious Pleasures*, p. 245. Brian Howard's letter to Driberg is dated April 29, 1945 (Driberg).

For Evelyn Waugh's later career, see Hastings, *Evelyn Waugh*, passim. The letter to Nancy Mitford about *Helena* is quoted in Carpenter, *Brideshead Generation*, p. 407. For the letter to Diana Mosley of March 9, 1966, see Amory (ed.), *Letters*, p. 638. "I quite liked old Harold . . . ," Anthony Powell to author. For Waugh on Henry Green's decrepitude, the letter to Diana Mosley quoted above. Anthony Powell's verdict on Green is in his *Journals, 1990–1992*, p. 95.

For Desmond Guinness's comment on his father, see Lees-Milne, *Prophesying Peace*, p. 201. Powell remembered the visit to La Pietra in *Journals 1990–1992*, pp. 6–7. On Brian Howard and the nightclub raid, see Lancaster, *Portrait*, p. 430. For his subsequent career, Lancaster, passim. On his visit to London of September 1955 and his death, see letters of Heywood Hill to Nancy Mitford, Saumarez Smith (ed.), *The Bookshop at 10 Curzon Street*, pp. 46 and 60. For Driberg, see Wheen, *Tom Driberg*, passim. For Gavin Henderson, Lord Faringdon, and Brenda Dean Paul, *New Dictionary of National Biography* entries by Gaynor Johnson and Philip Hoare respectively (Oxford, 2004). The remark about Brenda's younger acquaintances being "scared" of her was made by Marie-Jaqueline Lancaster to the author.

On Beaton's later life, see Vickers, *Cecil Beaton*, passim. Waugh's review of *The Wandering Years* is reprinted in Gallagher (ed.), *Essays, Articles and Reviews*, pp. 568–70. For Nancy Mitford, see Hastings, *Nancy Mitford*. The letter to Billa Harrod about Brian and Sam's visit to Paris, dated December 29, 1947, is reproduced in Mosley (ed.), *Love from Nancy*, p. 202.

On Diana Mosley, see Dalley, passim. For Tennant, see Hoare, *Serious Pleasures*. On Zita and Baby, see Evelyn Waugh, letter of May 1953 to Nancy Mitford, in Amory (ed.), *Letters*, p. 403, and James Lees-Milne, *The Milk of Paradise: Diaries, 1993–1997* (2005), p. 164.

For Connolly, see Jeremy Lewis, *Cyril Connolly* (1997). On the party given by Brian Howard to mark Eddie Gathorne-Hardy's retirement from the Foreign Office, see Lancaster, *Portrait*, pp. 556–57. Frances Partridge's account of her meeting with Eddie in France in early 1960 is in *Hanging On: Diaries 1960–1963* (1990), pp. 40–41. For Eddie in Greece during the 1967 coup, Saumarez Smith (ed.), *The Bookshop at 10 Curzon*

Street, p. 126. On Frances Partridge's stay in Suffolk in 1972, see *Life Regained: Diaries, 1970–1972* (1998), pp. 224–25. For the request to Angela Culme-Seymour see Gathorne-Hardy. For Alan Pryce-Jones's obituary of Hamish Erskine, *The Times*, January 12, 1973. All Howard quotations from Lancaster.

For Arthur Ponsonby's reflections on Elizabeth's death, diary entries of February 15, 1941; July 31, 1941; and July 31, 1943 (Ponsonby).

FICTION, DRAMA, POETRY AND ART

Harold Acton, *Cornelian* (1928)

Michael Arlen, *The Green Hat* (1924)

Cyril Connolly, *The Rock Pool* (1936)

Ronald Firbank, *The Complete Firbank* (1961)

Henry Green, *Party Going* (1939)

Bryan Guinness, *Singing out of Tune* (1933)

James Laver, *Ladies' Mistakes: Cupid's Changeling; A Stitch in Time; Love's Progress* (1933)

Nancy Mitford, *Highland Fling* (1931)

Nancy Mitford, *Christmas Pudding* (1932)

Nancy Mitford, *Pigeon Pie* (1940)

Beverley Nichols, *Crazy Pavements* (1927)

Anthony Powell, *Afternoon Men* (1931)

Anthony Powell, *From a View to a Death* (1933)

Terence Rattigan, *After the Dance* (1939)

Evelyn Waugh, *Decline and Fall* (1928)

Evelyn Waugh, *Vile Bodies* (1930)

Evelyn Waugh, *Mr. Loveday's Little Outing and Other Sad Stories* (1936), contains "Winner Takes All"

• • •

Marie-Jaqueline Lancaster prints a selection of Brian Howard's poems in an appendix to *Portrait of a Failure* (1968), pp. 574–601.

For a selection of Ed Burra's work from the 1920s and early 1930s, see *Edward Burra*, catalogue to the 1985 Hayward Gallery retrospective (Arts Council of Great Britain, 1985).

INDEX

Page numbers in *italics* refer to
   illustrations.

ILLUSTRATION CREDITS

The author and publishers are grateful for kind permission to reproduce the following illustrations in the text:

Illustrations from *Punch* (courtesy of *Punch* Archive): p. 7, December 14, 1927; p. 17, August 27, 1924; p. 80, November 27, 1927; pp. 98 and 99, July 20, 1927; p. 112, November 23, 1927; p. 190, October 8, 1930. The illustration on p. 23 is from the *Tatler*, August 29, 1928, and the illustration on p. 121 is from the *Bystander*, July 3, 1929 (both courtesy of the *Illustrated London News* Picture Library). The Christmas card on p. 155 from Evelyn Waugh, 1929, is reproduced courtesy of the Ponsonby family.

Printed in the USA
CPSIA information can be obtained
at www.ICGtesting.com
LVHW041045220324
775219LV00014B/118